A book in the series
Radical Perspectives
A RADICAL HISTORY REVIEW BOOK SERIES
Series editors: Daniel J. Walkowitz, New York University
Barbara Weinstein, New York University

History, as radical historians have long observed, cannot be severed
from authorial subjectivity, indeed from politics. Political concerns
animate the questions we ask, the subjects on which we write. For
over thirty years the *Radical History Review* has led in nurturing and
advancing politically engaged historical research. Radical Perspectives seeks to further the journal's mission: any author wishing to be
in the series makes a self-conscious decision to associate her or his
work with a radical perspective. To be sure, many of us are currently
struggling with the issue of what it means to be a radical historian in
the early twenty-first century, and this series is intended to provide
some signposts for what we would judge to be radical history. It will
offer innovative ways of telling stories from multiple perspectives;
comparative, transnational, and global histories that transcend conventional boundaries of region and nation; works that elaborate on
the implications of the postcolonial move to "provincialize Europe"; studies of the public in and of the past, including those that
consider the commodification of the past; histories that explore the
intersection of identities such as gender, race, class and sexuality
with an eye to their political implications and complications. Above
all, this book series seeks to create an important intellectual space
and discursive community to explore the very issue of what con-
stitutes radical history. Within this context, some of the books published in the series may privilege alternative and oppositional politi-

cal cultures, but all will be concerned with the way power is constituted, contested, used, and abused.

The region known as Assam, much of it now a state in northeast India, is likely to be known even to the academic public either for the type of tea that bears its name or for the ethnic violence that has erupted there in recent decades. In earlier historical and journalistic accounts both the lush tea plantations and the ethnic conflicts tended to be naturalized, to be seen as deeply rooted in the region. But as Jayeeta Sharma demonstrates in *Empire's Garden*, both "emblems" of Assamese identity are the result of relatively recent historical, not natural, processes. The British colonial venture to cultivate a highly lucrative imperial tea garden in a region previously regarded as wild and remote not only transformed Assam economically and demographically but in a sense reinvented the very notion of what and even where Assam was. To create this garden and make it profitable, the British brought in hundreds of thousands of laborers from other regions of India, forming a racialized workforce that became the "other" to an emerging regional identity promoted by local gentry eager to carve out a place for themselves in the booming regional economy, and then in the incipient nationalist movement. Ultimately it is the dynamic and unstable relationship between region and nation, further complicated by transnational influences, that lies at the heart of *Empire's Garden*. More than a regional history of Assam, this exhaustively researched and beautifully rendered study seeks to disrupt the Bengal-centered narrative that informs so much of India's colonial and postcolonial historiography, and invites us to think in terms of multiple Indian histories rife with the tensions seeded by local and imperial heralds of progress.

Empire's Garden

Jayeeta Sharma

Empire's Garden

Assam and the Making of India

DUKE UNIVERSITY PRESS DURHAM AND LONDON 2011

© 2011 Duke University Press
All rights reserved.
Printed in the United States of America on acid-free paper ∞
Designed by C. H. Westmoreland
Typeset in Carter and Cone Galliard by Keystone Typesetting, Inc.
Library of Congress Cataloging-in-Publication Data appear on the
last printed page of this book.

In memory of my father,
Sachindra Nath Sarma, who bequeathed
me his love of books and the best
education he could find

Contents

Preface

THIS BOOK HAS TAKEN many years to write and witnessed major changes and upheavals in my personal and professional lives. At its end, my thoughts are with my Deta (father), who acted as my field assistant through the project's inception but did not live to see his daughter finish her book. He would disagree with many of its arguments even while he took deep pride in it. Growing up in an environment where daughters were often second-class children, I remain deeply grateful for the loving care and first-class educations that my parents Sachindra Nath Sarma and Gita Debi gifted to their children, at personal and financial sacrifice, throughout their lives in Assam.

At the institutional level, I am grateful to the Association of Commonwealth Universities, the Government of India's Ministry of Human Resources and Education, St Catharine's College, and the University of Cambridge for facilitating my award of a Commonwealth PhD scholarship from 1998 to 2003. The Smuts Fund, Leche Trust, Mountbatten Memorial Trust, Eric Stokes bursary at St Catharine's College, and Berkman and Falk Trusts in Pittsburgh provided important additional funding from 2000 to 2005. In India, Britain, the United States, and Canada, the staff of the National Archives of India, New Delhi; National Library, Calcutta; Department of Historical and Antiquarian Studies, Guwahati; Gauhati University Library, Maligaon; Assam State Archives, Dispur; District Record Office, Jorhat; Dibrugarh University Library; Northeastern Hill University Library and Sociology Department, Shillong; Nehru Memorial Museum and Library, New Delhi; British Library; Cambridge University Library;

St Catharine's College Library, Cambridge; Cambridge Centre for South Asian Studies; London Guildhall Library; National Library of Scotland, Edinburgh; Hunt Library at Carnegie Mellon University, Pittsburgh; University of Pittsburgh Library; Yale University Libraries, New Haven; Burke Library at Columbia University, New York; Library of Congress, Washington; University of Western Ontario Library; and the University of Toronto Libraries provided invaluable help throughout my research years. I thank the Yale Agrarian Studies Program for providing me with a year of postdoctoral research, Carnegie Mellon University for research funds and leave, and the universities of Western Ontario and Toronto for their academic and staff support. I am grateful to the National Anthropological Archives and their amazing staff, especially Stephanie and Susie, for the images reproduced in the book, and to Bill Nelson for his maps. A specially warm thanks to Laurel Wheeler and Monica Hretsina, whose cheerful, efficient support has made my academic life so much easier, and to my two department chairs, William Bowen and Kenneth Mills.

The writing of this book owes a lot to Shahana, Asad, Nalini, Mintz, Bharati C., Ajay, Jinee, Sanjay, Janaki, Sumit, Tanika, Bhochka, Rinku, Saumya, Ravikant, Bharati J., Mukul, Rana, Ben, Prabhu, Suvrita, Anil, and Aparna in Delhi; Subhash babu, Rajat babu, Ian and Ben Zachariah, Amitava and Shaswati Bhattacharya, Sulagna Roy, Selwyn Jussy and family in Calcutta; Nikhilesh, Tarun, Urmila, and M. N. Karna in Shillong; Priya, Christina, Will, Perveez, Rachel, Francesca, Kate, Kevin, and Mustapha in Cambridge; Anitha and Paul in London; Natalie and Alejandro, Rick and Beth, Franca and Ian, Nida and Suvadip, Li, and Alison in Toronto; Nancy, Donna, Paul, Michal, John, Wendy, Marcus, Kate, Donald, Lara, the Labour and Working-Class History Group, and the Young Pittsburgh Historians in Pittsburgh; Jim, Kay, Radhika, Ravi, Mridu, Prakash, Sharika, Stefania, and Marco in New Haven; Manju and Vydhy in California; and my two families (Ma, Nimi, Mintu, Lipi, Roni, Chandan, Dibya, Sumi, Rion, Saki, and Mumu in Assam; Carl, Jessie, Michael, Tamara, Stephen, Alice, Bob, and Margery in St Louis and New York). My PhD supervisor Chris Bayly and my MPhil supervisor Sumit Sarkar have my deepest gratitude for guidance and unceasing support on all fronts. At various stages of this project I received encouragement and scholarly advice from Bob Frykenberg, Sugata Bose, Tim Harper, Polly O' Hanlon, Richard Drayton, Nandini Gooptu. John Zavos, Tanika Sarkar,

Sanjib Baruah, Aditya Sarkar, Rohan d'Souza, Vinita Damodaran, Richard Grove, Radhika Singha, James Scott, Donald Sutton, Julie Elkner, Christina Granroth, Rachel Berger, Indrani Chatterjee, Mridu Rai, Prachi Deshpande, Sumit Guha, David Offenhall, Donna Gabbaccia, Steve Rockel, Eli Nathans, Rod Chalmers, Riho Isaka, Francesca Orsini, Sudeshna Purkayastha, Arupjyoti Saikia, Jim Hagan, and the late Raj Chandavarkar. I also thank participants in the World History Workshop at St Catharine's College; the Commonwealth and Overseas History Seminar and the South Asia Seminar at Cambridge; the Yale Agrarian Studies seminars; my fellow panelists at the South Asia Conference (Madison); the British South Asian Studies Association meetings, and the American History Association annual meetings. I am grateful to the editors of *Modern Asian Studies, Indian Economic and Social History Review*, the Occasional Paper Series at the Centre for South Asian Studies, Cambridge, and the anthology *The British Empire and the Natural World* (New York: Oxford University Press, 2010) for allowing me to use some materials previously published by them.

A special word of thanks to Ramya Srinivasan for reading and commenting on the entire manuscript, and to Barbara Weinstein, Daniel Walkowitz, and Rukun Advani for their patience and support over the long gestation of this book. I owe much to the anonymous publishers' readers for their erudite, insightful, and encouraging reports, and to the editorial team at Duke University Press for its help and guidance. Any mistakes that remain are mine alone.

The final fruition of this project owes a tremendous amount to Daniel Bender, who has read more about Assam and South Asia than he ever imagined he would. To Danny, my dearly beloved life partner and intellectual companion, and our darling daughter, Piya Rose (Mili), thank you so much for your love and patience.

Illustration
Acknowledgments

IN CONTRAST TO SOME other regions of British India, photo-graphic images of nineteenth-century and early-twentieth-century Assam are difficult to find, except for privately held prints which can seldom be effectively reproduced. Official photographic efforts by photographers such as Benjamin Simpson tended to focus on ethno-graphic portraits of selected "savage" groups. For this book I was able to locate a trove of hitherto unpublished images of the "Assam garden" and its denizens from an undated collection of Bourne and Shepherd photographs held by the National Anthropological Ar-chives, Smithsonian Museum Support Center, at Suitland, Mary-land. There is no photographer or date listed for most of these images, but some are attributed to Colin Murray, who was the firm's head photographer from 1870 and eventually took control in 1884 when the founders retired and left India. All illustrations in this book are courtesy of the National Anthropological Archives, Smith-sonian Institution: NAA INV 04423901, OPPS NEG 79-14668 (p. 105); NAA INV 04423302, OPPS NEG 81-3611 (p. 106); NAA INV 04423002 (p. 107); NAA INV 04423502 (p. 108); NAA INV 04423501 (p. 109); NAA INV 04423702 (p. 110); INN INV 04422901, OPPS NEG 81-3607 (p. 111); NAA INV 04423401 (p. 112, top); NAA INV 04423402 (p. 112, bottom); NAA INV 04423202 (p. 113); NAA INV 04423600 (p. 114); NAA INV 04423800, OPPS NEG 79-14667 (p. 115).

Note on
Orthography and Usage

I HAVE CHOSEN TO RETAIN the common usage "Assam" in preference to recent variations such as "Asom" and "Axom." While I use "Assamese" to refer to the inhabitants of Assam, I use "Asomiya" for the language.

I use "tribe" and "tribal" in deference to common usage in northeast India, where these words are not yet politically incorrect, indeed are seen as a badge of honour as against references to "caste" populations. In other regions of India "Adivasi" or "Adibasi" (original dweller) has supplanted "tribal," but the former term is used in northeast India solely by the descendants of "coolie" labourers who wish to build political and other links with their brethren elsewhere. Even among them the term "Tea-Tribe" is in wider use.

Other terms such as "coolie," "savage," and "native," which convey opprobrium yet have historically specific meanings, are used with quotation marks at first appearance, but those are dropped thereafter in the interests of keeping the text readable.

Surnames such as "Barua," which are transliterated differently by different people, are used in a single form except in quoted matter. Given the many people with the same surname, first names and initials are used to distinguish one from the other.

Place names such as "Guwahati" and "Nagaon" are given in their current form. However, I have retained older, better-known spellings for places such as Calcutta and institutions such as Gauhati University.

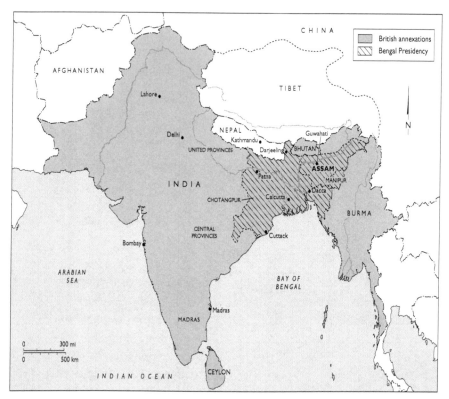

British India, showing the Bengal Presidency and Assam

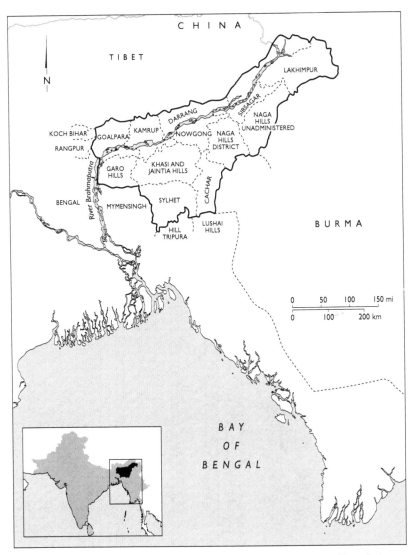

District map of British Assam

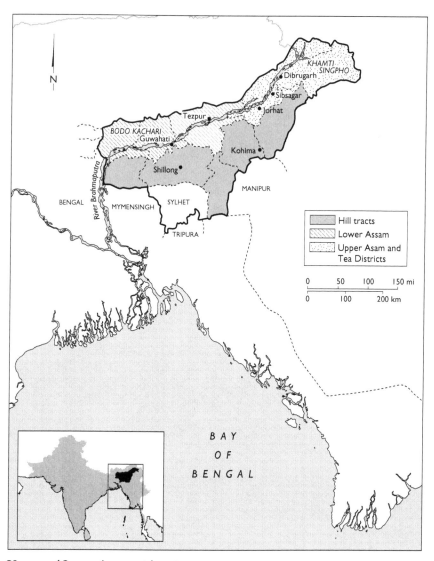

Upper and Lower Assam with main towns

Introduction

Passages along the Brahmaputra

IN 1841 A YOUNG MAN FROM ASSAM embarked on a lengthy journey along the Brahmaputra river. Voyaging in solitary splendour with an entourage of servants, Anandaram Dhekial Phukan had as his destination the city of Calcutta, where he aimed to join the prestigious Hindu School. Through the nineteenth century many young men across the Indian subcontinent undertook urban educational passages to cities such as Delhi, Lahore, Allahabad, Madras, Bombay, and Calcutta. Anandaram was the first inhabitant of Assam to venture upon such a novel journey. In Benedict Anderson's classic phrase, he was a pioneer of the new secular pilgrimage.[1] The new pilgrimages and urban encounters formed an essential component within a larger set of historical changes: they involved making an imperial "garden" and accompanying it, creating momentous encounters with modernity for Assam and India through British colonial rule.

For those officials, clerks, and migrants from British India who followed East India Company gunboats and explorers into Assam from the 1820s onward, the landscape of Anandaram's homeland lacked a sufficiency of urban concentrations and transport infrastructure. Nineteenth-century Assam's countryside was dotted with immense forested tracts and a large number of water bodies, interspersed with hamlets and small urban clusters. In place of nucleated villages populated by specialized cultivating and artisanal groups, the river-valley plains alternated small riverside hamlets with wooded and cultivated tracts. The largest urban settlements, Guwahati, Jorhat, Sibsagar, and Shillong, each possessed a few thousand inhabitants and blended into surrounding rural hamlets. Decades of political strife when the Ahom kingdom of Assam faced multiple internal and external challenges left a virtual absence of wheel-ready roads and thinned out the population. Hill tracts that bordered the river plains had even sparser populations and dense forested terrain. Peasants moved between shifting and settled agricultural modes, punctuated with extensive use of arable, forest, and water commons.

Anandaram's ship took two long months to reach Calcutta. Various transport bottlenecks long separated Assam from easy access to adjoining regions. A challenging topography aided rulers in maintaining independence from external political formations such as the Mughal Empire, while accentuating the region's ecological and economic distinctiveness. The natural frontiers of hilly tracts such as the Naga Hills separated the Assam plains from Himalayan and Sinic neighbours. Other natural obstructions, on both land and water, hindered long-distance connections with the Gangetic plains of Northern and Eastern India. Despite a length of over three thousand miles, year-round turbulence and seasonal floods limited navigation on the Brahmaputra river and its tributaries. Alternative land routes that linked the Brahmaputra and Gangetic plains had the disadvantage of crossing impenetrable, wooded, and high-altitude territories such as the Khasi and Jaintia Hills. Rains and floods made such territories almost impassable for long stretches of the year. All these factors hindered Assam's pre-modern trade and deterred many travellers. Historically such geographical inaccessibility also shaped external representations. Over the ages Sanskrit and Persian chroniclers depicted Assam as a remote periphery to which legend and hearsay attributed a fearsome reputation for supernatural wonders and esoteric witching rituals.

The British annexation of Assam in 1826 and the resultant economic and political restructuring necessitated overcoming transport hurdles. Despite the Brahmaputra's notorious reputation among navigators, commercially run steamers now joined country boats in plying the waterways. These steamers carried increasing volumes of people and commodities. However, improvements necessitated time and money. In the 1850s a frustrated official complained that a voyage from Calcutta to Assam took as long as a voyage from the Cape of Good Hope to London. A decade later — some twenty years after Anandaram's journey — a planter was dismayed that this voyage still required two weeks.

By this point in the mid-nineteenth century the discovery of Assam tea held the prospect of refinement for what seemed a wild, jungle-laden frontier, and promised to enhance the economic prosperity of the British Empire. Assam acquired strategic and economic import just as Britain sought to turn its Indian possessions to best account. Tea cultivation rapidly expanded into a million-pound industry bringing large colonial revenues. The name Assam became synonymous with tea, an everyday staple for households worldwide. A range of interlocutors, from British bio-prospectors to American missionaries to Assamese gentry, extolled the Edenic transformation under way, of a jungle into a garden. They conjured up a future ordered landscape of export-producing tea plantations, a stark contrast to the partially cultivated and imperfectly commercialized state of Nature that they saw in the present.

In the past the Ahom kings, ruling over the greater part of the Assam plains, successfully resisted most Mughal imperial incursions. However, they were weakened by internal strife, and much less capable when later forced to face an expansionist Burmese state. Burmese aggrandizers were expelled from Assam only after the East India Company's military intervention in 1825–26. This first Anglo-Burmese war, which the British undertook principally to safeguard adjoining Bengal possessions, eventually led to the annexation of Ahom Assam and neighbouring chiefdoms. Ultimately the British took over virtually the entire frontier region known today as north-east India.

Initially most of these annexations were incorporated into the Bengal Presidency of British India. From 1875 the British government instituted a separate province of Assam and adjoining it, separately administered northeast frontier tracts. Assam according to the common understanding (as distinct from Assam as defined by its fluctuating political boundaries) consisted of the valley plains of the Brahmaputra river-system and the hill tracts that immediately surrounded them. In addition, from the divisions of the Bengal Presidency (1905–12) up to the era of Indian independence and partition

(1947), the vagaries of colonial politics ushered the Sylhet plain, with ties to historic Bengal, directly into Assam's ambit. Long-term organic connections that had evolved through ecology and history meant that more distant hilly peripheries also played an important role in modern Assam's history and politics. After 1947 Assam's boundaries underwent further changes.

On returning from Calcutta, Anandaram Dhekial Phukan found that his experience of western education and his command over the English language eventually helped him become British Assam's first native magistrate. His family roots were in the Brahmaputra valley's second-tier élite, an upper-caste service gentry that served the Ahom state in a bureaucratic capacity. Like Anandaram, many members of this gentry managed to use administrative knowledge and a virtual monopoly over literacy to ease into British clerical service. In contrast, the top-ranking pre-modern élite, the Ahom warrior aristocracy, lost ground in political and economic matters.

A prolific writer in the Asomiya, Bengali, and English languages, Anandaram expressed the modernistic, patriotic, and improving desires of many locals. Beginning with his father, Haliram, and taking in Anandaram, his cousin Gunabhiram Barua, and their offspring, this gentry family contributed four generations of publicists, mostly men but also a few women. These were authors and commentators active in the burgeoning public arenas of colonial modernity. Anandaram, described as the most prominent representative of "Young Assam," publicly extolled new avenues for economic uplift while seeking progress for Assamese society, language, and culture. Succeeding generations of publicists, while they disagreed with Anandaram as to the state's willingness to promote local improvement, followed his lead in creating programmatic initiatives for social and cultural progress. Until the turn of the century most publicists were upper-caste males who had greater access to education and public life. But from the early twentieth century onward Assam's public arenas saw increasing visibility of educated lower-caste and tribal males, as well as women from different social groups.

From the mid-nineteenth century the British state nurtured an export-oriented tea enterprise as an essential part of the ideology of agrarian improvement that it enunciated for its Indian colony in general, and Assam in particular. However, it eventually neglected the overall development of the region and its infrastructure outside the European-dominated industry and its tea plantations. Partly the justification was what it claimed as the alleged lack of interest of most locals in economic advancement. The British stigmatized the Assamese as a lazy people, enervated by home-grown opium. As tea and rice acreage replaced verdant forests, the state created a legal apparatus to import plantation workers on indentured and penal contracts. The entry of over a million labouring migrants irrevocably changed Assam's social landscape and nurtured new notions of racial and cultural alterity. The consequences reached beyond an imperial labour regime to create intricate interplays between cultural constructions of race, social histories of resistance, and local imaginings of modernity and nationhood. ✱ *Thesis*

In this book I argue that a wide-ranging rhetoric of "improvement" and "progress" came to characterize both colonial efforts to order Assam into an imperial garden and local élites' responses to them. The varied, protean, and contested meanings of improvement and progress — whether plans for agrarian improvement dear to imperial scientists, policymakers, and tea capitalists, or projects of cultural and political *unnati* (progress) reiterated in the writings and speeches of local intellectuals and entrepreneurs — form a broad unifying theme to understand the modern making of Assam, and beyond that, the making of modern India and South Asia. The book seeks to elucidate such important processes intrinsic to the constitution of cultural capital and the political economy of colonial and modern India, as well as the complicated interactions between migratory and local groups within a regional field.

My subject is a febrile milieu where migratory and local groups generated, contested, and modified a host of identities around place, people, and community nodes alongside the immense changes that colonial modernity brought for Assam and India. Multiple improvement agendas provided inspiration for locals and migrants looking to circulate and mobilize around new and remade identities, even as the colonial establishment shaped Assam into a commodity-producing garden space. New and plural identities such as Bodo or Baganiya or Na-Asomiya developed in interaction with the dominant identity of Assamese, with each other, and with the larger field of local, provincial, and colonial discourses in the context of a rapidly changing political economy, social and cultural ferment, colonial state governance, and emergent nationalist ideologies.

Hirawidz (1995)

Nineteenth-century British colonial knowledge ranked indigenous societies as variously advanced and backward in relation to each other and European modernity. Within an older Indic knowledge system, Assam's borderlands location and comparative inaccessibility already gave it an image as a land of witchcraft and demonic people. Now, a seemingly modern vocabulary of utility and diligence added to this representation, with frequent condemnations of the region's inhabitants as backward, even in comparison with other colonial subjects. In sharp contrast to the negativity attached to lazy natives, colonialism promoted a glowing image of primitive diligence for the "aboriginal" men, women, and children recruited to Assam from distant, impoverished regions such as Chotanagpur. The book studies this racialization of local and migrant groups as shaped by, and in turn transforming, the Aryanist caste and Victorian race science ideologies that Tony Ballantyne depicts as central to European "imperial webs."[2]

The consolidation of an imperial tea garden both depended on and promoted these, and other types of movements, migration, and circulation. British Indian state space and the lived geographies that it generated, ranging from railways to standardized accounting, framed everyday experiences of colonialism for most colonial subjects.[3] By the end of the nineteenth century railroads reduced the journey from Calcutta into Assam to two or three days. This eased both tea exports and the influx of migrants. The majority of new arrivals still consisted of tea coolies — dispossessed migrants with little option but to stay and toil, despite harsh conditions that local labourers refused to countenance. Often they arrived in the wake of what Mike Davis terms the late Victorian holocausts of famine and drought, conditions exacerbated by the harshness of colonial revenue demands.[4] But increasingly there were other, better-off migrants, such as traders from Rajasthan, soldier-graziers from Nepal, and clerks from Sylhet and Calcutta. Thousands more settlers from densely populated East Bengal also entered: landless peasants attracted to cultivable lands on the last-remaining agrarian frontier of the subcontinent. In contrast to incoming groups, most Assamese travellers were sojourners who undertook secular urban pilgrimages into the Indic heartland and carried experiences of colonial modernity into Assam.

While this book focuses on the locality and the region of Assam, it locates this subject-field in terms of larger trans-regional and trans-imperial discourses and institutions. It argues that modern Assam, as it moved from being a previously peripheral frontier kingdom into an imperial tea garden and a key hinterland for British India, was made by and against a variety of Indic encounters. Many of these took place between Assam and Calcutta. The imperial city and port of Calcutta, which served as a key site for the circulation of commodities, ideas, and people, helped to shape processes crucial to South Asia's colonial modernity that affected manifold regions and peoples outside Bengal itself. An "imagined" Calcutta and a "real" Calcutta were central to many of the economic, political, and cultural transactions that fostered a sense of Assamese belonging, regionality, and national aspirations. Tea played an essential role in these transactions, whether in terms of commerce and the world market, labour mobilization of coolie workers, or cultural shifts around consumption and production. Élite and labouring groups evolved new understandings about locality, regions, and nation, while engaging with colonial modernity, cultural circulation, and commodity capitalism.

The book analyses a variety of state-generated archival and colonial documents as well as vernacular and local sources to explore this broad canvas. Some of its major themes and arguments are outlined below, followed by a summary of its chapters, and an account of its making.

Making Empire's Garden:
Labour, Colonial Modernity, and Public Arenas

Through the entire course of colonial rule, urban and infrastructure growth within Assam remained tardy, since state attention and private investment concentrated on the agro-industrial plantation sector. The export-oriented tea enterprise focused on forging intimate connections that were external to the region, centering around Calcutta and its port, and looking to the British metropole beyond. Rather than serve as agents within Assam, Calcutta's managing agency houses were the hub for Assam tea's capital accumulation and disbursement, higher-level recruitment, supplies, and marketing. On the eve of the First World War about three-fourths of the total British capital invested in India was still based in Calcutta. The city's managing agencies locked together the structures of commerce, finance, railways, collieries, as well as the jute and tea industries, to control the commanding heights of British India's economy. For instance, processed tea harvests were dispatched from Assam plantations by steamer and train to Calcutta's port, then onward to London and export markets worldwide. Tea equipment and managerial personnel for Assam were obtained all the way from Britain, via Calcutta. This created a unique relationship of dependence between Assam as an imperial garden undergoing development, and Calcutta as the sophisticated gateway for capital, expertise, exports, urban values, and trans-imperial circulation.

The hierarchical tenor of the economic relationship extended into a wider cultural and political realm. Until 1874 (and briefly during 1905–12) the British governed Assam as a part of Bengal. Well into the twentieth century Assam's élites depended on an external infrastructure of higher education in the absence of adequate local opportunities. As a new generation of gentry males sought college education to take advantage of colonial job openings, many became sojourners in the nearest metropolis, Calcutta. For most, this resulted in their first, momentous encounters with the materials of modernity, ranging from the printing press and the university to the railway and the restaurant. Exiles from home, these young men transcended caste, ethnic, and religious differences to develop strong affective ties to a *des* (homeland) and its Asomiya mother-tongue. Often this produced a complex situation in which economic links and newly created emotional attachments to Calcutta and Bengali culture jostled with regional pride and cultural nationalism. Thus journeys and passages into the urban realms of British India helped local élites to articulate their specific claims to the colonial modernity that they encountered, while at the same time they negotiated differing understandings of what was Assam and what was Bharat (India), and the spatial and emotive nodes of evolving identities.

Imperial capital and enterprise transformed Assam into a plantation economy characterized as much by rapid demographic change as by the visible emergence of ordered tea gardens and ricefields in place of forested, riverine, and commons lands. This immense socioeconomic transformation provided an important impetus for local élites to undertake parallel projects of cultural assertion and social demarcation, and lent urgency to their claims to be represented in the political sphere.

With this broad field of study, this book connects labour history and the exploration of colonial modernity. It argues that the racialized creation of the tea labourer was the catalyst for a larger South Asian project of cultural redefinition whereby members of Assam's gentry sought to insert their homeland into an imagined "Indo-Aryan" community and a modern Indian political space. Local élites sought to assert their distance from aboriginal labouring coolies as well as indigenous low-caste and 'tribal' groups. Simultaneously they claimed kinship with upper-caste Indic groups elsewhere on the subcontinent. As college-educated youths returned to Assam, now valourized as their beloved motherland of Asomi Aai (Assam the Mother), they presented themselves as modern representatives of Assam and India. Language became a fundamental part of the way they imagined the past and present. Based on their Asomiya mother-tongue's historical relationship to Sanskrit and Sanskrit-derived languages, the dominant gentry élite claimed intimate ties with a broad swath of high-status South Asian groups. A variety of historically framed linguistic and racial claims allowed local élites, Hindu and Muslim, to assert claims to modernity while simultaneously pushing the burden of primitiveness onto "non-Aryan" neighbours, whether indigenous tribals or migrant coolie plantation workers.

Jürgen Habermas's concept of the public sphere as one that mediated between society and state has long offered historians a useful framework for analyzing the structures of modernity.[5] The public sphere held out the potential for emancipation as well as for social, economic, and political exclusion. While this served well as a discursive model against which actual political and personal relations could be measured, Habermas's sole focus on the bourgeois liberal public elided important elements of contestation and unequal access. Subsequent modifications of Habermas's model, for example by Geoff Eley and Johanna Meehan, suggest that the public sphere instead be regarded as the arena where cultural or ideological or gendered contest or negotiation among a variety of publics took place in a single structured setting that advantaged some and disadvantaged others.[6]

Francesca Orsini's and Sanjay Joshi's explorations of the Hindi public sphere have proved particularly illuminating in studying colonial modernity in a specific South Asian context. Orsini's work focuses upon the socially subordinate vernacular élite (which constituted the bulk of North India's public), its ambitions and frustrations, and its inclination to establish dogmatic norms for linguistic and cultural standards and exclude certain social groups from equal participation.[7] Sanjay Joshi argues that a middle class constituted itself primarily through ability and desire for cultural entrepreneurship.[8] Modernity was not so much an ideology as a project that empowered its principal purveyors, the (mostly) male, colonial-era descendants of service élites, publicists active in the public sphere. These publicists were not necessarily distinguished in terms of access to economic or political power, but active involvement in public-sphere politics partially allowed them to fashion their own destinies, and the nation/s of which they dreamed.

By adapting such notions of overlapping and contending publics, this book explores the consolidation of an Assamese public sphere from the late nineteenth century onward, where multiple public arenas emerged, coexisted, competed, converged, and fragmented. It argues that print culture was an important instrument for extending communicative networks and the reach of these publics. Print had a considerable if limited democratizing impact in this colonial space. In Assam print had its origins with a nineteenth-century missionary periodical that standardized and popularized a pre-modern court idiom. It enabled the wide dissemination and circulation of improving vernacular writings from different ends of a broad social spectrum. Printed personal testimonies, autobiographies, letters, memoirs, and biographies allow an important, often overlooked entry into what Sumit Sarkar terms the fragile, doubt-ridden self-images and aspirations of colonial publicists.[9]

From the mid-nineteenth century Assamese élites became active users of the new media of public meetings, voluntary associations, and the printing press. Initially these media were dominated by gentry voices who articulated exclusivist claims to Indo-Aryan racial and cultural belonging. They portrayed tea labourers in particular as backward newcomers whose menial values and non-Aryan origins isolated them from future possibilities of progress. Nonetheless, by the 1920s this mindset gradually changed as Gandhian and other modernist pan-Indian and transnational ideologies of emancipation gained influence. Many men and women in Assam joined the Congress, Communist, and Socialist political parties. Gandhian ideals in particular now inspired many among them to propose a wholesale reform of society and a philosophy of national resistance and progress. At the same time they advocated local campaigns for temperance and improved treatment of coolies, tribals, peasants, and women. This reformism perforce involved élite rethinking about socially subaltern groups such as migrant coolies, previously stigmatized as incapable of mainstream participation and progress. This rethinking received increased urgency in the twentieth century as many subaltern groups themselves began to use public media and political forums to challenge dominant articulations of region and nation that excluded them from full belonging.

Élites responded variously to these challenges from below, sometimes negatively, at other times sympathetically, and often paternalistically, while the Assamese public arena expanded in scope and reach to accommodate the demands of newly vocal groups such as Bodo tribals and educated women. As various new groups became active participants in public discussions about history, progress, language, and community, late colonial and postcolonial attempts by local élites to consolidate a modern Assam faced a constant process of negotiation and disputation. Even while the dominant regional identity of Assamese achieved a strong public presence, a host of affiliated identities, whether of Bodos, Assamese Nepalis, or Na-Asomiya Muslims, developed to interact with, emulate, or contest that dominant one. All of these interacted too with other regional identities such as that of Sylhetti Bengalis, and most significantly with the novel concepts of a national Indian identity and of nation-states to which all might belong.

Improvement and Progress: Garden, Colony, and Nation/s

Gardens had long-standing associations with notions of paradise and civilization, whether in Indo-Persian or in European traditions. However, from the early modern period onward there appeared a remarkable change, as Europeans began to view gardens as receptacles of empire, filled with collections of flora and fauna accumulated from the lands they had discovered and colonized. The creation of botanical and zoological gardens linked with bio-prospecting explorations and imperial expansion was paralleled by global endeavours to transform seemingly nonproductive spaces into productive gardens. Assam appeared to be a promising example of such a space.

Assam's arrival as an imperial tea garden was in the first place inspired by a larger ideological doctrine of agrarian improvement. Progressive capitalism avowedly formed the fulcrum of British Indian socioeconomic policy, especially under Lord William Bentinck, a self-professed "practical agriculturist." However, this state-inspired improvement doctrine proved restrictive in its actual implementation. In Assam, for instance, full participation and benefits from the tea industry became virtually reserved for white denizens of the empire. Still, the slogan of improvement continued to generate some optimism among locals, particularly Assam's gentry. Over the nineteenth century, while many locals strived for a bright future for themselves through the new tea garden economy, increasingly their energies were directed toward a program of social and cultural regeneration. They called this objective unnati, a term increasingly in use all over the subcontinent. Even in the early twentieth century, when Assamese élites had come to bitterly contest most of the British claims to improvement, modified visions of unnati still shaped the mental horizon of most nationalists.

The classic contribution to the study of colonial improvement and progress is Ranajit Guha's history of the Permanent Settlement of Bengal in 1793.[10] He traces the origins of the British colonial faith in Indian landed élites as an improving class to the ideas of the French physiocratic thinkers and the English agricultural revolution. When Bengal's zamindar landlords failed to justify the faith which had bestowed on them the Permanent Settlement's landed estates, with the state's revenue claims fixed in all perpetuity, the British regime transferred hopes for agrarian improvement onto other landed groups such as prosperous peasant-proprietors, or "ryots." Over the nineteenth century the colonial state abandoned the model of Bengal's Permanent Settlement in favor of that of time-bound Ryotwari land settlements with peasant-proprietors. In his later writings Ranajit Guha makes an important polemical intervention when he argues that the idiom of improvement, in areas as varied as education, the factory, and marriage legislation, informed almost all colonial efforts to relate non-antagonistically to the ruled but in reality offered little but political sops to placate élites.[11] Subsequently a contest for hegemony defined the rivalry between bourgeois aspirants to power and the colonial rulers. In contrast to Ranajit Guha, another historian of modern South Asia, Peter Robb, asserts that colonial rule, however hollow its improving pretensions, made important beginnings in creating new forms of interested attachment to government, and through those generated an expectation of progress which outlasted colonialism.[12]

On the subject of improvement and agrarian initiatives, David Arnold points out that individual European administrators, missionaries, naturalists, and a variety of Indian groups played a significant role in extending and modifying this doctrine beyond the purview of the colonial state.[13] Ranajit Guha's work on the Permanent Settlement left unexplored such later incarnations that developed in regions other than Bengal, and in a variety of other hands. Richard Drayton makes an important intervention on the doctrine of improvement, using the lens of the newly emergent historiographies of science and environment and the "new imperial history."[14] He argues that agrarian improvement was a key instrument of British state policy, as it disseminated a range of improving ideas and practices, particularly those associated with the natural and agrarian sciences, from metropolitan Britain into its nineteenth-century colonial empire. However, Drayton's focus on Kew Gardens and British botanists is too restrictive: it needs to be amplified by expansive trans-imperial studies of how various local and metropolitan actors took the notion of improvement into new directions even as older initiatives failed. For instance, when Bengal's Permanent Settlement turned sour, British and Indian members of Calcutta's once-prominent Agricultural and Horticultural Society moved from advocacy of core agrarian innovations into a narrower horticultural agenda. In newly annexed Assam the doctrine of improvement inspired the ambitious project of an imperial garden based around tea. Individuals as diverse as the Bengali merchant Dwarkanath Tagore, the Assamese aristocrat Maniram Barbhandar Barua, the American missionary Nathan Brown, and the Calcutta-based British trader William Prinsep expressed faith in the transformative possibilities of tea enterprise.

For most Assam locals, tea eventually became the god that failed. Despite a brief window when improving British partnerships with a diversity of local individuals and groups seemed achievable, the late-nineteenth-century tea project of British India was consolidated as a predominantly white enterprise. Indeed, the supremacy of British capital and management in this sphere was such that its hold over the tea industry in India outlasted the era of formal empire, well into the late twentieth century. A combination of ideological, economic, and political factors caused the tea enterprise to be dominated by racialized constructions pertaining to entrepreneurship and labour. Historians of labour such as Ranajit Das Gupta, Rana Behal, Prabhu Mohapatra, and Samita Sen have shown how the coolie system of Assam's plantations developed along racialized and exploitative lines similar to disciplinary and legal regimes on other imperial plantations, creating a distinct enclave economy ruled by a "Planter's Raj."[15] The colonial state's obsession with the tea industry also derailed other improving efforts for the region. Although British officials introduced Ryotwari land settlements with Assam's peasant-proprietors to replace pre-modern land tenures, the tea industry's low opinion of locals and peasant society meant that the kind of optimism vested by British administrators in Punjab's cultivators, for instance, was absent in Assam. As a corollary, even the limited infrastructural investment that other regions received from the colonial state was absent, or benefited only the tea sector where it existed. For instance, railway lines in Assam failed to connect the region's towns and districts, and instead served only the needs of plantation managements. A previously vague expectation that British rule ought to bring improvement to India, Thomas Metcalf argues, was consolidated by the mid-nineteenth century into a distinctive ideology of imperial governance, inspired by the ideals of British liberalism.[16] The historiography of colonial South Asia provides ample evidence of the huge gap between this ideology and its fulfillment. Nonetheless, the hopes evoked among many colonial subjects by the slogan of improvement cannot be ignored, nor can the initiatives that it catalyzed, although it ultimately disappointed.

One of the first locals to articulate optimistic views of state-led improvement, in particular its agrarian agenda, was Anandaram Dhekial Phukan, the young Assamese magistrate and publicist. In his vernacular writings in the 1840s and 1850s Anandaram explicitly referred to the image of a blooming, productive garden which would transform Assam through a combination of British and local enterprise. At the same time he expressed his dreams for a wholesale rejuvenation of local society. He hoped to enlist British support for locals' reformist efforts in arenas ranging from educational and language innovation to agricultural and peasant uplift. Anandaram's vision received new impetus from a new generation of late-nineteenth-century Assamese gentry who placed progress at the centre stage of hopes for their homeland's present and future, eulogizing the transformation of Assam through the tea enterprise. However, by the end of the nineteenth century racially exclusionist colonial policies had gradually demolished local optimism about collaborative possibilities in the tea garden economy. While members of the Assamese gentry had initially aspired to become tea planters in their own right, most could become only hired clerical employees of British tea firms: the few who achieved planter status operated on a petty scale compared to their white counterparts. Nonetheless, the dependence of local élites upon the economic and political structures of colonial modernity meant that they had little choice but to look to the state for support, even when dissatisfied with its policies. In contrast to Anandaram's expansive hopes for agrarian development, later generations of Assamese publicists proffered few autonomous ideas for economic progress. This was a telling indicator of the increasingly restrictive circumstances for entrepreneurship in fin-de-siècle colonial India.

Sumit Sarkar has acutely analyzed how from 1870 to 1905 dreams of improvement and reform under British auspices were dashed without as yet being replaced by an alternative viable patriotic vision of nationalist activism which might end colonial rule.[17] A disjuncture of state and society, politics and community, began to appeal to many Indian intellectuals as a result of disillusionment with promises of improvement from above and with the futility of existing mendicant oppositional politics. Manu Goswami adds another important element to our understanding when she argues that this period also saw the elaboration of India as a spatially bounded national space and economy.[18] By the 1920s quests for individual and community advancement were able to lay the foundation for a broader, more optimistic agenda to seek cultural and political progress for region and nation. The Assamese élite objective of unnati was supplemented by other calls for progress — whether from Muslim peasant leaders or lower-caste and tribal publicists, who saw agrarian and economic improvement as an urgent prerequisite for broader social and cultural uplift and community redefinition. As P. K. Datta's work on Bengali Muslim publicists shows, such voices from below have often been overshadowed by urban élite and state discourses.[19] This book analyzes a number of early-twentieth-century improvement and identity initiatives to better locate the ground-level complexities of the quests for colonial independence and nationhood to which they led.

In the postcolonial period the expectations of progress that the colonial state had so singularly failed to meet were transferred onto its successors, the new nation-states of South Asia. In postcolonial India, Sri Lanka, Nepal, Pakistan, and Bangladesh (which incorporated some parts of erstwhile British Assam as well as East Bengal), the thwarting of these expectations often played a major role in creating volatile political situations. In particular, the twenty-first-century Indian state of Assam confronts multiple challenges from various insurgent groups, who accuse regional and central governments of perpetuating patterns of colonial exploitation long after the demise of the British Empire. Disillusionment with the slow pace of socioeconomic progress and perceived disenfranchisement has impelled different groups, from tribals to former coolies, to contest the legitimacy of the Indian nation-state and its local stakeholders. However, many of these contesting movements have themselves manifested weakness. Although critiques of the region's "economic backwardness and political marginality" have served as their rallying cry, they have often failed to enunciate broad-based programs for economic growth, social equity, and grassroots political mobilization for democracy. Instead nativist demands for territorial autonomy and a sectarian type of identity politics, lacking a proper class and gender critique, have been common. At times there have been attempts to seize power and territory through sectarian killing and ethnic cleansing. Contestatory groups have been riven with dissent while the viability of the twentieth century's national formations appears increasingly fragile. Meanwhile, India's Northeast remains buffeted by ecological, economic, and demographic pressures, with social inequities worsened by global commodity capitalism and migration, and political rivalries between the nation-states whose frontiers it demarcates.

This book examines local and imperial knowledge, economic improvement and social progress, racialized, ethnicized, and gendered identities, cultural and religious assertions, colonial exploitation, local resistances, and nationalist ideologies. For the most part its detailed regional archival study covers the period from the mid-nineteenth century to the mid-twentieth, but it ends with broader, urgent, and troubling questions which face twenty-first-century South Asia, and many other countries and regions of the global South.

Part I focuses on the British discovery of Assam tea and the establishment of an export-oriented enterprise based on plantation production using indentured migrant labour. Chapter 1 explores how the imperatives of plantation production reordered Assam's natural environment, in which commons, forested, and swidden lands, and people, were subjected to the scientific arguments, the economic pragmatism, and eventually the industrial discipline of creating an imperial tea garden. Chapter 2 discusses Assam's character as a historical borderlands distinguished by long-standing movements of commodities, people, and material cultures. Even as colonialism brought about the modern migration of coolies to serve as a docile work force for its garden, its construction of local indolence helped create a distinct, white-dominated enclave sector for tea production, and constituted the coolie migrant as a racial and cultural Other for Assam's inhabitants. Chapter 3 argues that the plantation production system introduced for the Assam garden decisively transformed the region's social demographics, far beyond the entry and settlement of labouring tea coolies. New opportunities emerged on this expanding frontier for Marwari traders, Nepali graziers, Sylhetti clerks, and East Bengali Muslim peasants to migrate and settle in Assam, and to create new social and political identities in the process.

Part II focuses on the social, cultural, and political circulation of people, ideas, and commodities that distinguished colonial modernity for the Assam region and the subcontinent as a whole. It explores how members of the Assamese gentry transformed themselves into a modern intelligentsia and dominated the new public sphere and its discussions around history, nationhood, and progress. The complicated, often fraught nature of the identities that developed on this Indic frontier meant an uneasy location within the parameters of a historical Assamese homeland and a new Indian nation in the making. Chapter 4 argues that the transition to colonial British rule engendered important cultural shifts and a variety of ideological and power struggles, particularly for the temporal and religious notables of the old order who faced cultural misunderstandings and economic conflicts with colonial functionaries. In contrast, the service gentry of the Ahom regime were able to use their literate and bureaucratic skills to gain employment under the British, and accumulate a new cultural capital of literature, language, and devotionalism. Chapter 5 explores the consolidation of a colonial intelligentsia and the emergence of key publicists within an urban associational culture and a

vernacular public sphere. The involvement of the Brahmaputra valley's predominantly caste gentry élites with the city of Calcutta, its
educational institutions, print culture, and consumption patterns,
formed an important impetus for a new social identity which sought
to balance local particularity with Indic cultural and religious belonging, in order to initiate a new agenda of improvement and progress. Chapter 6 focuses upon how a newly standardized vernacular
language emerged as the most visible component of this modernizing Assamese identity. It explores the social inclusions and exclusions
that this process engendered, and how the politics of empowering
language necessitated a vocabulary that stressed historical and emotional ties to a historicized and gendered mother-tongue. Chapter 7
argues that the constitution of Assam's multiple public arenas and
their claims to the twentieth century's nation-in-making operated
through a new language of gendered social improvement, and racial
and historical entitlements. Contestatory movements found new ad-
herents and political arguments within the volatile expectations generated by the achievement of independence from colonial rule, and
the disillusionments that the postcolonial nation and its structures of
regional governance subsequently generated.

The conclusion considers how Assam has evolved through the
fraught destinies of local nationalisms and regional configurations
within South Asia, as well as the impact of globalizing market processes. The making of modern Assam involved the making of the
Indian national formation of which it came to constitute a part, and
to which it poses so many challenges today. Assam offers a striking
example of how the interplay of global commodity flows, imperial
rule, and local cultural contestations has shaped the expression of
nationalisms in the postcolonial, multiethnic societies and states of
the global South. The lush, green appearance of the tea garden which
empire created still conceals deep fissures and conflicts, despite all
the hopes and promises associated with the postcolonial regimes
that succeeded it.

Global and Local Journeys: Personal and Political

In the course of my writing this book, a typical conversation would
go this way. "Hmmm. Writing about India . . . oh, Assam. Interest-

ing. Umm, where is it, actually?" Over my years as a student and professional in Britain, the United States, and Canada, I eventually evolved a strategy to deal with this sort of question. I would remind my interlocutor of her last trip to the supermarket, to its shelves of tea, where lay the packets marked Assam. There, I announced, was my subject. The conversation usually ended at this point. Packaged tea was central to the world marketplace, ubiquitous yet mysterious, travelling far and wide with evocations of distant places, depictions of graceful women picking the leaf. This, many questioners might have concluded, was the essence of Assam. This Assam existed in Cambridge, London, Pittsburgh, and Toronto, as it did everywhere yet nowhere.

Was Assam merely a label, like Darjeeling or Demerara or Madeira, an adjunct to the term "tea," for the world at large? I was reminded of my college days in Delhi. Whenever my Assam home was mentioned, my peers would exclaim, "Oh, yes, your father must be in tea." This was an assumption that I would hasten to correct, thinking of my sober parent and his middle-class government job, worlds away from the tea manager's quasi-feudal bungalow and lifestyle, an entrenched "Raj" relic in postcolonial India. In my family's existence Assam tea impinged mostly through tales of distant relatives living in "gardens" whose retinue of servants grew yearly, and whose children attended expensive boarding schools, and of course also through the CTC beverage that my economical parents continually drank, so different from the beautifully packaged, first-flush teas that I later encountered in the gourmet market of the global North. Tea workers, and the lives they led, meant little to me in my sheltered youth, although I was puzzled by the term "coolie manuh" (coolie people) employed by adults around me, usually in a disparaging manner.

Puzzlingly, the Assam history that I studied in my provincial Guwahati school resounded with kings and warriors, viceroys and commissioners, poets and freedom fighters, but said nothing about the universe of tea. When I made the journey to Delhi University, I connected with little that my fellow students from "mainstream India" associated with Assam. Certainly I was ignorant of any skill in performing the Assamese Bihu folk dance. That was the other image which every Indian knew, a vividly gendered fantasy circulated endlessly by national fetes celebrating the country's Republic Day, with demonstrations of the region's "folk" culture by supple, smiling youngsters clad in "ethnic" dress.

During those university years another Assam emerged in newspaper headlines and television screens, never to go away. This was the Assam of bombs and killings, massacres of Bangladeshi and North Indian labouring migrants, Bodo tribal insurgents, and the United Liberation Front of Assam (ULFA), joined by other militant groups variously claiming to represent tribals, tea labourers, and the descendants of East Bengali Muslims. The Indian armed and paramilitary forces, already ubiquitous in neighbouring Nagaland where "rebels" fought for Naga independence from India, were repeatedly deployed to curb this sort of resistance. After decades of seeming invisibility Assam entered mainstream India's consciousness, even that of the BBC and CNN, but yet again, as an aberration. In India's schools and colleges history had been taught for decades without reference to such a "periphery," a little corner of/f the map. Now twenty-first-century politics might incorporate Assam, sans history, as an example of primitivist ethnic insurgencies in a postmodern age.

I was born in Assam. I left it as a young adult, when in the manner of other young South Asians I travelled away, for study and work in a national metropolis and then in a global city. The Brahmaputra valley receded in my daily vision. I began to see it more clearly just when the never-never Assam of the mass media and the global shopping mall came closer to my life. As I shed the political indifference that my middle-class upbringing had bequeathed to me, the complicated and unbeautiful connections between tea, history, and politics came into sight. Assam's tea pickers and folk dancers were on display for the nation and the world, safely abstracted from class, race, and gendered contexts. Indian and international consumers could regale themselves with one or the other while Assam's dominant narratives erased both figures from history. In such manner were people and localities entered into the roll call of ethnicity, emptied of actual experience, the claims that imperialism, colonialism, nationalism, and globalization successively made on them.

Assam has been notably understudied in the modern scholarship on South Asia, partly because of its political volatility and strategic border location, partly because of its perceived remoteness from what policymakers and academics tend to view as the Indian normative paradigm. One of this book's arguments is that no such norm exists. Despite the rich recent crop of regionally and locally based historical and ethnographic studies of South Asia, there still exists an unfortunate tendency among some scholars to dwell defensively on an undifferentiated "India" and to elide the important constitutive links that particular regions and cultural groups developed with people and processes from other regions of South Asia and beyond. In this book I challenge these histories and seek to bring multiple archives of region, nation, empire, and postcolony into one frame of analysis, reflexivity, and understanding.

I. Making a Garden

1. Nature's Jungle, Empire's Garden

IN 1836 NATHAN BROWN and his fellow American Baptist missionaries journeyed up the Brahmaputra river into the remote recesses of
Upper Assam. For over four months they lived in country boats
beneath canopies of bamboo and palm leaves. At their destination,
Sadiya, its wild forested expanses inhabited by unlettered groups
deterred them somewhat. But Brown found optimism in the East
India Company's tea-growing efforts on this new northeastern frontier. He wrote, "If the means of grace are employed, may we not also
hope that [Assam] will become a garden of the lord?"[1]

[This chapter considers Assam's political and economic incorpora- ＊ *Time*
tion into the territories in British India ruled by the East India Com- *1820-1850*
pany between the 1820s and the 1850s and its parallel efforts at transforming the region into the British Empire's own tea garden.]The
British discovery of tea forests in Assam meant that a valuable commodity, previously a Chinese monopoly, could now be domesticated
within the British Empire. In this chapter I argue that the tea discovery catalyzed the making of Assam as an imperial garden for which
different groups — East India Company officials, tea entrepreneurs,
Baptist missionaries, and Assamese gentry — articulated their particular versions of improvement. Tea-growing Assam offered the East
India Company the opportunity to produce a commodity increasingly significant for world trade and the British domestic economy.
The ricefields of the Assamese peasantry began to be surrounded by
large tea estates, almost entirely held by European planters. British
officials and planters were the key players in this endeavour to convert the jungles of Assam into productive use for the imperial enter-

prise. Simultaneously, American missionaries aided this "civilizing" project as they sought souls to convert. Over the course of the nineteenth century Assam's peasants and forest dwellers found their lands and talents subordinated to the needs and desires of European entrepreneurs, while the local gentry attempted, with varying degrees of success, to carve out a role for themselves in the new garden.

Assam and the East India Company

The fertile plains of Assam were divided into distinct Upper and Lower regions. The two differed in many ways ecologically and culturally, but the mighty Brahmaputra river flowed through both. The rich silt deposited annually on the river's banks made these plains particularly suitable for rice cultivation. Prehistoric Neolithic horticultural cultivators were the first to cultivate rice in the Brahmaputra valley.[2] Over the centuries a rice diet remained central for Assam's inhabitants, colloquially known as *bhotua* (rice gluttons). The first domesticated rice variety was *ahu* rice, a dry variety, cultivated during the summers with a *kudali* (hoe). Later Indo-Aryan migrants from the North introduced higher-yielding and more labour-intensive *sali* rice (a wet variety), and its accompaniments, iron tools and cattle for ploughing. Indigenous communities of gatherers and cultivators in the Brahmaputra valley continued to make a living alongside new socially stratified agrarian polities.[3]

From the thirteenth century onward dynasties of Ahom kings ruled the fertile rice-growing territories of Upper Assam (their headquarters Gargaon and Rangpur were located near modern Sibsagar town). They sustained their rule through complex negotiations and alliances with neighbouring tribal and hill chiefdoms. As the early modern Ahom state expanded its hold into Lower Assam, it encountered migratory groups, cultural influences, and armed invasions from Bengal and Northern India. The Persian chronicler Mirza Nathan, who accompanied Mughal invading forces in the seventeenth century, graphically described Assam's hilly forests, torrential monsoon rains, and debilitating fevers which hindered them.[4] Assam's rulers successfully warded off most military threats while eagerly adopting some Indo-Persian courtly practices and fashions. By the late eighteenth century Assam was squeezed between two expansionist polities: the East India Company in Bengal and the Konbaung regime in Burma. Weakened by internal strife, the Ahom state was an easy target for Burmese armies. In 1825–26 the company's anxieties about a military threat to its Bengal territories precipitated the first Anglo-Burmese war. Its defeat of the Burmese annexed Assam to the Bengal Presidency. Initially the new rulers were dismayed at Assam's economic desolation after decades of political turmoil. Yet the new prospects for growing tea transformed British expectations. Instead of a profitless jungle, a new Eden beckoned.

Britain's engagement with Assam began at a pivotal moment in its career, as a modern British bureaucratic system gradually replaced military fiscal adventurism. New currents of morality and economical reform transformed public life. However, the East India Company had become notorious for financial profligacy and corruption. In 1784 William Pitt's government moved the East India Company directly under control by the Crown. Nevertheless, both public opinion and Parliament in Britain constantly attacked military expansion in India as imprudent and profitless. In defence the East India Company began to parade its commitment to the advance of science, knowledge, and morality. The tea discovery allowed it to claim an imperial triumph for both science and economics. Assam tea vindicated the vast potential of empire for the British people.

Agrarian science, immensely important for eighteenth-century Britain, also played a vital role in shaping imperial policies and their improvement agendas. The establishment of botanical gardens became part of the consolidation of new conquests. Historians of science such as David Mackay, Roy MacLeod, and Bruno Latour have described botanists of that age as agents of empire whose service to the colonial enterprise influenced the character of their scholarship.[5] In the words of Londa Schiebinger, "global networks of botanical gardens, the laboratories of colonial botany, followed the contours of empire, and gardens often served its needs."[6] For example, Robert Kyd's scheme for a Garden of Acclimatization proposed to cultivate varieties of cotton, tobacco, sugar, and tea in India to enable the British to outstrip rivals in the production of every valuable commodity.[7] Kyd's proposal was approved and a Royal Botanical Garden established at Calcutta in 1787. At the same time, a new breed of colonial governors and administrators transmitted post-Enlightenment ideas on governing land and people to Britain's possessions.

For instance, Lord Wellesley, the governor general of India from 1797, combined older Whig notions of the basis of politics in land with a new Physiocratic devotion to agrarian science. In this spirit Wellesley commissioned agrarian surveys of newly conquered lands. In the imperial historian Richard Drayton's words, these endeavours inaugurated a complicated theatre of virtue through which the Crown and the East India Company offered to the British people and their colonial subjects living testimony of improving colonial administration.[8] Its activities helped the East India Company to position itself as a dedicated patron of learning. But endeavours which advanced commercial interests still received priority. In the case of tea, its commercial importance helped propel the plant to the centre stage of imperial science and governance.

Trade in tea was the most profitable component of the East India Company's commerce with Asia. Through its tea exports from China it supplied rapidly growing western demand. Despite still high tea duties in Britain (an average of 12 shillings on the pound), per capita consumption grew rapidly. Tea drunk with sugar, previously a luxury, rapidly became indispensable for the British working-class public. Between 1792 and 1828 the Canton tea trade provided a quarter of the company's profits. As tea became more and more popular, British botanists interested themselves in the tea plant's provenance and dissemination.[9] At first the East India Company ignored their efforts. It concentrated on its profitable trade. Yet the increasing dominance of laissez-faire economic doctrines in Britain made commercial monopolies seem obsolete. In 1813 the Charter Act divested the East India Company of its trading privileges. Although the act permitted the company to continue its monopoly over the China trade, this would last only for another twenty years. The company realized the urgency of finding an alternative source for tea. Clashes with the Chinese Qing state over the East India Company's involvement in opium smuggling made China commerce increasingly volatile. Among the British mercantile public a strong conviction emerged that "some better guarantee should be provided for the continued supply of this article, than that at present furnished by the mere toleration of the Chinese government."[10]

After the abolition of the East India Company monopoly in 1833, the new plan mooted for tea, as for other botanical resources considered of national importance, was to cultivate it under the British flag.

One observer noted, "We can scarcely doubt that when the skill and science of the Europeans, aided by thermometers etc. should once be applied to the cultivation and preparation of tea in favourable situations, the Chinese tea will soon be excelled in quality and favour."[11] Fears that tea would grow only with the unique qualities of Chinese soil and climate were dispelled as botanists and travellers declared that the only real requirement for tea was high altitudes.[12] By the 1830s the Burma and Nepal wars had brought under British control large tracts of the Himalayan foothills, which seemed suitable for the tea plant. If this imperial tea project was successful in growing tea in India, the particular advantage of possessing Britain's own harvest would be added to the general one of using otherwise unproductive hill regions.

The accession of Lord William Bentinck to the governor-generalship of India in 1828 provided immense encouragement to the proponents of agrarian science and tea cultivation. A self-professed practical agriculturist, Bentinck constituted an official Tea Committee for India in 1834. At the head of the committee was the influential director of the Calcutta botanic garden, Nathaniel Wallich. Calcutta's mercantile world provided two Indian members, Raja Radhakanta Deb and Ram Comul Sen. The opium trader George Gordon was valued for his contacts in China. These men were made aware of the economic importance of finding a suitable locale in which to grow tea in British India. "If we should succeed . . . Bengal would be possessed of an additional staple for export nearly equal in value to that of the aggregate mass of indigenous articles now shipped to England."[13] The committee commenced its mission with a circular to district commissioners asking for particulars of lands which might fit the scientific criteria for tea. Gordon was dispatched to China to collect tea plants and seeds, and to Java to gather information about Dutch tea ventures.[14] As fate would have it, long before these enquiries bore fruit, a new tea plant would be authenticated, growing wild on the Assam frontier.

Science, Tea, and the Native "Savage"

The newly industrializing societies of the West were responsible for transforming tea into a global beverage. But the Chinese had a head start of many centuries, both in the cultivation of tea and in consumption. While tea grew wild in different parts of Monsoon Asia, its need for extensive processing meant that use as a beverage was rooted in a particular set of settled agricultural mores. Tea was in early use along Indo-Sinic peripheries, including Kashmir, Bhutan, Tibet, and Mongolia, but there seem to be no records of regular tea drinking in the Indian subcontinent proper.

In Assam evidence of pre-modern tea use comes from the Singpho and Khamti tribes, pre-literate groups who lived in the forested areas of Upper Assam. As discovered by Charles and Robert Bruce, pioneering explorers into the region, the wild tea plant grew on the Assam-Burma frontier in abundance. Locals used its leaves to brew a beverage, probably medicinal in character. The Bruce brothers witnessed this use of tea as early as 1823 but did not succeed in obtaining scientific recognition for their discovery.[15] The potential of Assam's forests remained unknown. Almost a decade later the credit for the tea discovery went to Lieutenant Andrew Charlton of the Assam Light Infantry. Charlton, like Bruce, acquired local forest lore and identified the tea plant. He observed that "the Singphos and Kamptees are in the habit of drinking an infusion of the leaves, which I have lately understood they prepare by pulling them into small pieces, taking out the stalks and fibres, boiling and then squeezing them into a ball, which they dry in the sun and retain for use."[16] Unlike Bruce, he was fortunate enough to obtain official notice for his discovery. Charlton sent to the newly constituted Tea Committee at Calcutta the seeds and leaves he had grown. He reported that the plant was indigenous to this place and grew wild everywhere, all the way to the Chinese province of Yunnan. Subsequently, in December 1834 the Tea Committee announced a "discovery . . . by far the most important and valuable . . . on matters connected with the agricultural or commercial resources of this empire [that] the tea shrub is beyond all doubt indigenous to Upper Assam."[17] Two years later a scientific delegation headed by the botanists Nathaniel Wallich and William Griffith formally examined the Assam tea forests on behalf of the East India Company and established a strategy to cultivate tea in British India.

The urgent task, these experts agreed, was to improve upon what nature had provided them. They viewed the indigenous tea plant of Assam, like its populace, as unacceptably savage. The significance of this tea discovery lay in signalling the region's suitability for cultivating the crop. The wild plant itself was entirely dispensable. In its place the Tea Committee sought the importation of Chinese tea seed and plants. The botanist Griffith declared, "I imagine that the importation of even the inferior kinds would be more likely to lead to the produce of a marketable article than the cultivation of a wild, or (to use our Indian notions) a more expressive term, jungly stock."[18] Griffith's use of the vernacular term "jungly" indicates how colonial scientists blended indigenous notions of primitiveness and civilization with western typologies borrowed from race science. Griffith's opinion fitted well into a contemporary agenda that located different parts of the Orient in a hierarchy of civilization. A purported wilderness such as Assam ranked far below China, or more settled parts of the Indian subcontinent. British officials and planters introduced the China tea plant into the Himalayan tracts of Darjeeling and Kumaon. The wisdom of the age dictated that nature's bounty, the wild Assam plant, could be of proper use only after its modification by Chinese culture and western science. The East India Company agreed to fund this scientific experiment into tea cultivation.

Charles Bruce was placed in charge of the experimental tea enterprise. The company's officials viewed the "country-born" Bruce's acquaintance with the natives of Upper Assam and the local language as ample compensation for his lack of formal botanical learning. As a beginning Bruce arranged to procure seedlings from China, and Chinese growers to tend them. The Chinese plant was used to hybridize the native one and eventually replace it. His initial plan was to harvest wild tea leaves to blend with the Chinese supply. Bruce's auxiliaries were the local hill chiefs who controlled the tea tracts, and the Chinese growers who cultivated tea in those experimental gardens. His was the all-important responsibility of conveying the processed tea leaves in good order to Britain. The *Times* published a dialogue between Bruce and Chinese cultivators on tea growing, to establish for the London reading public the "similarity between the soil and teas of Assam and China."[19] After all, it was that very public, so far cognizant only of China tea, which was expected to buy the new commodity. London auctioneers and British consumers would be the ultimate arbiters of Indian tea's commercial future.

From Upper Assam, Bruce sent his first batch of processed tea on its long voyage, first on country boats to Calcutta, then on steamship to London. In January 1838 this tea reached London. Experts provided a cautiously positive verdict. They declared that it was entirely satisfactory for a first experiment. At the auction the British public showed patriotic zeal with a record price of 21 to 38 shillings a pound. This was about twenty times the usual price for China tea. Clearly the British consumer was receptive to Empire tea. This was the green light for metropolitan investors. In February 1839 the provisional committee of a newly established Assam Tea Association met in London. It resolved to gather information about tea production and ascertain what support the East India Company might provide. Its promoters exulted that Assam tea only required the application of European capital and enterprise to make it a great source of profit.[20] *Importance of finance and investment capital*

These London merchants quickly formed a new joint-stock enterprise, the Assam Company. It was capitalized at 500,000 pounds, in 10,000 shares of 50 pounds each, of which 8,000 shares were earmarked for Britain and 2,000 for India. Yet Assam tea had already begun its commercial life in India. The firm of Carr, Tagore and Co. had established a Bengal Tea Association which comprised a diverse group of Calcutta merchants. They included the famous "Bengali Merchant Prince" Dwarkanath Tagore, and William Prinsep, from a prominent British-Indian family. Finally the London and Calcutta merchants agreed to amalgamate in July 1839 into a single Assam Company. The promoters intentionally left "tea" out of the firm's name, since they hoped to extend their reach to Assam's oil, timber, and coal reserves. In the spring of 1840 the East India Company granted approval to the Assam Company's proposal to produce tea. The Assam Company was granted two-thirds of the experimental tea establishment rent-free for ten years, along with permission to settle on other lands.[21] Soon it was joined by other entrepreneurs. For the next fifty years the Assam Company remained British India's chief tea producer. At the Great Exhibition in London in 1851 visitors to the Crystal Palace thronged to admire the medal-winning display of imperial tea from the Assam garden.

Improving Assam

The East India Company's annexation of Assam in 1826 did little to improve economic prospects for the majority of inhabitants. The Burmese invasions had drastically reduced an already sparse population. Large numbers were killed, kidnapped as slaves, or forced to flee to remote hills and forests, or into neighbouring British-ruled Bengal. Warfare severely damaged much of the rice-growing economy, as well as the infrastructure of dykes, irrigation tanks, and roads built by the Ahom. British entry also meant a painful transition from a largely non-monetized economy to a cash-based one. The Ahom revenue settlement was based on corvée services and other payments by *paiks* (peasants). The East India Company introduced new cash payments of land revenues, which local functionaries called *mauzadars* were placed in charge of collecting. Peasants faced a heavy tax burden, often arbitrarily fixed.

Over the early years of colonial rule the entire region suffered an acute cash crisis. The Ahom mint was defunct and there was a shortage of British-Indian currency. This worsened the strain of the transition to a cash economy. In barter-oriented, money-short Assam, rice was cultivated for subsistence. Opium and mustard were the only cash crops. Since the East India Company's money revenues were annually remitted to Calcutta for recoinage, the local cash shortage continued. That remittance represented a surplus of revenue over local disbursements. It resulted in the withdrawal of a considerable quantity of circulating currency from Assam.[22] This money crisis made it difficult for peasants to pay their dues in cash to the new government. Many defrauders fled to inaccessible hill regions not yet under British control.

In 1830 David Scott, Assam's first colonial administrator, mourned the state of the economy: "The want of coin is . . . such that cloths of certain fixed dimensions, salt, iron hoes and other articles in general use pass currently instead of money. Since the accession of the British government, the labour of paiks is commuted for a money payment without any considerable addition being made to the currency . . . grain . . . almost ceases to be saleable when offered in any quantity."[23] To alleviate the economic crisis, Scott's plan sought to develop Assam's export potential based on resources and skills available in the region. He encouraged Assamese peasants to increase production of indigenous cash crops such as opium, mulberry, and muga silks. He argued that since these enterprises already existed locally, they only needed government encouragement to thrive. Such a strategy would avoid the upheaval that the colonial imposition of indigo cultivation had caused in Bengal and Bihar.[24] But Scott's early death in 1831 prematurely halted these plans to encourage Assamese enterprise.

Scott's successor, Colonel Francis Jenkins, took advantage of the

Charter Act of 1833 to moot new plans for Assam. This act introduced European land ownership into India, allowing Jenkins to mount a different strategy. He preferred to encourage British rather than local agrarian enterprise in Assam. In his view, "The settlement of Englishmen of capital on its wastes of these frontiers seems . . . to offer a better prospect for the speedy realisation of improvements than any measures that could be adopted in the present ignorant and demoralised state of native inhabitants."[25] Jenkins echoed Lord William Bentinck and the members of his council, who had decided that an active policy of European colonization was the only effective agency for India's reform and modernization.[26] Jenkins, a member of the Agricultural Society of Great Britain, sought to introduce into this distant colony of Assam the "agrarian imperialist" ideas currently fashionable in Britain.[27] Unlike his predecessor Scott, he viewed Assam's economic future as dependent upon European agrarian enterprise. The region's lands were termed wastelands, open for exploitation. Colonel Jenkins's desire for European enterprise to cultivate those Assamese wastelands laid the foundation for the colonial tea enterprise.

Therefore the East India Company now offered attractive terms to the Assam Company and other European applicants who wished to grow tea. Wastelands Rules, promulgated in 1838 and revised in 1854, provided for long-term leases of land to applicants who possessed capital or stock worth at least Rs 3 per acre and who applied for not less than a hundred acres. While the rules did not expressly discriminate against Indian applicants, these requirements ensured that only Europeans possessed sufficient capital to avail themselves of government concessions. In the rare cases that Indians qualified for long-term concessionary leases, they faced considerable harassment and refusals.

In 1853 the East India Company appointed Justice A. J. Moffat Mills to report on Assam's administration and outline future policies for the region. In his report Mills supported Jenkins's strategy to discourage non-European agrarian involvement. In his view only Europeans possessed the capital reserves and the vision for long-term improvement: "Natives have no capital and their only resource is to settle other ryots to settle in these grants so that as much or even more becomes waste in one place than is reclaimed in the other."[28] Over the next few decades the Assam government encouraged hundreds of British speculators to acquire land on ridiculously low terms, expecting these tea entrepreneurs to procure a better labour force. Just as the Chinese tea plant was finer than the native one, imported labour was thought to be far superior to that of local agriculturists. Jenkins denigrated Assam's locals as brutish raw material: "We have . . . an unlimited range of wastes, wastes enough for three or four millions of people, which implies, of course, that our population is very scanty, and what is worse, they are very rude; fine, able, strong men, but without the introduction of a more civilized race they are not convertible to immediate use."[29] A primitive population seemed particularly unsuited to cultivate the delicate tea plant acquired from China.

Chinese Skills in the Assam Jungle

From the seventeenth century tea was one of the few staples of European commerce with Asia. In the mid-nineteenth century, despite their excitement at locating indigenous tea forests, the British were pessimistic about the abilities of Assam's "savage" inhabitants to successfully nurture tea. The conviction grew that Chinese skill and labour were essential to transforming the Assam forests into tea gardens.

By the early nineteenth century, as Europeans expressed hostility and contempt towards the Chinese Qing government, China's "tea planters" were held in awe. Chinese peasant households which cultivated tea worked alongside seasonally employed specialists who possessed the expertise needed to process the leaves.[30] Their processing skills were much in demand. After the Tea Committee authenticated the tea plant of Upper Assam, the East India Company tried to obtain wild tea leaves locally. However, it also decided to establish a parallel, experimental venture to cultivate tea in nurseries. This was done using seeds and plants smuggled out of China, which seemed necessary since botanists believed that only the cultivated China plant was acceptable as a marketable beverage. Its wild Assam cousin required either hybridizing or uprooting. The normally miserly East India Company had to open its purse to recruit Chinese tea experts.

Lord William Bentinck was an important supporter of Chinese involvement. He visited the East India Company's settlements in the Straits of Malacca and Singapore to observe the Chinese "character."

He declared that their superior energy, industry, spirit of speculation, and ability to calculate profit equalled that of any European nation. Bentinck endorsed the recruitment of Chinese labour to grow tea: "My idea is that an intelligent agent should go down to Penang and Singapore, and concert measures for obtaining the genuine plant, and the actual cultivators who shall then be employed, under the promise of liberal remuneration, to carry on the cultivation."[31] He emphasized that India urgently required Chinese tea growers, artisans, and labourers. The Assam Company commissioned the London bio-prospector Robert Fortune, the Calcutta opium trader George Gordon, and a China missionary, the Rev. Gutzlaff, to obtain these workers. For interpreters and supervisors the company tapped Calcutta's Chinese population.

The first set of reports, letters, and other documents about tea in British India, later collated for the British Parliament, described these Chinese as "tea planters" or "tea growers." This was an indication of the regard in which their skills were still held, and strikingly different from the pejorative, all-encompassing epithet of "coolie" applied to Chinese migrants to the Straits labour market. Little is known about the Chinese tea growers recruited to Assam, whether in supervisory or labouring capacities. The earliest mention of a Chinese "planter" is of A-mong. In 1832 he helped start the East India Company's first experimental Assam estate, Chubwa, and he later purchased the property outright, but he failed to make a sufficient living. In 1849 he resold the estate to James Warren, who established a long-standing British tea dynasty in India.[32]

There is a little more information about Lumqua, a physician from Calcutta's Chinese community, who was reported to be "a kind of Captain with Magisterial powers among his countrymen."[33] Indeed, the Tea Committee recommended that he should be paid at least Rs 400 for his duties as a manager and interpreter. But the East India Company was reluctant to continue to employ Lumqua at this high salary. Instead it advocated the employment of a Chinese carpenter from Calcutta who would accept just Rs 40 for his "practically useful" skills.[34] The carpenter's interpreting abilities proved nonexistent,[35] and when the new Assam Company inherited the East India Company's tea assets and responsibilities it retained Lumqua as an overseer.

At Lumqua's recommendation the tea enterprise hired E-kan, a "very respectable Chinese merchant," formerly a resident of Upper

Assam, to recruit "volunteer labourers" in Penang and Singapore.[36] Other recruiters were asked to enlist capable hands from the China junks.[37] Labourers were paid Rs 16, artisans Rs 45, and apprentices Rs 20, the rates prevalent in the straits market. A few hundred Chinese workers were recruited on these terms. They mostly hailed from Malaya and Singapore. Their origins eventually became a contentious matter. The botanist William Griffith agreed with Bentinck about the need for Chinese cultivators and manufacturers. However, he disagreed on their provenance: "I found that among all the so-called Chinese, who are to be met with at Mogaung, Bamo and Ava, as well as those among those who form the large annual caravans that trade with Burma there is not a single genuine Chinaman."[38]

Griffith's use of the term "genuine" to characterize labour is revealing. This word first appears in the Parliamentary discussions over Assam tea. Bentinck used the term to refer to the authenticity of the wild tea plant. Griffith's objections to the overseas Chinese expanded the discussion from plant to people. The East India Company had become the master of vast wastelands. The Charter Act of 1833 permitted them to be used by European enterprise.[39] The Assam tea plant could be grown on these lands, but only after careful nurturance by genuine Chinese tea growers. What did the category "genuine" denote? Was it a racial connotation for the people of the entire China mainland? Or did it simply denote the inhabitants of China's tea-producing regions, people who were accustomed to the cultivation of the crop? A useful exercise is to consider the people whom Griffith excluded from the category of genuine. Those were the immigrants who lived outside the country. Therefore, in Griffith's perception a genuine Chinaman was one who was racially, ecologically, and climatically based in China. Overseas migration excluded a person from that category. This was a crude and early foreshadowing of late-nineteenth-century race science theories, which held that transplantation to other locations and climes produced racial degeneration. Since the Assam Company's agents found it easiest to bring in Chinese labourers from the coolie networks in Singapore and Malaya, their bona fide status seemed open to question. Certainly Chinese workers from the Straits did not all possess tea skills, but Griffith's objections made no mention of this. In practice the difficulties in obtaining artisans from mainland China meant that Straits and Macao Chinese were the only recruits for Assam.[40]

In Upper Assam the "once mysterious and still curious process" of tea production began. When Charles Bruce sent the first batch of Assam tea made by "our China manufacturers" to England in 1838, it arrived in a blaze of publicity and praise.[41] The Assam tea enterprise's optimism about the Chinese proved short-lived. The Assam Company's prized employee, the Chinese physician and manager Lumqua, died in August 1840.[42] In a sense his death marked the beginning of the end of the Chinese involvement. The British desire for Chinese labour gradually ebbed in the face of desertions, deaths, and disillusionment. The Assam Company's British employees increasingly complained about what they saw as the obstreperous character of Chinese recruits to the tea enterprise. Deeming them incorrigibly "turbulent, obstinate and rapacious," the Assam Company returned many Chinese workers to Calcutta. It retained only the "most experienced tea-makers and the quietest men."[43]

Europeans had previously praised the Chinese as universally skilled and refined. Their association with tea, a commodity linked with luxury and civilization, provided them with further cachet. But after actual contact with its Chinese recruits, the Assam Company managers condemned them as gentlemen too great to undertake certain kinds of work.[44] J. W. Masters, the Assam Company superintendent, grumbled when they objected to doing anything else but making tea. The tea enterprise refused to acknowledge that its recruits' expectations about work and livelihood were intrinsic to the long-standing employment and migration networks in Southeast Asia. These workers had firm notions of their dues.[45] Although they were hired to grow and process tea, the scarcity of general labour meant that they were often called upon for all kinds of gruelling tasks, to which they objected. In this first stage of creating the Assam garden, an essential but difficult task was to clear the extensive forest undergrowth. Clearing the region's luxuriant jungles required considerable and wearisome manual labour. These demands caused Chinese recruits to perceive the Assam Company as reneging on customary employer obligations, the norms set by the Straits credit-ticket system.

In contrast, the British began to praise Upper Assam's indigenous inhabitants as well suited to such labouring tasks. In the region's hilly tracts various "wild" groups were accustomed to employing fire and axes to clear jungle for shifting cultivation. For example, at the Hookumjooree station the Assam Company's Mr. Parker reported that "by presents and good treatment, many of these wild Naga people have been induced to help in the labour of clearing the jungle. A few cowrie shells and a buffalo feast have established a very amicable feeling with these people which may be serviceable hereafter."[46] Bruce, Masters, Parker, and others were delighted by these Nagas who had no use for money (given their barter economy) and were content to be paid in "shells, beads, rice &c."[47] However, they also found that "a wild people" would not work steadily, but appeared and disappeared without prior warning. Therefore the British tried their best to recruit from among other local, more settled groups. In addition to the Nagas and the Chinese, the tea enterprise began to employ almost a hundred more labourers every month, mostly peasants from nearby Brahmaputra valley villages. The Assam Company attempted to bring these labourers under engagement for a fixed term. It was difficult to retain these workers for long. It proved even harder to trace them, "so as to bring them back to fulfil their engagements when they have once deserted."[48]

Over these early years the colonial tea enterprise was constantly plagued by desertions. This was not surprising, since it offered punishing work in a famously inhospitable terrain and climate, for wages that it tried to keep as low as possible. Both Chinese and local workers deserted in droves. While on the job they vented their resentment whenever they found an opportunity. In 1841, in the midst of the optimistic predictions submitted to tea directors and shareholders, appeared the Assam Company management's acknowledgement that there was "on every payday a general strike among the taklars (local tea makers), and some have left the employ, refusing to sign a covenant."[49] Grudgingly managers agreed in the following year to provide "an increase of Rs 1 p.m., on their present salary after they have signed a covenant for three years, and have served one year, and a further increase of Rs 1 p.m. for each succeeding year."[50]

Assam's cash shortages and the low availability of waged work allowed local labourers to be employed at such meagre wages, but these could not earn their loyalty. Many labourers worked against their will, since often "the Gaon Bura (headman) of the local village supplied the labour."[51] Assam's ecology also imposed a high cost. During the insalubrious monsoon months, many labourers fell ill from malaria and other ailments. In the absence of medical or dietary care, the attrition rate was high. For instance, in 1840 more than half the numbers on the payroll were off due to sickness.[52]

Once the active intervention of the East India Company and its attendant scientific experts receded, British managers chose to hire the cheapest of the local labourers rather than recruit the skilled Chinese. While condemning Chinese "obstreperousness," they cast around for alternatives to those highly paid tea growers. As a result, by the 1860s Chinese labour almost disappeared from Assam. The Assam Company halted the recruitment of new Chinese labour. Existing Straits Chinese workers mostly died or deserted. In their place planters sought to identify an alternative workforce which would be both cheap and easily disciplined. At the same time, the Assam Company and the colonial state aimed to control the ways Assam's locals might be involved in the new imperial garden.

The "Native" in the Garden

The early years of the colonial enterprise reveal a significant linguistic shift, from "tea forests" to "tea gardens." In his correspondence with the Assam Company, Charles Bruce pioneered the use of the term "garden," alongside its vernacular equivalent *bari*. In pre-colonial Assam bari and *basti* had a very particular denotation: they referred to the raised or high lands used for homestead and garden sites. Peasants possessed hereditary proprietary rights over these sites. The bari was distinct from the low-lying lands used for wet rice cultivation. These ricefields were communally owned. Peasants held only usufruct rights over them. The tea baris of the Assam Company and other planters could thus be understood as their private property. This was an important claim, considering the vast expanses of previously common land which the tea enterprise obtained from the state. Large portions of these tea grants remained fallow. Such uncultivated lands gave the plantations free access to timber and other natural resources. The vastness of these tea grants also served to minimize land availability for local peasants.

Even more significantly, the colonial enterprise began to view the garden in opposition to the forest. The initial discovery of tea was in the lands of the "aboriginal" Singpho people on Upper Assam's forested frontiers. In its first euphoria over this tea discovery, the East

India Company envisaged some kind of partnership in harvesting the forests. A Singpho hill chief, Ningroola, collected over a thousand pounds of wild leaf, which eventually made its way to London. Wild Assam tea was seen as a useful supplement to the newly cultivated crop. About Chief Ningroola's involvement the Assam Company at first hoped that "the price that his Tea fetched, will no doubt so well satisfy him, that he will probably be induced greatly to increase his cultivation, and a reasonable hope may be entertained that he and other Singphos similarly situated, may eventually become valuable auxiliaries to the objects of our Company."[53]

The Tea Committee's scientific experts expressed strong opposition to this sort of commercial partnership. The botanist Nathaniel Wallich urged Colonel Jenkins to speedily annex these tea forest tracts instead. Such resources were too valuable to be left in native hands. While acknowledging the cooperation that the British had received from local chiefs such as Ningroola, Wallich wrote darkly of the destruction that natives were prone to unleash upon Nature: "In my humble opinion, the gamers or chiefs who own the Singfo tea tracts will not object to our leasing or purchasing them . . . Considering, however, the destructive manner in which the tracts in question have been hitherto treated by the natives and the injuries which most of them are at this time almost daily undergoing, I beg most earnestly to urge the necessity of immediate and effective measures."[54] Such guardianship, the notion of Nature as property, fitted well with a growing British conviction that Indians were incapable of government. For this and other reasons an economically valuable territory seemed to require direct colonial rule.

Meanwhile these Singphos already resented the British intrusion. Their chiefs ruled over a hill community at the margins of settled society. In the past other such communities had possessed much more control over labour power and forest resources than plains peasants did under the Ahom state. British attempts to control the tea forests led to violence. In 1843 a large number of Singphos rose up in arms. At Sadiya they attacked troops and drove out newly arrived American Baptist missionaries. Eventually British reinforcements overpowered the Singphos. The East India Company now needed little excuse to annex their lands outright. Colonial sources were quick to attribute this clash to the savage and treacherous nature of the Singphos; British cupidity went unacknowledged. A chief poignantly wrote in a letter of protest to the East India Company, "Now it is said that where the tea grows, that is yours, but when we make sacrifices we require tea for our funerals; we therefore perceive that you have taken all the country, and we, the old and respectable, cannot get tea to drink."[55]

Ironically, once these tea forests were theirs the British colonizers changed their minds. They realized that the malarial character of Sadiya, its remote location, and the intransigence of the Singphos meant that tea would always face labour difficulties there. After 1843 the British decided to move tea production to the erstwhile Ahom territory of Upper Assam, away from the unruly frontier.

Previously, at the time of the British conquest in 1826, Upper Assam, the Ahom kingdom's historic heartland, had appeared remote and poor after the Burmese depredations. It seemed less desirable than Lower Assam, which lay contiguous to British-ruled Bengal. Thus in 1833 the East India Company agreed to install Purandar Singha, a prince of the dispossessed Ahom dynasty, as the ruler of Upper Assam, on payment of a large annual tribute. With Purandar's accession bright prospects seemingly opened for the élites of yore, the displaced *dangariyas* (lit. great men: pre-colonial aristocrats). Before the British takeover of Assam many of them had already sought refuge in British-ruled Bengal from the Burmese invaders. One such exile was Maniram Barbhandar Barua (1806–57), son of a high-ranking Ahom minister. While self-exiled in Bengal, Maniram served the British as an interpreter. He rapidly rose through the ranks. When Purandar Singha ascended the throne of Upper Assam, he appointed Maniram as his prime minister, with the blessings of his overlord, the East India Company.

Shortly afterward British land surveys revealed that the Jorhat and Sibsagar districts in Purandar's territory were ideally suited for tea. Centrally located near the Brahmaputra river, they possessed fertile, acidic soil and gently sloping plains. Steamers and country boats could transport labourers, supplies, and tea leaves. Following Maniram's advice, Purandar Singha welcomed the British tea enterprise and expressed a strong desire to participate: "Raja Poorunder Sing makes no hesitation in placing the Gubroo hill at the disposal of Government; but he is anxious to retain one-half of the hill, that he may carry on the cultivation of the tea plants, on that half, simultaneously with us on the other, and that the superintendents and overseers of the Government should instruct his people in the management of the plant and manufacture of tea."[56]

The tea partnership between Purandar Singha and the East India Company proved stillborn. The prince's throne was in danger as soon as the British discovered the tea-growing potential of his lands. Already the East India Company demanded a large annual cash tribute that was difficult to pay. High revenue demands upon the peasantry created popular unrest. Purandar Singha's nobles nurtured high hopes for advancement, which his empty coffers failed to satisfy. They then turned against him. The new tea potential of his lands gave the British government the reason it needed to dethrone him. In 1838 the East India Company ousted the Raja on charges of "misgovernment." While Purandar Singha then had few defenders, the British opportunism did not go unremarked. A local chronicler, Dutiram Hazarika, attributed the end of Ahom dynastic rule to the white man's desire to turn Assam into a vast tea garden.[57] Years later the king of neighbouring Manipur pleaded with the British political officer to abandon plans for growing tea. He feared that he would lose his kingdom to tea planters, in the same manner as Purandar Singha.[58]

The British abandonment of the wild tea zones on the Sadiya frontier illustrates how the emergent terminology of garden distinguished between the wild, "jungly" variety of tea and the superior strain cultivated by Europeans. In this vision savage forests would be transmuted by European capital and science into a cultivated tea expanse. An influential voice here was John MacCosh, an East India Company surgeon turned an Assam "booster." He eulogized the introduction of tea cultivation as the prelude to transformation of a wild, unhealthy, and jungle-laden region into "one continued garden of silk and cotton, of tea, coffee and sugar."[59] His idyllic vision of unordered Nature blooming into ordered gardens openly articulated the doctrine of imperial expansion and improvement which Drayton calls the "economics of Eden."[60] As Kavita Philip shows for the Nilgiri Hills, colonial Assam's gardens became significant ideological spaces, both metaphorically and materially.[61]

Significantly, some of the most fervent support for this garden project came from non-British missionary auxiliaries to empire building. In colonial Assam's new Eden, East India Company officials and planters were joined by a handful of missionary brethren.

They were Baptists from the United States, sent by the American Board of Commissioners for Foreign Missions. The board was established after the famous Haystack Prayer Meeting of 1806 with the objective of spreading the Protestant gospel overseas. Its pioneering preacher, Adoniram Judson, originally intended to work in India, but when he landed at Calcutta in 1812 the East India Company refused to allow him to preach. The British still feared that missionaries would jeopardize commercial activity in India. Instead Judson established a Baptist mission in Burma. After many years of scant success this mission began to achieve conversions among the Karen people in Upper Burma. But by 1830 the growing antagonism of the Burmese government impelled Judson's successors to seek an alternative field. Assam, geographically contiguous to Burma, seemed the brightest prospect.

Meanwhile, a decade after Judson's abortive landing at Calcutta, the East India Company's transformation from a trading to a ruling power had altered its attitude toward missionaries. Many high-ranking officials, such as Charles Trevelyan, now professed evangelical sentiments. Missionaries were particularly welcome to undertake their work in a remote region such as Assam, where few white people wished to go. The Americans were told to begin work at Sadiya, which lay close to Burma. At that time the tea enterprise was still there. Trevelyan advised the missionaries that they might be able to use their Burmese language skills and, in the future, expand into Burma and China.[62]

In 1836, armed with a printing press and high hopes, the American Baptist Mission established a base at Sadiya. Its missionaries soon realized that their British advisers had little comprehension of the region's complexities. Assam's languages were completely different from those of Burma. Sadiya's populace consisted of unlettered hill people who used a variety of pre-literate tongues. Nonetheless, Nathan Brown tempered his disappointment upon finding among the natives "very few, if any, who can read" with his excitement at the new tea venture. After its manager Charles Bruce gave him a tour, Brown wrote, "Tea trade will produce a great change in the country — will fill it with a dense population, and convert these almost impenetrable jungles into the happy abodes of industry."[63] Assam's forests seemed so impenetrable that for both officials and missionaries the region's improvement through the establishment of a commercial tea garden seemed the prerequisite for a more general order of civilization.

This civilizing project needed local allies. For this role Assam's caste Hindu gentry seemed the best possibility. The British hoped that these literate groups might be more adaptable to new institutions than the region's unlettered hill chiefs and Ahom nobles. This did prove correct. In the manner of other subcontinental scribal groups such as Kashmiri Pandits, Kayasthas, and Deshasht Brahmins who joined British service, by the late nineteenth century so did the majority of Assam's gentry, who had earlier served the Ahom kings (the upper-caste groups of Brahmins, Daivagnas, and Kalitas, as well as a few élite Muslims). This transition was not uncomplicated, as evinced by the ups and downs in the career of a prominent member, Maniram Barbhandar Barua.

When Purandar Singha lost the Upper Assam throne, Maniram also lost his prime ministership, but he quickly found a new opportunity as the Assam Company's *dewan* (land agent). Maniram's local knowledge speedily enabled the tea enterprise to establish itself on a sound footing. For instance, he helped it to obtain more regular supplies of scarce rice through his establishment of weekly *haats* (markets) near the tea gardens where villagers brought goods to sell. The proximity of the haats was essential for feeding labour, given the limitations of rural Assam's market economy for staples, and its transport bottlenecks. Uncultivated lands held by the tea enterprise were also handed over to local tenants in return for supplies of rice, wheat, and sugarcane.[64] A director of the Assam Company, William Prinsep, on a visit from Calcutta, was delighted with Maniram's endeavours: "I find the Native Department of the office in the most beneficial state under the excellent direction of Muneeram, whose intelligence and activity is of the greatest value to our Establishment."[65] To circumvent the other major problem for the Assam Company, the perennial scarcity of labour, Maniram suggested putting out tracts of tea cultivation to local *hazarees* (supervisors) who would be responsible for getting them worked. Those men would report monthly to the superintendent, in the manner of his European assistants. This was a radical measure to suggest, but a sensible one, given the high turnover of Europeans, difficulties of obtaining and retaining local labour, ravages of disease upon newcomers, and frequent scarcities of marketable food grains. Through this and other measures Maniram advocated that local gentry and peasants play a leading role in establishing an Assam tea garden, alongside British capital and science.

Sadly, despite Prinsep's praise of Maniram's initiatives, the moment seemed already past when the British would welcome local initiative. After 1841 Maniram no longer appears in the Assam Company's records as its land agent. The records provide no clues as to why or when he was dismissed. Assamese folklore claims that he retaliated with interest when a British employee slapped him and that subsequently the Assam Company dismissed him.[66] Another tale has it that Maniram's establishment of his own tea estates offended the Assam Company. Allegedly he was suspended on charges that he had purloined his employer's seed and labour. Ironically, a number of new tea estates were established by the Assam Company's British employees, who liberally pilfered its resources.[67] Maniram's guilt in this matter cannot be proved or disproved, but certainly not one of his European colleagues was similarly penalized for entrepreneurial activity.

In the early years of colonial rule Maniram Barbhandar Barua proved a useful mediator with locals, who provided the colonial state with information about resources as varied as gold and silk. His local biographer even avers that he was the person who first brought the Assam tea plant to the notice of the Tea Committee.[68] Once tea cultivation expanded, Maniram ably used his skills to promote it. But as colonial institutions penetrated deeper into the region, Maniram's powerful local connections made him appear dangerous to British control. For instance, Upper Assam's inhabitants revered him as the Kalita Raja (king of the Kalita caste), a title unlikely to be welcome to the British.

After he left the Assam Company's employment, Maniram delivered a scathing critique of colonial policies which confirmed his pariah status for the new rulers. Maniram's criticisms were directed to the enquiry conducted in 1853 by Justice Mills. This body was entrusted with collecting information on Assam's economy and society and establishing guidelines to improve colonial rule. Maniram wrote a lengthy memorandum which castigated British rule for bringing unprecedented suffering. In response Justice Mills branded Maniram as "clever but untrustworthy and intriguing,"[69] and he was kept under surveillance. Eventually Maniram's involvement with the

Great Rebellion of 1857 led to his execution for treason. His fate revealed the risks inherent in openly challenging the new regime.

Maniram's break with the Assam Company fits a larger pattern within changing colonial structures. From the second half of the nineteenth century indigenous participation in South Asia's mercantile capitalist networks was subjected to many obstacles. This tendency was particularly marked in the Calcutta trading world, the commercial progenitors of the tea venture. The character of the Assam Company's management was altered. William Prinsep, its representative from the famous Indo-British firm of Carr, Tagore and Co., retired to England. Soon after his departure the Indian names on the Calcutta board started to disappear.[70] Previously the patrician Bengali merchant Dwarkanath Tagore was an influential promoter of the Assam Company. The wealthy Tagore had earned the rare privilege of a royal audience when he visited England in 1842. London newspapers carried headlines for every day of his visit, an accolade not enjoyed by any Indian until Mahatma Gandhi's visit in 1931.[71] No nonwhite businessman acquired such renown until the empire waned. Lord Auckland, during his tenure as governor general (1836–42), had in fact hailed Assam as "a country of vast promise" whose development might occur through the joint application of European and Indian capital.[72] But colonial attitudes soon changed. Over the next few decades British rule circumscribed, controlled, and stifled indigenous capital, and enterprise.[73] After his conviction for treason in 1857, the East India Company confiscated Maniram's tea estates. These estates were sold at a throwaway price to Captain Williamson, the founder of the managing agency house of Williamson and Magor.[74] (Today the Williamson Magor Group calls itself the world's largest producer of tea of high quality.)

Maniram's growing distrust of the new regime was not universal among his peers. In the first half-century of British rule many among Assam's gentry expressed enthusiastic support for British rule and by extension for the tea enterprise. A good example is the young Calcutta-educated Brahmin Anandaram Dhekial Phukan (1829–59). In 1847 he published an influential essay in the new missionary-run Assamese periodical the *Orunodoi* which eulogized the virtues of England. Anandaram's fondest hope was that England's progress could be replicated in Assam. His wish was that his compatriots would soon acquire "the desire to render their land civilized, wise and pious . . . when Assam will cease to be a forest and become a garden of flowers."[75] This language is very similar to the garden metaphors that appear in the writings of colonial boosters such as John MacCosh. Anandaram's cousin Gunabhiram Barua (1837–94), who also had close links with Calcutta's reformist intelligentsia, was even more laudatory of the garden project. He gave it high praise in his history of Assam, *Assam Buranji*, which was widely prescribed as a school textbook and went into many editions. His history's narrative began with Assam's mythical links to the pan-Indian epic the *Mahabharata* and ended with the favourable economic prospects for a British-ruled future of the region. "Almost fifty years ago, the news was received that the tea plant was growing in Assam. Its cultivation has made substantial progress. Huge expanses of forest have been transformed into blooming and productive land."[76]

Publicists like Gunabhiram Barua, active participants in Assam's nascent public arenas, grew to adulthood in different circumstances from Maniram. For them Ahom glory represented bygone times. Their prospects lay ahead, in British service, and they were eager to optimize opportunities. The displacement caused by the Ahom-Burmese conflict had already meant that the subsequent British annexation of Assam did not elicit much direct political opposition. During the first fifty years of colonial rule this gentry's differences with British policies tended to be obliquely delivered, as when Anandaram censured measures more suited to "an Asiatic Government rather than enlightened England."[77] Colonialism's reiteration of Assam's backwardness acted powerfully on such upwardly mobile groups. They were keen to proselytize for their homeland's improving potential, even as they denigrated its present. As the colonial tea industry moved from strength to strength, locals developed a complicated relationship of dependence, cooption, and eventually resistance to British rule. Throughout, the seductive power of the tea garden as the model for Assam's progress persisted.

2. Borderlands, Rice Eaters, and Tea Growers

✱The making of the Assamic peoples

HISTORICALLY, ASSAM WAS A BORDERLAND on the margins of Indic culture. Over the centuries Indo-Aryan migrants bearing wet-rice technology, Sanskritic caste, and ritual norms settled there along-side indigenous groups practicing diverse technologies and belief systems. Textualized representations of difference and alterity be-tween Assam and the Indic heartland were generated and extended even as military, commercial, and cultural encounters strengthened the links between these spaces. With the annexation of Assam in 1826 and the discovery of tea thereafter, Assamese élites soon deemed it necessary to prove their Indic credentials. This chapter argues that boundaries for Assam's inhabitants, once permeable, became more rigid over the colonial period as élite local groups began to emphasize their racial distance from social subordinates and seek a place in the Indic sun.

In 1881 the census showed Assam's population to be 4,881,426, a considerable increase of 376,550 over the estimates of 1872.[1] A large part of this increase was due to the operations of the tea plantation economy. British planters were now importing a large number of labourers annually into Assam. These "coolie" newcomers were sup-plemented by European planters, "Marwari" traders, Bengali Hindu clerks, Nepali graziers, and East Bengali Muslim traders and peas-ants. Migration into Assam was not in any way a new phenomenon, but its scope and prominence were greatly amplified under colonial modernity. Local reactions to this population increase were mixed.

In 1885 a writer for the periodical *Assam Bandhu* declared, "Apart from the people of our own land and the people of the hills, everyone else is a Bongali [lit. inhabitant of Bengal]. The very word denotes an inauspicious and unholy jati."[2] This statement should be read as an aggressive response to the rapidly changing demographics in British-ruled Assam, rather than as a statement of fact. Neighbouring Bengal had historically functioned as a symbolic and real space where flows of people and cultures encountered the Brahmaputra valley. Conventionally the terms "Bongali" and "Bangal" denoted residents of Bengal. But within Assam these terms were used to refer to outsiders, denizens of an indeterminate space beyond Assam's western limits. The use of these terms allowed Assam's inhabitants to make a conceptual differentiation between their des (homeland) and other Indic lands. This distinction acquired force in the medieval period and retained sway until the nineteenth century. People, rather than space, formed its referent. Yet the writer for the *Assam Bandhu* now employed the term "Bongali" to articulate his negative feelings toward new migrants into Assam, whether from Bengal or beyond.

In the past Assam had connected with other regions of the subcontinent through occasional flows of people and long-distance commerce, alongside seasonal links for trade and pilgrimage with Himalayan regions such as Bhutan and Tibet. While successive waves of Indo-Aryan migrants from the North and East into Assam helped to establish wet-rice technology and caste ideology, the Indic world continued to imagine Assam as a distant, ritually ambiguous frontier zone. Dominant literary representations, whether in older Sanskrit or later Persian texts, continued to recycle images of a fabulous and mysterious periphery inhabited by practitioners of the occult, yoga, and black magic. This textualized imagery obfuscated the actuality of a mobile frontier where material goods, people, and ideas circulated and mingled in Assam with existing institutions and discourses.

The impact of Indic knowledge upon the region itself was to harden internal social and cultural hierarchies. By the nineteenth century Assam's élites flaunted Indic genealogies of élite descent and caste purity as a sign of racial distinctiveness from social subordinates, even as they prized local indicators of social capital such as titles bestowed by Ahom rulers, and Asomiya vernacular prowess. Through the workings of the new colonial economy, this hierarchy combined with Victorian notions of race science to create a situation in which local élites racialized

tea's new labouring migrants as ritually impure and primitive aboriginals, and sought to prove the impeccability of their own Indic and
Aryanist credentials.

"Indo-Aryan" Agriculturists and a Moving Frontier

Sanskrit literature of the later Vedic period described Assam as a distant land toward the East. The *Satpatha Brahmana* deemed the region impure for ritual sacrifices, and therefore for Indo-Aryan settlement.[3] In fact, as the historian Richard Eaton's work shows, textual
taboos notwithstanding, Indo-Aryan groups in early South Asia gradually settled the upper, the middle, and finally the lower Gangetic
region. Plough-bearing migrants pushed first into Bengal and later
into Assam.[4] In the Brahmaputra valley they settled amid existing
inhabitants who, by contrast, used stone hoes to cultivate rice crops.
Assam's rich mythology about local figures such as Raja Narak-Asur
and Usha-Ban interacting with Indic figures such as the god Krishna
reveal the tensions, as existing groups of "Mlecchas, Danavas, and
Asuras" (lit. demons — that is, people outside the ritual pale) were
absorbed into the world of Indo-Aryan newcomers.[5]

Historians disagree on when these Indo-Aryan migrations from
northern and eastern India took place, and how far their wet-rice
cultivating, iron plough technology penetrated. The archaeologist
Nayanjot Lahiri cites more than thirty Sanskrit inscriptions of the fifth
to fifteenth centuries which recorded privileges and lands granted to
Brahmins. Based on them she postulates the presence of a highly developed agricultural civilization in Assam in which peasant life revolved
around homesteads, paddy fields, dry fields, and ponds.[6] Yet scholars
such as Amalendu Guha dispute her conclusions. They warn that
epigraphic sources from ruling groups eager for ritual and territorial
aggrandizement need to be treated with caution. Amalendu Guha
describes Assam's Sanskritization as slow and patchy. Early settled
agriculturists long formed isolated outposts in a sea of shifting hoe
cultivation and forest land. Different levels of technology and culture
probably coexisted in early Assam, even in the fertile Brahmaputra
valley. Near the Ambari (Guwahati) temple complex, where the
finding of fine wheel-turned pottery brought claims of an ancient
Brahmaputra valley civilization, archaeologists also found contem-

poraneous evidence for crude stone hoes. His view is strengthened by the tendency of this mix of plough and hoe cultivators, and wide variations in material and social culture, to remain characteristic of Assam until the mid-nineteenth century.[7]

In addition, Upper and Lower Assam developed quite differently. Known to late Vedic lore as Kamarupa, Lower Assam was closer to Bengal and allowed closer links to the Gangetic plains. The historian Kunal Chakrabarti argues that Lower Assam produced a number of *Upapurana* and *Tantra* literary texts, which were Brahminical attempts to integrate ritually peripheral lands. The *Kalika Purana*, *Jogini Tantra*, and other works valorized local shrines such as that of the Kamakhya mother-goddess (near Guwahati) and linked them with worship of newer Indo-Aryan gods such as Shiva, Vishnu, and their consorts.[8] The relatively late appearance of locally produced Sanskrit texts between the fourteenth and seventeenth centuries supports the thesis of Assam's tardy and incomplete incorporation into the Indo-Aryanist world. The older Sanskrit inscriptions can then be taken to refer to the smaller groups of early migrants who brought wet-rice, plough-based agriculture, caste ideology, and Sanskritic rituals into Lower Assam. These pioneering Indo-Aryan migrants interacted with extant tribal groups who possessed a range of technological and belief systems. While some local cults such as that of the Kamakhya mother-goddess were incorporated into the Brahminical belief system, others such as the Kachari and Chutia worship of the Bathou and Tamreswari deities stayed on its fringes.

Outside of belief systems, divergent groups of Assam's inhabitants found an important element of cultural unity insofar as *bhaat* (cooked rice) represented a common staple food. In the Assam plains rice, fish, and *saak* (wild greens) collected from common lands formed the essential diet across the social divide. In the hills meat was substituted for fish, and bamboo for greens. For all except ritually orthodox upper castes, this diet was supplemented by home-brewed *lao pani* (rice beer). Newcomers usually signified their absorption when they adopted these dietary and other living habits. Yet notwithstanding the entry of successive waves of migrants and Indic cultural influences, Assam's ecology and location rendered it for the most part a mysterious, impenetrable frontier until well into the colonial period.

Borderly Transactions

The terms "Bongali" and "Bangal" as indices of externality also reveal how pre-modern territoriality was often linked with a notion of community. The historians Romila Thapar and Hermann Kulke see early state growth as tied to an emergent sense of territoriality.[9] Often territoriality was defined through interactions with external forces rather than rigid spatial or ethnic parameters. For instance, the category Bangal first appears in local chronicles that narrated military conflicts with medieval Indo-Turkish forces. Later the British were called *boga* (white) Bangals.

Often this sense of alterity worked both ways. Those whom the Assamese saw as Bangals had their own views of Assam as a foreign, alien space. Persian chroniclers who accompanied invading armies into the Brahmaputra valley annexed older Sanskrit lore about Kamarupa as a land of *jadugiri* (black magic) to their own experiences to fashion a potent, alienating image of Assam. They tacitly denied any affinity to other parts of the subcontinent when they located Assam alongside other fearsome lands beyond the Himalayas. For example, the Persian poet Mulla Darviah's ode of 1663 declared: "Assam, which lies on the border of China and Cathay; It is another world, another people and other customs; its land is not like our land, its sky is not like our sky."[10] Assam's witching reputation was such that the Rajput prince Ram Singh arranged to have his expedition, mounted on behalf of the Mughal emperor Aurangzeb, accompanied by several *pirs* (holy men) and the Sikh guru Tegh Bahadur.[11]

Nonetheless, continued transactions between Assam and the Indic world did substantially extend zones of exchange and mutuality, even as different sides employed a discursive vocabulary of alterity. Between 1494 and 1533 Bengal's Hussain Shahi regime dominated a large portion of Lower Assam. The Ahom kings forced its retreat in the course of their own expansion down the Brahmaputra valley from their original base in Upper Assam. In addition, over the sixteenth and seventeenth centuries there was a long history of military struggle between Ahom and Mughals. One effect of this conflict was the long and gradual permeation of courtly and administrative Indo-Persian mores, as well as a steady influx of Muslim migrants from Bengal and North India. These migrants were often sponsored by rulers for building, brass-working, scribal, priestly, and Persian skills.

Brahmin priests, Sufi teachers, and Bengal artisans were particularly welcome. The Ahom king Rudra Singha patronized a talented crafts-man, Ghanashyam, who is said to have introduced Bengal's brick ornamentation style in place of wooden buildings.[12]

Many of these Muslims settled and intermarried with existing populations. Testimony for this comes from Shihabuddin Talish, the chronicler who accompanied Mir Jumla's Mughal expedition in 1663. He observed sourly that of the "Musalmans who had been taken prisoner in former times and had chosen to marry [here], their descendants act exactly in the manner of the Assamese, and have nothing of Islam except the name; their hearts are inclined far more toward mingling with the Assamese than toward association with Muslims."[13] Talish's reaction probably stemmed from finding that his co-religionists were in the trusted service of the enemy. His asser-tion that local Muslims were not allowed to perform their religious duties certainly ran counter to the evidence of an eighteenth-century folksong which narrated how the Ahom king Siva Singha built a mosque big enough to house six score devotees at a time.[14] The most important Islamic shrine was the Hajo mosque in Lower Assam, adjacent to the tomb of the Sufi teacher Ghiyasuddin Aulia. The shrine was known as Poa Mecca, since a pilgrimage bestowed a *poa* (one-fourth) of Mecca's blessings.[15] Sufi preachers such as Azan Fakir who migrated to Assam from Baghdad in the seventeenth cen-tury propagated a faith and a way of life based on devotional princi-ples quite similar to local Vaishnavite teachings.[16] Azan Fakir's real name was Shah Milan, but he took his sobriquet from the Azan (call to prayer). A large number of *jikir* (Assamese Sufi songs) are at-tributed to him.[17] Local lore speaks of Azan Fakir's initial persecu-tion by Ahom officials, soon followed by royal rehabilitation with grants of revenue-free lands.[18]

Long-distance trade represented another channel of interaction with the Indic world, although its character and volume often de-pended on political circumstances. Luxury goods were the original mainstay of the trade between Assam, Bengal, and North India, since everyday staples were locally produced. The best-known of these luxuries was a condiment, salt. Lacking adequate local sources, As-sam's pre-modern élites consumed expensively procured imported salt. Common people depended on home-made substitutes such as *khar* (plantain bark-ash). Talish was horrified at the absence of markets for staples, finding that betel nuts were the only edible goods for sale. As he remarked, "the inhabitants store in their houses one year's supply of food of all kinds; and are under no necessity to sell or buy eatables."[19] Until the seventeenth century Bengal merchants sailed on large boats into Lower Assam. There Assamese traders and some Vaishnavite monasteries took a leading role in sending long-distance goods upriver.

Ongoing rivalry between Ahom and Mughals caused the Assam kings to prohibit foreign traders' entry into the kingdom. This forced them to exchange goods at the border. "Once a year, by order of the Raja, a party used to go for trade to their frontier near Guwahati; they have gold, musk, aloe wood, pepper, spikenard, and silk cloth in exchange of salt, saltpeter, sulphur, and other products."[20] Urbane Mughal courtiers were understandably amazed that "their kings neither allow foreigners to enter their lands, nor permit any of their own subjects to go out of it."[21] In reality, traders often did manage to evade such restrictions.[22] Also, Ahom control extended only over the Brahmaputra valley; other routes to Bengal were open. For example, a key route connected the Bengal district of Sylhet to the Khasi and Jaintia hill states. Cotton, iron, wax, ivory, betel leaves, and cloth were exchanged at Jaintiapur for Bengal's salt, tobacco, rice, and goats.[23]

In the absence of political rivalry, there were no prohibitions on free movement of people and commodities across the hilly territories which linked Assam with Tibet, Yunnan, and Burma. Another Persian chronicle, the *Tabaqat-i-Nasiri* by Minhaj-i-Siraj, mentions regular caravan routes used mostly by Tibetan pilgrims and traders.[24] Assam's traders travelled through territory controlled by Bhutia chiefs to reach Geegunsheer, about two months' journey from Tibet. There they sold rice, silk cloths, iron, lac, skins, buffalo horns, and precious stones. Again, from Bhutan, Bhutias and Tibetans journeyed to Hajo for religious and trading purposes.[25] They also timed their journeys so as to take advantage of markets and fairs such as the Udalguri one held annually at the foot of the Bhutan hills. The last Ahom capital, the town of Jorhat, was named after the two *haats* (markets) held on the banks of the Dikhow river in Upper Assam.

Right into the nineteenth century barter held the key to these transactions, since cash coins played only a minor role in Assam's economy. Local coinage appeared from the sixteenth century, mostly in higher denominations. In the late seventeenth century the Mughals found that *kauri* (conch shells), silver, and gold coins circulated in the Ahom kingdoms, but no copper coins.[26] Since the volume and value of salt imports from Bengal alone exceeded local products, Assam had a long-standing outflow of slaves and gold. Subsequently, King Rudra Singha set up a revenue farming system that allowed a steady exchange of commodities between Assam and Bengal, but minimized direct contact. He appointed revenue farmers called *Duariya Baruas* at the Hadira Chowky frontier outpost opposite Goalpara. These functionaries were in charge of exchanging Assam's goods with Bengal's traders. The Duariya Baruas were assisted by *Bairagis* (customs officials). These revenue farmers paid the Ahom state an annual rent of ninety thousand rupees for their monopoly over the Assam-Bengal trade. In effect they supervised Ahom relations with neighbouring Bengal, and with the traders, Indians and Europeans, who congregated on the Assam-Bengal border. The Assamese magistrate, Anandaram Dhekial Phukan, hailed from a line of such wealthy Duariya Baruas. By the eighteenth century the Bengal salt trade was controlled by European traders such as Jean Baptiste Chevalier and John Robinson. This trade provided the West with its first regular contacts with Assam.[27] In the early nineteenth century Francis Buchanan Hamilton reported to his employer, the East India Company, that salt headed the list of imports into Assam. Others were ghee, fine pulses, sugar, stone beads, precious stones, spices, paints, copper, English woollens, and fine Banarasi fabrics. These high-value goods were exchanged for Assamese silks, lac, black pepper, cotton, ivory, bell-metal vessels, iron hoes, and slaves.[28] A commodity much in demand was Assam's lustrous muga silk.[29] Ahom functionaries paid the balance in gold dust and silver coins.[30] This trade later suffered much disruption during the strife with Moamoria rebels and Burmese invaders.

As early as 1771 the English East India Company had shown interest in trading with Assam and Bhutan. It sponsored the explorer George Bogle on an expedition which aimed to collect information about Tibet, the Brahmaputra river, and Assam. In 1774 the East India Company appointed Hugh Baillie to the border town of Goalpara as its agent to oversee the Assam-Bengal trade. British observers remained lukewarm about trading prospects with Assam, given the barriers to free trade imposed by the Ahom regime. Nonetheless the number of European and Bengal merchants on the Assam-Bengal border gradually increased, even though commerce was often marred by the European traders' infighting, and by their allegations of nonpayment against Assamese creditors. Their confrontations led to defiant incursions by Europeans into Assam, causing the first official communications between the English East India Company and the Ahom state. In 1780 the newly appointed governor general, Warren Hastings, expressed his determination to prevent the disputes. He promised to offer protection to the Assam traders from their European counterparts so that commerce might continue for mutual advantage.[31]

Meanwhile the late-eighteenth-century Ahom state was troubled by both internal rebellions and the depredations of military mercenaries from Bengal. After repeated Ahom protests, the British governor general Lord Cornwallis agreed in 1792 to help eject "gangs of vagabonds belonging to Bengal."[32] Captain Welsh, previously distinguished in the Mysore wars, was appointed commander of an Assam military expedition. His medical officer J. P. Wade exulted, "Today we shall enter a kingdom scarcely if ever trodden by Europeans before."[33] Once Welsh achieved his political mission to expel the Bengal mercenaries from Ahom territory, he attended to the East India Company's main concern: commercial relations. He proposed the abolition of monopolies, a fixed duty of 10 percent on imports, and a similar duty on exports. But Welsh's early recall by Cornwallis's successor Sir John Shore renewed internal turmoil in Assam, and the Burmese invasion of the Ahom kingdom meant that the Assam-Bengal border and its commercial transactions remained unstable.

Through this period newcomers to Assam were still called Bangals, but they lost that ascription once they settled down. Usually they entered into local marriages and gradually adopted living habits, religious norms, and dietary customs similar to those of their neighbours. The political scientist Sudipta Kaviraj terms similarly derived pre-modern conceptions of community "fuzzy," in contrast to the more recent "enumerated" type, born from the marriage of colonialism and modernity. He sees community as a notion necessarily predicated on some conception of difference. People handled their daily experience of social complexity through some system of rules by which people could be classified as similar or different.[34] Yet there are tensions and ambiguities inherent in this notion of fuzzy community. Pre-modern classifications such as Bangal represented relative distance rather than a permanent essence. They could easily be acquired and often as easily lost if location changed. When a vestige of externality remained, it was as a marker of status and difference, real or fictive.

Ambiguity in representing the self and the other is evident from the internal differentiation of categories within Assam itself. Between the hills and the plains there were a number of ways for people to see themselves as different from other groups. The labels "Naga" and "Abor" for hill and frontier groups denoted naked and rude. Plains inhabitants often used these pejorative names for neighbours whom they regarded as *a-sabhya* (uncultured), but this sort of identification was often contingent upon habitat and way of life, rather than signaling a permanent unchanging condition. Plains groups often applied the name "Abor," signifying barbarous, rude, or independent, quite imprecisely to a number of distant, independent hill clans.[35] The term was a shorthand label for groups living at the furthest distance from Ahom kingly authority and influence. In contrast, the name "Naga" was applied to those hill dwellers who inhabited nearby peripheries and existed within a complex intermeshing of exchanges. Therefore terms denoting indigenous alterity were fairly amorphous. As a British army official noted, "a Naga in the middle of the Naga hills" might "point out some distant and unknown village or country" in even more distant hill territory as inhabited by savage Abors.[36] The flexibility of these labels is clear from the tendency of individuals and groups from the hills to acquire different names when they entered the Brahmaputra valley's social life more closely. For instance, under the Assam kings meritorious state service earned for a few high-ranking individuals who originally hailed from hill communities the prestigious status of Ahom. Again, the collective adoption of Sanskritized lived practices and a shift of habitat might serve to transform a hill clan of Nagas or Kacharis who previously existed outside the caste order into a plains community of lower-caste Hindus.

In this manner the pre-modern relationship between the Brahmaputra valley and its bordering territories was characterized by degrees of alterity, fluidity, and flux. This was especially true of Assam's plains and the surrounding hills, where an intricate net of relationships and perceptions, rather than a rigid set of binaries, knit the inhabitants together. For example, in a Naga tale an old man asked the three sons of an ancestor what they would do for a living. The eldest decided to till the soil, the second to be a writer, the youngest to be a hunter. From the tiller of the soil was born the Naga tribal people; the hunter disappeared into the forest; and the writer became the ancestor of the plains Assamese.[37] Overlapping frontiers of technology, ecology, and migration thus shaped the multiple and contextually shifting contours of social identities in Assam.

Colonial Changes:
Élite Pedigrees and Hill "Savages"

Colonial rule was the catalyst for change in this flexible social landscape, as political and economic incorporation into British India brought closer social and intellectual contacts with other regions. Assam's repertoire of Sanskritized cultural and political ingredients had cohabited and partially overlapped with patterns tied to hill, Sinic, and Tibeto-Burman cultures. But from the late nineteenth century, as Assam's gentry fashioned themselves into a colonial intelligentsia, they evinced a new, strong desire to be Indian, and "Aryan."

High-caste claims of Aryan descent became central, with the gentry's self-representation now anchored to a distant, migratory origin in the Indo-Gangetic plains. Such claims are not surprising. As the historian Sumit Guha shows, fictive claims of immigration from the core areas of Islam and Hinduism were a well-established device in South Asia for constructing a high-status identity.[38] In their new location as Indian subjects, Assamese élites wished for this key to an Indo-Aryan heritage.[39] By asserting their status as historical Indic migrants, these élites aggressively denied kinship with Assam's lower castes and hill groups, who ranked low in the Sanskritic ritual hierarchy.

These genealogical fictions reflected racial ones, as modernizing Indian and British intellectuals interpreted a Vedic "Arya" cultural lineage as Indo-European or Aryan racial belonging. Assamese publicists now claimed historical Indic migrants, the Bangals of yore, as "Aryan ancestors."[40] Their assertions served to buttress their other, locally rooted claims to prestige, such as the ranks, offices, and titles acquired through past state service in the Ahom kingdom. When Prafulla Chandra Barua compiled his father's memoir, for example, he appended to it a *vamsavali* (genealogy) that detailed thirteen generations of his ancestors.[41] While his family's local status was linked to its Ahom-conferred Bujar Barua gentry rank, it still claimed original ancestry from Mithila (now in Bihar), famous as the land of

Sita in the *Ramayana* epic tradition. Almost every high-caste family boasted intricately inscribed palm-leaf genealogies which linked it to ritually sanctified Indic locations such as Mithila and Kanauj. Similarly, Assam's small Muslim gentry declared their descent from élite Shaikhs of Gaur (Bengal) who accompanied Turkish armies. Under the Ahom rulers many Muslims acquired high official rank, as modern family names such as Ali Hazarika and Rahman Barua reveal.[42] Others traced their origin to *khalifas* (preachers) who entered the Brahmaputra valley and settled there with honourable titles and landed endowments.[43] With claims of Persianized Gaur origins, colonial-era Muslim gentry racially distinguished themselves from lowly co-religionists such as Moria brass-workers whom they stigmatized as aboriginal converts to Islam.[44]

In a similar fashion, Ahom élites took pride in their own myths of origin outside the space of Assam. As local intellectuals and British officials transmuted older chronicles into printed knowledge, another set of legends about noble migrants to Assam acquired currency. These narratives centred around Ahom warrior ancestors whom they claimed as followers of the heroic Sukapha, the first of Assam's Ahom kings. One version claimed that Sukapha was a Shan prince from Upper Burma. Another described Sukapha as descended from the sons of the Lord of Heaven, Indra, who arrived on earth by an iron ladder, bearing a magic sword. By the early twentieth century a consensus emerged that in the thirteenth century, a royal prince, Sukapha accompanied by his band, had made his way into Assam. In the course of this journey he vanquished and allied with tribal groups such as the Barahis, Morans, and Nagas. The Ahom line of kings that he founded subsequently ruled over the fertile rice-plains of the Brahmaputra valley with the help of their warrior followers and a caste Hindu service gentry. From the late nineteenth century this was the explanation of Ahom rule, widely circulated by the British administrator Edward Gait in his *History of Assam* (1906),[45] and his one-time research assistant Golap Chandra Barua, an Ahom aristocrat in British service.[46] This view later received support from anthropologists and linguists who studied Tai migrations in early Asia. As Tai groups carried wet-rice and irrigation technology into Laos, Yunnan, Burma, and Assam, they intermarried with existing settlers to lay the foundation for dispersed kingdoms.[47]

Overall, in colonial Assam's changing cultural landscape, myths of origin and distance, whether for Brahmins, Muslims, or the Ahom warrior élite, emphasized a common theme of élite superiority over subordinate groups whom they viewed as autochthones. Colonial appropriation of local chronicles gave greater currency to these myths. These views achieved further importance when, from the mid-nineteenth century, Assam's upper-caste gentry accrued a significant amount of cultural capital through their scribal and literate skills. They gradually adapted an existing repertoire of Indic affiliation to fit in with newly racialized, pan-Indian narratives of Indo-Aryanist belonging, and distance themselves from lower castes and tribes. They simultaneously distanced themselves from neighbouring hill groups.

When the British became Assam's rulers their authority was confined mostly to the plains. Subsequent colonial attempts at "pacifying" the frontier produced an escalated rhetoric of Nagas as hill savages responsible for bloody raids on the plains. For the British rulers, one political solution was the installation of the Inner Line Restrictions of 1873, which cordoned off the hill areas. These regulations prevented ingress into the hills except with special permission. Like the rest of Assam, the hill districts also came under the Non-Regulation system of administration, which concentrated vast powers in official hands, often British military cadres, with little accountability. Yet the low revenue-generating possibilities of the hill districts meant that colonial officials paid heed primarily to maintaining the rule of law, and little or not at all to health, education, and general welfare in the hills. Later those responsibilities were made over to Christian missionaries. This isolation and administrative singularity caused political, economic, and racial boundaries to rigidify. Measures such as the Inner Line Regulations which restricted movement into the hill districts further reified perceived differences between Assam's hills and plains. An older economy of exchange and interaction gradually withered away. Over the modern period the dominant Brahmaputra valley discourse hardened to ascribe civilizational and racial externality to neighbouring hill dwellers as savage, marauding tribal autochthones.

"Lazy" Peasants and "Opium Eaters"

In early British-ruled Assam the cultivated portion of the Brahmaputra valley was covered by small-scale peasant holdings. Most inhabitants practiced a multi-tiered system of plough-based cultivation.

They grew higher-yielding wet-rice varieties on fertile *rupit* lands, and used dry *faringati* lands for other, inferior crops. Hoe-cultivating communities lived in the valley's hilly peripheries. They grew inferior varieties of dry rice and often practiced shifting cultivation. All over Assam people collected timber and other necessities from the non-arable, forested commons which were plentiful all around. The scarce factor of production in Assam was labour rather than land, given the low population and abundant uncultivated territory. Large estates were few, usually owned by religious heads or nobles. Previously these estates used servile labour. After the British abolition of slavery in 1843 the remaining large estates were cultivated by tenants and sharecroppers.

Rice was grown by all, almost entirely for subsistence, but in the new cash economy introduced by the British, peasants needed marketable products. Peasants initially turned to mustard, grown to obtain oil and sold to traders for cash. In the virtual absence of a rice market, mustard sales enabled peasants to pay colonial taxes and buy goods such as salt. Mustard as a marketable crop was speedily overtaken by opium. Migrant commodity traders, known as Kayas or Marwaris, aided this changeover by providing cash advances to peasants only if they grew opium.[48]

Historical evidence on opium use indicates that by the eighteenth century Ahom notables consumed it in emulation of North Indian courtly fashions. In 1792 Captain Welsh found that it was grown abundantly in Lower Assam. He noted that "a great quantity of opium is produced and used by the inhabitants. In point of purity it is probably equal to that of Patna or Benares but it is prepared in a different form, being reduced to a dry state by exposure to the air spread on narrow strips of cloth, which are afterwards rolled up into small balls and called Kanee or Kappa."[49] These opium cloths were soaked in water to form a decoction. Numerous peasants began to grow small amounts of opium. They consumed some of their harvest in decoction form, and marketed the rest. During the early decades of British rule Assamese peasants solved the cash shortage and the excessively heavy demand of government dues when they cultivated more opium. While the rice crop maintained the peasant household, the opium crop brought in scarce cash. In contrast to mustard, the demand for opium had the potential to rise every year, as did its price. While opium's average after-harvest price in the 1840s was Rs 5

Mustard and opium as cash crops

a seer, the retail price might rise to Rs 80 a seer during the lean months.[50] By 1852 Nagaon, the main opium-growing district, had more than three thousand acres, about 2 percent of cultivated acreage, under the plant.[51]

During the same period the Assam Company was attempting to enlist local peasants to work in the tea enterprise. A good many peasants responded positively. To meet an urgent need for cash, or as a source of extra income in the slack season, there were few other options, since most local work was paid in kind. Occasional tea work filled the need for cash. Yet these peasants would not stay for long periods and risk neglect of their ricefields. Mostly they chose to labour only when the tea gardens were near their own hamlets. Sometimes planters arranged with village headmen to round up a few daily labourers. Even such ad hoc arrangements became less attractive as the arduous work and discipline of the tea enterprise was better known.

Given abundant land availability, it was quite logical that most Brahmaputra valley peasants should not have been overly attracted to wage labour as a way of life. An early British report acutely stated that it would be rare for an Assamese living at a distance to leave his home for the mere inducement of working on a tea plantation: "Their taking such work at all is generally attributed to temporary necessity, as for instance, inability to pay their revenue, wanting to get married and not having the necessary means, being in debt to a Kaya [trader], or as more commonly happens, pawning their freedom, being in want of a yoke of buffaloes for cultivating purposes."[52] Such clearsighted reporting became less common as the colonial regime became entrenched. As the tea venture's need for a regular, disciplined labour force became urgent, its frustration with locals grew. British officials increasingly speculated that it was an innate indolence in Assam's people, perhaps a climatic or racial trait, which made labouring work so unpopular. Missionaries concurred, eager to fault local people in a place where their proselytizing activities were as yet quite unsuccessful. In this manner colonialism discovered Assam's lazy natives. They acquired the epithet of *lahe lahe* (slowly slowly). → Due to redual to work be a lot of land

The essentialist explanation of local indolence gained scientific and medicinal credence from the peasant's easy access to opium. Not only were Assamese peasants lazy, but Nature seemed to compound their weakness with a fertile soil. All crops, particularly opium, grew in easy profusion. Captain Rowlatt articulated the new colonial orthodoxy about the lazy native when he argued that Nature's bounty added a fatal element to human failing: "It is the low cost and great ease with which every ryot [peasant] is able to procure a supply of opium that so thoroughly demoralizes the whole people . . . This, if it produces no worse consequence, most certainly induces great laziness . . . the peculiar characteristic of the Assamese people."[53]

Such opinions of officials, planters, and missionaries tended to ignore the material necessity that drove peasants to opium cultivation. Opium as a homegrown, morally dubious luxury was their focus. Some medical men already argued for opium's medicinal value in a malarial climate, but most colonial observers simply castigated indigenous society for sloth and indulgence. Homegrown opium was a needless luxury for Assamese peasants, just as alcohol was for Britain's factory workers. The perceived moral turpitude was all the more extreme since this luxury was obtained at virtually no cost from the peasant's own garden, in such abundance that peasants, observers alleged, even fed opium to their wives and children.[54] For western observers opium was the definitive sign of the profligate native. Not content with wasting Nature's bounty, peasants abused it to reinforce their moral and physical inadequacy. Captain John Butler declared, "The utter want of an industrious, enterprising spirit and the general degeneracy of the Assamese people are greatly promoted by the prevalent use of opium."[55] Concurring with British officials, some local élites did express perturbation that opium use had spread to ordinary people.[56] But these sentiments differed in nature from the moral outrage of colonial officials who chose to ignore the economic logic behind the newly increased domestic cultivation of opium and its connections with colonial revenue policies. Instead they condemned opium addiction as a congenital defect of the Assamese people.

Notwithstanding the moral rhetoric of its officials, the East India Company itself had a long-standing relationship with opium. The prosperous trade between China, Britain, and India largely depended on the sale by British traders of Indian opium in China. Since 1773 the silver that Britain obtained from China in return for Indian opium was remitted as profit back to Britain. After Britain's success in the Opium War with China, the supply of Indian opium smuggled into China rose sharply, as did Chinese consumption of opium. But the East India Company was still not satisfied. It desired other, closer markets in Eastern India where surplus opium supplies from Bengal, Bihar, and Malwa could be marketed. As early as 1837 the Malaya expert John Crawfurd pointed out that "the countries lying between India and China" would be great marts for its consumption.[57] Accordingly, from the 1840s the East India Company arranged to sell imported opium in Assam through government agents. These sales remained limited, since there was an abundant and cheap local supply.[58] At the same time, some British officials expressed concern about opium's debilitating effects. To limit opium use, both David Scott and Francis Jenkins suggested that the tax on homegrown opium should be gradually raised. Instead Justice Mills's recommendation was adopted: "Opium they should have, but to get it they should be made to work for it."[59]

By the 1850s the two main problems for the colonial state were what it saw as local indolence and the shortage of tea labourers. Mills's suggestion effectively linked these problems and suggested a solution. Following his advice, in 1861 the British banned opium cultivation in Assam, while the colonial state established a wide network of licensed outlets. Those outlets would sell imported opium. The necessity to purchase opium from them, the state anticipated, would forcibly drag indolent peasants into the labour market. This policy received support from officials, planters, and many missionaries. The Rev. Mr. Higgs of the SPG Mission in London reassured officials that their policy was morally and economically right: "The abkarry [state-distributed] opium is only supplying the place of the indigenous drug, and by forcing the lazy natives to work to gain the money to pay for it, it tends more than anything to bring Assam under cultivation."[60] Interestingly, this dubious logic did not carry conviction with Higgs's American Baptist missionary colleagues, whose periodical the *Orunodoi* publicized local opposition to this new opium policy.[61] The temperance-minded Americans approved of colonial improvement initiatives but could not bring themselves to see opium as one such. Meanwhile Upper Assam peasants, whether opium consumers or not, mostly resisted incorporation into the tea garden's regimented labour ranks. In their place socially and economically subordinate Kachari cultivators from Lower Assam momentarily formed the plantation's workforce.

Kachari Tribals: "Primitive" Exceptionalism

These labouring discourses and practices in the Assam locality need to be placed in the larger context of the colonial construction of racial differences. Over the nineteenth century European race science became extremely influential in South Asia. The perceived physicality of race was extended and modified as colonial administrators ordered and separated South Asian populations into tribes and castes. Their discursive framework was built around ideas about savages and primitives, and about hunting, pastoralism, agriculture, and commerce. The historian Ajay Skaria has shown how by seizing upon and magnifying racial and cultural differences among different groups of people, the British prepared an exhaustive list of the "tribes of India." In almost all cases the so-called tribes shared more cultural, social, and economic practices with their caste neighbours than with other, distant "tribes" with which British officials grouped them. Skaria claims that this listing of tribes represented the colonial invention of primitive societies in South Asia.[62] Significantly, this invention occurred just when the colonial regime withdrew from its earlier promotion of "skilled and civilized" labour for the tea industry. The colonial quest for an amenable labouring class now led to a new interest in the "primitive virtues" of the subcontinent's tribal populations.

Assam's "heterogenous" population provided an array of additions to the list of tribes. Thus it was not difficult to find a local group which seemed more promising for the colonial tea enterprise than the usual lazy native. The British were especially interested in the Kachari people of the Lower Assam districts of Kamrup, Lakhimpur, Darrang, and Goalpara. Several colonial commentators already distinguished Kacharis from other locals because of their capacity for toil: an "aboriginal race of Assam" who were "cheery, good-natured, semi-savage folk."[63] The SPG missionary Sidney Endle recommended his Kachari flock as being well fitted for all forms of outdoor field and factory labour which might require strength rather than skill: Assam's "navvies."[64]

Notably, these late-nineteenth-century observers of the Kacharis were influenced by an older tradition of colonial ethnography which emphasized distinctions between India's "Tamulian" and "Caucasian" races, in particular the work of the pioneering Himalayan explorer Brian Hodgson (1800–94), the first commentator to bring the Kacharis to scholarly notice. From his residency in Kathmandu,

Hodgson contributed over eighty papers to the *Transactions of the Asiatic Society of Bengal*, many about the "aboriginal" inhabitants of the Bengal Presidency. He sought to systematize the study of racial difference by linking it with language.[65] The historian David Arnold argues that when Europeans explored the interiors of the subcontinent, they distinguished between Indians of the plains, seen as an Indo-Caucasian race, and indigenous groups inhabiting hilly and forested territories, seen as aboriginal or tribal. Ethnographers such as Hodgson ascribed several traits to tribals: a minimal use of clothing, hunting or shifting cultivation, and lives spent in jungle habitats. These traits also differentiated tribals from caste society.[66] Hodgson collected a large variety of vocabularies from the sub-Himalayan regions of India and Nepal, and relied on these to classify local populations. He argued that the non-Caucasian inhabitants of these frontier lands belonged to a unique race. He termed this race the Tamulian and asserted that its members were India's original inhabitants, forced to flee into hills and forests by racially and linguistically distinct newcomers who usurped the fertile lowlands.[67]

Colonial race science changed considerably after Hodgson, the pioneering scholarly figure of the early and mid-nineteenth century. By the twentieth century other names appeared, such as Herbert Risley, whose emphasis on physical and biological traits considerably downplayed the linguistic features of racial groups. In this later period Hodgson's work had much more impact on George Grierson's *Linguistic Survey*[68] than it did on Risley's Anthropological Survey of India and his magnum opus, the *People of India* volumes.[69] Nonetheless, from Hodgson's research on "the Koch, Mech and Dhimals" of the Himalayan foothills, the missionary Sidney Endle and other late-nineteenth-century ethnographers borrowed the notion that these peoples were fragments of a larger Bodo Kachari race, itself an offshoot of the larger Tamulian race. Hodgson had also called attention to the physical suitability of Tamulians for life and work in territories inhospitable to the Caucasian races. This idea was developed further by his intellectual heirs. By the second half of the nineteenth century Kacharis were deemed to possess a "share in the marvellous freedom from the effects of malaria which characterizes nearly all the Tamulian aborigines of India, as the Kols, the Bheels and the Gonds."[70] This was an important consideration for tea industry recruiters wishing to minimize labour deaths.

Previously, Assamese élites had played a key role in identifying

Kacharis as potential labourers. The last Assam ruler, Purandar Singha, first drew British attention to the Kacharis. When the East India Company asked to use his lands for tea, he gave permission. He recommended that it recruit "Cacharee" workers whom he called the labouring class of the country.[71] Assamese folklore, with ubiquitous tales of Kachari servants and Brahmin masters, bears testimony to a long-standing hierarchical relationship between the high-status caste society of Upper Assam and the Kachari peasants who made a sparse living from the submontane lands of Lower Assam.[72]

In the labour discourses that subsequently circulated in colonial Assam, there is a definite similarity between the ritual purity-obsessed superiority displayed by Assam's high-caste groups, who disdained alcohol use as a lowly habit, and the British condescension toward primitiveness. Assam's pioneering administrator Francis Jenkins felt that it was because "the Cacharee consume so much of their rice in making spirits that they are obliged to labour to pay their rents."[73] Unlike the high-status, Hinduized groups who shunned alcohol consumption, Kacharis, Mishings, Nagas, and other tribal people regarded rice beer as an essential staple. Jenkins claimed that this custom forced Kacharis onto the labour market, since they brewed up their rice crop: "Cacharie labourers almost invariably engage on an agreement to receive Rs 6 per month for single task work, and very frequently they stipulate for double task work for double pay."[74]

Therefore colonial observers tended to cite the same "aboriginal" habits of alcohol consumption and non-settled agriculture that marked off "tribe" from "caste," and the Kacharis from the Assamese, as proof of an equally "primitive" habit of diligence. Industriousness seemed a trait intrinsic to many primitive Asian peoples which distinguished them from primitive groups in Europe and North America. Ecology and climate had caused people who lived in India's "enervating plains" to be lethargic, since "the fertility of the soil is such that one month's labour is enough to maintain a family in comfort for a year."[75] It was aboriginal groups, driven out by more civilized peoples into less productive hills, who remained industrious, since they needed to work hard to live.

Of course there were many inconsistencies in these opinions. Quite often the same observers bemoaned a vagabondage that they saw as peculiar to "savage" people. Nonetheless, for Kacharis and later for other "Tamulian aboriginals," ethnography defined industriousness as a prime attribute. The supposed Kachari appetite for work excited the tea industry. One planter described how "they travel in gangs of ten to twenty, from garden to garden, and will not take a job unless they are assured of being allowed to do at least a double day's work in one day. After a garden is got into a good condition, and the work falls short, they will frequently pack up and move off to another place."[76]

British commentators constantly cited racial difference as the ultimate determinant of work capacity. Some did, however, note the marked differences in technology and resource base between Kachari tea labourers and Upper Assam peasants. Most Kachari workers originated from communities that depended on hoes to cultivate crops. Their caste Hindu neighbours, by contrast, possessed superior cattle-driven plough technology. District officials observed: "The population in Dhurmpore are mostly Assamese who cultivate only with the plough, Cacharees and Mikirs who cultivate much of the lands by the hoe alone, without the assistance of plough cattle, changing their grounds every three to four years and allowing their old fields to run to jungle and remain fallow nine to ten years."[77] These Lower Assam Kacharis, a community low down the ladder of pre-colonial status and power, lived in hilly, less fertile tracts. Because their lands were marginal they had been exempt from customary corvée services. Most households held land suitable only for dry rice varieties, which yielded less than wet rice and required fallowing every three years. Under Ahom rule these Kacharis often supplemented their incomes by labouring for prosperous neighbours who paid them in kind. With the arrival of the British these Kacharis were pushed into plantation wage contracts by the cash-short economy of Assam, where wage-earning opportunities were limited. Therefore in contrast to Jenkins's observations, Kachari peasants were forced into seasonal labour migrations by an insufficient resource base, not by improvident drinking habits. When they could, Kacharis also availed themselves of other wage-earning channels, either as "a strong element in the military and police forces"[78] or as "tenants of the Government or on the Gosains' lands."[79] Generally they retained household links in their home villages. One son usually lived in the village while his siblings seasonally moved to plantations. They often volunteered to work at double tasks so as to return to their villages with an ample supply of cash.[80]

The British tea enterprise's fascination with the Kacharis soon faded. Despite colonial officials' lavish eulogies, planters became increasingly dissatisfied with Kachari workers. The reality was that local workers tended to come and go as they pleased, whether they were Kachari migrants from Lower Assam or Upper Assam peasants from villages adjoining plantations. Local workers were unwilling to start work without a wage advance. Planters complained that "after working a few days they go home."[81] In 1854 the tea enterprise became totally disenchanted with its once cherished Kachari workers when the Assam Company's entire workforce, "thousands in number, and all Cacharees, struck work for an increase in pay."[82] These workers clearly had good reason for the strike: even the capital-minded *Times* newspaper rebuked the Assam Company, which maintained "rather too strict a control over its rate of wages."[83] This dispute was resolved, but employer-labour relations definitively soured. In 1861 Kachari peasants joined the Phulaguri uprising against opium prohibition and a new agricultural tax. When a British officer was killed, colonial opinion branded Kacharis "bloodthirsty" as well as primitive.[84] Such an unruly workforce with a potential for violent resistance seemed uncomfortably reminiscent of the Chinese workers of yore.

Over the nineteenth century, encouraged by the British state, tea firms such as the Assam Company had sought to control large swaths of land, and to discover how to subordinate human skills to an industrial regime. British enterprise gradually reduced the basics of tea manufacture learnt from the Chinese to a large number of simple yet arduous tasks. The new agro-industrial enterprise of tea took shape. Once planters escaped the trap of high wages for Chinese workers, they sought, in their place, low-waged, unskilled labour from the Assam locality. Instead of Rs 16 a month that the Chinese earned, the wage rate for locals was a low 2 annas a day. But low wages alone were not enough to create all the attributes of a proletarian workforce. Local labour's ability to leave without notice enraged colonial capital. Planters complained that they lacked the power to discipline workers who left after taking advances. After 1859 employers could invoke the new Workmen's Breach of Contract Act, but planters still claimed that "tedious civil cases" were useless when defendants had practically no attachable property.[85] Workers might have had different imperatives and lived practices, but their common role as local labour made them equally unsuitable for the plantation's needs. Assam's peasants could not be reduced to total dependence. Ultimately the simple, hardworking Kachari and the indolent Assamese seemed equally inconvenient for tea's labouring requirements. Although racial logic failed in its advocacy of the Kacharis, it remained critical, as the British colonial regime searched for yet another source of tea labour. Primitiveness necessitated looking further afield for the right type of worker.

Inventing the Tea Coolie

During the first few years of the tea enterprise Charles Bruce and his colleagues depended on China, its tea plant, and its tea growers. But once the British learnt how to cultivate tea, Chinese growers became expendable. Moreover, the China-Assam hybrid plant which imperial botany had created was discovered to be ill suited to its environment. By the 1870s British planters witheringly referred to this China-Assam hybrid plant as the "plague." In its place they replanted the indigenous Assam species. Thus the China tea plant too proved dispensable. While the British initially learnt to grow and process tea from the Chinese, they later created a different system. Rather than perpetuate the Assamese tea forests, or Chinese household production, British entrepreneurs learnt how to grow tea on an industrial scale. Under the white man's supervision the plantation's prime requirement became a vast pool of cheap, docile, easily reproducible labour.[86] To find such a workforce the Assam industry relied on the assistance of the colonial state and the expertise of other imperial plantation enterprises.

In the wake of the British Empire's slave emancipation in the 1830s, subcontinental labourers were recruited to the sugar plantations of the Caribbean and Mauritius as replacements for African slaves.[87] Most of these workers, known as coolies, were recruited from tribal groups which lived in Central and Eastern India. The anthropologist Kaushik Ghosh describes how the nineteenth-century British conquest of Bengal's "wild frontier," the Chotanagpur-Santal hill territory, physically and economically dislocated its inhabitants. Local groups such as the Kols rebelled in 1831–33, followed by the Santhals in 1855–56. The British state harshly suppressed these uprisings, and the rebels lost most of their lands. Colonial policymakers were determined to "pacify" the region, and plains migrants who operated as moneylenders, traders, and landlords assisted the state in this endeavour. A long, ugly process of depeasantization took place. The displaced groups subsequently became known as compliant and hardworking labourers on mines, roads, and plantations. As with the Kacharis, facile racial explanations by more powerful contemporaries must be read against the grain if we are to comprehend how the colonial dispossession of Chotanagpur's inhabitants transformed them into the British Empire's labour reserve.

Newly labelled as hill coolies, these migrants were praised as far as the British House of Commons for their primitive traits of obedience and toil.[88] Colonial race thinkers once again revised their views on primitiveness as they observed these new labouring groups arrive on the plantations. In the early nineteenth century Brian Hodgson had classified the tribal inhabitants of Assam and Chotanagpur together as Turanian aboriginals belonging to the Tamulian race. But by the 1860s ethnographic manuals separated the two groups, to match their differential status as colonial labourers. George Campbell, later Bengal's lieutenant governor, pioneered this modification, adapting Hodgson's scheme to reflect changed realities. Campbell now distinguished between two groups of aboriginals: Kolarian people of Chotanagpur and Kacharis of the northeast frontier.[89] He employed the tenets of race science to argue that the Kolarians were far superior to their fellow aboriginals the Kacharis as tea labourers.

Campbell praised Chotanagpur labourers as a simple, industrious people. Unlike other aboriginal groups who succumbed before the onslaught of modern civilization, these groups steadily multiplied and supplied British India's labour markets in abundance. These Kolarians worked on indigo plantations and on railway and road construction, and were the favourites for Assam tea work. Campbell speculated as to why they were so prized. "Partly on account of the cheapness of labour in their country, partly on account of their tractable disposition and freedom from all caste and food prejudices, and more especially, I think, because of that want of attachment to the soil which distinguishes the Aboriginal from the Arian."[90] Campbell opportunely forgot that the equally primitive Kacharis had displayed too much of an attachment to their soil for the planters' liking when they chose to return to their home villages. His theories effectively erased history and the impact of colonial policies. In reality, dispossessed Kolarians had little alternative but to migrate from their home region of Central India. By contrast, Kachari peasants often had some land and some control over their labour. Campbell translated this social reality into racialized distinctions between Kolarians and Kacharis.

Both Chotanagpur Kolarians and Kachari workers became known as tea's archetypal coolies. The term "coolie," which apparently originated from the Tamil word for wages "kuli," was long used to denote low-level workers in the Indian Ocean labour market.[91] Now it acquired a specific racial sense. Colonial ethnographers began to plot an essential link between the term and Chotanagpur's labourers, also known as Dhangars. In Campbell's influential *Ethnology of India* he suggested that the term was in fact derived from the name Kol, or Kolarian. He mentioned in his listing of tribes "Dhangars; that last term being one the proper meaning of which I cannot ascertain, but which, as far as I can learn, is applied generically to the aboriginal labourers in Calcutta."[92] Following his lead, in 1883 the influential Anglo-Indian lexicon *Hobson-Jobson* defined Dhangar as "the name by which members of various tribes of Chutia Nagpur [*sic*] are generally known when they go out to distant lands to seek employment as labourers (coolies)."[93]

Over the nineteenth century tribal labourers from Chotanagpur and Central India were subsumed into this identity of Dhangar, or hill coolie. Their migratory existence became another defining characteristic. Recruiters from all over the British Empire made their way to this region. During the 1830s and 1840s sugar planters in Mauritius and Trinidad were the pioneers in recruitment from this region. A recruitment team for Assam met little success in 1839 as it competed against established networks of overseas recruiters. However, after a few years high shipboard death rates forced the state to impose stricter medical checks on overseas recruitment. In response, labour contractors dispatched recruits to Assam, where regulations were lax. Tea plantations joined the overseas sugar colonies as a prime labouring destination. Steamers and roads, and at a later date railways, carried men, women, and children to the jungles and gardens of Upper Assam. Sent to Assam wearing the red jackets that many associated with degrading prison life, most Chotanagpur peasants viewed Assam as an unknown wilderness, "the end of the world." Yet the circumstances of their home region left little choice but migration.[94] British policies had caused immense political and socioeconomic dislocation. Colonial observers asserted that "movements of this kind are due to take place from one province to another whenever there is a great demand for labour on the one hand, and a crowded population on the other."[95] This was a disingenuous argument that ignored the state's role in accelerating "push" and promoting "pull."

British India's promotion of "forced commercialization" caused an ever increasing amount of landlessness and indebtedness and forced many labourers to migrate outside existing seasonal circuits. By the end of the nineteenth century the recruitment area for coolie labour, once restricted to Chotanagpur, encompassed more and more of the subcontinent. Natural calamities and livelihood losses pushed starving people into distant coolie work. The famine of 1873–74 in North Bihar caused fresh migration from there to Assam.[96] Similarly, famine conditions in the Central Provinces in the 1890s caused large numbers of its lower classes to migrate: 28.2 percent of Assam recruits came from there in 1896, 37.7 percent in 1900, and 39.2 percent in 1901, compared with only 5.6 percent in 1894.[97] Economic crises fell disproportionately upon lower-caste and tribal groups. For example, in a famine-affected district tribal groups such as Gonds suffered a 17.3 percent population decline and untouchable Mahars a 6 percent decline, compared to only 0.3 percent for high-status Brahmins.[98] An observer noted: "Hard times, so to speak, have driven Khonds, Savaras, Gadahas, and others from their own to other jungles."[99]

From the 1860s the British state worked closely with Assam planters to establish a legal regime of coolie indenture buttressed by harsh penal provisions. Planters now attributed earlier labour problems to incorrect recruitment policies. In contrast to Chotanagpur coolies, earlier tea labouring groups such as the Chinese, Assamese, and Kacharis were regarded as aggressive, congenitally lazy, or addicted to opium. Taming the jungle might require "aboriginal" traits, but it also required labourers to submit to control and discipline. Neither China's nor Assam's local workers were willing to do that. While the Chinese clung to their contracts for protection, locals collected their advances and deserted the plantations. By the second half of the nineteenth century the tea regime devised a way to bring labourers of its choice to the plantations — and to keep them there. Starting with the Transport of Native Labourers Act (1863), the colonial state passed numerous laws to facilitate the recruitment and control of Assam's migrant workforce. In Mauritius, the Caribbean, Natal, and Fiji, indentured coolies became essential for sugar planting, and in Assam for tea production.[100] By the end of the nineteenth century Chotanagpur labourers acquired the highest rank among Assam coolies. They were known as "Class I junglies" in the planter's lexicon.[101] In the recruitment market, aboriginals were the most prized and the most expensive: planters ranked them high in terms of resilience, labouring ability, and resistance to disease.

Initially most tea labour recruitment was in the hands of professional recruiters (*arkattis*) who journeyed to Central Indian villages to recruit labourers for the plantations. When the arkattis became notorious as unscrupulous "coolie catchers," tea planters sought around for alternative recruitment strategies. Individual plantations began to send coolie *sardars* (overseers) back to their home villages to raise fresh recruits. The sardars were especially successful in using kin and local ties to recruit newcomers. By the 1890s most arkattis moved to recruitment of coolie labour to work Bihar's mines and collieries.[102] Eventually the tea industry established its own organization to oversee labour recruitment and retention, the Tea Districts Labour Association.

A special correspondent of the *Times* lyrically reported on the tea coolie: "The labourer has been withdrawn from the fierce battle of the millions amid the storm and stress of varying seasons into the constant shadow of prosperity and peace. For him and his like alone among the poor of India the problem of life is solved."[103] This account purported to depict the estimated 700,000 and 750,000 recruits for the tea industry who came to Assam between 1870 and 1900. About 250,000 were from Chotanagpur. Yet the reality of their new life under the penal regime of indenture was as far removed as possible from the "prosperity and peace" that London's press described. Given an almost total absence of state regulation, labour abuses were staggering in scope.

The "he" adopted by the *Times* and most other official documents concealed the large number of women and children included within the term "coolie." The plantation system divided the hundreds of tasks involved in tea production along lines of gender and age.[104]

Use of female and child labor

High labour coercion

Planters employed semi-feudal methods of discipline and coercion to subject ostensibly free labourers to a new kind of serfdom. Indentured coolies were open to oppression in a way that earlier tea recruits had not been. They were virtually imprisoned in the squalor of the housing lines and locked in at night. These migrant workers found themselves living in the middle of remote, forested terrain, allowed little or no contact with neighbouring villagers. Flight was well-nigh impossible, since migrants' ignorance of the terrain, coupled with bounties offered to hill people to track fleeing coolies with dogs, ensured that they would stay.[105] The archives provide some records of the frequent floggings, beatings, and even killings of coolies but are usually silent about other forms of exploitation. Fragmentary anecdotal accounts testify to the many ways female coolies were sexually exploited by Assam's white masters, and of the mixed-race, illegitimate children who often resulted.[106] These regressive aspects of coolie life had an enduring, negative impact on the migrants' status among local populations.

The plantation hierarchy consisted of the European manager at the top, with the coolie workers at the bottom. In between were European assistant managers, aided by a number of native supervisors, or *mohurirs*. Most of the latter were Assamese or Bengali caste Hindus. A. R. Ramsden's estate, for example, employed five mohurirs, described as "Assamese and agriculturists by birth."[107] Their main task was to oversee the workforce of three thousand coolies. Ramsden's clerks earned an average of one rupee a day as well as a monthly commission "on the payment for work done by those they supervise."[108] Considerable distance and antagonism separated coolie labourers and the caste gentry who disciplined them on behalf of the white "sahibs." Many mohurirs possessed a full share of racial prejudices and class antagonisms to vent upon these migrant labourers, scorning the tribal coolies as alien, ritually low intruders. Census reports detail how local clerks, when sent as enumerators, refused to enter coolies as Hindus, but indifferently lumped them together with Christians or Animists, because, they said, "they eat anything."[109] A mohurir, Someswar Sarma, wrote a traditional verse panegyric, *Assam Companir Biboron* (Description of the Assam Company), notable for its groveling praise of the tea gardens' picturesque beauty, in complete disregard of the wretched reality of the coolie lives.

Despite planters' complaints about the high cost of importing la-

An animosity

bour, their state-conferred ability to impose starvation wages and a draconian work regime, as well as to prevent desertion by these migrants, was quite unprecedented.[110] As the historian Samita Sen suggests, in the manner of other sectors of colonial capital, planters could minimize labour costs since the burden of reproduction was usually passed back to the rural hinterland.[111] Only later did the state and the industry evince concern at the low birth rate and infant survival rate and the high number of abortions among coolie women.[112] The tea industry was immensely successful in evading the costs that participation in a truly "free" labour market would have entailed. In 1864, while a labourer in the Public Works Department earned Rs 7 monthly, the going rate in the Assam Company was only Rs 4 to 5. In this manner the indentured labour and penal contract systems permitted planters to bypass prevailing wage structures.[113]

The significance of the Assam tea industry to the British Empire was reflected in the large body of legislation enacted to facilitate labour supply. The Transport of Native Labourers Act of 1863 was followed in quick succession by the Bengal Acts of 1865 and 1870, the Inland Emigration Act of 1893, the Assam Labour and Emigration Acts of 1901 and 1915, and finally the Tea Districts Emigrant Labour Act of 1932. As with the overseas sugar industry, the state claimed that these laws would facilitate the recruitment and retention of labour and also allay humanitarian concerns. For the tea industry the only relevant parts of this legislation related to labour recruitment and discipline. Penal privileges such as the right of private arrest formed the foundation of Assam's notorious "Planters' Raj." Minimum wages remained the same for forty years. Legal provisions which limited work to nine hours a day and six days a week, or stipulated the construction of a hospital on every plantation, existed only on paper. The state did not attempt enforcement of these benefits, while workers had little knowledge of their legal entitlements. They had no way to make a claim even on recruitment promises. Given the isolated, regimented, and illiterate conditions of labour, planters easily enforced their writ. Although the penal provisions underlying tea recruitment were removed in 1926, almost four years later the Royal Commission of Labour found that workers still believed they could be arrested by their employers if they left before their contracts expired.[114]

This tea enterprise visibly transformed Assam's landscape and ecology. The gazetteers described the Sibsagar district as "a wide plain on which there is hardly any jungle to be seen. On the lower levels, the staple crop is transplanted rice, while the higher levels have been planted out with tea."[115] At the turn of the century this tea landscape represented the "second nature"[116] of ecological transformation, resulting from plantations cultivating the alluvial slopes of the Brahmaputra valley. Upper Assam's forests were steadily replaced by European-owned tea plantations and the numerous ricefields required to feed a growing labour population. In 1858 Sibsagar already possessed fifteen tea estates to which the state granted 13,977 acres from its estimated 1,612,636 acres of wasteland holdings.[117] By 1901 the tea enterprise covered 164 plantations over 244,653 acres, while the cropped area under rice and other crops was 357,135 acres.[118] Assam tea acquired a leading position in the world market. By 1888 India's tea production outpaced that of China. By 1901 Indian tea obtained 57 percent of the British market.[119]

3. Migrants in the Garden
Expanding the Frontier

DURING THE 1860s John Carnegie was one of the many British young men who joined the Indian tea industry as planters and assistants. In his letters home Carnegie expressed his shock at the spartan conditions of travel to Upper Assam. The steamer cabin that he boarded at Calcutta had only "a stretcher, no bed, no sheet, no pillows nor any one thing. No basin but simply the four bare sides of a stretcher and thousands of mosquitoes."[1] Despite these drawbacks, his austere cabin bore little relation to the terrible conditions in which the steamer's labouring passengers travelled. But Carnegie had little sympathy to spare for them. "Worse than all," he declared, "we have 500 coolies on board. The dirtiest beasts in creation swarming with lice and one had cholera last night."[2] In his new employment Carnegie was in charge of those coolie labourers who survived this dreadful journey. Plantation conditions in these early years were primitive for white planters and their assistants, but they were almost unbearable for the workforce.

By 1901 nearly 13 percent of Assam's population was born outside the region.[3] The majority were coolie labourers dispatched under indentured contracts to work the Assam garden. Carnegie's coolie co-passengers hailed from a diverse range of communities in Central India. They had in common their ascribed "aboriginal" status and the proletarian labouring existence that the colonial economy forced upon them. Those recruits who survived the harsh journey faced a rigorous disciplinary regime enforced by European planters and caste Hindu supervisors. In addition to coolie labourers and British planters, colonial Assam attracted a host of other migrant groups. From the mid-nineteenth century to the mid-twentieth, Marwari traders, Bengali clerks educated in Calcutta and Dhaka, Nepali soldier-graziers, and East Bengali Muslim peasants journeyed to Assam to seek a livelihood. The majority settled there. This chapter examines how these transregional newcomers reformulated their identities in this new frontier, how the migratory experience affected their way of living and being, their role within larger discussions about improvement and progress, and the mediating roles that locals and colonial officials played in this migratory process. It argues that the various improving visions in colonial Assam were articulated through and against these demographic shifts, which transformed the region's social landscape and natural ecology. Complex understandings emerged of Assam and Assamese, and constantly shifting categories of "indigenous," "local," and "migrant" constrained and complicated the existence and identities of different groups in the region.

Moving for Tea

Steamers played a pivotal role in facilitating the movement of goods and people between colonial Assam and other regions. In the first decades of colonial rule steamers operated on the Brahmaputra river only at irregular intervals. After 1861 two private British firms, the India General Steam Navigation Company and the River Steam Navigation Company, operated weekly steamer services for passengers and freight. From 1886 government subsidies and the growing demand from the tea industry sustained two lines of weekly steamer services between Assam and Calcutta. Another line of mail steamers operated from Upper Assam up to Dhubri (Goalpara) on the Assam-Bengal border, where they connected with the Bengal railways. By the 1880s Dibrugarh (Upper Assam) could be reached in six days and Guwahati (Lower Assam) in three days by steamer from Calcutta. Yet rail transport was slow to arrive. The Assam Railways and Trading Company's first routes were only designed to carry passengers and goods connected with the tea industry over short distances. From the 1880s its lines linked Upper Assam's collieries and tea estates with steamer landings on the Brahmaputra river. Only after 1911 was there an Assam-Bengal train line which enabled thorough rail transportation for passengers between Assam and the rest of India. As the rail network expanded from the 1920s onward, the centrality of the Brahmaputra river to translocal transport lessened.

As steamers and, later, trains moved tea equipment and products in and out of Assam, they greatly facilitated migration. Tea coolies were the largest migrant group. In 1858–59 four hundred labourers arrived from Benaras, Ghazipur, Chotanagpur, and Bihar.[4] Subsequently, as the state aided labour imports, numbers steadily rose. Planters managed to lessen their dependence on local labour. In 1867–68 two-thirds of labourers were already imported, 22,800 out of 34,433.[5] By 1901 about 645,000 indentured labourers lived in Assam.[6]

During the 1860s a typical steamer might carry a few hundred coolies into Assam in addition to its other passengers.[7] In later decades, as traffic and profits increased, facilities improved substantially for upper-class passengers, but hardly at all for coolie freight. Carnegie's disgust highlighted how cholera was the great killer on the long journey from the recruiting depots in the Bengal Presidency. Observers blamed high death rates and cholera outbreaks upon recruits' dirty habits. In 1867 the *Times* noted the high mortality upon the Assam plantations. It compared Assam's death rate of 21–30 percent unfavourably to the rate of 2.5 percent in British Guinea but attributed the higher figure solely to the poor quality of labour.[8] These high mortality rates eventually forced the state to regulate the recruitment process. The Bengal Legislative Council enacted Act III of 1862 for the "regulation of emigration to the districts of Assam, Sylhet and Cachar, to make sure that the labourers recruited for the tea district had not been deceived by the contractors or their agents; and, to lessen the fearful mortality previous to arrival at the tea districts."[9] This objective remained incompletely realized: in 1886–99 the mortality rate averaged 5.32 percent, an improvement over previous years but still much higher than in other plantation regions. In a report the civil servant John Edgar acknowledged the disparity between recruiters' promises to coolies and the reality of a plantation life: "They have been told that they were going to a garden in a country where the means of living were plentiful and cheap, where they would receive very high wages and have little to do. They have found themselves set down in a swampy jungle, far from human habitation, where food was scarce and dear, where they have seen their families and fellow labour struck down by disease and death, and where they themselves, prostrated by sickness, have been able to earn less by far than they could have done in their homes."[10]

Unlike the general run of colonial officials, Edgar acknowledged some culpability for the oppression inflicted by British planters. He observed ruefully that it was unpleasant to write of their abuses: "I must reflect unfavourably upon the past conduct of a body of men for whom I have unfeigned respect and esteem, among whom are some intimate personal friends."[11] Most officials exonerated planters for the high mortality rates. They blamed high deaths on recruiters' greed or coolies' ignorance. The social ties which linked officials and planters, the fellowship incumbent upon white men in an alien land, and the unquestioned importance of the imperial tea industry served as blinkers for state representatives. In the rare cases where officials questioned planters' actions, they were powerless to enforce their rulings. In 1902, for instance, in a rare case of opposition to industry interests, Assam's chief commissioner Henry Cotton advocated a wage increase for coolies, but the tea lobby blocked this reform and subsequently impeded Cotton's career.[12]

From the late nineteenth century the Indian tea industry attracted thousands of British applicants: most were directly recruited at London or Calcutta for managerial posts. The majority's class background is evident in the entrepreneur William Nassau Lees's assurance to readers that "planting, though a hard life, is eminently a profession which gentlemen's sons may follow."[13] Warnings about the planter's arduous life did little to discourage Britain's surplus middle-class young men. Industry veterans emphasized that a managerial position in the tea industry required acquiring agricultural expertise and the ability to supervise large, intractable bodies of workers.[14] Manuals written by retired planters provided advice to newcomers on the best way of growing and treating plants as well as proper labour organization, describing every detail from the division of tasks by sex and age to the hierarchy of payments.

Most plantations employed at least two European assistants to work under the manager. One assistant usually supervised the labourers doing outdoor work such as planting, weeding, and harvesting. The other assistant was in charge of the plantation's factory, leaf processing, machines, and skilled factory workers. Labour discipline was the dominant concern. David Crole sadistically described how "an obstreperous and refractory coolie is given nice hard pieces of wood to cut into firewood for a month or two. He can be made to work from sunrise to sunset at this exhilarating exercise, but as he can never accomplish the full task except by superhuman toil, he draws short pay in consequence, and so his stomach reproaches him for his sins."[15]

The coolie population varied from a few hundred to a few thousand, depending on the size of the estate. Usually plantations deployed 1.5 to 3 adult coolies for each acre of outdoor work. For optimum supervision the whole labour force was divided into various *chillans* (gangs) of men, women, girls, and boys. Each gang worked under a *sardar* (overseer). Sardars were almost always men, promoted from coolie ranks. Sardars in turn were supervised by caste Hindu Assamese or Bengali mohurirs (clerks and supervisors). Mohurirs answered to European assistant managers. At the apex of the plantation pyramid was a European manager, often with more than one estate in charge.

The first plantations grouped their workers as "Assamese, Cacharees, and imported Bengalees."[16] Samuel Peal recollected that at first he employed only local labour, Assamese and Kacharis.[17] By the 1860s British planters no longer valued locals. Migrant coolies were held to be ideal workers. By 1884–85, 44.7 percent of workers were from Chotanagpur, 27.2 percent from Bengal, 21.6 percent from the United Provinces and Bihar, 0.2 percent from Bombay, and 0.7 percent from Madras. Only 5.5 percent were from Assam.[18] Dr. Charles Forsyth of the Tea Districts Labour Association listed "hardy aboriginal races" as the best.[19] His list covered indigenous groups living all over the subcontinent, outside of Assam. He asserted their immunity to malaria, willingness to work, and docility.

Planters' relatively high outlay on the recruitment of indentured labourers from distant lands was easily offset by the shockingly low wages they paid. The coolie workforce was placed under constant surveillance, night and day. Handbooks recommended two watchmen for each line of coolie houses, and the houses were built in straight rows, or "lines," so that the watchmen could get about easily among them.[20] This degree of control was far removed from the planters' situation with local workers, who were caustically observed to be "what they term themselves, mon khushi coolies, or labourers who do as they please."[21] Surveillance and control prevented coolies from deserting and halted acquaintances with locals. Plantations became restricted zones where outsiders were not permitted entry. Locals referred to Upper Assam as the land of "Planters' Raj."

Gradually people in the older recruiting districts became aware of these harsh conditions. By the turn of the century Chotanagpur's inhabitants referred to the act of Assam migration as "being sold." Their children learnt of Assam as a "death trap" whence their ancestors never returned.[22] While former coolies who returned to their home districts spread this negative message, their peers on the plantations took every chance to challenge planters. The tea industry now complained about indentured coolies working slowly and spoiling tea bushes, clear tactics of everyday resistance. Coolies also resorted to violent protest. Cotton noted that "there is a growing tendency in the Coolie class to resent a blow by striking a blow in return and this soon leads to serious results, as the Coolies act in combination among themselves, and armed with formidable weapons, the implements of their industry."[23] Such violence occasionally culminated in workers' setting fire to the manager's bungalow, the seat of the power they sought to challenge.[24]

Planters' punishments of protesting workers were extremely harsh. Still, they failed to arrest the increase in assaults, rioting, and unlawful assembly. Between 1904–5 and 1920–21 there were forty-one reported cases of rioting and unlawful assembly. A worried state established tea enquiry commissions in 1906, 1921, and 1929, but the commissions' recommendations to improve work conditions remained on paper, given the industry's opposition to any substantive reform. Planters blamed nationalist agitators associated with the Congress and Communist parties for labour unrest. They attempted to prevent Assam's local Congress activists from contacting tea workers. They harshly suppressed attempts at labour organization. Nonetheless a mix of worker grievances, anticolonial sentiment, and something akin to millenarian fervour inspired many incidents of resistance, including the famous Chargola walkout in 1921, when thousands of coolies in the Cachar district deserted their posts in the name of Gandhi, greatly alarming the British government.[25]

Unlike the densely populated Gangetic plains, the Brahmaputra valley was still an expanding agrarian frontier well into the second half of the nineteenth century. The wastelands grants policy of the colonial state meant that tea plantations, mostly owned by big firms, controlled more than a quarter of the total settled area of the Brahmaputra valley. Planter's land grants were freehold, with an especially low rate of rent fixed for all time to come. These grants were unencumbered by any stipulations about cultivators or subtenants.[26] About 85 percent of plantation land was obtained on this privileged freehold; only for about 15 percent of their holdings did tea planters pay the higher rates that the state levied on local cultivators.[27] Planters constantly sought to extend their freehold land. Despite vast areas of unused land adjoining existing clearances, tea firms still applied for more land. They hoped to control most of the cultivable land around them. Having surplus land helped to attract labourers, since plantation managements could promise to lease them cultivable land after their indenture term was over.[28]

The practice of leasing cultivable land to tea workers came into vogue during the early years of the indentured labour system. The local gentry also found it profitable. In 1868 Lees noted that "natives . . . especially the court officials, are going in for tracts of lands at Rupees 2–8 an acre in the neighbourhood of villages, with a view of leasing them out."[29] Settled areas increased by 15 percent between 1881–82 and 1891–92, as did the tenant labour population. The census of 1901 showed a substantial rise in cultivating tenants, a rise attributed to the "practice which is growing up among the Assamese of leasing out the land lying near a tea garden to the coolies."[30] Taking advantage of their surplus freehold land, plantations began to rent plots to coolies who finished contracted terms, i.e. time-expired labourers. The state also directly leased wasteland. By June 1920 it leased 223,331 acres of land in the Brahmaputra valley and 34,592 acres in the Surma valley to former coolies, who held a further 21,683 acres in the Brahmaputra valley and 13,180 acres in the Surma valley as tenants of private landholders.[31] Former coolies preferred to lease lands from the government or private landlords rather than from planters. Government or private leases did not entail the extralegal labouring obligations that planters' leases did. However, the former coolies were constrained to accept plantation leases if planters controlled the only available lands.[32]

By the end of the 1920s there were about 1,200,000 time-expired coolies in Assam, about 50,000 of whom held land outside the plan-

tations.[33] Plantations rented no less than 139,207 acres to these labourers.[34] This meant that for a large number of coolies, their lives
remained intertwined with the plantation long after their term of
indenture was completed. Planters referred to the time-expired labourers as *faltu* (free; at a loose end) workers. The availability of
cultivable land was a considerable asset when plantations recruited
migrant coolie labour. Despite the harsh conditions on Assam tea
plantations, the ability to offer land leases proved a major incentive
to attract labouring migrants from parts of the subcontinent where
land was extremely scarce. As numerous village (*basti*) settlements of
time-expired coolies emerged, they proved a useful labour reservoir
for the plantations. Hiring such faltu or basti labour became the
cheapest option for specialized plantation tasks such as clearing forest land. This was especially valuable at times of high labour demand
such as the harvest.[35]

Overall population density in Assam fell sharply after the *kala azar*
(black fever) epidemic of 1897. Yet in tea districts with higher immigration and settlement rates the population stayed steady. Plantation
and time-expired labour demand for food grains and other goods
transformed the rural economy. Weekly village *haats* (markets) grew
substantially in number. In Upper Assam many haats were located
near plantations whose workers could buy goods.[36] As a planter
remarked, "The Assamese instead of labouring at our factories grow
rice and vegetables which they sell to our Bengali coolies."[37] Through
such everyday contacts, coolie society gradually developed closer, if
not always amiable, ties with locals. As census officials noted, "Assamese with variations" became the lingua franca for diverse plantation groups. Communication with planters and supervisors and with
neighbouring villagers was undertaken through the plantation vari-
ant of the Asomiya language, termed coolie baat.[38]

From the early twentieth century many Upper Assam hamlets
showed a diverse population of Assamese caste Hindus, local tribal
groups, former coolies, and newer peasant migrants from Nepal and
East Bengal. The amount of good land for cultivation was fast shrink-
ing, a situation aggravated by the presence of large tracts unused but
controlled by plantation managements. Former coolies often lacked
the skills to bring riverine char lands under cultivation, unlike the
East Bengal peasants who were used to such an ecology. The scarcity
of other rural waged employment kept time-expired coolie households dependent upon plantations for a livelihood. Baganiyas (peo-

ple of the garden) remained, for the most part an economically and socially disadvantaged group. Well after Indian independence they were a labour reserve for the tea sector, since most lacked the skills and opportunities to venture outside the plantation.[39] Former indentured labourers, now often calling themselves Tea Tribes or Adibasis, continued to be mere foot soldiers for improvement, as in their coolie past.

"Kaya" Newcomers and "Marwari" Traders

In contrast to the immiserated coolies, colonial Assam's most visibly prospering migrants were Kaya traders, better known today as Marwaris. For centuries traders from Rajasthani trading lineages participated in the long-range trade and high finance of North India.[40] During Mughal rule several such semi-permanent migrant communities had already settled outside Rajasthan. The most famous were the Jagat Seth bankers and the traders of the Oswal caste who settled in Murshidabad (Bengal). These traders and their countrymen who entered Assam were locally known by the ethnic tag Kaya, and eventually by the pan-Indian community name of Marwari.[41]

For these Rajasthani merchant clans involvement in expanding commercial networks around primary commodities provided a powerful impetus to migration. British rule opened new trading opportunities even as it constricted older financial and trading avenues.[42] Looking outward from Rajasthan, they were helped by the changing, transregional character of the colonial economy. British economic expansion penetrated local trading networks. New land settlement policies required cash tax payments and resulted in the greater commercialization of agriculture. In the absence of formal banks, these migrants intervened. For money lending and trading tasks they developed complex, multi-circuited travel and migration patterns, facilitated by marriage and kinship ties. Many lineages had sent several generations to the United Provinces, Bihar, and Bengal before they entered Assam.[43] In the 1820s Francis Buchanan Hamilton remarked on Kaya traders at the Goalpara border.[44] While pioneer firms such as Mahasingh Rai Meghraj Bahadur arrived in Assam before 1850, the bulk of the region's Rajasthani migrant households migrated after the railways opened, in the early twentieth century.[45]

Nonetheless, even a few years after the British takeover there was at least one Kaya merchant in every Assam town of importance. Their *golas* (warehouses) to store goods became ubiquitous landmarks. In 1854 a fire at the Hunatram Kaya warehouse in Jorhat spread to at least twelve other golas.[46] Reports indicate a substantial trading presence, with the warehouses storing staple commodities such as salt, oil, lac, and grain. In the absence of significant local competition, Kaya traders acquired a virtual monopoly over the export and import of almost all primary commodities. Assam's peasants took money advances from the traders to pay revenue dues, providing in return cash crops such as mustard, cotton, pulses, opium, and jute. As the district gazetteers noted, "[Kayas] purchase their surplus products from the raiyats and supply them in return with cloth, thread, salt, oil, and very often, opium."[47] In his report in 1854 Justice Mills observed that these traders distributed Assam's entire supply of imported opium.[48] Given the peasants' lack of alternatives, these were asymmetrical exchanges. In Upper Assam, as the tea industry expanded, so did the Kaya's trade. Each plantation had a provision store run by Kayas which sold everything from rice to opium. A classic Asomiya novel about tea life vividly described the centrality of such a store to coolies' everyday existence.[49]

By the late-nineteenth century, as far as distant hill districts, these traders controlled the wholesale trades in Assam's unique muga and eri silks, cotton, metalware, and rubber.[50] In 1880 the province's annual report noted, "The enterprise and endurance of the Marwaris is surprising. They live the whole year round in miserable houses, sometimes in mostly unhealthy situations and slowly store what they collect from the hill tribes and country produce for export."[51] Links between Assam and Calcutta through important Kaya firms meant that traders also provided credit to the British-owned plantations (which had head offices at Calcutta). In this way these business houses actually financed a large portion of the tea trade, even though they did not directly export tea out of Assam.

Urban commerce in Assam was largely in Kaya hands. At Sibsagar the folklorist Benudhar Sarma (1895–1981) recollected Sylhetti and Kaya vendors opening the first shops selling ready-made sweets at the turn of the century.[52] Historically, Assam lacked the *ganj* (market town) settlements of eastern and northern India. Instead administrative centres such as Guwahati, Barpeta, Tezpur, Bishwanath, Nagaon, Jorhat, and Dibrugarh became important locations for commerce. In the 1850s Guwahati had four main markets, including Fancy (or Phasi) Bazaar, already the epicentre of Kaya business and residence.[53] In Jorhat's bazaar the largest shops were owned by Kayas who did a flourishing business with plantations.[54] The only exceptions to their ascendancy were the furniture and haberdashery trades, dominated by East Bengali traders, and print shops run by educated Assamese, Bengalis, and Nepalis.[55]

Young male Kaya migrants usually joined established firms as clerks and later set up independent ventures. They were helped by their access to capital, a wide credit resource base, and long-standing commercial skills. They displayed a readiness to travel and to live separated from family for years at a time. An early (and atypical) entrepreneur was Navrangram Agarwala of Churu (Rajasthan), who began his career in 1829 with the Ramdayal Poddar firm on the Assam-Bengal border. Taking advantage of the British annexation, Poddar established a new Lower Assam branch at the military outpost of Biswanath. Navrangram was sent to manage this branch but soon launched out on his own. He traded in a variety of commodities, which included elephants, rubber, cane, mustard seed, and rice. He also supplied British military rations. By 1855 Navrangram accumulated Rs 50,000 worth of capital, and his business ventures dominated the Brahmaputra's north bank.[56] His usefulness to the new regime impelled the British district magistrate to appoint him as a *mauzadar* (rent collector). "Respectability of character" was the main criterion for appointment, since mauzadari posts were meant to provide "employment for the better class of Assamese."[57] Since the commission was only between Rs 10 and 50, mauzadars were usually appointed from among prosperous gentry who held substantial lands. In 1881 there were two hundred mauzadars who received commissions of Rs 50 or more, a hundred who received between Rs 50 and Rs 20, and fifty-seven who received less than Rs 20.[58] A mauzadari represented an axis of local power and gentrified respectability beyond its financial returns. Navrangram's assumption of mauzadari duties represented his aspiration to local gentry status rather than business gain. Another break from standard community practice was his marriage to Sadari, a high-caste Assamese woman. When she died he married Sonpahi, from a similar background. Navrangram took another important step toward Assamese gentry status when a local Vaishnavite Gosain initiated him as a disciple.

Still, he continued to maintain links with his birth community. Navrangram's hybrid lifestyle was most visible at his death. He died while visiting kin in Calcutta, who organized a funeral along Kaya lines. Later, at his home in Assam, a local Brahmin priest performed the last rites.

The cultural assimilation of Navrangram and his descendants into Assamese society provides a rare insight into the assimilative possibilities that this borderland offered. In 1885 a publicist declared, "Because the marriage rules are lax in our country, *bidesi* [those from outside the homeland] people find it easy to settle in our country . . . Our people generally do not mind marrying their daughters to men from outside. Often, jati and kul [caste and lineage] are disregarded."[59] Certainly Navrangram's migrant Agarwala lineage was absorbed relatively painlessly into the local Kalita caste. Fascinatingly, in his family's retelling of their history, only Navrangram figures as a Kaya: his offspring are called Assamese. For instance, Navrangram's son, Haribilas (1842–1916), born of an Assamese mother and married to an Assamese woman, Maloma, was a devout practitioner of local Vaishnavism. Unlike his vegetarian father but like his Assamese in-laws, he ate fish. These social practices visibly marked out his local identity. Nonetheless, other elements of cultural hybridity remained, notably Haribilas's retention of Kaya business practices. Rajasthani traders traditionally kept accounts in large, red cloth ledgers and used the *parta* system, according to which cash and credit standings were counted and recorded at the end of every business day. The community's young men learned arithmetic and accounting and calculated sums in their heads without paper. Haribilas's descendants recall how he continued to use this accounting system and its Nagri script for his business activities. In the manner of other prominent Kayas, Haribilas assisted later migrants to establish their own enterprises. In all other respects, however, Haribilas completed his father's journey into Assamese gentry status. Local observers eulogized him as Assam's "illustrious saudagar" (merchant).[60] Patronage of the Asomiya language for literary and Vaishnavite religious writings added to his reputation. In the Darrang district Haribilas continued to administer mauzadari duties, alongside various trading ventures. His manifold business interests included tea, opium, and rubber enterprises. The Agarwala home at Calcutta provided a welcoming refuge for many a homesick Assamese student. "Poki" (from *pucca*, or concrete), Haribilas's home in Tezpur, was renowned as the first brick house owned by a native. Assam's plantations and subdivisional towns possessed many half-timbered and brick bungalows of the Assam type, but those were the abodes of Englishmen.

Through this hybrid lineage some of the wealth from Kaya enterprise was channelled into Assamese cultural capital. There were other cultural patrons among local businessmen, such as the prominent timber merchant Bholanath Barua and the Khongiya Barua planter clan of Jorhat. Among them the Agarwalas earned a unique place as moneyed patrons who also made their mark as artistes and cultural producers. Haribilas's son Chandrakumar (1867–1938) expanded this cultural engagement by his involvement in Calcutta's Asomiya literary public sphere and, after his return to Assam, through his journalistic and poetic achievements. Thanks to him, the Agarwala family published Assam's first successful newspaper in the vernacular, the nationalist-leaning weekly paper *Asomiya*. The third and fourth generations of Agarwalas earned fame as planters, businessmen, publishers, writers, artists, and supporters of Gandhian nationalism. Chandrakumar's nephew, Jyotiprasad (1903–53), carried the family's cultural entrepreneurship further, into the medium of film. He made the first Asomiya film in 1935 on his family's tea estate. It claimed the dual objective of propagating Gandhian ideas and Assam's heritage. His multifarious achievements caused a highly popular genre of song (Jyoti Sangeet) to be named after him, and made him a nationalist icon popular throughout Assam. This Agarwala family became an exemplar of migrant assimilation into Assamese culture.

Nonetheless, economic power over locals earned many Rajasthani businessmen the opprobrious image of parasitical exploiters. Kayas provided cash advances to peasants at a high rate of 1 anna per 1 rupee per month, the equivalent of 75 percent interest. Since their objective was to source commodities at the most advantageous rate, they were usually uninterested in acquiring peasant land. They preferred to seize crops for nonpayment.[61] Not surprisingly, this practice incited local anger. Rural Assam's uprisings in 1894 were directed primarily against the state, in protest against a huge revenue increase, but they also attacked Kaya traders and moneylenders. Resenting Kayas was a common feature of rural unrest all over the subcontinent. In David Hardiman's study of the Deccan riots of

1875, the outsider middleman was the most visible target.[62] Urban traders were a target for protests at times of rising food prices. During Assam's food shortages of 1896, for example, the state called out the army to suppress a riot against traders who had allegedly cornered the grain market.[63]

By the early twentieth century the pejorative image of Assam's migrant traders was accentuated by their active role in the opium retail trade, whose prohibition was the main objective of Gandhian nationalists. When non-cooperators fanned out into towns and villages, they often clashed with traders who ran opium marts or sold foreign cloth. Colonial administrators evinced little sympathy for this migrant community, despite its usefulness. Marwaris, as they were now called, were not British subjects since they belonged to Rajasthan's princely states. They were enfranchised only in 1923.[64] British official disdain was especially acute in the 1920s and 1930s, when paternalist officials such as J. P. Mills and J. H. Hutton attempted to halt what they saw as pernicious upcountry exploitation of the simple hill tribes. Instead of improvement, Marwaris seemed to promote exploitation. Colonial officials and Assamese élites alike blamed Marwari traders as the sole cause of social and economic dislocation, rather than taking into account the changing conditions engendered by the political economy of colonialism and its complicated linkages to the worlds of national and global capitalism. Assam's Kaya-turned-Marwaris, like their pan-Indian counterparts, became a community known for financial success and cultural differences from their neighbours.[65] For most locals the economic and social successes of the Agarwala clan counted solely as Assamese achievements, their Kaya ties relegated to a distant past.

"Gorkhalis," "Graziers," and "Nepalis"

In the nineteenth century many of Nepal's inhabitants joined Kaya traders as voluntary migrants to colonial Assam. Historically, groups from Nepal's crowded central hill areas had often settled in the northern and eastern parts of India, known as Mugalan.[66] Colonial policies further accelerated and encouraged such movements of people through this Himalayan zone, especially into sparsely populated Assam.

The Gurkha valley in western Nepal lent its name to the kingdom ruled by the expansionist king Prithvi Narayan Shah. After the Anglo-Nepal War in 1814–16 the British realized that the Gurkha king's hardy hill fighters could be a valuable military adjunct, and the peace treaty provided that "Gurkhas" could volunteer for service in the East India Company's army. Gurkhas proved such an asset during the Revolt of 1857 that they were awarded the title of riflemen, to differentiate them from Indian sepoys.[67] These impecunious and resilient soldiers had already made their mark during the extension of British rule into Assam. In 1817 a combined corps of "Hindustanis and Gorkhas" fought for the British in a military operation in Sylhet. Another corps fought in the Anglo-Burmese War of 1825. Such local corps were raised cheaply under the command of a few European officers to deploy in difficult and unhealthy areas, so as not to risk regular troops.[68]

Gurkha was initially a loose generic term used by the British for the indigenous hill population of east and west Nepal. Inhabitants of a region short of arable land, Gurkhas soon joined British irregular units in increasing numbers. Many served as load-bearing coolies for colonial expeditions. As one explorer noted, "Our string of coolies &c is a terrible long one now and every nationality to be found on the Eastern frontier: English, Hindustani, Hazaribagh, Assamese, Bengali, Garo, Cachari, Khasi, Mikhir, Naga Angami, Naga Tangkol, Munipuri, Kooki, Goorkha."[69] In the early years of recruitment men from almost every caste became Gurkha soldiers, but the British soon developed an ethnographical preference: the best Gurkha troops were said to be the Magar and Gurung hill groups. When those were not sufficient, Rais, Limbus, Sunuwars, and Khasas could be recruited. Significantly, Newar Buddhists were altogether omitted, stigmatized as peace-loving because of their faith. By the 1870s Magars, Gurungs, Rais, and Limbus acquired the name of Gurkha, as distinct from their other countrymen, known as Nepalis.[70] The British praised Gurkhas as a people inured to jungle and hardship. They approvingly noted their taste for the manly sports of cricket, football, and shooting. One sporting officer declared, "When properly led, they are fully equal to Europeans."[71]

The real beginnings of Nepali settlement lay with David Scott's policy in the 1830s, which allotted land on easy terms to Gurkha soldiers with families. Since newly annexed Assam was depopulated by the years of strife, officials advocated the settlement of "Gurkhas and others who may feel inclined to colonize."[72] By 1832 "there was an extensive village of Goorkhas established with a flourishing crop of paddy on a spot which before was a jungle."[73] Many retired Gurkha soldiers settled in the salubrious town of Shillong in the Khasi Hills, soon to become Assam's capital.

In his district gazetteers B.C. Allen described the majority of Nepali migrants as graziers—keepers of buffalo and cattle. They settled on the sandy alluvial banks of the Brahmaputra, and on its shoals and islands. These were called *char* or *chapori* lands. The riverbanks flooded in the monsoon, but once waters receded the lands were covered with fertile silt. Previously these areas were barely used, except for Mishing tribals who established *pam bastis* (temporary settlements) in the dry season. These remote, empty tracts were a new and attractive frontier for Nepali graziers, who introduced a hardy buffalo breed. *Mokhutis* (grazing camps) became a familiar feature, with buffalos swimming in the river.[74]

In W. W. Hunter's account (1879) there were fewer than a thousand Nepalis in the Brahmaputra valley. The majority then lived in Kamrup, Sibsagar, and Lakhimpur districts.[75] By 1901 their numbers had increased to 21,347.[76] In 1906 Allen noted that Nepalis had also moved into sparsely populated Darrang: "Many of them are graziers, sawyers, and rubber tappers, but they are also taking to cultivation."[77] Nepali settlers found new opportunities to use Assam's abundant forest resources and its deserted riverine tracts. The settlers received official sanction and approbation. For instance, the Assam Forest Regulations of 1891 and the Indian Forest Act of 1920 allowed "forest villages" within the newly created reserved forests. To meet its labour needs, the government's forest department settled dozens of villages, with each resident allotted eight hectares. Many Nepalis were attracted by this type of land allotment.

Gradually, official perspectives on Nepali migration into Assam changed for the worse. Until the latter half of the nineteenth century British officials were preoccupied with increasing Assam's revenue potential and therefore its settled population. Migrants such as Nepali graziers were welcomed and often explicitly recruited. But as Nepali numbers increased, new migrants moved into petty trades. Some of these, such as illicit distillation and poaching, went beyond the bounds of the law. Settlers were often encumbered by heavy loans from moneylenders to build cowsheds. A typical Nepali grazier had to borrow about Rs 2,500, usually from a Kaya trader. The loan obliged him to supply a certain quantity of ghee a year to the lender at less than the current price. He could not sell to anyone else, and he was required to buy stores at high prices from the lender. By 1930 Assam's chief secretary described Nepali migration as an administrative nuisance.[78] By then there were over eighty thousand Nepali settlers.[79]

The colonial state was also perturbed when migrants moved beyond the valley districts into remote interiors. Increasingly, paternalist officials in hill districts began to blame Nepali newcomers for corrupting simple tribals with supplies of opium and liquor. The tour diaries of the Naga Hills district commissioners Hutton and Mills make scathing references to Nepali chicanery and dishonesty. Nepali cattle-keeping activities often caused clashes with shifting cultivators. Hutton, when he adjudicated a dispute between a Nepali grazier and a Naga village, tersely noted, "Like all Nepali graziers he is a curse to cultivators and decent folk."[80] As graziers desperately tried to avoid paying rent, and to find more cattle land, their actions incited local conflicts and official condemnation.[81]

Ironically, colonial voices still applauded the bravery and sense of Gurkha soldiers. British observers argued that not only was the Gurkha far superior to the indolent Assamese, but his qualities of mind, honed by British training, enabled him to get the better of the local hill men in battle. For colonial officials there emerged a clear distinction between the Gurkha soldier and the Nepali grazier. They took to denigrating graziers as belonging to effete upper-caste groups of "Jaisis and Upadhyay Brahmins or Chhetris of non-martial classes."[82] Sons of Nepali graziers who wished to become Gurkha soldiers were rejected, as were sons of Gurkha soldiers who had settled in Assam.[83] A racial and climatic logic was at work here. Recruiting officers claimed that Assam life caused Gurkhas to degenerate racially. W. C. M. Dundas, the inspector general of police, declared that "Gurkhas deteriorate quickly outside their own country, and the generation born in this province has not the qualities that we look for in our Assam Rifles Battalions."[84] While acknowledging that migration from Nepal was an ongoing process, Dundas argued: "It is surely more desirable that we take the best of those [migrants] in our battalions than that they should find menial service as cowherds under Nepali graziers, or as coolies and watchmen under contractors and other civil employees."[85] This was a strange tautology. It tacitly acknowledged that the military castes would not disdain grazier employment. But army recruitment preferred Gurkhas direct from Nepal to their migrant cousins.[86]

The colonial dichotomy created between Gurkhas and graziers also obscured the gradual emergence of a small Nepali middle class in Assam, similar to its counterparts in Darjeeling, Benares, and Kalimpong, drawn from both occupational groups.[87] At a more general level the British failed to recognize that Nepali migrants were becoming part of the region's social fabric. Colonial records tended to emphasize Nepali differences with local society. Nepali graziers often clashed with the state, with revenue collectors, and often with agriculturist neighbours. Yet British preoccupation with these clashes ignored how the majority of long-standing Nepali settlers, whether in the plains or the hills, adopted many of the same cultural practices as their longer-established neighbours. These included celebrations of the Assamese Bihu springtime harvest festival, the Durga Puja festival that Bengali settlers had originally introduced, and reverence of the historic Kamakhya mother-goddess. As they adopted the Asomiya language in the Brahmaputra valley, or intermarried with Angami women in the Naga hills, Nepalis established roots and identities in their new habitats.[88] Even as many migrants actively participated in the emergent Nepali literary public of Eastern India, Nepalis who settled in Assam viewed themselves as different from larger Nepali communities of the eastern Himalayas, and of Nepal. They saw themselves as distinctively Assamese, but also Nepali.[89] Educated Nepalis studied and favoured the Asomiya language for local literary activity while using the Nepali language at home and favouring its instruction in Assam schools for their children. A number of names from this community appeared in the annals of Assam's freedom fighters.[90] For instance, Chabilal Upadhyay established the Tezpur Graziers' Association in 1933, to organize Nepali graziers and participate in the nationalist struggle.[91] By the early twentieth century, while Assam's Nepalis resisted colonial attempts to stereotype them as loyal Gurkhas or troublesome settlers, they sought active involvement in the agenda of progress that local élites had begun to articulate.

Bengali "Babus" and Sylhetti Sojourners

Given the contiguous location of Assam and Bengal, it is not surprising that the longest historical traces of migration should be from Bengal. Under the Ahom kings there were movements of priests, mendicants, artisans, and occasionally Bengal traders into Assam. Well-known Brahmin families such as the Parbatiya Gosains of the Kamakhya shrine proudly traced their lineage to Bengal's pilgrimage town of Nadia. Yet patterns of migration altered dramatically when the institutional changes of British annexation brought a steady stream of entrepreneurial Bengalis. Local perceptions about these migrants then changed, as did the Bengali migrants' views of their new location.

A local publicist wryly observed, "Even if it was British rule, ordinary people called it rather the time of the Bangals."[92] Many new arrivals were clerks, the archetypal Bengali *amlahs* who accompanied the colonial regime. With few white officials in Assam in the first years, Bengali clerks formed the visible face of the new colonial regime. They dominated many new jobs in schools and offices, since the Assamese gentry were as yet unschooled in western education. Many Bengalis had already acquired the needed skills over the half-century of British rule in their home region.

There is so little information about individual amlahs that it is difficult to determine whether any particular Bengal district dominated recruitment. As the colonial state established new educational institutions, clerks were joined by Bengali schoolteachers, mostly upper-caste Hindus. Assamese pupils' narratives tell us that schoolteachers played an important role in acculturating local élites into so-called Bengali ways, in reality the new urbanized modes of British-ruled Bengal.[93] Already by the mid-nineteenth century Assam's "advanced" young men donned *chapkans* (long coats) of the kind worn in Calcutta and subscribed to Bengali books and periodicals. At Guwahati and Shillong, Muslim and Hindu shopkeepers from East Bengal established haberdasheries and bakeries to meet demand from expatriates. Well-to-do locals soon emulated these urban consumption mores. Bengali *luchi* (fried puffy bread) and *kaliya* (spicy fish curry) became integral to dietary norms in fashionable homes. Such cultural changes made many locals uneasy. The periodical *Assam Bandhu* debated whether Bengali fashions had driven out *desiyo* (country) clothing.[94]

Two state measures greatly encouraged the influx into Assam of Bengali-speaking settlers. One was the official use until 1873 of the Bengali language in government offices and schools. The other was the joining of the Sylhet district to Assam in 1874. This administrative reorganization, while resented by Sylhettis and many Bengalis, ultimately helped educated Sylhetti job-hunters to find positions in the Brahmaputra valley. Previously at a disadvantage compared to their more polished counterparts from Calcutta and Dhaka, these newly domiciled residents of Assam now had greater access to government jobs. Thus the census of 1901 concluded that "Sylhettis who are good clerks and enterprising traders are found, in small numbers, in most of the districts of the province."[95] In the historian Anindita Dasgupta's study of Sylhetti settlers, her interviewees recounted how over the early twentieth century they moved to district headquarter towns such as Shillong, Guwahati, and Silchar, and to smaller towns near plantations.[96]

The growth of Assam's main urban centres, Shillong and Guwahati, was centrally linked to the presence of new Sylhetti and Bengali middle-class inhabitants. Although Sylhet remained the homeland where they retained a *desher baari* (rural rentier homestead in the homeland), Sylhetti male sojourners established secondary households in Assam's towns, where they serviced government and plantation offices. One family member usually supervised rentier properties in rural Sylhet, while other males moved for clerical livelihoods. Newcomer Sylhettis lived and dined in urban boarding houses and "messes." Neighbourhoods such as the busy Panbazar (Guwahati) acquired tea shops and *addas* (social circles), which resembled their counterparts in Calcutta. Outposts of the reformist Brahmo Samaj religious group were established. Homesick clerks encouraged the formation of Bengali-language drama troupes, also popular with Asomiya-speaking town dwellers.[97]

Consciousness of difference between these migrants and other locals became acute as the number of Bengali speakers grew in the Brahmaputra valley. Often this was due not so much to language or regional origin per se as to prejudices and rivalries between locals and newcomers. In his memoir the gentry official Uttam Chandra Barua recorded his pleasure when Bengali-speaking colleagues attended his marriage.[98] His joy was a rare instance. Personal narratives of social and professional interactions between Assamese, Bengalis, and Sylhettis often dwelt on slights and retaliations. For instance, the Aso-miya literatteur and Ahom politician Padmanath Gohain Barua re-counted his persecution by a Sylhetti superior in the educational service.[99] Often derided as rustic by other Bengalis, Sylhettis took pride in their superiority of educational achievement over the As-samese. In 1912 only 18,214 inhabitants of the Brahmaputra valley were literate in English, as compared to 1,098,022 in Sylhet.[100] Com-petition for scarce colonial educational and clerical employment ac-centuated existing cultural differences.

Charua and Na-Asomiya Musalmans: The "New Assamese" Muslims

Conceptual distinctions between old and new migrants are most evident with Assam's Muslims. As in other parts of South Asia, the colonial British constantly remarked on the gap between doctrinal Islam and the practices of Assam's older Muslim population, known as Thalua Musalmans (Muslims of the place). Mostly simple village converts, the majority of rural Muslims in the Brahmaputra valley followed customs similar to those of their Hindu neighbours. While some practiced circumcision and offered prayers, most of these illiter-ate folk could not read the Koran. Services were held in the open fields. Until the late nineteenth century, Muslims in the Brahmaputra valley mostly dressed, shaved, and worshipped like their Hindu neighbours, and eschewed beef. During sickness and trouble they resorted to a common repertoire of folk remedies and devotional practices.[101] As in Bengal, the upper classes among Assamese Mus-lims claimed a lofty Indo-Persian pedigree. They asserted that they were the descendants of Indo-Persian warrior nobles who served the Ahom kings. But unlike in Bengal, there were few linguistic and cultural differences between the Muslim gentry and the lower classes. Their common language was Asomiya, interspersed with a scattering of Arabic and Persian terms.[102] Sufi beliefs were popular among élites and lower classes. Local Sufi songs (*jikir*) resembled in their lan-guage and devotional sentiments the verses (*naam kirtan*) associated with Sankardeb and other Vaishnavite preachers.[103]

From the late nineteenth century rapid changes occurred in Assam-ese Muslim society, largely because of the influence of pan-Islamist and other revivalist movements which entered Assam from North India. For instance, in Darrang during the 1880s a preacher called Zalkad Ali (Safi Saheb) inspired the adoption of many orthodox Islamic practices. "Fired by his example, the Muhammadans abandoned their Hindu superstitions, allowed their beards to grow, and took to eating beef."[104] With thatched houses erected as mosques, many villagers conformed to standard Islamic practice. Nevertheless, when cholera or smallpox appeared they recited folk incantations.

After the late nineteenth century the Muslim gentry, like their Hindu counterparts, began to travel outside the region for education, work, and pilgrimage. In 1922 Maulvi Muhammad Shah Haji, a local mauzadar, wrote an account of his district in Lower Assam, *Lukir Buranji*, in which the changes that local society experienced are quite evident. As an alumnus of the University of Dhaka, Shah dedicated his work to a pan-Indian figure, Nawab Salimullah of Dhaka, a founder of the Muslim League. However, as befitted the title, his was a local chronicle rather than an Islamic narrative. His account of the "Musalman jati" was framed within an extremely localized narrative of the Luki neighbourhood, alongside descriptions of "other Assamese jatis." The author proudly narrated tales of some devout Muslim gentry but observed that most of Luki's Muslims were fairly lax in their religious observances. While showing pride in his status as a pilgrim returned from the Haj, Muhammad Shah used both the Persian term "khuda" and the Sanskrit-derived "niranjan" to refer to the divine.[105] And even as ideas inspired by Taghlibi and Wahhabi doctrine created a template of Islamic purity and the notion of a larger *umma* (Islamic community), these still coexisted with the distinctive syncretism of Assamese Sufism associated with preachers such as Azan Fakir and sites such as the Hajo Poa-Mecca shrine.

From 1902 onward the rail link between Assam and Bengal made transport quicker and cheaper. Taking advantage of this, Muslim peasant immigrants from East Bengal entered Assam in large numbers. Marked differences in language, lifestyle, habitat, and religious observances initially differentiated them from other local and migrant groups. In contrast to their middle-class Bengali Hindu predecessors, these migrants were peasants in search of cultivable land and an agrarian livelihood. Entire households moved into Assam from the East Bengal districts of Mymensingh, Pabna, Bogra, Rangpur, and Rajshahi. They were part of a large landless or marginally landed Muslim population in those districts. These "farm settlers" were attracted to the Brahmaputra valley by reports of its fertile, underpopulated lands, a sharp contrast to densely populated East Bengal. The district of Mymensingh, for instance, in 1901 had the second-densest population in Bengal, 618 persons to the square mile. In contrast, Assam still possessed vast tracts of empty land and had only 41.12 persons to the square mile, one of the lowest population densities in South Asia. This was partly due to the ravages of the *kala azar* (black fever) epidemic of the 1890s, which drastically reduced Assam's population and left cultivated lands vacant. Moreover, land ownership in East Bengal was concentrated in upper-caste Hindu hands; 73.2 percent of its Muslim peasants were dependent tenants; and only 1.7 percent of East Bengal peasants owned any land. In 1890–1910 East Bengal also experienced a marked rise in food prices, which further encouraged peasants to move.[106]

During the early twentieth century East Bengal peasants first migrated to the district of Goalpara, geographically contiguous to Bengal. Goalpara landlords, desperate for cultivating tenants, offered attractive inducements.[107] But as East Bengalis learnt more about Assam, they preferred to move into the interior valley districts under ryotwari settlement, free of the control of landlords. By 1902–4 the new Assam-Bengal railway enabled a direct journey between the East Bengal terminus of Chittagong and the Brahmaputra valley towns of Guwahati and Dibrugarh.[108] One central aim often overlooked in the general imbroglio over Lord Curzon's controversial partition of Bengal is that Assam was to be linked with East Bengal so that its "culturable wastes" could be reclaimed more easily. The Assam government welcomed this influx of thrifty, hardworking peasants. By 1921 East Bengali peasants settled all over the Brahmaputra valley.[109] The tremendous surge in arable land expansion, about 47 percent (over 83,000 hectares) between 1930 and 1950, clearly revealed the region's attraction for these farm settlers.

This migration not only augmented population but also created important changes in the agrarian landscape. East Bengali peasants introduced jute, an important new cash crop that they grew commercially by 1913–14 in the districts of Sylhet, Goalpara, and Kamrup.[110] Arriving from a region where scarce arable land accustomed them to cultivating in marginal conditions, the East Bengali peasants saw new possibilities in Assam's underused riverine (char) belt. In the past Mishing peasants sometimes used char lands for cultivating and fishing. From the 1860s Nepali graziers set up cattle camps. But these were only temporary uses of the low-lying lands that river currents made available. The East Bengalis' innovation, which earned them the sobriquet of "Charua," was to reclaim these riverine lands as a new agricultural frontier for permanent cultivation. Jute thrived in such soggy environments.[111] Cultivating char lands involved the annual slashing and burning of grass and reed jungles before they could be ploughed or hoed. As they prospered, newcomers also acquired better lands close to existing villages, where they grew vegetables, pulses, sugarcane, and of course rice.

Many early migrants from East Bengal were initially funded by prosperous élites from their home villages, known as *matabbars* (headmen). Later, Marwari traders and Assamese mauzadars offered them credit and leased land. Migrant men generally arrived first, in groups from a single village. Once they raised a homestead, families followed, all working the fields. Where local peasants could grow only one crop a year, the East Bengali migrants often raised three, using crop rotation and green manure.[112] Just as Nepali migrants expanded the dairy economy with buffalo milk, the East Bengalis introduced poultry farming. Chicken meat formed an important part of the East Bengali Muslim cuisine. By the 1920s chicken was accepted into the caste Hindu Assamese diet as ritual prohibitions gradually loosened. East Bengali peddlers of chicken and eggs became a familiar sight in towns on weekly sales trips from the countryside.

Originally grouped together as Mymensinghias, these peasant settlers became known as Charua Musalmans, Muslims who lived in the char (riverine) lands, as distinct from the older, settled Thalua Musalmans.[113] There was little tension between Assamese peasants and the newcomers, as long as the latter stayed in the uninviting char areas. But as East Bengali cultivators prospered they aspired to buy better lands. Many Assamese gentry found it profitable to engage in land speculation. Reports described how locals employed labourers to clear wasteland near their villages and sold these cleared lands to newcomers. These dealings violated the colonial Line System, devised in 1916–20 and introduced in 1923, the main objective of which was to limit migrant settlements to the underpopulated parts of certain districts.[114] As the historian Rinku Pegu shows, the government hoped that when it prevented East Bengali peasants from acquiring land in inhabited areas, newcomers would be forced to open up wastelands for cultivation. Migrants were technically permitted to buy land only from the state, at the high rate of Rs 25 per bigha. At a time when Gandhian nationalism had gained wide popularity among locals in Assam's countryside, the administration deemed it politic to concentrate revenue-raising efforts upon this migrant peasantry.[115] But officials could not prevent local speculators from selling lands. Also, the state machinery failed to stop land-hungry migrants from illegally occupying grazing and forest lands. For all these reasons the Line System proved unworkable. Its failure provoked a public outcry in Assam. Local newspapers and representatives in the Legislative Assembly fulminated about how East Bengalis encroached upon locals' lands.[116] Assam's public blamed corrupt revenue functionaries for the Line System's failure, but it was evident that locals had also profited from illicit land sales. Migrants' agrarian innovations found little mention in accusations and counter-accusations of a demographic and religious takeover.

In this manner, from the 1920s Muslim immigration into Assam became a politically volatile, communally sensitive topic. Competition between the Congress and the Muslim League, disputes between politicians in Sylhet and the Brahmaputra valley, and inflammatory British official rhetoric on "Mymensinghias overrunning Assam" had serious consequences for East Bengali settlers. Influenced by fiery peasant demagogues such as Maulana Bhasani, many East Bengali migrants chose to support the Muslim League, led by Muhammad Sadullah. They were attracted to the League by its liberal land-grant policy, which promised to remove all restrictions on land sales to migrants.[117] But these League promises of land to Muslim immigrants inflamed Assamese Hindu public opinion. The declaration by prominent Muslim League leaders such as Muhammad Ali Jinnah that Assam would form part of a new Muslim homeland called Pakistan caused Assamese Hindus to fear that East Bengali Muslim migrants living in Assam might support such a scheme.

After 1947 Assam was retained within India, while Sylhet went to East Pakistan. The bulk of the East Bengali Muslim peasant migrants remained in Assam. They gradually adopted a new identity as Na or Natun Asomiya Musalmans (New Assamese Muslims), whose language was Asomiya and whose religion was Islam. The recasting of their cultural identity accentuated a distance from middle-class Sylhetti settlers, the majority of whom continued to represent themselves as Bengalis, and staunch Hindus, even more so after India's Partition caused the loss of their Sylhet homesteads and their sojourner self-image. As they settled in urban linguistic enclaves, Sylhetti "optees" (who had opted for India rather than Pakistan) often sought to retain the ties to Bengali high culture that political boundary making had sundered. By contrast, the East Bengali Muslim peasantry largely assimilated into Assamese linguistic and cultural modes as Na-Asomiyas in the first decades of their migration. However, by the late twentieth century continued migration from the new nation of Bangladesh created ugly political and sectarian antagonisms within Assam, and in other Indian regions which experienced considerable flows of cross-border labour migration — antagonisms which affected these groups as well as their relationships with Assam's other inhabitants and later waves of migrants.

Men and elephants in the jungle

Loading the garden's tea

The daily wage

The manager's bungalow

White plantation staff and wives

MANAGERS AND ASSISTANTS IN TEA. 2646.

Coolie "lines"

Mustering coolies

(above) Picking leaves; *(below)* Weighing leaves

Sorting leaves

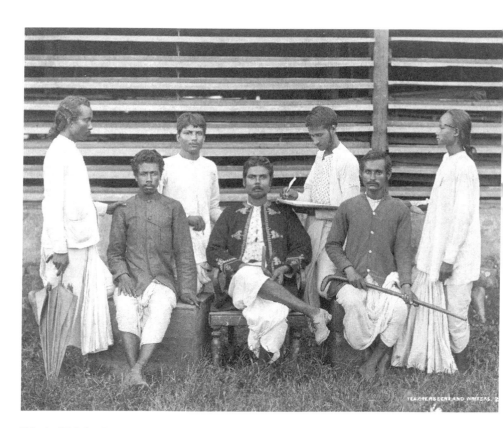

"Native" Mohurirs

The coolie in the garden

II. Improving Assam, Making India

4. Old Lords and "Improving" Regimes

IN 1825, ON THE EVE OF THE BRITISH TAKEOVER, the East India Company official David Scott issued a momentous proclamation to the people of Assam. At that moment Assam was beset by an invading army from Burma. Scott drafted his proclamation with help from Haliram Dhekial Phukan (1802–32), a prominent member of the caste Hindu service gentry.[1] Written in the Asomiya and Bengali languages, Scott's proclamation assured the people that the British had entered Assam only "to restore peace and security to your distracted country."[2] Scott urged them to rise up against the Burmese invaders. He declared: "we will never consent to depart until we exclude our foe from Assam and reestablish in that country a Government adapted to your wants and calculated to promote the happiness of the people of all classes."[3]

Assam's political history had only occasionally overlapped with that of other parts of the subcontinent. Aided by the ubiquitous monsoon rains and fevers, the past kings fought off Indo-Turkish and Mughal armies. The Mughals conquered parts of Lower Assam in the seventeenth century, but Ahom generals quickly recovered them. Only the Goalpara and Cachar districts, adjoining Bengal, stayed loosely under Mughal sovereignty. But over the course of the eighteenth century, as religious dissent and economic dislocation weakened the Ahom state, it became an easy target for Burmese and British imperial ambitions. Local warrior élites could do little to resist ambitious neighbours. From 1817 to 1824 Burma sent in a series of armed levies. For decades afterward popular lore recounted tales of the Maan (Burmese) atrocities. The *Weissalisa* chronicles, by the scribes Cha-ang and Thaomung, who accompanied the Burmese armies, acknowledged the tremendous bloodshed that their compatriots had unleashed in this land of "golden Weissali."[4] While some Ahom nobles allied with the Burmese, the king and most of the gentry decamped to Bengal. The dethroned ruler, Purandar Singha, tried to raise reinforcements, but the Burmese retained their hold. The obvious interest of the Burmese Konbaung rulers in expanding into Bengal territory alarmed the ruling power, the English East India Company. During the ensuing First Anglo-Burmese War in 1824–25, Scott was given dual charge as collector of Rangpur district on the Assam-Bengal border and as newly appointed Agent to the Governor-General for the northeast frontier.

Scott presided from 1824 to 1831 over the Burmese ouster, the company's annexation, and gradual incorporation of Assam into British India. Initially this territory seemed "of little value."[5] Assam's acquisition seemed to confirm the historian P. J. Marshall's theory that expansion by the East India Company often occurred haphazardly, instigated by the short-term opportunism of the men on the spot.[6] But the prospect of growing tea drastically altered how the British viewed Assam, while colonial institutions simultaneously transformed the lives and destinies of its inhabitants. The nineteenth-century British tea industry in effect reintroduced Assam to the rest of India.

This chapter argues that the process of state transition engendered important cultural shifts for the region as the same time as a variety of power struggles took place among local élites and the functionaries of the new colonial regime. The British state's chief claim was that it had introduced a regime of liberty and improvement to replace the existing despotic rule of Ahom rulers, dangariya lords, and Gosain priests. Among pre-colonial élites the group that did best under this new regime was the service gentry, whose bureaucratic talents proved well adapted to British service. The gentry's monopoly of literacy and education allowed them to appropriate the resources that colonial modernity made available, whether through clerical jobs in the revenue offices or missionary access to print technology.

Administering Assam

David Scott's proclamation raised high hopes for gentry families displaced by the Burmese. In his memoir the Assamese official Harakanta Barua (1813–1900) described how exiles returned from Bengal while the British fought the invaders. These gentry returned with high hopes of preferment. Some, like Maniram Barbhandar Barua, quickly found employment as interpreters and guides during the war. Others, like Harakanta's elder brother, found clerical posts in the wake of the Treaty of Yandaboo (1826), which transferred Assam into British suzerainty.[7] In the first years of British rule the East India Company attempted to build an alliance with pre-colonial élites, and the British incorporated existing revenue functionaries such as Chaudhuris, Rajkhowas, and Phukans into their administration. In these early years a mere handful of British officials were appointed to Assam. To assist Scott there were three army captains, Davidson, White, and Neufville. Initially revenue assessments were still based on eighteenth-century Ahom surveys, with the exception of a few measurements hastily undertaken in 1825.[8] Tributary chiefs of small territories were left undisturbed. The former Ahom king Purandar Singha became the tributary ruler of Upper Assam.

If élites momentarily regained some power, the transition to colonial control exacted a heavy economic toll on plebeian inhabitants, already dislocated by the Burmese invasion. Peasants fled to Bengal and Bhutan to avoid the high British rent exactions, even more onerous because of the commutation of the corvée into cash payments.[9] The British mediated the transition from labour to cash rents by appointing influential, well-to-do locals as rent collectors, or mauzadars of a *mauza* (revenue circle). A mauza could be anywhere between 8 and 200 square miles, depending upon the number of villages. Ideally each mauza paid revenue of about Rs 10,000 and comprised between two thousand and ten thousand people.[10] Rent collectors' tenures lasted about five years, on renewable terms. Since mauzadars were paid by commission on the amount of their collections, they had an incentive to press hard on the peasantry.[11] Their motive was short-term gain rather than the promotion of long-term land improvement. Many mauzadars became very prosperous. A mauzadar's son recorded that his father at his death left a large estate of sixteen thousand bighas of land, and much other property.[12]

For peasants, mauzadars represented the colonial state in a direct and visibly oppressive guise. To mitigate mauzadar tyranny, Harakanta Barua advised his British superiors to conduct a long overdue cadastral survey of cultivated lands. He advocated introducing longer leases, since more secure tenure and income might interest rent collectors in the long-term goal of improving land.[13] The Assamese magistrate Anandaram Dhekial Phukan prudently suggested that the "public authority" keep a close watch over mauzadars' actions.[14] His advice was ignored. As the Assam correspondent for a Calcutta newspaper reported, the "ryot is obliged to keep survey officers and mauzadars in good humour by presents of sugar, butter, milk, goats etc, otherwise is sure to find that in surveying his holding, waste land has been classed as land under cultivation."[15]

During the mid-1830s, after the British resumed the charge of Upper Assam from Purandar Singha, the East India Company organized the Brahmaputra valley's administration into a district system based on the standard British-Indian model. Each district came under the charge of a British principal assistant to the commissioner. He functioned as judge, magistrate, and collector, with the help of a junior assistant. Apparently this restructuring resulted from the Assam commissioner's pleas to his superiors to provide him with more European assistants.[16] As Captain John Butler stated, "Once his representations were acceded to, the revenue has consequently increased, and the people, as far as their vices will permit, have thrived in peace, security and comfort."[17] However Butler, a military officer posted in Assam for most of his life, was more sanguine than Indian Civil Service (ICS) officials who surveyed the region from without. For instance, in 1858 H. H. Wilson noted that the region might present future promise, but at the moment had limited prospects: "In an economical point of view . . . these territories are in a state of progress to still greater improvement; while they have a real political value in constituting a difficult and well defined frontier, presenting a ready access to Ava and Siam, and promising at some future period convenient intercourse by land with the opulent empire of China."[18]

Unlike boosters of the tea industry, Wilson and his ICS colleagues believed that the Assam tea discovery was unlikely to yield adequate returns without further "improvement." In their eyes this objective was hindered by the region's sparse population and archaic revenue system. The first census of Assam, in 1872, counted only fifty inhabitants to the square mile.[19] The census rated the region's direct revenue-generating possibilities as low, because the inhabitants had very slight acquaintance with a market economy. Over the nineteenth century further territorial expansion into the hill districts caused officials to constantly bemoan the region's "revenue-deficit" status. The introduction of the Non-Regulation system confirmed the assertion that unlike other Bengal territories, Assam possessed a "rude and simple state of society."[20] Instituted in 1822, the Non-Regulation system allowed British India's newly annexed territories, inhabited mostly by "aboriginal tribes," to be governed directly by officers who were exempt from the general regulations. Although Assam remained within the Bengal Presidency, in practice the Non-Regulation system meant that it was ruled by military men appointed as civil officials, largely unfettered by the rule of law.[21]

In 1874 Assam was separated from the Bengal Presidency and given the status of a chief commissioner's province. Yet the Non-Regulation system persisted.[22] Assam now comprised the Brahmaputra valley districts of Kamrup, Nowgong, Darrang, Sibsagar, Lakhimpur, and Goalpara, the hill tracts of the Naga, Khasi, Jaintia, and Garo, and the Surma valley districts of Cachar and Sylhet. The colonial regime hoped that populous Sylhet, newly separated from Bengal against its inhabitants' wishes, would compensate for the scanty population and revenue of Assam proper. Including Sylhet, Assam's total area was 54,000 square miles. The total population was 4,150,000, with gross revenue of 52.5 lakh rupees.[23] The gentry of the Brahmaputra valley welcomed Assam's new provincial status and independence from Bengal, since they expected less competition from Bengal's middle classes. But the bulk of Bengali public opinion opposed the new province. In particular, Sylhet's Bengali-speaking inhabitants disliked this political change. Sylhet's élites submitted numerous memorials to the British government protesting the joining of their district to "backward" Assam, and the severing of its historical and cultural ties with Bengal.[24] They hoped for a reamalgamation of Assam and Bengal. Such a reunification occurred in 1905, but for other reasons. Lord Curzon's creation of the new province of Eastern Bengal and Assam aimed at suppressing Bengali nationalist sentiment by separating Bengal's western and eastern halves. Facing immense political opposition, this partition of Bengal proved short-lived.[25] Assam and Bengal were restored to their pre-1905 boundaries in 1912, but Sylhet and its adjacent Surma valley tracts remained in Assam for the remainder of British rule.

There continued to be a huge disparity between the different parts of the new chief commissioner's province of Assam. The census of 1881 showed that the population density of the Surma valley was 335.82 per square mile, as compared to 105.03 for the Brahmaputra valley and only 20.54 for the hill tracts.[26] Newspapers in Calcutta accused the government of having allowed tea's "powerful commercial lobby" to extend despotic rule, aided by the legal minimalism of the Non-Regulation system. The *Bharat Sangcharak* remarked, "It is well known, that in such provinces, the administration of justice is not quite pure. The case would have been otherwise if it had continued to form part of Bengal, as the judicial officers then would have had to proceed according to law, and might at times punish offending planters."[27] Despite British claims to have delivered liberty to a benighted region, the support lent by colonial officials to Assam planters' harsh labour regime lent credence to these accusations.

Labour and the Lords

Through the nineteenth century the rhetoric of liberty emerged as an essential part of the British imperial imagination, and an important justification for military and financial expansionism. Needing to bolster itself in British public opinion, the East India Company could not afford to ignore the language of liberty, in particular the impulse toward emancipation. The East India Company's moral strictures against slavery distinguished it from older regimes and practices in India. Thus its court of directors declared in 1830 that "slavery in every form is peculiarly revolting to the moral feelings of Englishmen."[28] In Britain a strong abolitionist current turned its attention to eradicating slavery in the colonies after its victory over the metropolitan slave lobby. In 1834 it helped create a Parliamentary committee to examine slavery in the East Indies and enact prohibition.[29] Act V of 1843 emancipated thousands of plantation slaves in the sugar-growing Caribbean colonies. In British India too, slavery became illegal even as the colonial administrators' tendency to insist upon the rights of masters and the sanctity of property tended to moderate the act's effect.[30]

In newly conquered Assam élite groups had long controlled large numbers of servile men and women. Given the region's sparse population, forced labour retained considerable economic importance. Exemption from manual service was a privilege only for those entrusted with some office or status. Most of the remaining population bore stringent corvée obligations, directly to the state or to high officials. In addition, there were slaves, male and female, known as *bandis* and *betis*. The historian Amalendu Guha estimated that at the close of the Ahom period about 9–10 percent of the total population held this servile status. They mostly worked on agricultural estates which belonged to the aristocracy and the holders of *devottar* and *brahmottar* (religious endowment) lands.[31]

The term "slave" as used by British observers is misleading. It conflated war captives and agrarian and domestic bonded labour, as well as debt slaves. The last category was probably the largest, and growing, owing to economic dislocation. East India Company officials found "astonishing the number of people who from the pressure of rent have sold themselves for a trifling sum and become bondsmen with their wives and families until the original sum which they can never have the means of realizing is obtained."[32] This situation was actually encouraged by David Scott's decree of 1825 that permitted peasants to sell themselves to their creditors.[33] His decree passed muster at a time when Assam was not formally British territory and was distant from public knowledge. By the 1830s Scott's policy caused tensions with his superiors. He ran foul of the general emancipatory current in the British Empire when he proposed to allow the continuance of the Ahom system of bonded servants who cultivated élite estates.[34]

Scott justified this continuity partly on grounds of economic necessity, and more strongly in terms of civilizational logic: "From the records of history, Jewish, Classical, Asiatic and European, it appears that slavery has everywhere prevailed in the less advanced stages of civilization; and I apprehend Assam, according to European notions, may be considered as a country exhibiting a still ruder state of society . . . Were the country further advanced in the career of improvement, and capital more widely diffused . . . this system of slavery and bondage would gradually diminish of itself."[35] Scott and his local officials were convinced that the condition of the slaves was not the most urgent issue facing them in war-ravaged Assam, being more or less "comparable to the dissolute paupers in England."[36] But his sentiments were out of step with the tide of reformist ideologies seeking to banish vices from the body politic, at home and abroad.

As Scott had warned, Assam's élites greatly resented the British decree of 1843 that announced the abolition of slavery.[37] With status taboos against ploughing, the upper classes had long depended on servile labour. The labour shortages that resulted from the Burmese depredations became even more critical when the British announced the cessation of forced labour. A shortage of cultivating hands caused a breakup of many large estates. Sizable tracts of land were surrendered to the state by nobles who could no longer afford to cultivate them or pay the revenue. A paucity of sources makes it difficult to trace the subsequent fate of the erstwhile serf labour. Given that land was abundant but capital short, many became sharecroppers and tenants. The number of tenants showed a steady rise under British rule. At the same time, the practice of mortgaging labour to settle debts continued, relatively unaffected by legislation.[38]

In 1830, when Scott wrote to his superiors in Calcutta on the issue of slavery in Assam, he had stated his desire to canvass the opinion of intelligent natives. He opposed the outright promulgation of the slavery decree. In its place he advocated its gradual introduction, so as to avoid a general disruption among the upper classes. As Scott predicted, Assamese élites quickly showed their displeasure at the outlawing of slavery. Harakanta Barua's memoir describes his attempts to convince his British employers of its ill-judged nature. He narrated how the Brahmin landholders of the Kamrup district held a protest demonstration and submitted to the authorities a petition in which over a thousand signatories sought permission to retain their "slaves and bondsmen."[39] In 1853 the issue of slavery remained a major grievance when Maniram Barbhandar Barua submitted his views on East India Company rule to Justice Mills. In Maniram's view the British rulers initially undertook to maintain "all respectable people in honour and affluence."[40] Now, under their altered policies, Assam's élites, "whose ancestors never lived by digging, ploughing, or carrying burdens," were forced into ignoble work to live.[41]

In his robust critique of the colonial takeover Maniram singled out its adverse impact upon his own class, the notables whose displacement was exacerbated by the British decision to free their slaves.

Undoubtedly he was unaware of the larger context of this measure: that it was part of the British Empire's far-reaching anti-slavery initiatives, which culminated in the Emancipation decree. He reacted solely to the labour shortage and its deleterious impact upon his class-fellows. Their main source of income was their estates, so far cultivated by servile labour. Loyal to his British employers, Harakanta privately sought out his superior, the commissioner at Guwahati, to warn him about the damaging effects of the emancipation decree. Maniram's harsher remonstrations had no effect other than to render him an object of suspicion. Most probably, he came under state surveillance. Harakanta mentions that his superiors warned him not to keep company with Maniram, and that he in turn passed on the warning to others. This was a prescient warning, as a few years later, in 1857, Maniram's dissatisfaction led him to join hands with North Indian military rebels against the British in 1857. His objective was an Ahom royal restoration. However, Maniram's conspiracy was quickly detected. In the post-1857 hysteria this erstwhile British favourite ended on the gallows.

Disapproval in Calcutta and London of David Scott's attempts to prevent an abrupt break with an older political economy provides an interesting insight into the British desire to extend the liberty of the "free-born Englishman" liberty to his less fortunate brothers elsewhere.[42] The colonial regime was keen to emphasize the contrast between the liberties it had introduced and its Ahom predecessors' despotic restrictions. When a memorial to the viceroy from the inhabitants of Guwahati and Sibsagar complained of the decay of old families, it earned a crushing putdown. "The nobility of Assam as of other parts of India was maintained chiefly by class privileges and by slavery, which are opposed to the whole spirit of British rule and the resuscitation of which would be an unmixed evil."[43] Official reports on the "State of Public Opinion" reinforced this view of British rule as promoting a free market. "The upper class of the Assamese's opinion is that times are very hard for them as they cannot get servants to cultivate their lands and everything is so dear. The lower classes say that times are good, as they can make lots of money on tea gardens and can eat opium as much as they like."[44]

That the abolition of slavery had turned the Assam world on its head was argued even by the new generation of the gentry who joined British service, but their arguments often differed from Maniram's. Gunabhiram Barua, who later retired from British service with the rank of extra-assistant commissioner, compared the Ahom past and the British present, to the former's disadvantage: "According to the present laws of the land, the grihastya [householder] and the ghulam [servant] enjoy the same status. Talented people, even if of low caste, have received high rank. In this regard, older people look at the Ahom days and say, this could not happen in the old days."[45] For Gunabhiram as for his British superiors, freedom was apparently the watchword of the day. The assumption was that the tea labour market would be the first beneficiary, as emancipated bonded servants might flock there for employment. But in their first flush of enthusiasm for this purported emancipation, local élites overlooked the harshness of the penal labour system that the British tea enterprise had introduced. Nor did labour emancipation go far enough in its impact. As the newspaper *Assam Mihir* noted in 1873, poor parents still mortgaged daughters to wealthy families, with "scarcely a man of substance in Guwahati in whose home there are not one or two slaves."[46]

Spiritual Lords and Service Gentry

Pre-modern authority in Assam took two distinct forms, military and spiritual. As in other pre-modern states, Assam's kings acquired cultural capital through their relationships with Indic religious practitioners. These were the Gosains, the heads of *satras* (monasteries).[47] By the sixteenth century the Ahom royal court patronized select aspects of devotional worship and nurtured a rich tradition of vernacular literary production. Royal bestowal of landed estates and servile labour on local religious sects created a powerful spiritual aristocracy. It helped to expand the kingdom's settled agrarian frontier, as followers of the sects extended cultivation into fallow and forested lands.

The majority of these local sects followed Vaishnavite practices and beliefs. In its broadest form Assamese Vaishnavism was a monotheistic, congregational form of religious practice which rapidly superseded older forms of worship.[48] The legendary founder of Assamese Vaishnavism was the fifteenth-century bhakti preacher Sankardeb. Within this faith the relationship between devotee and preceptor

was modeled on that between God and man. This tie was institutionalized through the *saran* (initiation) ceremony, in which devotees received formal spiritual indoctrination from a preceptor,
usually known as a Gosain, a term that served as a synonym for God.
By the seventeenth century the Gosains, or heads of Assam's three
hundred odd monastic satras, were the linchpins of the faith. They
usually ruled over large communities of *bhakats* (monks) and servile
labourers.[49] Satra lands enjoyed concessional revenue terms from the
state and were often rented to cultivating lay tenants. Satra domination also extended over larger networks of villages inhabited by *shish*
(tithe-paying lay disciples). By the late seventeenth century four
competing *samhatis* (sects) emerged: the Brahma, Purusa, Nika, and
Kala, with a marked social differentiation in doctrine and membership. The Brahma sect comprised the Auniati and Dakhinapat satras,
located on the Majuli riverine island in Upper Assam, with close ties
to royalty. Its social and ritual conservatism appealed to the Ahom
rulers, especially its endorsement of Vedic rites and idol worship.
Unlike members of other Vaishnavite sects, celibate Brahmin re-
nouncers dominated the Brahma order, which accepted only upper-
caste and high-status lay devotees, mostly from the service gentry
and Ahom aristocracy.[50] In contrast, other sects were headed by non-
Brahmin householder Gosains, and their membership came from a
similar, middling cross-section of society.

While royal patronage enabled the Brahma satras to become very
wealthy, so did many satras belonging to other sects. Satra wealth derived from a combination of land grants from the state, unpaid labour services, and tithes from lay disciples.[51] The spread of satras
helped to extend the Ahom state's reach and that of its cultivated
lands, particularly over remote, frontier areas.[52] Yet periodic clashes
still erupted between state and spiritual authority. In this sparsely
populated frontier region, control of labour was imperative for any
regime. While the Ahom state imposed the corvée on its peasant population, satra initiates were exempt from this labouring obligation.
Over the eighteenth century hard-pressed peasants often sought refuge from state service by taking on the identity of a satra initiate. This
subtle form of resistance increased the tensions between these two
nodes of local authority, the Gosains and the Ahom kings. The latter
resented the pretensions of the spiritual lords and refused to become
their disciples. Instead they imported Bengali Brahmins from the

sacred town of Nadia to officiate as royal preceptors. These Brahmins were given the title of Parbatiya Gosains and installed as heads of the historic Kamakhya shrine, a famous centre of Sakta worship.[53] These Brahmin priests and a few Muslim Sufi preceptors were the Ahom kingdom's non-Vaishnavite landed spiritual lords.

It was with the Moamoria order, the newest and the most socially diverse of the Vaishnavite sects, that the Ahom state openly clashed. Followers of this order were drawn from tribal and lower-caste groups, people whom other sects deemed unacceptably low. Encouraged by their Brahmin preceptors, late-eighteenth-century Ahom rulers scorned the Moamoria Gosain. His disciples, many from a lowly fishing community, took up arms to protest royal insults to their spiritual lord.[54] This uprising began in 1769 and was not suppressed until 1805. It shook the very base of Ahom power and twice forced the rulers to flee the capital. After the Ahom kings regained their throne, the state's bloody reprisals decimated the rebellious order. Other Vaishnavite sects held aloof from the Moamorias and condemned their social, political, and religious radicalism. Nonetheless, the long-term impact of the Moamoria revolt was considerable. This uprising greatly weakened the Ahom state and contributed to its eventual demise.

The late eighteenth century and early nineteenth century were years of immense political and economic strife in Assam. The upheavals caused by the Moamoria rebellion, the Burmese invasions, and the ineptitude of the last Ahom rulers made this a difficult period for Assam's common people. These events did adversely affect the Gosains, but on the whole they managed to retain most of their wealth. Even after the British slave emancipation the Gosains were less hard hit than other aristocrats by the loss of servile labour. Their social and religious domination over lay tenants and sharecroppers gave them access to cultivating labour. Tenants were also attracted by satra lands' lower rents, since Gosains enjoyed concessional revenue rates under the British state.

In contrast to the Gosains, by the 1850s the condition of the Ahom royalty and the rest of the lay aristocracy was so dire that the East India Company government at Calcutta expressed shock and unease at their collapse. Assam's administrative head, Colonel Jenkins, insisted that this decline of the Ahom élites was inevitable, given their inability to adjust to changed times.[55] The talents of the Ahom dangariyas (great men) seemed redundant in a new age. In the past they were content to relegate tasks requiring literacy and numeracy to their social inferiors, the caste Hindu gentry. Now, with the loss of courtly offices and their absence of literate skills, most Ahom aristocrats had little to sustain themselves. They had little to offer to the British regime.[56] The abolition of slavery meant that they lost most of their labour, rendering their lands fallow and unprofitable. Unable to pay the land revenue, many aristocrats resigned most of their holdings. Unlike their erstwhile service gentry subordinates, these aristocrats found that their lack of marketable educational and literary skills prevented them from earning a livelihood.

Noting the changed situation for Assam's aristocracy and its gentry, Colonel Jenkins remarked, "The members of the late ruling class, the Ahoms have hitherto shown, with few exceptions, little aptitude for learning or qualification for our offices."[57] In contrast, the service gentry which previously held middling ranks prospered under the British. Comprising both high-caste Hindus and a few high-status Muslims, members of the service gentry carved out a livelihood in British-ruled Assam on the basis of the same recordkeeping skills which had previously made them indispensable to the Ahom state.[58] For example, Harakanta Barua steadily ascended the British regime's clerical ranks, retiring with the rank of Sadar Amin, while his patron Ghanakanta Yuvaraj, an Ahom royal prince, was reduced to penury. In his memoir Harakanta described how the prince struggled to sustain his large household with no income other than a meagre British pension.[59] *Admin, fradion and privilege*

The local gentry did face considerable competition from the established clerical cadres from Bengal who accompanied the East India Company into Assam. But the locals' detailed knowledge of the region's land tenures was a key advantage that allowed them to be appointed to many of the subordinate revenue and judicial posts in the British administration. The Assamese gentry's firsthand knowledge of *lakhiraj* and *nisf-khiraj* pre-colonial grants (providing charity and religious land on revenue-free or concessional terms) was particularly important for the new administrators as they struggled to understand the local complexities of land rights and dues. Justice Mills wrote, "The officers who had the preparing and keeping of the lakhiraj records were Mozemdar Burrooahs and Mozemdars, in whose families the appointments were hereditary."[60] These men possessed invaluable experience with these land records, since either they or their fathers had administered the grants for the Ahom monarchy.

In this manner the gentry's specialized knowledge of land records greatly benefited the colonial regime while facilitating their employment in its new revenue and judicial offices. Rent-collecting (mauzadari) rights over land were a further component of gentry incomes, quite apart from their remuneration. Appointment to clerical offices allowed the gentry to further consolidate their hold over mauzadari rights. Harakanta Barua frequently referred to the mauzadari rights he held over certain villages and the periodic renewal of those rights by the government. The gentry's control over land records and rent collection not only benefited them materially but proved an invaluable advantage for their spiritual lords, the Gosains. Their strategic placement in revenue offices proved important in smoothing the satra transition into the new order. By the 1840s the prominent satras recovered most landed privileges. For example, in 1841 satra lands in the Kamrup district accounted for "nearly one-half of its cultivated area . . . besides including an immense extent of garden and other lands of great value."[61]

Nonetheless, the first generation of colonial officials still distrusted the spiritual lords. The early British, in line with Protestant sentiments, held stereotyped opinions about Gosains as cunning, manipulative priests, and suspected their links with the old regime. They also disapproved of the satras' wealth and influence over the common people. For all these reasons the East India Company feared the satra lords as potential troublemakers. In 1854 Captain John Butler warned Justice Mills of the danger from these wealthy and influential Gosains: "Possessed of great power over the minds of the people, bigoted, ignorant and avaricious, they do not, in the smallest degree, through the means at their disposal, aid in the education of the people . . . they may truly be said to be the only disaffected subjects of the government in the plains of Assam."[62] In 1843 the Political Department dispatched a confidential memorandum that "all the principal priests and Mahantas are dissatisfied towards our Government and would be glad of any change."[63] A decade later, in 1857, these fears seemed justified when Maniram Barbhandar Barua's conspiracy with North Indian soldier-rebels to overthrow British rule was unearthed. The evidence against him included letters of support from key Gosains.[64]

Shortly after the British discovered the plot, Maniram was speedily tried and hanged. The administration decreed severe punishments for those found guilty of involvement, but unlike in epicentres of the rebellion such as Delhi, there was no necessity to mete out wholesale retaliation, and the rebellion made little impact on the life of Assam's general population. Rumour and discontent were certainly rife, both among élites and commoners. Contemporary sources such as Harakanta Barua's memoir, the diary of a British soldier, George Carter, and letters circulated among the American Baptist missionaries provide vivid testimony of the tense atmosphere. The few white men in the Assam countryside, whether officials, soldiers, planters, or missionaries, nervously anticipated trouble from their suddenly sullen native subordinates. But active rebels in Assam were relatively few. Coordination remained poor given the immense bottlenecks of transport and communication. Maniram was already under surveillance as a malcontent. The British discovered his plot with the sepoys in its preliminary stages. Rumours circulated that Maniram's captor Captain Holroyd had declared, "We will hang you first and try you later."[65] The British hanged another aristocrat, Piyoli Barua, for his part in the attempted uprising. Other conspirators were imprisoned in the Andaman islands' penal colony. The teenaged Ahom prince Kandarpeswar Singha, whom the rebels planned to enthrone, was exiled.

Yet the state took no punitive action against any of the Gosains involved with these rebels. Clearly the colonial rulers feared the tremendous power vested in the Vaishnavite sects, which enjoyed the allegiance of "almost all people of middle and better lower classes" and "most of the lower classes."[66] Their immense reach was reason enough to allow the Gosains to rest undisturbed, for the time being, in their "arrogance and disaffection."[67] While the East India Company's punishment of other rebels did not provoke open hostility, Assam's public might have reacted very differently if the colonial rulers had chastised the spiritual lords. The Gosains' lands remained untouched. As a result, they enjoyed much better prospects than their former royal patrons. Many years later a planter noted that the Gosain's word was still paramount for most people—"no right-minded co-religionist would think of questioning his decisions."[68] Nonetheless there were heightened political tensions, as the British state and the Assamese spiritual lords continued to jostle for power.

Moreover, the satras faced spiritual and cultural competition from a new direction: Christian missionaries.

Preaching and Print: Missionary Ventures

In the 1830s British officials extended an invitation to American Baptist missionaries. The East India Company hoped that missionary activity would "elevate the character of the people" in newly conquered Assam.[69] The Americans had established their first overseas mission in Burma in 1812. When political opposition forced them to retreat, these missionaries sought a new venture in British India. They were excited by reports that hill groups in Assam were related to the Karen people of northern Burma, among whom they had achieved many converts. In 1836, armed with the first printing press in the region, the American Baptists opened a new mission at Sadiya in Upper Assam, close to the experimental tea tracts. Initially the American Baptists viewed Sadiya as a foothold enabling future penetration into other parts of Asia. But they soon confronted difficulties. A fundamental principle of the Baptist philosophy was that the Word should reach people in their own language. They found that this was no easy matter in a region with such diverse, polyglot cultures. Their notion of a unilingual field in Asia proved to be a chimera. Burmese dialects were of little use among Sadiya's inhabitants. Instead the Baptists were forced to learn many local dialects (of the Tibeto-Burmese language family). Sadiya lay in a hilly, remote area sparsely populated by preliterate groups. To use their precious printing press, the Baptists needed to first transpose spoken dialects into new, written alphabets. As the discrepancy between their expectations and reality became obvious, the missionaries became disheartened.

Nor was this new terrain politically secure. After attacks by angry Singpho tribals who had lost their rights to land, the British tea enterprise decided to move from remote Sadiya into the mainland of the Brahmaputra valley. With the British retreat the missionaries were isolated. At this point they realized that in contrast to Sadiya, the valley below was inhabited by a settled agriculturist population of Asomiya speakers. In 1841 the American Baptists followed the British tea enterprise out of Sadiya. They chose Sibsagar town, once the capital of the Ahom kings, as their new base. The peaceful Brahmaputra valley and its dominant language, linked to a Sanskritic script and the Indo-European language family, appeared to be the best possible vehicles for Baptist proselytizing. The missionary Miles Bronson enthusiastically described their new flock to the home board of the American Baptist Foreign Mission: "The Assamese are a most encouraging and inviting field; they are in great measure a civilized people."[70]

From Sibsagar the American Baptists decided to convey their message through Asomiya, the lingua franca for most élites and commoners in the Brahmaputra valley. This language had the advantage for the missionaries of an established script and a long written tradition. After their tours of the valley, the missionaries concluded that "[though] as many dialects are spoken . . . as were heard at Jerusalem on the day of Pentecost . . . each of the tribes has a language of its own, while the Assamese is the common medium of trade."[71] This important conclusion set the mission at loggerheads with British language policy. In 1836 the East India Company had already ruled that for administrative convenience Bengali would be the standard language all over the Bengal Presidency. This decree disregarded the many local languages and dialects in use over the huge Presidency area, comprising Bengal, Bihar, Orissa, and Assam. According to the decree, proceedings in Assam's courts and offices were henceforward to be conducted in Bengali, marking a drastic break from the pre-colonial use of the Asomiya language for administrative purposes. William Robinson, the British government's inspector of schools, ordered that children should be educated through the Bengali medium.

For the American Baptists, the goal of conversion clashed with the expediency of colonial administrators. Bronson urged them to reconsider the language policy: "I believe that so long as the courts and schools are in Bengali, there will be the greatest impediment to the education and improvement of the people."[72] The East India Company ignored this plea, but the missionaries decided nonetheless to use the local language for their activities. "We have by every means in our power endeavored to make ourselves acquainted with the people, and by daily familiar intercourse acquire their language, so as to be able to communicate to them in the most direct manner the blessings of science and Christianity."[73] The hierarchical nature of the official colonial project confronted the more assimilative approach of the missionaries.

The missionary objective was to win over the gentry, the most influential section of the Assamese people. In 1846 the American Baptist mission decided to publish a periodical in the Asomiya language, titled the *Orunodoi*. Through it the Baptists planned to disseminate their notions of "Religion, Science, and General Knowledge." This became the motto for its masthead. Concurrently they established mission branches at Guwahati, Jorhat, and Nagaon. After the remote, sparsely populated, and densely forested tracts where the missionaries had spent their first years, these localities seemed to offer better scope for Christian improvement. Rather than the lower-caste villagers whom they had so far acquired as converts, the Baptists desired a more élite constituency. The high schools and courts in these towns attracted precisely those educated youths whom the missionaries hoped to wean from traditional beliefs. As Cyrus Barker optimistically noted, "The principal government of the district is invested in this court, which brings together the most active, learned and intelligent part of the people . . . the population is a reading one."[74] The *Orunodoi*, the only periodical published in the entire region, seemed the best way to win their hearts and minds.

In 1858 the missionary Samuel Whiting informed the secretary of the Foreign Mission Board at Philadelphia, "Our paper is now in its thirteenth year and is regarded by Young Assam at least, as one of the institutions of the province."[75] The periodical's contents were fairly eclectic. It clearly aimed to expand its readers' horizons about the wider world as well as acquaint them with the Holy Word. As Whiting noted, "A brief sermon or exhortation, a chapter of church history, a chapter of the Life of Mohammad . . . of the history of Bengal, of the life of Luther, a geographical article, a chapter of Isaiah, together with the news of the month, contributions on various topics such as the marriage of widows, duties of wives, duties of parents, from Christian and other contributors, make up each monthly number."[76] The mention of "other contributors" is significant. The focus on enlightenment through religious exhortations and secular truths was supplemented by contributions from a local reading public. Their inclusion reflected shared concerns about education, language, and Assam's social regeneration.

But apart from its literary appeal, it was as yet unclear whether and how the *Orunodoi* might actually win Christian converts, who remained few in the Brahmaputra valley. The missionaries tended to blame this failure on the defective character of the local people rather than on any shortcomings of their own. Much as they disagreed with colonial policymakers on the language issue, as fellow white men they rallied to the side of British law and order, and civilizing imperatives.

Gosain, Mission, and State

Even as the American Baptist missionaries evolved their strategies to win over the Assamese, India came directly under the British Crown. In 1858, Queen Victoria's proclamation to the princes, chiefs, and people of India formalized this handover from the East India Company. As the Queen's representative and British India's first viceroy, Lord Canning undertook a series of tours in different parts of the country to make manifest the new British relationship with Indians. This presence of the queen's representative was a symbol of the reestablishment of political order after 1857. An important feature of these tours was the holding of official receptions for Indian notables and British and Indian officials, glorified as durbars in the tradition of Indo-Persian public audiences. In Canning's place lesser plenipotentiaries were assigned to outlying regions. Assam's turn came only in July 1862, when Cecil Beadon, the new lieutenant governor of Bengal, voyaged there from Calcutta. Beadon's main objective was to study the condition of the Assam tea industry. At the same time he wished to impress local élites with the majesty of the British crown.[77]

Harakanta Barua was in that year a Munsif (subordinate judge) at the collector's office in Guwahati. His description of Beadon's durbars depicts them as momentous encounters between the old and new regimes. Like most of his contemporaries Harakanta executed a complex set of maneuvers between changing structures, and his memoir provides a rare direct insight into this process. Based on daily diary entries, the memoir was the first personal testimony in the Asomiya language. In all probability Harakanta wished for it to remain within his immediate family circle. Certainly he made no attempt to publish it, although he did publish another work, a buranji history of Assam.[78] His memoir reached the public domain long after his death, through his grandson's efforts. A strong sense of the author's preoccupation with issues of hierarchy and deference permeates the text, as he describes interactions with various social superiors. They included the Ahom prince Ghanakanta Yuvaraj and his wife Padmabati Kunwari, the British commissioner and his wife (referred to as the memsahib), and his spiritual preceptor, the Auniati Gosain.

Harakanta wrote at length about Cecil Beadon's shipboard reception for Assam's dignitaries at Guwahati. This proved an occasion when figures representing different interests actively competed for allegiance. Harakanta and his colleagues, in their dual capacity as disciples of the Gosains and clerks to the British, faced a moral dilemma. What took place at Beadon's reception made visible the cultural and political transition from the old to the new lords of the land. The Gosains, Assam's spiritual heads, faced a new order in which the British regime took unto itself an entirety of authority. During the period after 1857 tangible changes entered the equation between colonial rulers and local notables in British India. The colonial state maintained some external forms of deference to local élites, but in a form domesticated within the increasing pomp of imperial authority. The new rulers granted the Gosains a share in this authority as long as they accepted subordinate roles. Élites in other regions faced a similar situation. This accommodation between old lords and a new regime took time to evolve and involved many a slip.

Harakanta's narrative opened rather cryptically, with a mention of the lieutenant governor's imminent visit accompanied by the author's confession of his nervousness. His anxiety was focused upon one particular occasion: Beadon's shipboard durbar at Guwahati. Harakanta mentioned his reluctance to attend. He appeared only when his superior, Captain Lloyd, sent for him. "I had no wish to be present there, when the Gosains would all be sitting."[79] His nervousness was due to his having to sit alongside the lords. In the 1830s David Scott had recorded that "Gosains or archbishops residing at or near Gowahatty get chairs when they call upon European officers, but those in Upper Assam prefer to bring with them their own particular seats as prescribed by ancient custom. No other individuals are permitted to sit in the presence of the archbishops."[80] The day of Scott's respect for local precedents had long since passed.

At Beadon's durbar, ushers showed Harakanta and his fellow clerks to chairs near where the Gosains and the erstwhile royals were seated. British officials sat at the other end of the ship. The occasion passed without any overt ripple, but Harakanta rightly anticipated that a reckoning would come. It arrived the next day, in the form of a furious note from his preceptor, who cursed Harakanta for his impudence at sitting on a chair in his presence. Harakanta nervously informed Captain Lloyd that a serious breach of custom had occurred. Lloyd flew into a passion. "I've never encountered such a land before. Respectable people like a Deputy Collector to sit upon the floor. Your Rajas and others may have been rulers once, who created aristocrats and Gosains around them. Maharani Victoria is at the head of India. She has created Deputy Collectors and others. Don't they have rank and honour too?"[81]

The Gosains would not leave this affront unchallenged. Cecil Beadon held his next durbar at Sibsagar. During the event Duttadeb Goswami, the powerful Gosain of the Auniati satra, vociferously objected to having natives sit in his presence. The Assamese deputy magistrate, himself Goswami's disciple, hastily moved to squat on the floor, but the commissioner, Major Haughton, angrily ordered him back to a chair, and the durbar continued.[82] Subsequently the Auniati Gosain wrote to Haughton, avowedly apologizing for his refusal "to be seated equally with the natives."[83] He attributed the entire misunderstanding to a failure to inform the British authorities of local customs: "I had been told that no native would take chair in the Muzhib except me, but upon entering the hall, I perceived the contrary. I declined to sit, for natives were not authorized by ancient Rajas to accept any respectable seat in my presence."[84] When forwarded to the government of the Bengal Presidency, the Gosain's explanation vouchsafed a stern response: "The Rajas of Assam had ceased to have any power long before British rule commenced and all honours that are now enjoyed in the British Durbar can only be enjoyed in so far as they are conceded by the British Government which seeks to elevate all of its subjects and desires the abject degradation of none."[85]

This exchange was significant, as it revealed the limits that the colonial government imposed upon older élites. It asserted the British throne as the sole emanation of power and as the guarantor of an egalitarian status for all its subjects. In a sense this evoked the tone and spirit of the queen's proclamation of 1858. As the anthropologist Bernard Cohn shows, that proclamation functioned as a cultural statement encompassing two divergent or even contradictory theories of rule. One sought to maintain India as a feudal order, while the other anticipated changes which would inevitably lead to the destruction of the order. Each theory incorporated ideas about the

*Divying Harris of Imperpath and colonialism

sociology of India, and the relationship of the rulers to individuals and groups in Indian society. If the British ruled India in a feudal mode, then an Indian aristocracy had to be present to play the part of loyal feudatories to the British Queen. On the other hand, if the British ruled India in a modern mode, then a new kind of civic or public order had to be developed. In both modes, although Indians might become associated with British rulers as feudatories or as representatives of specific interests, the British would make all effective decisions.[86]

This fraught encounter between the Auniati Gosain, the representative of pre-colonial dignity, and the lieutenant governor, the spokesman for the queen, brought to the fore the contradictory impulses of these theories. It also illuminated the specific role that the British fancied for themselves in Assam, as emancipators of a people from a retrograde system of slavery. This logic allowed the chief commissioner to reject a petition for pensions from the old aristocracy, since "the nobility of Assam as of other parts of India was maintained chiefly by class privileges and by slavery, which are opposed to the whole spirit of British rule and the resuscitation would be an unmixed evil."[87] Ironically, after the British introduced an indentured labour system into the tea industry, they faced charges of having revived slavery under a new name.

The British admonishment of the Gosain revealed another delicate balancing act. British administrators and an emergent intelligentsia sought to promote modern notions of merit as opposed to inherited privilege, of education as opposed to ancestral status. They viewed these as the reigning precepts of a new modernizing order. But in the aftermath of the revolt of 1857, the colonial state saw traditional élites as suitable supporters of the social and political status quo. The incident at Cecil Beadon's durbar showed the tensions that could emerge even as the state socialized traditional élites into a new role. The Gosains had to realize that the uneasy oscillation between accommodation and challenge that characterized their relationship with the Ahom state was no longer permissible. The British regime claimed all authority for itself. Elites could share in that authority only insofar as they accepted their allotted place.

Throughout the consolidation of the British Raj after 1857, tensions between state and temple still surfaced. Notably, a British court issued a summons to the wealthy Auniati and Dakhinpat Gosains who had allowed opium to be grown upon their lands.[88] Local rumours swiftly circulated that the Gosains had retaliated by placing a curse upon the unfortunate officer concerned with the case. The matter grew serious enough for official concern.[89] In response to a query from Calcutta, the assistant commissioner reported that soon after the Gosains had been summoned and penalized, the deputy commissioner of Upper Assam, Captain Sconce, became seriously ill. Assamese public opinion believed that this was due to the Auniati Gosain's curse.[90]

In this fresh fracas between state and Gosain, the normally circumspect American Baptist missionaries publicly interceded, through the editorial pages of the *Orunodoi*. Usually they avoided polemics against local religious authority. They believed that "the most effective way of defeating the purpose of the Brahmins is not to attack them personally, but to enlighten the masses."[91] However, there had long been tensions between the missionaries and the Gosains. Ever since their move to the Brahmaputra valley, the American Baptists recognized the Assamese Vaishnavite faith and its Gosains as their main rivals. An early missionary dejectedly noted the power of "proselytizing mahants in Assam . . . they give a discourse on initiation, forms of Hindu worship and the shastras [scriptures] to local people, they ask for a house to be built for them. People then become bhakats or believers."[92] The authority that these religious specialists exerted over the people was evident in Nathan Brown's wry comment after a visit to a Gosain in 1843: "The young man who was in attendance was somewhat displeased that I did not address his master by the title of 'God' as is their custom."[93] Far from acknowledging the missionary's god, these locals wanted the missionaries to pay obeisance to theirs.

The missionaries had hoped that their printing press would prove a secret weapon. Through the *Orunodoi* the Baptists delivered enlightenment in affordable and popular monthly print installments in the local language.[94] There was a growing readership among "Young Assam." A Brahmin letter writer to the *Orunodoi* extolled the periodical as a *gyan bhandar* (store of wisdom).[95] Similarly, a British planter noted the popularity of the *Orunodoi* among locals: "It has been in circulation for twenty years, and is largely read and apparently really appreciated by all those who can afford to take it in. I subscribe for a number for each of my factories, and I was much pleased to see some fifteen or twenty coolies assemble nightly of their own accord, after their day's work was done, to hear the Mohurir [supervisor] read it to them."[96]

Despite their periodical's popularity, the American Baptists remained aware of the need to avoid being too heavy-handed with their religious agenda. Like other missionary periodicals, the *Orunodoi* promoted "improvement" by linking Christian accounts with apparently secular and quite objective facts.[97] News headings included "Turko-Russian hostilities; War in China; Revolution in Spain; Telegraph from Calcutta to Bombay." Educational articles on astronomy, geography, and natural history appeared alongside homilies on temperance, veracity, self-reliance, and family government. In this manner the periodical offered morsels of useful knowledge artfully scattered amid Christian teachings. The American Baptists followed the lead of other missionaries by offering writings especially on astronomy, designed as a combination of secular information and religious propaganda. Missionaries approved of disseminating scientific factuality partly as a laudable end in itself and partly as an effective means to ridicule indigenous cosmology and its guardians.[98] The mission's annual report smugly declared, "The Assamese, Brahmins as well as others, think it impossible to measure the distance of an inaccessible object . . . From the errors of the shasters on these . . . points, the people will readily see that they are only the work of man."[99] Still, these erudite measures did not bring actual conversions, even if they furthered the cause of rationality.

The missionaries were especially eager to convert Young Assam, the region's literate and influential gentry youth. This focus on élites was common to almost all missionaries of this period, who evinced a profound distrust of the motivations behind the conversion of lower classes. The historians Antony Copley and Duncan Forrester have drawn attention to the missionary obsession with Brahmin conversions in different regions.[100] Optimism was rife after even the slightest overture from a "higher class" of would-be convert. For example, Mrs. Bronson anticipated the conversion of "Two pundits . . . representative men of the educated Assamese. One is an old Brahmin, deeply read in Sanskrit . . . He seems to be like one of old, anxious to bow in the house of his god for appearance' sake, while in his heart he worships the only living and true God. The other is a representative of young Assam. He is bound hand and foot by the chains of custom

The place of the mission in society

and caste, like the old man, but he seems to have a conviction that there is truth in the new religion, and that he must seek for it."[101]

Judging by the number of actual conversions, Mrs. Bronson's hopefulness was somewhat misplaced. Despite the missionary desire to win élites, Baptist converts in the Brahmaputra valley were almost all from a lower-caste, unlettered background. These converts largely depended upon the mission for sustenance. Usually converts to Christianity found it impossible to continue with their occupations in the face of social ostracism. Kolibor, an early convert, was a washerman, but the Sibsagar church had to employ him as a preacher, since he could no longer make a living. The usual channels for mobility were fairly restricted even for educated Christians, since they came from humble backgrounds. For Assamese Christians the ultimate post within reach was that of a low-level clerk or school inspector. Hardly any were appointed to the coveted revenue jobs that most gentry youths obtained through patronage.

For almost three decades the American Baptist missionaries retained hopes for respectable converts to man "God's garden" in the Brahmaputra valley. The reading public of the *Orunodoi* was their main target. Baptists argued that only this educated class could intellectually accept the Christian creed; missionaries remained suspicious of the materialistic motivations of lower-class converts. At the same time, missionaries also believed in a "filtration" theory according to which subordinate groups might emulate higher-class converts. Yet there were comparatively few converts in the Brahmaputra valley, of whichever class. Peasant society in Assam, lacking strong landlord-tenant ties, had developed a powerful substitute in the patronage links maintained by the satras dotting the countryside, with tithe-paying disciples from every rank of society. Close ties between spiritual preceptors and their disciples were difficult to break for both peasants and gentry. Even more than the ubiquity of caste ties, these links may account for the scanty harvest that the mission achieved, and also for the frequent complaints of "backsliders."[102] Unlike in Punjab or the Madras Presidency, Assam's looser caste structures meant there were no pariah groups to whom Christianity might offer deliverance. In 1858 there were only fifty Assamese Christians, after twenty-five years of exertion by twenty-two missionaries.

It is not surprising that the arrogance of the Gosain's curse should have evoked pent-up missionary spleen. The missionary editor of the

Orunodoi roundly condemned a people so credulous as to attribute powers of life and death to priests, as well as the allegedly godly personages who encouraged their beliefs.[103] But better sense later prevailed. The periodical's next issue carried a disclaimer of the curse in a letter from the Gosain.[104] The Gosain's curse was depicted as an example of bucolic foolishness and rumour mongering. In the aftermath of this incident the colonial state took pains to mend its relationship with the major spiritual lords. The contrast could not be sharper between Captain Butler's low opinion of Gosains in the 1840s and the eulogy delivered in B. C. Allen's district gazetteers in 1906. Allen observed, "The Gosains have always been distinguished by their loyalty to Government and render a real service to the administration by encouraging purity of life and obedience to the authorities."[105] The deputy commissioner's annual tours now culminated in his stay as an honoured satra guest at the newly built guesthouses on the Auniati and Dakhinpat estates at Majuli.

Still, an important distinction should be made between the prominent landholding satras and the many petty Gosains with precarious economic positions and a large following among the lower castes. In 1894 these petty lords apparently "instigated" peasant protests at the *raij mels* (village assemblies) against an inflated revenue assessment.[106] In contrast, almost all the major, wealthy satra heads stayed aloof from any kind of political activity.[107] For the most part British incorporation of these grandees was successful. Most prominent Gosains were unwilling to defy the Raj. Their role as social leaders was gradually usurped by their disciples, the service gentry turned intelligentsia.

Once it became clear that the *Orunodoi* was not making inroads into the Gosains' social constituency, many locals were ready to applaud its patronage of the vernacular. Almost a century after its inception, an author remarked that local villagers were still in the habit of referring to any periodical paper that they came across by what they regarded as its generic name — as an Orunodoi.[108] Rather than face a head-on collision, the periodical saw its unique position gradually eroded as local groups began to employ similar techniques. The anthropologist Jean Comaroff's argument is pertinent: while missions helped to establish the conditions on which the colonial state was founded, they simultaneously communicated "a language for contesting the new mode of domination."[109] In the 1870s the Auniati Gosain acquired a printing press at Jorhat, the Dharma Prakash Press. The satra circulated a vernacular paper, the *Asom Bilasini*, as well as an assortment of devotional texts.[110] In addition, Gunabhiram Barua and other members of a new generation of gentry publicists, who had started their careers writing in the *Orunodoi*, subsequently launched their own ventures such as the *Assam Bandhu* periodical. By the late nineteenth century an Assamese intelligentsia based in Calcutta evolved a variety of print enterprises in the Asomiya language. Indigenous cultural entrepreneurs almost completely displaced missionary-controlled print modernity. To borrow a term used by the historian Rosalind O'Hanlon in describing western India, missionary periodicals had articulated a "crisis in legitimacy."[111] This crisis facilitated the emergence of small but vocal groups of social reformers who selected from an eclectic variety of ideas to form their own independent critiques of Hindu society.

As the influence of the *Orunodoi* waned, some Baptist missionaries began to look beyond the Assamese plains communities which had provided such limited gains. The shift in priorities by a fresh generation of missionaries in the 1870s is obvious. The *Orunodoi* was issued very irregularly, until its demise sometime in the 1880s. The mission press moved from Sibsagar to Guwahati and gradually "rusted away," with the occasional print job farmed out to commercial concerns.[112] New missionaries blamed the valley's barren harvest on its people's innately "conservative" character. "Their history proves them to have been always timid of innovation. When the Mohammadan faith spread like a flood over Southern Asia, it never gained a strong foothold here . . . This extreme conservatism has been one of the chief hindrances to the progress of missions."[113] The mission's attention turned full circle, back to earlier attempts at claiming preliterate hill tribes. In place of intellectual activity, missionaries undertook to provide basic medical and educational facilities to these groups, especially in remote tracts where state infrastructure was practically nonexistent. For instance, Edward Clark began work in the Naga Hills in 1871. As the hill districts became the new centre of Baptist activity, condemnations of the Brahmaputra valley's caste society increased, making it a scapegoat for the missionary failure to achieve conversions.[114] The failure in the plains made the prospect of learning hill and tribal tongues more attractive. Missionaries now eagerly anticipated working among "non-idolaters" with "no distinctions of caste, or priesthood."[115] The missionary O. L. Swanson noted encouraging responses from unlettered communities such as the "Kols and Mundaris" of central India, then entering Assam as indentured coolie labour for the tea industry.[116] Another hill people, the Garos, also entered the Baptist orbit. Garos voluntarily sought out the Guwahati mission and returned to their villages as preachers for a new god. American Baptists began to avow that "missions seem to have been more successful among the aboriginals proper."[117] The gentry of the Assam plains gradually receded in importance, as missionaries decided that hill tribals and "aboriginal" migrant coolies were their true flock in place of the unresponsive caste gentry.[118]

5. Bringing Progress, Restoring Culture

IN THE 1870S AN ASSAMESE YOUTH, Lakshminath Bezbarua (1864–1938), began his college career at Calcutta. Lakshminath came from a prominent gentry family which in the past had provided physicians for the Ahom kings. In the new circumstances of British India, the family's elder sons had all proceeded to Calcutta for a college education. But the father, Dinanath, was grieved when Lakshminath, his third son, made the same choice. He had hoped that this younger son might carry on the family's medical tradition. But like his brothers before him, Lakshminath did not wish to become a traditional healer.[1] In the manner of most of his contemporaries, Lakshminath's sojourn away from home nurtured a dream of modern *unnati* (progress). Even as he married into the prestigious Bengali Tagore family and carved out a career outside Assam, Lakshminath Bezbarua constructed his public image as an Assamese patriot—a champion of the Asomiya language and its cultural heritage of devotional religion.

The Asomiya language's print and literary efflorescence from the second part of the nineteenth century bore eloquent testimony to the self-consciously modern public which generated it. This public's most visible constituent was the Brahmaputra valley's élites. In colonial Assam that class, which provided both the Ahom and British regimes with their service gentry, was regrouping as a colonial intelligentsia. Its publicists wrote and imagined into existence a new Assam. The colonial state took almost a century to create modern transport, communication, and even a proper educational infrastructure for the region. In their absence Assam's élites largely depended on educational facilities in the nearest metropolis, Calcutta, the quintessential centre of commercial and cultural entrepreneurship. There they would "mess" together (sharing a house with a common kitchen rented by students from the same district or region) to acquire college degrees and a love of the motherland. In the colleges, bookshops, streets, and messes of Calcutta, they withstood the snubs meted out to them as provincial nobodies. There they found solidarity of brotherhood linked to region and mother-tongue.

Using the abundant and cheap infrastructure offered by the city's presses and meeting-halls, a new Assamese public gradually formed, its goal being to create modernity for the homeland. Its members dreamed of creating progress and restoring the impressive cultural credentials that they glimpsed in Assam's past. The ease and relative cheapness of print technology helped them to achieve their objective of creating a modern oeuvre for the Asomiya language. Their literary mission was accompanied by a reformist campaign to eradicate the stigma of opium consumption and thus of Assamese indolence. Just as they sought to replace the opium consumption of their fathers with temperate tea, they wished to substitute the vagaries of old-style religious heads with the deified figure of a historical spiritual leader. These publicists wished to restore local Vaishnavism to its pristine state under its founding father, Sankardeb. This, they hoped, would install Assamese Hinduism to its rightful place alongside other types of Indic devotional religion. That in turn would emphasize the gentry's kinship with caste élites in other regions of the subcontinent, and its distance from Assam's tribal and coolie population.

This chapter analyses how this regional élite engaged with notions of progress and patriotism as something that could be learnt in the colonial metropolis and transported home. Their tools were voluntary associations, clubs, public meetings, petitions, and pamphlets. Step by step they carried their task and its tools back to their homeland, to inspire an expanding audience and motivate younger generations of publicists with new aims and objectives. Education, religion, and culture served as the means to connect emerging regional and national identities and concerns, and as vehicles to achieve improvement and progress. To achieve their goal of progress, they initially sought state support. However, British obduracy on issues such as opium sales and the racism of tea's emergent Planter's Raj gradually drew this local agenda of progress away from a colonial vision of improvement and toward alternative nationalist dreams.

Education and Urban Mobility

In his memoir the Assamese official Harakanta Barua (1813–1900) described the ease of obtaining government employment in the 1820s. It was enough for his clerk brother to introduce him to the British district collector.[2] Through much of Harakanta's working life the colonial regime continued to rely on such informal networks of patronage and rank to staff its institutions. But from the late nineteenth century there was an increasing professionalization of government structures. Social connections remained important, but appointment to clerical and other "respectable" service jobs increasingly needed certificates. Even for the sons of mauzadars (revenue collectors), usually assured of succession, higher education was crucial to expanding social capital. Educated caste Hindu men were the most favoured for these new educational and service opportunities. The occasional scion of Muslim or Ahom gentry also obtained them. As yet, "tribal" names were few in the roll of educated employees.

Assamese gentry increasingly sought new education along western lines as the key to better jobs and speedier promotions in the colonial administration. Service jobs were important to augment family income and status. Relatively few Assamese households possessed connections or wealth of the magnitude of landed families in other regions. Even spiritual lords of the upper echelons, who possessed sizeable rent-free estates, often found it worthwhile to invest in higher education for their sons. Less well-to-do members of the gentry struggled to finance some amount of secondary education. Often a college degree was beyond their reach. Clerical remuneration from government employment was especially important for gentry households which possessed some land but few sources of cash income. Plantation clerkships provided other, albeit less coveted openings. Daughters were rarely sent to school until the early twentieth century, but many girls learnt to read and write the Asomiya language at home.

For the generations that succeeded Harakanta Barua, involvement with teachers, schoolmates, and urban life played an increasingly important role in their transition to adulthood. Despite the popularity of western pedagogy, the basics of reading and writing usually began in a domestic setting. During Harakanta's childhood his elder brother taught him to read and write in Asomiya at home. By that time the political turmoil of the Burmese invasion had shut down

Assam's *tols* and *pathshalas* (traditional schools). In later years Anandaram Dhekial Phukan's cousin Gunabhiram Barua (1837–94) described how the family's sons were taught the Sanskrit and Bengali alphabets at home, by older male relatives and specially appointed pandits.[3] His Brahmin family's close ties to Indic high culture explained these language choices. The father of Padmanath Gohain Barua (1871–1946) instructed him in Asomiya alphabets even before school began. His sister taught him to write with quills on banana leaves.[4]

Proceeding further into the educational system necessitated a novel degree of interaction with colonial institutions. From the 1840s most high-status males attended, whenever possible, new institutions offering western education. A pioneering advocate of such education had been Anandaram Dhekial Phukan's father, Haliram Dhekial Phukan (1802–32), who represented the cream of precolonial society. Well versed in Asomiya, Bengali, and Sanskrit lore as David Scott's right-hand man, he had helped to establish the Guwahati Collegiate English School in 1835.[5] The growth of these schools was slow. Unlike in Calcutta and Bombay, where colonial educational structures penetrated earlier and deeper, in Assam the starting age for institutional schooling remained late, depending upon available infrastructure and family resources. Padmanath Gohain Barua joined a lower primary school only at the age of eight. Officially the primary school syllabus, "reading, writing, fundamental rules of arithmetic, bazaar and zamindari accounts, and elements of mensuration (land surveying)," was intended for the lower masses of the population.[6] In reality it was mostly the gentry that availed itself of such an education. Primary schooling was an investment that allowed genteel yet impecunious youths to qualify for positions as village accountants. Poorer and lower-caste students lagged in enrolment, needing to earn a living. Even among the gentry, only more affluent youths could afford to join the Middle English level, where instruction was in Bengali and English. Asomiya replaced Bengali as the official language in 1874, when schools began Asomiya and English instruction.

The number of schools in Assam increased during 1884–85 from 1,656 to 1,800, and of pupils from 56,858 to 58,755. Most of this growth was at the primary level. In 1884 there were just nine high schools. By 1886 there were fourteen.[7] In 1875 Assam had eleven normal schools to train teachers, some run by the government, others by missionaries. The teacher-training schools run by the S.P.G., American Baptist, and Welsh Presbyterian missionaries mostly catered to members of their flock: pupils "from three aboriginal races, Mikirs, Garos, and Kacharis."[8] Well into the twentieth century Assam's new educational institutions were few in number. High schools were in only a few towns. Because of this, the acquisition of colonial education necessitated sojourns beyond village and natal households. Kin and caste ties were tapped in the quest for accommodation. Even so, students faced hardship, sacrifices, and emotional dislocation over their scholastic years. Padmanath left home to attend the nearest high school, at Sibsagar, where he lodged with relatives. Lambodar Bora (1860–92) obtained no formal schooling until he was twelve, when a primary school opened in his village. When he proceeded to the Middle School at Tezpur he lived in a friend's shed, where he cooked his own meals.[9] Government reports darkly insinuated that "a boy who had no relatives or friends to take him in is almost compelled to find shelter in one of the quasi-monastic institutions, which are reported to be generally little better than brothels and dens of vice."[10] This insinuation referred to the practice of several satras (Vaishnavite monasteries) of housing schoolboys who assisted the celibate monks. There is no evidence that the warning had any basis other than British suspicion of monastic morals.

From the 1870s the government established a few student boarding houses. By 1883 nine were open, with a total of 127 boarders.[11] The education report mentioned that "free lodging is supplied at the Government boarding houses, with some servants, and a master of the school is placed in charge with free quarters assigned to him; but the inmates make their own arrangements as to food and meals."[12] But these boarding houses, like the high schools, were too few to cater to the entire region. Also, public prejudices about common living across caste and sectarian boundaries remained strong. The difficulty of suitable accommodation explained "why so large a portion of the high school students are sons of government officials and of traders residing in the town."[13] This problem was much more acute for girls, since most parents were unwilling to send them away from home.

College education was an even more ambitious and expensive venture. Even well-to-do families whose sons had access to high schools hesitated before they sent their sons to college. College education was unavailable in Assam for a long time. For most of the nineteenth century obtaining a college education necessitated a long, expensive journey and a long sojourn in Bengal proper. Government policy dictated, partly as economy and partly as ideology, that Assam should not require a separate infrastructure for higher education. Administrators believed that "natives of the province should resort to Bengal to prosecute their studies, and thus enlarge their minds by contact with a higher civilisation, than that an expensive Government college should be maintained for them in Assam."[14] In 1892 a landlord in Sylhet endowed the Murarichand College. Only in 1901 did the government establish the Cotton College at Guwahati.

A sojourn at Calcutta or Dhaka for college study meant a significant material investment, although the state provided small scholarships. Lambodar Bora financed his college education by teaching in a school in the remote Naga Hills, where better-qualified instructors were difficult to recruit.[15] Upendra Nath Barua put himself through law college by working as a postal clerk.[16] Other obstacles might block entry into the new urban world. Some families were reluctant to allow sons to cross local and ritual boundaries. After he passed the college entrance examination, Bolinarayan Bora (1852–1927) ran away to Calcutta with the help of a Bengali mendicant. When he won a prestigious Gilchrist scholarship to the Cooper's Hill engineering college in England, his orthodox father forbade him to accept it. For the rest of his life Bolinarayan remained an outcaste to his ritualistic family after he crossed the ocean.[17] Many college-educated youths justified these fears when they transgressed ritual bounds. Gunabhiram Barua's behaviour was deemed scandalous when he married a widow and joined the heterodox Brahmo sect. In another departure from accepted custom, he sent his daughter to be educated at Calcutta's Bethune School. Lakshminath Bezbarua married Pragyasundari Devi, a granddaughter of the Brahmo reformer Debendranath Tagore. Incensed, his orthodox family contemplated a lawsuit. Bolinarayan Bora's outcaste status was confirmed when he married a daughter of the Bengali civil servant and writer R. C. Dutt.

In 1841 Anandaram Dhekial Phukan had travelled to the Hindu School with an entire ship to himself and his retinue of Brahmin cooks and a Bengali clerk. The splendour of his lifestyle earned him the sobriquet "Assamese Raja."[18] Later generations of students had more modest means and little access to Calcutta's élite society. The quasi-domestic camaraderie of the "mess" system, rather than family or caste ties, helped them to adjust to urban life. As the historian Pradip Sinha notes, urban practices of dining together and commensality diluted caste norms to some degree for the young men who messed together.[19] Padmanath described how new students had to brave the perils of steamer and train travel. They ate strange food in wayside hotels until they finally arrived at an Assamese mess in Calcutta. Often an address was the only information that the new students had about the city. There the comfort of familiar food and language was backed up by the expertise of seniors. The mess was an introduction to an "associational culture" that created bonds of mother-tongue and motherland.[20] Still, a *chatra samaj* (student community) remained circumscribed by caste and gender.[21] It was entirely male, and lower-class students were mostly absent. Decades later, dormitories at Cotton College still segregated lower-caste and tribal students in separate buildings.[22]

A comparison between Harakanta's and Padmanath's memoirs reveals a significant shift in emphasis from relationships founded on ties of kinship and social hierarchy to a stress upon comradely ties and relationships of affect. The new consciousness of a common language and nation developed alongside this shift. The Assamese student community in Calcutta led the way as it negotiated the infrastructure of urban modernity. By 1862 over 56 percent of all undergraduates in Calcutta colleges were from outside the city. After the 1870s the Bengali gentry founded four new colleges, Metropolitan Institute, Albert College, City College, and Presidency College (later Ripon College), whose affordable fees and lenient admission requirements attracted poorer, provincial students.[23] While Presidency College charged Rs 12 a month and missionary colleges charged Rs 5, new colleges such as Metropolitan charged only Rs 3.[24] Students from Assam, Bihar, Orissa, and East Bengal enrolled in these colleges in Calcutta. The mess became the chief space for socializing these provincial sojourners. It was managed on strictly democratic lines, and the "voice of the majority" was decisive.[25] The Congress politician Bipan Chandra Pal, who hailed from Sylhet, described in his autobiography how mess managers were elected monthly by all the students. Disputes were settled by a "court of the Whole House."[26]

Benedict Anderson's notion of the "secular pilgrimage" seems apposite to characterize the sojourners' experiences of the colonial city.

A college education and its attendant urban processes precipitated a perceptible shift in the Assamese gentry's mental landscape.[27] Harakanta Barua's and Padmanath Gohain Barua's accounts of their lives, written half a century apart, make this shift clear. Harakanta seldom mentioned educational experiences and friendships. Interactions with kin and social superiors were the main subject of his narrative. In contrast, Padmanath chose to structure the story of his life around friendships as well as his educational and associational life.[28] His account shows how the creation of a homeland within the city fostered a strong sense of oneness of language and heritage. During their stay in Calcutta these young men articulated a sense of an Assamese nation. Later this consciousness worked its way back into Assam's towns. Given the uneven urban development in British India, only a sojourn in teeming Calcutta could provide the excitement of urban modernity for Assam's nascent intelligentsia, as it did for other provincial sojourners.[29]

Like their counterparts from Bihar and Orissa, Assamese students often criticized Calcutta's inhabitants as devoid of courtesy. Assamese and Oriya students were particularly scorned when they spoke in their own tongues, which Calcuttans likened to rustic Bengali dialects. Even courteous friends and well-wishers stumbled offensively on this sensitive issue of language. Lakshminath described how he became friendly with two Bengali youths who brokered his marriage with their cousin. They, and their famous uncle Rabindranath Tagore, while appreciative of Lakshminath's literary talents, felt that they would be wasted if he wrote in Asomiya. They advised him to write in the Bengali language, since it offered greater scope for fame. To counter such accusations and to improve and modernize Asomiya, several young men, led by Chandrakumar Agarwala, Lakshminath Bezbarua, and Hemchandra Goswami, formed the Assamese Students' Literary (ASL) Club and sponsored weekly tea parties. Meetings, pledges, and oral perorations on bringing about Assam's progress led to social improvement campaigns and print productions. The club's paper *Jonaki*, started in 1889, soon superseded the *Orunodoi* as the periodical of note. Succeeding generations termed this the "Jonaki Age." For Padmanath, the alienation engendered by city life and Bengali hegemony was countered by ties of affect created with improvement-minded peers. Even when this student community was dissolved by the imperatives of adult life and careers, the bonds created during his existence in Calcutta endured through subsequent careers.

Replacing Opium with Tea: Making Progress

⌈For the young members of this new public there was an urgent task close at hand: to rescue the Assamese from the disgrace of being known as *kaniya* (lazy) opium eaters.⌋Colonial officials summarily condemned the region's population as "indolent sensual non-pro-gressive beings"[30] because of their "continued attachment" to "a single article of commerce, opium."[31] In the eyes of the jaundiced British observer, "kanee or opium [was] consumed by all classes, high and low, rich and poor, old and young, men, women, and even children."[32]

Opium smoking began as a Mughal-inspired fashion among As-sam's élites. As the antiquarian Benudhar Sarma observed, "during those days, among the things that denoted a dangariya [big man], one was the use of opium."[33] During the 1830s a medical survey found opium in use among 80 percent of the Assamese population.[34] Expanding use gradually modified élite attitudes to this habit, espe-cially as the availability of imported refined opium increased the possibility of addiction and diffused consumption across class lines. Maniram Barbhandar Barua initially distinguished between the older, aristocratic consumption of opium as a luxury, imported from beyond Assam's borders, and the subsequent prevalence of local cultivation and consumption.[35] He expressed indignation at only one class of opium eaters: "low people as Doomnees, Gorionees and Meereonees [Dom, Goriya, and Miri women]."[36] Rather than con-demn opium per se, he condemned popular dissemination. Opium's moderate use remained acceptable for upper-class males for a while. Through the nineteenth century opium continued to be widely con-sumed, not unlike *bhang* (hashish) elsewhere. It enjoyed religious sanction through the *kaniya sabhas* (opium assemblies) of local Vaishnavism. High-caste norms frowned upon rice beer and other kinds of alcohol, tea was still an urbanized, expensive good, but opium was familiar, and tolerated.

British attitudes to opium were divided. Well into the 1890s colo-nial medical opinion held to its necessity in malarial areas and its efficacy for stomach remedies. Yet many district officials viewed Assamese opium use in a negative light, as one of the worst "social evils" in the countryside. They echoed Maniram's argument that opium consumption by peasants and lower-class women was the ultimate proof of social disorder.[37] This moral disapproval set the stage for a ban on local opium cultivation in 1861, but consumption was still permitted. Officials hoped that local peasants would turn to plantation labour to earn the cash needed to buy imported opium. In this manner the colonial morality on opium consumption stood revealed as a mere platitude. Instead of a sincere opposition to opium, the ban on cultivation was inspired by a dual set of economic imperatives: to provide labour for plantations, and to increase excise revenue.[38] Opium sales to cash-strapped peasants helped to promote colonialism's two most important commodities, tea and opium. Officials sought to mask this agenda with a vocabulary of temperance, thrift, and industry — virtues absent among the Assamese, in their judgement.

With support from American Baptist missionaries, segments of local opinion gradually coalesced against the cynical colonial policy on opium. In its very first issue in 1846, the *Orunodoi* published an approving report about a meeting of Sibsagar's gentry on opium prohibition.[39] Its anti-opium stance shows that these missionaries did not hesitate to oppose the British state on matters of conscience. Also, the Baptists had another motivation to oppose opium's continuance. They gleefully reported a government penalty imposed on the Auniati Gosain for his condoning of opium cultivation.[40] The mission's temperance campaign was encouraged by its satra rivals' links with opium.

The Vaishnavite institutions' encouragement of opium use infuriated young Assamese reformers, some of whom were already critical of the satras' religious exactions upon the peasantry and called for a return to an original, pure, devotional faith. Hemchandra Barua (1835–96) powerfully expressed these sentiments in his play *Kaniyar Kirtan* (Song of the Opium-eater). When it appeared in 1861 this play introduced into Assam the genre of didactic social drama, already familiar to the Calcutta urban public but new to Assam. Dramatic works in the Asomiya language were so far limited to handwritten religious texts. Gosains wrote religious dramas as a sign of devotional virtuosity. Their works followed in the tradition of

Sankardeb, the Vaishnavite founder, who had composed a number of devotional one-act plays called Ankiya Nat. Satras regularly performed religious-themed compositions upon festive occasions. In contrast, Hemchandra Barua's secular play was a modern, reformist innovation which other young writers emulated with plays that advocated widow remarriage, lampooned new Bengal-inspired fashions, and portrayed legendary figures from a heroic past.[41] The dramatist himself was a self-professed atheist with a minimum of formal education.[42] He articulated a pungent critique of high-caste superstition and clerical corruption through an idiom of rational scepticism. The play's title, *Kaniyar Kirtan*, alluded to the *kirtan*, the Vaishnavite genre of devotional song. The play itself was a cautionary satire about Kirtikanta, a rich mauzadar's son whose frequent enjoyment of the opium assembly, in the company of a lewd woman and a hypocritical *bhakat* (monk), reduced him to utter poverty. In consequence, Kirtichandra was unable to pay his revenue dues to the government, took recourse to stealing, and finally died a repentant death in prison. This plot was clearly inspired by the Victorian temperance tracts which missionaries circulated. However, it also marked the first appearance in print of a long-standing folk tradition of lampooning religious authority, personified by the gluttonous, tyrannical monk. Hemchandra gave this tradition a new significance when he linked it to a critique of the opium consumption that his generation viewed as morally reprehensible and socially wasteful. Scenes set in colonial institutions such as the revenue office and the prison framed this narrative of degeneracy and redemption in which the author declared, "The opium-eater has destroyed the Assam homeland."[43] The moral message garnered patronage from the reform-minded. Despite the government's ambivalence on opium, Utsavananda Goswami, a deputy inspector of schools, financed the first printing. Its second edition was supported by another official, A. C. Campbell.

Even after the play gained approval from high quarters, the colonial state's forked tongue on opium policy continued. It encouraged the sale of imported opium, which was more refined than the banned domestic variety and caused a more pronounced degree of addiction. In 1874 the state introduced retail sales at licensed outlets. In that year 5,070 shops received a license to sell opium. Opium sales, excise revenues, and consumption sharply rose. The price almost tripled, from Rs 14 in 1860 to Rs 26 in 1879 and Rs 37 in 1890. For the Indian government in 1870–71, of 51 million pounds in revenue, 8 million was from opium sales.[44] Once the imported opium was sold in Assam, excise revenues increased. By 1880 opium was the highest contributor to state coffers.[45] Of Assam's excise revenue of Rs 19 lakhs, more than Rs 15 lakhs was from opium sales.[46] Still, the state looked the other way: "it is impossible to be strict among the Assamese where the habit has grown inveterate, nor is there any sufficient evidence to show that opium is generally consumed to an extent which is injurious to health."[47]

In Britain itself public opinion and medical expertise began to be concerned about the dangers of opium consumption. In 1868 the Pharmacy Act restricted the sale of opium in Britain to professional pharmacists. From 1874 the Anglo-Oriental Society for the Suppression of the Opium Trade opposed the British diffusion of opium in India and China.[48] Eventually, in 1893, the pressure of British prohibitionist opinion caused the creation of a royal commission to enquire into opium use in India. The Assam hearings extended over a week. A large number of witnesses were summoned to Calcutta, including British government officials, planters, and several members of the Assamese gentry. The European witnesses asserted that Assam's common people had always believed in the medical efficacy of opium, and that it would be cruel to prohibit all opium sales, as reformists had urged. Assamese planters echoed this opinion. These arguments hinged on the nature of work and the common worker's habitual use of opium. The veteran planter Samuel Peal told the commission that he used to pay his local labour force over half their wages in opium.[49] The commission's star witness was Assam's excise commissioner J. J. S. Driberg. He argued that opium was a locally important medicine, that "rightly or wrongly, the people certainly believe [opium] to be an antidote against fever, malarial diseases and bowel complaints."[50] In a strange contradiction of the usual view that the Assamese were indolent and weak because of their opium-eating habits, Driberg asserted, "A man who has had his opium will do his work, whether in the garden or in the field, much better than a man who has not."[51]

At the other end of the spectrum were men such as Gunabhiram Barua and Upendra Nath Barua, who represented the ASL Club of Calcutta. Keen to rehabilitate Assam and its people from the drug, they vehemently denied that opium had any medicinal properties against malaria, dysentery, or black fever. According to them, opium eating was losing social acceptance. In contrast to Driberg's tale of how a habitual opium eater was able to be summoned for any arduous task, they declared that nowadays such a man was one "who commits all sorts of vices, and he is looked down upon."[52] In the past opium had been widespread in Assamese society, "either to treat some disease, or for pleasure,"[53] but respectable people now opposed it. These members of the ASL Club also argued that opium use was dangerous since it reversed the natural gender order: "Everyone must have heard that it is opium that has gone to make man woman, and woman man in Assam."[54] Upendra Nath Barooah even translated Hemchandra Barua's *Kaniyar Kirtan* into English and presented it to the commission to show the strength of anti-opium sentiment among Assam's new public.

Nonetheless, there was no simple dichotomy between the British advocacy of opium and opposition from locals. This was clear from the evidence given by two Assamese tea planters, Jagannath Barua and Munshi Rahmat Ali. Jagannath Barua (1851–1907) was the president of the Jorhat Sarvajanik Sabha, Upper Assam's leading organization of landholders. He declared that opium was necessary to treat many diseases. Prohibition would bring great hardship to opium users.[55] His planter colleague Rahmat Ali observed, "Well-to-do or respectable people have given it up, and the coolies who cannot avoid it must take it."[56] In Ali's view Assam's poor tribal labourers, Mikirs and Kacharis in particular, depended on opium to sustain the hard manual labour that brought them a livelihood, and would suffer immensely if it were suddenly unavailable.

Jagannath Barua, colloquially known as B. A. Jagannath, was a well-known figure, Upper Assam's first college graduate and an early member of the ASL Club who subsequently received the prestigious rank of Rai Bahadur from the British government. His disagreement on this matter with other Assamese gentry educated in Calcutta illustrates the social complexities created by colonial policy. He declared that if opium sales were ended, people would not tolerate more taxes to replace the excise gap. Under his leadership in 1884 the Jorhat Sarvajanik Sabha appealed for revocation of the opium cultivation ban to avoid increased taxes.[57] Unlike British planters, local non-white planters (and other landholders) did not enjoy revenue concessions: they held their lands at ordinary rates. The Jorhat Sarva-janik Sabha's opposition to opium prohibition was therefore due to fear of a revenue shortfall which the state might seek to rectify with additional taxes. For these local landholding élites the supposed moral degradation of the opium-consuming labouring classes was a small price to bear for a lower tax burden. In Jagannath Barua's words to the commission, "At the present moment, it is the people who take opium who pay the tax. If opium is abolished, the whole population will have to bear the cost."[58]

In both Britain and India, by the late nineteenth century represen-tations of opium had changed. Once regarded merely as a stimulant, it was now condemned as a pernicious drug. Advocacy of its stimulat-ing and medicinal qualities rapidly lost ground before criticism of its addictive, harmful ones, particularly as technological advances en-abled its refinement to dangerously pure levels. From the mid-nine-teenth century Assam's reforming public agitated against opium, but local opinion remained sharply divided. The peasantry stayed indif-ferent to the progressive message of the élites. Tea coolies obtained ready supplies of alcohol and opium from the Marwari traders' shops on every plantation. Yet most élites, concerned about the economic costs of reform, were willing to sacrifice the health and well-being of working-class opium eaters. For instance, the tea planter and opium merchant Haribilas Agarwala, influenced by his ties with the reform-minded intelligentsia, advocated the gradual easing out of opium, but not an outright ban. In 1894, after interviewing a host of individ-uals and organizations, the Royal Commission retained the status quo for British India on opium. It declared, "The movement in England in favour of active interference on the part of the Imperial Parliament for the suppression of the opium habit in India has pro-ceeded from an exaggerated impression as to the nature and extent of the evil to be controlled."[59] The operation of this Royal Commission on Opium underscored the complex institutional attitudes to opium consumption. The colonial state undertook the role of opium pro-curer. Its ostensible agenda was to curtail consumption, but in reality it connived at exactly the opposite result. The commission's ultimate failure to act was mainly due to the overarching importance of opium revenues to the British Empire.

Despite the state's failure to act, the anti-opium campaign in As-sam only increased in force. A majority of young people gradually joined its ranks. The deputy inspector of education noticed the generation gap on this issue: "Every pathshala [school] boy is taught to hate opium eating and I have never come to know of any instance of a schoolboy being addicted to that vicious habit."[60] The eradication of the Assamese opium eater became inextricably associated with the task of bringing progress. Eventually the Assamese students in Calcutta renamed their ASL Club the Asomiya Bhasa Unnati Sadhini Sabha (ABUSS, or Society for the Progress and Regeneration of the Asomiya Language). Their ambitious objective was to regenerate Assamese language, literature, and society.[61] In pointed refutation of their elders' habits, they met, temperately, at a weekly tea party. Over the next few decades their tea-drinking sessions gradually spread into the homeland. They ousted the opium of the caste Hindu (although not the rice beer of the tribal peasant). While participation in the older opium assembly revolved around religious sociability, the new public was bound by ties of affect to *bhasa* (language) and *des* (homeland). The young men of the ABUSS returned to Assam from their colleges in Calcutta as clerks, schoolteachers, writers, and struggling lawyers. Back in their homeland they proselytized against opium at the same time as they preached love of mother-tongue.

By the early twentieth century opposition to opium constituted the essential link between Gandhian nationalism and the local desire for progress. The socialist poet and Gandhian nationalist Jyotiprasad Agarwala was the grandson of the pioneering Kaya trader-turned-Assamese, Haribilas Agarwala. In the past Haribilas had invested his profits from the opium trade in a tea plantation at Tamulbari (Tezpur). In a neat instance of historical symmetry, his grandson Jyotiprasad became a major figure among the nationalists campaigning for freedom from opium addiction and foreign rule. While school and college students harangued women, elders, villagers, tribal, and coolie brethren against this social evil, an innovative mail-order trade advertised remedies for opium addiction on book jackets and in newspaper advertisements.[62] A fiery woman activist and schoolteacher from a lower-caste background, Chandraprabha Saikiani (1901–72), was the first to move an anti-opium resolution at a public meeting in Assam, that of the Asom Chatra Sanmilan (Assam Students' Conference) at Tezpur in 1919, with the eminent Bengali seer Acharya Prafulla Chandra Roy in the chair.[63] By the 1920s the

Congress-led anti-opium political campaign received prominent coverage in the region's first well-established vernacular newspaper, the *Asomiya*, financed and run by the Agarwala clan. Columnists drew parallels for readers with the larger international battle against opium spearheaded by the League of Nations, and with Chinese struggles.[64] At the local level, under Chandraprabha's leadership the women activists of the Mahila Samiti (Women's Association) organized public awareness campaigns about opium's ills. One global commodity, tea, flourished in the Assam garden. But it was the fight against another, opium, which allowed the Assamese imagination to locate itself within a larger global and Asian community which envisioned modernity and progress through "self-strengthening."[65]

"Babus," Local Entrepreneurs, and "Coolie" Subjects

In his autobiography Lakshminath Bezbarua recollected that tea was the usual beverage offered to visitors in his boyhood home during the 1870s.[66] Such lavish use of tea was then rare in rural homes. Reflecting on his own childhood in the second decade of the twentieth century, Benudhar Sarma observed that *sah-pani* (tea made with hot water) was too expensive except for special guests and that his modest household usually drank fresh cow's milk from their own animals.[67] This practice contrasted with that of the Bezbaruas and other wealthy families who early adopted "Calcuttiya" consumption mores. The use of tea was widespread in Calcutta, as shown by the ASL Club's "Tea Party" meetings in the 1870s. By the 1920s brewed tea was commercially available in many Assam towns. At Shillong, the hill-station capital, Khasi women traders sold cups of hot, sugared *cha* (tea) at the Bara Bazaar market.[68]

But in domestic settings in the early twentieth century, tea was not yet cheap enough for mass consumption on a large scale. Tea became the ubiquitous Indian beverage for élites and commoners alike only after independence, when domestic sales rose to rival exports in volume. In earlier decades among ordinary Assam households, it was in homes connected to its production where tea was most likely to be daily consumed. These included coolie households, which received a tea-dust ration alongside an equally low-grade ration of cheap rice as part of their remuneration. Low-grade tea was also widely available

as a perquisite of employment in the households of mohurirs (clerks)
and other supervisory staff on the Assam plantations.

Plantations recruited these clerical and supervisory employees
from local Assamese and Bengali-speaking families. The majority
came from the middling and upper castes, which sent the majority of
students to Assam's schools. These plantation jobs seldom demanded a high school diploma. Reports by the education department bemoaned that as soon as they learnt the rudiments of reading
and writing and reached middle school, students abandoned their
school education for these clerical jobs. It was "a general complaint
of schoolteachers that many of their pupils, when raised to the
higher section, leave in order to get appointments."[69] Plantation
clerkships were less prestigious and paid less than equivalent government positions. But since the demand for government jobs far exceeded the supply, these supervisory openings provided useful incomes for sons of the poorer gentry. Tea supervisory jobs included
those of the *burra mohurir*, who wrote letters and kept accounts; the
hazra mohurir, who counted how many coolies were working and in
the evening gave them their daily wages; and the *godown mohurir*,
who gave out new materials and tools, and weighed tea leaf.[70] Native
doctors formed another segment of this supervisory babu class. The
majority were Bengalis, since Assamese medical students were as yet
few in number. New European planters were cautioned about the
difference in social standing between these caste Hindu employees
and their subordinate coolies. Edward Bamber's account of tea plantation life observed that these babus had "on account of their caste
and occupation, a social status to which the pay they are drawing is
no guide."[71] Bamber warned novices that these garden babus were
the "middle classes" of local society, even if the most senior clerk
earned a mere Rs 20 a month. These supervisory staff owed their
relatively high status in local society to their caste position and the
respectable nature of their work. They were "styled in the vernacular
by a phrase which may be translated as 'respectable classes,'" in con-
tradistinction to the coolies.[72] In 1896 one such clerk, Durga Prasad
Majumdar Barua, wrote the comic play *Mohurir*, which sympathetically portrayed a tea plantation clerk who existed on Rs 15 a month
and was bullied by his British manager. In his account the oppression
of coolies received short shrift, preoccupied as he was with the interests of his own class.

The largely negative feelings of Assam's local élites toward tea labourers received wide public dissemination through an essay on the coolie published in 1887.[73] Its writer was the former Calcutta student Bolinarayan Bora, now an engineer educated in England who co-published an Asomiya periodical, the *Mau*, from Calcutta. Bolinarayan was an ardent believer in British rule as the harbinger of modernity for a benighted Assam. He supported the plantation system as an essential part of this modernity. But he scorned coolies as uncivilized savages and refused to believe the stories of their sufferings which the Bengali press had disseminated. Bolinarayan's essay graphically revealed the disdain with which many locals regarded coolie newcomers: "Reader, listen, to what manner of creature the coolie is, and how it lives. That whose body hue is blacker than the darkest hour of the night, whose teeth are whiter than even pounded rice, in whose home are to be found bird, pig, and dog, in whose hand is a bilati [foreign] umbrella, and in whose hands are held a hoe and basket among the tea bushes, that is what is called a coolie." What the historian Tony Ballantyne and other scholars have called the delusion of Aryanism then overtaking South Asian élites[74] is visible in the way Bolinarayan distanced his readers from the darker-skinned migrants whom they encountered in the Assam countryside. His essay relegated coolies to animal status. Simultaneously, Bolinarayan ridiculed the coolie adoption of western dress while they existed in filthy living conditions. Coolie consumption of meat, opium, and alcohol formed another mark of lowly status.

Bolinarayan's distasteful invective was reflective of another strand of opinion among Assamese élites: faith in the modernity which tea enterprise represented. Well-known intellectuals and social reformers such as Gunabhiram Barua remained silent about the "new slavery" linked with tea progress. Instead they exalted the egalitarianism which colonialism claimed to promote.[75] Paeans to the colonial tea industry were common in Asomiya works used as school readers, such as Padmanath Gohain Barua's *Assam Buranji*, first published in 1899. This first generation of Assamese publicists mostly concurred in the colonial claim that British rule in Assam had replaced premodern slavery with free labour. Paradoxically, this claim placed Assamese élites in opposition to a growing body of outside observers, especially Bengali intellectuals, who widely disseminated their knowledge of the semifeudal modes of coercion on tea plantations.

As Bengali observers critiqued the violent and inhumane tea system, they reverted to metaphors of bondage to expose its evils.[76] The initial exposés of the tea industry's abuses came from Bengali missionaries who visited Assam in the 1870s to proselytize on behalf of the modernistic religious organization the Brahmo Samaj, which had its headquarters at Calcutta. Ramkumar Vidyaratna was one of these missionary visitors.[77] Horrified by what he saw and heard of coolie conditions, he sent a searing exposé of planter abuses to the *Sanjibani*, a newspaper in Calcutta.[78] His article was followed by another English-language account of tea oppression by a Brahmo missionary, Dwarkanath Ganguli, *Slavery and British Dominion*. The title itself was a pointed rebuttal of British libertarian pretensions. Rather than the idyllic picture of Edenic redemption that planters claimed, the book recounted appalling details of coolie oppression. Yet another Brahmo activist, Gagan Chandra Home, wrote a novel in 1888, *Kuli Kahini*, widely compared to *Uncle Tom's Cabin*.[79] Bengal's vernacular newspapers such as the *Dacca Prakash*, *Shome Prakash*, *Hindoo Patrika*, *Amrita Bazar Patrika*, and the *Sanjibani* took up the cause of the Assam tea coolie. They printed a steady stream of articles, editorials, and letters that protested against planter atrocities, coolie kidnappings, and ill-treatment.[80] This issue offered nationalists an opportunity to flagellate colonial institutions on irreproachably humanitarian grounds. Their anti-colonial and anti-planter sentiments were echoed on the Bengali stage. Theatres in Calcutta staged a number of plays which attacked oppression by white planters, whether on Bengal's indigo plantations or Assam's tea plantations. The best-known was Dinabandhu Mitra's *Nil-darpan*, followed by Dakshinacharan Chattopadhyay's *Cha-kar-darpan*. These plays impelled the British to institute the repressive Dramatic Performances Act in 1876, which empowered the Bengal government to prohibit performances it deemed unsuitable for public viewing.

By contrast, many Assamese élites in the late nineteenth century still defended the tea enterprise, and by extension the planters. They claimed that tea ameliorated the lives of Indian peasants and regenerated Assam's economy. On the condition of coolies they were mostly silent. The only substantial contribution on this topic was Bolinarayan Bora's hostile piece in the periodical *Mau*. It did publish a dissenting note on Bora's sentiments, written by Lakshminath Bezbarua, the noted timber merchant and Asomiya litterateur, then based in Sambalpur (Orissa) and Calcutta. As yet, his was the lone local voice to acknowledge that the Assam garden was built upon migrants' life blood.[81] Since Assam still lacked a sustainable newspaper culture, the entire tea coolie debate took place in Calcutta papers. Hemchandra Barua's short-lived *Assam News*, published from Guwahati, did address the coolie issue, but only to protest the inconveniences that locals suffered when mistakenly impressed for labour. It remained silent on migrant coolies. Bolinarayan Bora's condemnation of "our newspaper writing friend of the coolie, the Bengali babu" expressed the tension between these two factions of the colonial intelligentsia. Unlike Bengali intellectuals, nineteenth-century Assamese publicists saw themselves as weak and lacking in influence. In their eyes the policies of the British state so far represented Assam's best possibility for progress.[82] For now Assam's élites, far from condemning the plantation system, still sought a place in the colonial sun.

While many sons of the Assamese gentry moved into urban employment and residence, their families maintained a base in the countryside. Brahmin and other noncultivating proprietors who had lost labourers with the end of slavery entered into sharecropping arrangements for their lands. The Auniati and Dakhinpat Gosains, the largest landowners in the Brahmaputra valley, held large estates on the Majuli island, cultivated by Mishing tribal peasantry. As the tea fervour spread, lawyers, traders, and retired clerks bought land with their savings. William Nassau Lees observed, "The natives . . . many of them, especially the court officials, are going in for tracts of lands at Rupees 2–8 an acre in the neighbourhood of villages, with a view of leasing them out to the ryots."[83] Local peasants and time-expired tea labourers both entered into such leases.

Some among the Assamese gentry ventured into the tea industry. Mostly they were hampered by lack of capital. They also lacked access to the privileges that the colonial state offered to British entrepreneurs. Racial barriers made it impossible for them to join white planters in organizations such as the Indian Tea Association. The often precarious economic condition of these local élites made it difficult to withstand slumps in tea prices. A British official noted that during the difficult years of the 1860s "a large number of respectable natives burnt their fingers in tea speculation and have been shy of retiring into any other since."[84] But since tea was practically the only outlet for economic entrepreneurship, others succeeded them in shouldering its risks. Savings accumulated from government service or professional earnings were used to buy tea lands. For instance, the revenue clerk Rudram Bordoloi held title for forty-five *bighas* at Haiborgaon (Nagaon), and smaller plots in other areas. He established a tea plantation on some of his land.[85] Similarly, Sheikh Danish Mohammad, a lawyer, used his savings to start a small plantation on forty-five acres.[86] Often petty planters leased additional land from the government or from big landlords. Debeswar Sarma got his start when the Auniati Gosain leased him land from the satra's considerable holdings near Jorhat. By 1903 fewer than 20 of the 112 estates in Sibsagar and Jorhat were in local hands. While British firms employed an average of 1,000 coolies (distributed among several gardens), native gardens usually had between 10 and 150. The biggest local planters were Jagannath Barua, with 400 coolies who worked 800 acres (he held 2,811), and Bisturam Datta Barua, whose 173 coolies worked 246 acres (he held 823).[87]

The Khongiya Baruas, the tea dynasty founded by Bisturam Barua, were the most successful among Assamese entrepreneurs. Bisturam began by supplying seeds to big colonial firms. As mauzadar of the Thengal area near Jorhat, he was able to coerce local Kachari peasants to grow tea on his lands. This was a quasi-feudal relationship that had Bisturam extracting unpaid labour from poor tribal clients.[88] Since Assamese planters like Bisturam lacked resources to set up factories, they usually had little option but to operate as subsidiaries of bigger British-owned gardens to which they supplied tea leaves and seeds. This strategy was risky, since big planters could arbitrarily increase or decrease quotas and set prices as they wished. The Khongiya Barua family managed to establish a secure hold only because of its long-term subordinate relationship with the powerful British managing agency Williamson, Magor and Co., which helped Bisturam set up a tea factory with its obsolete equipment.[89]

Assam's development as an imperial tea garden fostered hopes among its élites that all-round prosperity would follow. They resented any attacks on the industry as a threat to the prospect of achieving it. Yet locals began to chafe under the arbitrary racialism of the white planter establishment. Irrespective of status, every native was forced to stand at attention if a white person passed by. Since plantation grounds were closed to outsiders, villagers were compelled to take long, circuitous routes. Assamese planters were at the mercy of British tea firms to process and sell their harvest. From the

1880s the state granted a small degree of local self-government to Indians through the creation of municipal boards and legislative councils on which a few seats were elected. But since nominated members and the tea lobby's representatives together opposed substantive reform, these bodies were even less effective in Assam than in other regions.

By the early twentieth century many among the Assamese gentry openly critiqued the Planter's Raj. Mahatma Gandhi's visit to Assam in 1921 made his teachings widely popular throughout the region. Influenced by Gandhian reformism, Assamese nationalists condemned the racist, exploitative practices of European planters and in particular their treatment of migrant coolies. In 1924 the newspaper *Asomiya* ran pieces on the exploitation of workers on British plantations as many as six times over a period of three months.[90] Subsequently, in 1926 the Indian National Congress held its 41st annual session at Guwahati. Congress volunteers dedicated themselves to promoting temperance and reformist agendas among plantation coolies even as British planters sought to thwart them. The colonial state obstructed Congress and Communist attempts to unionize tea workers for as long as it could.[91] As many more middle-class political activists encountered planters' repression and arrogance firsthand, they became highly critical of the British-run tea industry and of colonialism.[92] Many, like Sankar Chandra Barua and Kushal Konwar, left plantation clerical jobs to join the nationalist cause.[93] Still, for the majority of Assam's gentry, the hope of progress and modernity from the tea enterprise, independent of colonial control, remained essentially inviolate.

Print, Progress, and Devotion

In his autobiography Padmanath Gohain Barua graphically described the genesis of the first Asomiya novel. His messmates at Calcutta, when they realized that there was not a single modern novel in the Asomiya language, locked him in until he finished writing his historical novelette *Lahori*. Thereupon they passed around the hat for the publishing expenses and rushed to the nearby Samya press to print the book, aided by a handout from Phukan, Majindar & Co., an Assamese trading firm based in Calcutta.[94] In this hand-to-mouth manner Padmanath and his messmates in Calcutta created the first self-consciously literary texts for modern Asomiya. Under the auspices of the ASL Club and ABUSS they aimed to fashion a modern print culture for the Assamese people.

From their abodes at Mirzapur, Harrison, and Middleton Streets in Calcutta, these youthful publicists addressed their peers in the city, and beyond it in Assam. They established informal networks to disseminate ideas, periodicals, and pamphlets. Their writing quality varied, since fervour often outstripped inspiration. Money was always short, but the youthful promoters were ready for immense sacrifices. Padmanath Gohain Barua almost bankrupted himself when he used his meagre reserves to publish the periodical *Bijulee*.[95] As the literary scholar Francesca Orsini observes, the colonial intelligentsia used language and literature as the means to define and communicate their agenda for progress. These then became metaphors for the nation: the strength of literature showed the strength of the nation, while the life of the language was the life of the nation.[96] The ABUSS subsequently sprouted branches all over Assam as members finished their studies in Calcutta and returned home to begin their careers.

However, this new Asomiya vernacular milieu lacked capital, both symbolic and material. In an absence of rich *zamindar* (landlord) patrons, members of the Assamese intelligentsia depended on their own slender resources. While they did try to harness what remained of traditional patronage networks, doing so had limited potential. Traditional wealth was represented by the pre-colonial aristocracy and the spiritual heads of the Vaishnavite satras. Most of the old aristocrats had fallen on hard times. By contrast, the continuing wealth and authority of the major satras, their traditional connections to scholarship, and organic ties with gentry intellectuals did bring some degree of involvement with the new print culture. Hemchandra Goswami, from a Gosain family, took a leading role in obtaining satra patronage for literary ventures. Through his efforts the wealthy Auniati Gosain made a substantial donation when the region's key literary organization, the Asom Sahitya Sabha, was instituted in 1917.[97] Even before the Calcutta print productions in Asomiya took off, the Auniati Gosain established the Dharma Prakash Press as a counterweight to the new kind of cultural patronage that missionaries had initiated. But without a viable machinery of production and distribution, the Gosain's serial productions had brief lives. The administrative report of 1888–89 mentions, "One new paper, a monthly Assamese, *Assam Tara* printed at the Dharma Prakash Press at the Auniati Satra in Sibsagar, and treats of religious, historical and literary subjects." Earlier, in 1883–84, another satra periodical, the *Asom Bilasini*, had faded away.[98]

From the 1870s various small presses appeared in Assam itself.[99] The major centres of this publishing enterprise were Goalpara, Nagaon, Guwahati, Sibsagar, and Jorhat. They included the Assam News Press, the Chidananda Press, and the Hitasadhini Press.[100] Their publications supplemented the Asomiya works that appeared from presses in Calcutta. The Assam-based presses operated on shoestring budgets and usually required authors to cover their own costs. An exception was made if the education department prescribed a work as a school textbook, a form of indirect state patronage that helped cover the publication costs for well-known works such as Gunabhiram's *Assam Buranji*, as well as translations of traditional didactic works such as the *Hitopadesa*.

Among Asomiya-language periodicals the best-known was the *Jonaki*, first published at Calcutta in 1889 and then at Guwahati from 1901. Others were the *Bijulee*, which first appeared from Calcutta in 1890 and then from Shillong, and the *Bahi*, which appeared from Calcutta in 1909 and then from Guwahati. The *Sadhana* appeared for a few years in the 1920s in Guwahati under the aegis of the All Assam Muslim Students Association. These were weekly or monthly periodicals with a limited circulation and print run. Nonetheless, as one disappeared another took its place. The *Asomiya* was a weekly that was the first vernacular newspaper to circulate all over Assam, from 1918 to 1947. It had deeper financial reserves than its predecessors thanks to its owners, the Agarwala business clan.

Without well-honed distribution and publicity channels, Assam's periodical and book trade was mainly conducted through the post office. Prospective readers ordered a book to be delivered through the post and had to pay postage costs in addition to the cover price. This discouraged many purchasers. The historian and poet Surya Kumar Bhuyan (1894–1964), himself a prolific writer, bemoaned the small reading public and the slow progress of literature: "The Assamese author publishes a book at a loss, and he is naturally shy in repeating his financially unprofitable experiment by publishing another book. To ensure a large circulation of his book, the Assamese author has to adjust the manner and matter of his writings to suit the mind of all readers ranging from the most highly educated scholar down to his semi-illiterate countrymen."[101]

Commercial logic also played an important role in shaping the contours of Assam's print culture. The same accessibility of print that encouraged intellectuals to engage in literary production also allowed the wide dissemination of cheap copies of religious texts. Many authors turned to the devotional genre of Asomiya publications, which offered better sales prospects than literature. Literary and social reformist texts by the new intellectuals, despite their prominence for future literary scholars, actually accounted for a minority of Asomiya publications. Vernacular readers preferred to buy printed versions of older, devotional texts, such as Vaishnavite scriptures such as the *Bhagavat Purana*. Although the satras continued to produce copies of handwritten religious manuscripts, those had limited scope. A new variety of devotional text — cheap editions of Vaishnavite scriptures and commentaries published by small local presses — were the most common printed material entering the Assamese home.[102] The *Orunodoi* carried an advertisement for two works by the Vaishnavite saint Madhabdev, published by the Dhekial Phukan family's Calcutta New Press.[103] Another pioneer in producing devotional printed works was the Dharma Prakash press in Jorhat. Steady demand for religious texts encouraged other, more commercially motivated presses to publish them. Businessmen such as Haribilas Agarwala showed their piety by financing the printing of canonical Vaishnavite scriptures. Another entrepreneur, Harinarayan Dutta Baruah (1907–58), was able to establish a successful publishing and bookselling business based on the publication of such texts.

This spread of devotional print culture accompanied and accelerated a transformation of religious belief and practice. In the Brahmaputra valley, where large landed proprietors were few in number, wealthy Gosains (monastery heads) wielded both spiritual and temporal influence over their flock. As notions of contract and good government provided an expanded basis for British authority, Gosains, the upholders of an indigenous social order based on cosmological concepts, proved important to the state through their role as local landlords. British administrators resolved the practical issues of rule as they developed links with these localized nodes of religious

✳ *Spread of devotional texts*

authority. These links helped to legitimize and sustain colonial state power. But by the late nineteenth century the popular acceptance of Gosains as omnipotent arbiters of social and religious authority was assaulted through abstract, overarching systems of print and associational culture.

Through the agency of print, older forms of authority gradually lost ground, while newer kinds of sacred authority came to the fore. Wide circulation of the textual message of Vaishnavism went hand in hand with a gradual dilution of the "godly" veneration of the Gosains. Popular oral culture often lampooned the stock figure of the bhakat (monk) as the epitome of corruption through its proverbs and folktales. This oral satirical tradition was newly disseminated through the medium of print.[104] Writings such as Hemchandra Barua's play *Kaniyar Kirtan* criticized monastic corruption and linked it with the evils of opium consumption. Lakshminath Bezbarua in his popular satires went even further by lampooning the awe-inspiring figure of the Gosain, the spiritual lord of Assamese Hinduism, as part of his call for a devotional reformation.[105]

While portraying Gosains as mortal men with mortal failings, these publicists invoked the name of Sankardeb, Vaishnavism's legendary founder, as the fount of Assam's unique cultural, religious, and literary traditions. Frequently these intellectuals needed to challenge competing versions of history which questioned the distinctiveness of Assam's religious heritage. For instance, the ABUSS waged a long struggle against British officials who had described the Bengali saint Chaitanya as the Vaishnavism's founder, with Sankardeb a mere follower. Their campaign to rehabilitate Sankardeb eventually triumphed, as the Census Report of 1911 acknowledged: "One point in connection with the Vaishnavism of Assam is worth considering, i.e., whether Sankardeb its founder, drew inspiration from Chaitanya, the great reformer of Bengal, as stated in the last two Census Reports of Assam. The Society for the Improvement of the Assamese Language has taken up the issue and strongly objects to the accounts hitherto given. It claims that Sankardeb was anterior to Chaitanya in birth and reforms."[106]

Through such campaigns these young publicists placed the fifteenth-century figure of Sankardeb at the centre of modern public veneration. They extolled the foundational role that Sankardeb and his disciples played in the development of Assamese culture and civilization, particularly the Asomiya language. The variety of Vaishnavite texts in print showed Sankardeb's importance as the pioneer who created Asomiya as a literary language. Gentry publicists created a literary canon and envisioned themselves as the saint's heirs, whose writings would usher the Asomiya language and Assamese society into a "modern age" and prove Assam's cultural distinctiveness, particularly vis-à-vis Bengal. To support their assertions they cited Indological scholarship which held that Asomiya derived from Sanskrit, as did Hindi, Marathi, and Bengali. Publicists used this linguistic genealogy to reiterate that the Asomiya language was "a sister of Bengali and not a daughter," an implicit denial of Bengali linguistic historicity and superiority.

This genealogy concealed the fact that a large part of Sankardeb's oeuvre was originally composed in another language, Brajabuli. Similar to Sanskrit and Pali, Brajabuli was a literary language, not a spoken one. It first gained prominence in the works of the fourteenth-century poet Vidyapati, in the Mithila region of Bihar. After him Brajabuli became popular as a poetic medium for devotional poets in northern and eastern India. Sankardeb's use of Brajabuli signified his close connections to this wider pan-Indian culture of bhakti religion and devotion to the god Krishna. But for the most part Assamese publicists elided Sankardeb's use of Brajabuli. Despite their eagerness to cast Sankardeb as an important figure in the canon of Indic devotional religion, they chose to underplay his use of a transregional linguistic idiom.

This elision sprang from the publicists' mission to acquire a higher status for the Asomiya language. Without the long historical pedigree for literary Asomiya that Sankardeb's writings provided, they were not confident that they could challenge the attribution of an inferior dialect status. When cast as the language of sacred worship, Asomiya became a formidable ingredient in assertions of the unique local identity of Assam. One writer asserted, "The religious books are in this language. So long as there will be Hindu religion and Hindu society, Assamese will be the language of Assam."[107] While publicists enthusiastically participated in imagining a larger Indic sacred landscape that encompassed previously marginal sites such as Assam, they simultaneously articulated a strong desire for local cultural particularity.

By the turn of the century Sankardeb moved from text to spiritual ancestor. Even as publicists glorified the unique heritage of Assamese Hinduism derived from Sankardeb's teachings, they recognized the shortcomings of the monastic satra institutions and their heads, the Gosains. Some began to openly criticize Gosain pomp and authority, oppression of disciples, and discrimination against lower castes. They viewed these practices as unsanctioned deviations from Sankardeb's egalitarianism. By the early twentieth century an organization dominated by non-Brahmins, the Sankardeb Samaj, established itself as a popular rival to the satras. In the name of a return to Sankardeb's original faith, the Samaj offered an alternative to satra rituals. For instance, it introduced a simple marriage ceremony independent of the customary Brahmin priest.

An important figure who sought to revive and modernize Assamese Vaishnavism was Lakshminath Bezbarua. His involvement with Vaishnavism stemmed from his father's close ties to the Kamalabari Satra. Lakshminath's memoir recounts the crucial importance of this devotional faith to his upbringing.[108] But after leaving Assam for his college education at Calcutta, Lakshminath began to revise the uncritical attachment to the satra culture that had characterized his childhood. In particular, his exposure to the Vedantic faith of the Adi Brahmo Samaj, the modernized Hinduism espoused by his Tagore in-laws, proved critical. Influenced by the Brahmo Samaj, he sought to integrate the teachings of Vedantism with the seemingly pure, egalitarian faith that he associated with Sankardeb. Through most of his adult life Lakshminath embarked upon a recovery of Assamese Vaishnavism's past through writings that celebrated Sankardeb's life and teachings.[109] Through these writings he also advanced a strong claim to place Assamese culture and devotional religion at the centre of a larger Indic universe.

Lakshminath's essay "Asomiya Bhasa aru Sahitya" (1910) purported to be about Assam's language and literature. In reality it was a history of the Assamese people, whom he depicted as spiritual heirs to ancient Hindus.[110] The most significant section of this essay covered the period from the mid-fifteenth century to the mid-sixteenth. Lakshminath characterized this era as the "age of revival of learning and Renaissance in Assam, as in Europe."[111] For righteous India (*dharmapran Bharatvarsha*) and Assam, he traced a cultural renaissance that differed from that of Europe. Rather than the arts, the Indic renaissance's key elements were the reformation and propagation of knowledge and learning (*gyan vidya*) and righteous religion (*dharma sanskar*). Lakshminath declared, "Everything for Hindus is

mingled with dharma, so how is it surprising that their cultural renaissance and reformation takes the form of righteous religion?"[112]
His lengthy list of Hindu spiritual leaders included the Buddha,
Shankarcharya, Ramanuja, Ramanand, Kabir, and finally Assam's
own Sankardeb. In his view the spiritual life of India's Hindus
reached a zenith with Sankardeb's Reformation in Assam.[113]

Apart from this seminal essay, many of Lakshminath's other writings helped shape the contours of a modern neo-Vaishnavite religion.
An influential series of articles published in his periodical *Bahi* provided devotional discussions, biographies of Vaishnavite holy figures, and historical information about the satras. Lakshminath also
used the genre of satire to great effect in his reformist efforts. Under
the nom de plume of a bumbling figure called Kripabor Barua, he
published a large number of satirical essays in serial form.[114] In these
satirical essays Lakshminath lampooned monks and even some revered satra heads. Stung by this, the powerful Auniati Gosain publicly rebuked him and stopped financial assistance to *Bahi*.

Within the close-knit circle of Assamese sojourners in Calcutta,
Lakshminath gained fame for his public celebrations of Sankardeb's
tithi (birthday).[115] These fetes derived inspiration from his Tagore
in-laws' commemoration of Brahmo festivals, and popularized a new
form of public ritual that focused on the individual saint. In 1924,
when the book-trade entrepreneur Harinarayan Dutta Baruah compiled a new version of the *Assam Buranji* chronicle, he added a chapter on the historical role of Sankardeb.[116] Subsequently Dutta Baruah collected and edited the writings of Sankardeb and his followers,
as well as publishing a number of old Vaishnavite manuscripts stored
by satras.

In 1934 Lakshminath's fame as a religious thinker led to a prestigious invitation from the learned Gaekwad ruler of Baroda (in
western India) to present a series of lectures about Sankardeb. Lakshminath was overjoyed. He hoped that this recognition could rescue Assam from opprobrium as the land of "opium-eaters" and "law-
less barbarians from the hills."[117] Instead Assam would become
known as the "land of Sankar bhakti," an important part of Indic
civilization and religion.[118]

From the late nineteenth century the efforts of Lakshminath and
other publicists brought Sankardeb a new role as Assam's cultural and
spiritual icon. They sought to restore Sankardeb to his rightful place as

Assam's representative within a lineage of Indic bhakti saints that included Chaitanya, Kabir, Nanak, Tuka, Mira, and others, drawn from different regions. While Sankardeb and other Vaishnavite preachers such as Madhabdeb, Damodardeb, and Harideb reached public deification, the Assamese satras lost most of their political and economic power, becoming instead custodians of the region's cultural and spiritual heritage. Lakshminath and other publicists discarded an older kind of identity that was dependent upon an established relationship with sacred geography and ritual boundaries. Instead they turned to an identity grounded in the newly minted categories of culture and progress. Paradoxically, this refigured identity was itself placed within an invented archaism of Bharatvarsha-India as nation. The bhakti saint Sankardeb became a potent symbol of local particularity within a pan-Indian pantheon of heroic spiritual icons.

6. Language and Literature
Framing Identity

ON 9 APRIL 1872 the lieutenant governor of Bengal, Sir George Campbell, received a memorial signed by over two hundred influential residents of Assam asking that the Asomiya language should be declared the official vernacular in place of Bengali. The memorial was the climax of a long campaign to convince British policymakers that the Bengali language was unacceptable to most inhabitants of Assam. This campaign was a joint effort by the American Baptist missionaries based in Assam and members of the local gentry. The missionary, Miles Bronson, headed the list of signatories. Exactly one year after this memorial the British state capitulated. It agreed to use the Asomiya language alongside English in the region's schools and courts.

Colonial encounters in the empire's garden were mediated by complex discussions involving language and race. Inspired by Romantic philosophy and the philological science to which it gave rise, nineteenth-century intellectuals viewed language as a product of nature and the fundamental defining parameter of culture.[1] Missionaries, colonial administrators, and local élites armed with this vision examined languages to discover the basic principles which demarcated one from another.

In pre-modern South Asia administrative, literary, and religious élites consciously selected languages for public use from a broad repertoire.[2] In sixteenth-century North India the same person might use Sanskrit for ritual purposes, Persian for administrative purposes,

Hindavi for leisure writing, and a local dialect to communicate with kin. Different linguistic registers were used for dissimilar purposes within the same region, even as many languages reached widely across regional boundaries. In the mid-nineteenth century ideas about language began to change. People still recognized variations of dialect and idiomatic usage. But now each language was believed to possess a standard root form. That standard form alone deserved state and public patronage. As a result, local élites helped to modify the acceptability of a previously multifunctional linguistic repertoire. In British India they promoted the notion of a *matri-bhasa* (mother-tongue) as the rightful linguistic choice for each region.

Mother-tongue was a novel, gendered identity conferred upon nineteenth-century vernacular, "literarized" languages. On the one hand intellectuals valorized mother-tongues as the property of home and hearth. On the other, they advocated the standardized, polite, and literary forms of these mother-tongues as most suitable for modern administration and public use. This differentiated them both from colloquial, localized, and lower-class dialects and from the languages of yore, now bestowed classical rank. An all-important question in a world of many mother-tongues was which ones had primacy. To ward off criticism from rivals, the chosen languages were portrayed as natural and timeless. Champions of a particular language astutely deployed a vocabulary of historical and emotional entitlement. This language strategy represented its subject as eternally true. Supporters portrayed a mother-tongue's claim as universally valid and commonsensical.[3] Until the early nineteenth century Assam's linguistic practices showed fluid, situational shifts in register and idiom. This chapter discusses the changes that occurred when the colonial state first gave a monopoly of official use to the Bengali vernacular. Assamese publicists opposed this measure and advocated the Asomiya language as the language of choice for the progress of homeland, literature, and family. Subsequently these élites deployed a newly discovered racial vocabulary of Indo-Aryanism to denigrate local languages and socially subordinate groups to which they ascribed non-Aryan status. Language became an essential means by which élites could imagine the past of Assam and aspire to its progress in the future.

Colonial Encounters with Language

The East India Company began its political career as a successor state to a weakened late Mughal regime. Having acquired the Diwani of Bengal in 1765, the company now had new responsibilities as a revenue collector and dispenser of justice that required its employees to possess a fair degree of linguistic proficiency. A command of Persian, North India's chief administrative language, was deemed essential. The historian Muzaffar Alam shows how the sixteenth-century Mughal emperors, the descendants of Chaghtai Turks, deliberately chose Persian as the public language of their dominions to buttress their cultural stature. In contrast to their native Turkish, the Persian language had a long and prestigious association with literature, culture, and diverse ruling classes. Unlike North India's Hindavi dialects, Persian possessed a rich and fairly standardized vocabulary and an accepted script. Persian also differed from Sanskrit, the sacral "language of the Indian gods," in its ease of use. Administrative and literary élites across Mughal lands became proficient in Persian but continued to use Sanskrit and other regional languages for literary, religious, and domestic purposes.[4] Even in Assam, a distant region which the Mughals repeatedly tried to conquer, rulers strategically patronized Persian scribes.[5] Unsurprisingly, the East India Company deemed it essential to continue this Persian linguistic and administrative tradition.

From the late eighteenth century British linguistic attitudes changed as the East India Company broadened its territorial and ideological reach. While the administrative use of Persian continued, many company employees were attracted to the Sanskrit language. Sanskrit seemed to provide the key to a vast reservoir of indigenous knowledge. Initially their quest to learn it was beset by difficulties. The main obstacle was the Brahmin pandit élite's reluctance to teach a sacred language to "unclean" foreigners. In the early years even the noted Orientalist William Jones, later Sanskrit's champion to the western world, was unable to employ a Brahmin scholar. Yet over the next decade Brahmin pandits experienced economic reverses as indigenous patronage decreased. The next generation of British officials easily employed Brahmins as Sanskrit teachers. During the 1780s Warren Hastings's tenure as governor general established an educational infrastructure which added Sanskrit to Persian within

British Orientalist learning. The new science of philology supported an emphasis on Sanskrit. A momentous occasion arrived in 1786, when William Jones declared to the new Asiatic Society of Bengal that Sanskrit belonged to an ancient Indo-European language family. Not only did Sanskrit share a lineage with European languages, but it possessed "a wonderful structure; more perfect than the Greek, more copious than the Latin, and more exquisitely refined than either."[6] Generations of scholars studied Indo-European languages as the birthright of Aryan races which diffused them worldwide, from England to India.

Since the literary vernaculars of northern and eastern India derived from Sanskrit, scholars eulogized them as heirs to its Aryanist legacy. While the Sanskrit language was not suitable for everyday purposes in schools, courts, and offices, it seemed that colonial intervention might render vernacular languages suited for quotidian usage. As a result, mid-nineteenth-century British India experienced a momentous change in linguistic and print cultures. Assisted by native informants, philologists compiled vernacular wordlists, grammars, dictionaries, and primers. Interactions between colonial administrators, missionaries, and scribal groups produced standardized print-ready forms. As literacy and official use based upon these print languages expanded, so did a publishing industry for each vernacular. A circular set of processes appeared: local languages responded to the new "civilizing" and "ordering" imperatives; realizing these imperatives, in turn, seemed to depend upon the transformation of language.[7]

In Assam the extension of British authority dramatically transformed language policy and usage. Until the early nineteenth century Asomiya, Kamrupi, Sanskrit, Bengali, and Persian functioned as local literary languages. They existed alongside a huge variety of spoken languages. From the mid-nineteenth century colonial officials categorized local populations within various linguistic and racial categories. Like colonial policymakers elsewhere, the new regime tried to decide which natives possessed a distinct history, and whether their cultures could be classified as civilizations.[8] In response, the members of Assam's colonial intelligentsia, like their counterparts elsewhere, asserted the longevity and uniqueness of their cultural heritage. Language was critical in this assertion. Élites claimed their mother-tongue, Asomiya, as the single, authentic vernacular language of Assam. Eventually they were willing to sacrifice the autonomy of other local idioms to protect Asomiya's authentic status.

At the onset of colonial rule many Assamese gentry élites deployed their multilingual skills to gain a foothold with the British. The political upheavals of the early nineteenth century gave them the role of *dubhashis* (interpreters, lit. speakers of two languages). A typical example was the Assamese official Haliram Dhekial Phukan (1802–32), who sought refuge in Bengal from the Burmese. This brought him into direct contact with the East India Company as its forces advanced into Assam. His command of Bengali, Asomiya, and Sanskrit proved invaluable.[9] Company officials esteemed him as "a man of large property and extended information who professes some literary celebrity."[10] Haliram engaged intensively with Calcutta's new print milieu, as a periodical subscriber and author.

In 1829 the Samachar Chandrika Press in Calcutta published Haliram's *Kamakhya-yatra-paddhati* (Description of a Journey to Kamakhya) and *Assam Desher Itihas Orthat Assam Buranji* (History of Assam). Although these works described Assam, Haliram chose Sanskrit and Bengali as their medium. In doing so he distanced himself from the linguistic practices of Assam's pre-modern literary traditions. The choice of Sanskrit for his description of the Kamakhya shrine made for a sharp contrast with the bulk of devotional literature produced by Assamese Vaishnavite satras. Most satra texts were in Asomiya, the chief vernacular of the region, which emerged in written form from the fourteenth century.[11] This vernacular literarization played an important role in widely disseminating Vaishnavism's textual message. But unlike satra writers who produced locally focused devotional texts, Haliram sought a readership beyond Assam's rural populace. Through a devotional work written in Sanskrit and published from Calcutta, he ambitiously addressed a broader Indic audience.

In *Kamakhya-yatra-paddhati* Haliram chose the Sanskrit language to describe his sacred subject, the Kamakhya shrine. The goddess Kamakhya's worship had begun in the distant past as a local fertility cult of a mother goddess. By the early medieval period this cult became linked to Indic worship patterns through an identification of Kamakhya as a form of Parvati, the god Shiva's consort. The shrine's holiness stemmed from the legend that when the god Vishnu cut the corpse of Sati, Shiva's first wife, into fifty-one pieces which landed all over the subcontinent, her vagina fell on a hill near Guwahati. Although late medieval Sanskrit texts such as the *Kalika Purana* stressed Kamakhya's importance, its remote location removed the shrine from most pilgrim itineraries. For the Bengali-reading public Haliram's text provided a timely new introduction to this potent, yet less frequented site for devotion. Haliram rightly anticipated that pilgrims from "Bengal and Hindustan" would be eager to visit the site now that it was more accessibly located in British India. Kamakhya's localized worship now figured prominently on the all-India itinerary of *tirtha yatra* (pilgrimage). The shrine became renowned as the farthest sacral point to the east. In the past "no person was allowed to make any offering at the above temple except the representatives of the Assam Raja."[12] In contrast, Kamakhya's patrons in the colonial era were important pan-Indian figures such as the Maharaja of Darbhanga (in Bihar). The Sanskrit register of Haliram's work was vital to reaching this broad audience.

In language and theme Haliram's other published work, *Assam Desher Itihas Orthat Assam Buranji*, provided a contrast. Through this historical account of Assam, Haliram asserted his place within the new colonial knowledge. "A huge amount of vidya [learning] has emerged out of the printing presses in the city of Calcutta through the efforts of many talented gentlemen who have come out with many kinds of books, including ones describing different lands but, there is as yet none about Assam."[13] He drew readers' attention to the increasing interactions between Assam and the larger Indian hinterland. "After the British takeover, people from many lands have started interacting and coming here, but they have no way of learning about it, so for the benefit of all, I have published this book."[14] Haliram called this work a *buranji*, after the pre-modern Asomiya chronicles commissioned from scribal élites by the ruling class.[15] There were only a few extant manuscripts of these older works. Each was slightly different because of the idiosyncrasies inherent to a scribal text. These chronicles focused mainly on political events, as did Haliram's text, but this resemblance in content was overshadowed by Haliram's innovation in language, his use of Bengali. Unlike the older chronicles, his buranji was produced for a new age and for a transregional audience. Through this text Haliram self-consciously engaged with the colonial rulers and the Bengali print public. His new print buranji made strategic use of the Bengali language to describe Assam to Calcutta's "learned readers."[16]

It also signaled the advent of a new colonial order. In past buranjis the Asomiya vernacular used by scribal élites reflected the Ahom state's patronage of a local speech idiom that acquired written form as part of the widespread "vernacularization" of medieval South Asia.[17] While older buranjis remained rooted in a local context through their linguistic usage, Haliram's chaste, modern Bengali idiom introduced Assam to a new print public both in and outside the region. Bengali-reading intellectuals and colonial officials formed the bulk of Haliram's audience. With a broader remit than its localized predecessors, his was a local chronicle which sought a place within the new genre of useful knowledge. Haliram's choice of the "high" register of the Bengali language marked a momentous transition to colonial modernity as well as an attempt to incorporate Assam into an Indic hinterland.

Championing Asomiya, Asserting Lineage

Today Assamese nationalists revere Haliram's son, Anandaram Dhekial Phukan, as Asomiya's first modern champion. His efforts to establish his mother-tongue as the public vernacular contributed to a conviction among modernizing local élites that land, language, and literature were all-important for social belonging. Ironically, Anandaram's efforts to promote the Asomiya language ensured that his father's Bengali writings were relegated to obscurity. Assam's new generation of writers chose to look inward. In sharp contrast to Haliram, they used the Asomiya language to reach an audience within the homeland. Anandaram Dhekial Phukan's actions, aided by the American Baptist missionaries who worked in Upper Assam, catalyzed this change.

The thorny issue of Assam's vernacular language choice brought the American Baptist mission on a collision course with the colonial state. By the 1830s British Indian policy decided to replace Persian by local vernaculars wherever feasible. Act 29 of 1837 allowed the East India Company to replace "the use of the Persian language in any judicial proceeding or in any proceeding relating to the Revenue" with the vernacular language of each administrative region. The rationale was that local people would be better served if the official machinery was accessible to them in their own mother-tongue. As a result, colonial officials struggled to identify the local vernacular best suited for use as an administrative and educational medium in a

✳ Pushing local language w/o local knowledge

particular region. Often their choices were controversial. For instance, this policy brought about an adversarial relationship between the newly standardized Hindi and Urdu languages of North India.[18] Unlike other Mughal-ruled regions, pre-modern Assam used Persian minimally. The region's pattern of vernacular language use was uniquely its own, and was dominated by the Asomiya dialect of Upper Assam. At first British courts relied on clerks who used their own native languages, Asomiya and Bengali. Then in 1837 the colonial state sought administrative simplicity through the use of a single vernacular, Bengali. This policy became the root cause of long-lasting linguistic discord.

The choice of the Bengali language as the official vernacular for Assam strongly relied upon the opinions of the inspector of schools, William Robinson. He believed that the Asomiya was merely a rustic spoken form of the Bengali. Robinson declared that even Bengali in its native state was "clumsy and uncouth [and] it needed a literature to render it compact, energetic and harmonious."[19] He advocated that the newly refined literary form of the Bengali vernacular be used in Assam, in place of "slovenly" and "crude" local spoken varieties.[20]

Robinson's opinions and the direction they set for colonial language policy clashed with those of Baptist missionaries and locals. While the Baptists acknowledged that "Bengali and Assamese derived from Sanskrit [and] bore close affinity to each other,"[21] they contested Robinson's assumption that the local language was a rustic Bengali dialect. Instead the missionaries declared Asomiya a centuries-old spoken and written language. Their close interactions with common people revealed that Bengali was totally incomprehensible for them.[22] The missionary Nathan Brown had Robinson in mind when he wrote, "finding so large a proportion of words common to Bengali and Assamese, and not considering that this similarity necessarily results from the derivation of these languages from Sanskrit, the common parent of both, it has been hastily concluded that the Assamese is an uncouth jargon, formed by incorporation of Bengali with various dialects of the country."[23]

The American Baptist conviction that the Brahmaputra valley possessed a distinct script, language, and history formed the basis for a new print modernity that these missionaries sought to introduce through a partnership with Assamese élites. Among the local gentry Anandaram Dhekial Phukan was the first to intervene on these issues of language, education, and state policy. Unlike members of his father's generation, Anandaram came into contact with colonial schools and the English language at a relatively early age. As befitted his Brahmin ancestry, Anandaram was formally initiated into Sanskrit learning at home at the age of five, in 1834. Later he joined the new English-medium school at Guwahati.[24] His pivotal educational moment occurred when his father sent him to Hindu College in Calcutta. Family problems forced Anandaram to return home after two years, but a British official arranged for him to continue the study of English at home. Anandaram began to "memorize a few pages of Johnson's Dictionary everyday, give his wife lessons in reading and writing, and learn Persian and Urdu from a Munshi."[25] Interestingly, from this multilingual repertoire Anandaram chose Bengali to write a number of volumes compiling legal cases.[26] Given Assam's minuscule reading public, it seemed only sensible to produce such works for the Bengal Presidency at large, as his father had done. Anandaram's only substantial work in the Asomiya language, the primer *Asomiya Lorar Mitra* (A Companion to the Assamese Boy), long remained unpublished. The work was intended as a complete course of elementary education in the Asomiya language, but publication costs exceeded projected sales. So far, in the absence of state patronage, only the Baptist Mission published works in the Asomiya vernacular.

In 1853, when called upon to assess East India Company rule before Justice Mills, Anandaram delivered a powerful indictment of British failures in language and educational policy.[27] The language he chose for his statement was English, the language of the colonial rulers to whom it was addressed: "Little argument is necessary to prove that popular education will never advance in the country unless the system at present pursued in the vernacular schools be remodeled."[28] The educational shortfalls of the Assamese people were entirely due to a defective language policy. The British erred when they introduced primary education in the Bengali language. The benefits of modern education were outweighed by an alien language of instruction completely at odds with the ostensibly popular focus of the schooling system. Anandaram declared, "It is not through the medium of a language refined and elevated in imitation of the Sanskrit, above the comprehension of the mass of the population, that we should try to educate the people, or strive to give them a popular literature; but by means of the language spoken and understood by all classes."[29] He viewed the Asomiya language as the most suitable medium to introduce a truly popular and modern educational system. While Bengali and Sanskrit might be somewhat accessible to élites, the common people lacked any knowledge of these languages. In Anandaram's eyes Asomiya's very lack of refinement made it the best vehicle for a popular system of education. "Instruction in [vernacular] schools in a foreign language, viz., the Bengalee which is imperfectly understood by the teachers themselves, not to speak of the pupils" blocked local progress.[30]

In 1855 Anandaram's magnum opus appeared: *A Few Remarks on the Assamese Language and on Vernacular Education in Assam*. This slender pamphlet made a weighty case — in English — for Asomiya as a modern vehicle for progress. Published at Anandaram's own expense, this work confronted the British unwillingness to consider Asomiya as a proper language. As a new strategy, Anandaram claimed the science of philology as the basis for his arguments favouring Asomiya. He first aimed to provide a "copious vocabulary, a literary genealogy, and historical origin" for Bengali and Asomiya.[31] Then he demonstrated that both languages derived their lineages from Sanskrit. Anandaram further traced a lengthy historical tradition for the Asomiya language and its literature. Asomiya's long use of prose, he speculated, exemplified in the buranji chronicles, proved that it might be a more modern language than Bengali, whose prose works were more recent. As a climax to his arguments he arranged Bengali and Asomiya vocabularies in parallel columns. He demonstrated that of 287 words in Asomiya, 112 were unconnected to Bengali and 98 were derived from Sanskrit. Only 77 words were either derived from or had a resemblance to words in Bengali. As Anandaram compared the literary histories of Assam and Bengal, he cited the Serampore Baptist missionary and language scholar William Carey to remind readers that Bengali too was once considered a vulgar dialect.[32]

Over these years Anandaram managed to refine and modify his arguments in favour of Asomiya. In the statement he delivered in 1853 Anandaram advocated it for Assam's schools and offices because it was the colloquial language of use. In particular, he argued that common people would benefit from the colonial system of popular education only if it was available in their mother-tongue. Then, in *A Few Remarks on the Assamese Language*, he began to historicize

the Asomiya language and construct a lengthy literary history. Subsequent publicists followed Anandaram's lead, as they established a
community structured around a standardized language, albeit one
contoured along fault lines of gender and class. Given the public
nature of language contestation, late-nineteenth-century intellectuals could no longer profess a dual affiliation to Bengali and Asomiya. Just as Hindi and Urdu became part of a competing set of
linguistic dualities, so too did Bengali and Asomiya.

Love, Mother-Tongue, and the City

From the mid-nineteenth century Assam's new intelligentsia gradually negotiated a modernistic language agenda through and against
the colonial state's establishment of a hierarchy of subjects, languages, and cultures. Yet arguments about vernacular utility or history or literary merit did not seem adequate on their own. They were
often bolstered with rhetoric about the emotional debt of love owed
to one's mother-tongue.

One of the first public invocations of love for Asomiya appeared in
1853, when the missionary-run periodical *Orunodoi* published a series of epistolary articles on language use by a writer using the nom
de plume "A Countryman based in Calcutta."[33] Through exhortations and admonishments, this author explicated the connections
between his mother-tongue, learning, love, and service toward the
homeland. Each epistle began with the salutation "Dear friends."
This phrase bound together author and reader in a community of
affect even as the author bemoaned the *on-aador* (lack of affection)
shown toward the Asomiya language.[34] While the anonymous author, in all likelihood an upper-caste man and a college student,
asserted his love for Asomiya, he made clear that his agenda was to
improve and modernize it. To that end he advocated that Asomiya
should be enriched with judicious borrowings from related languages, especially Sanskrit: "In this country, there are so many languages and the root of them all is Sanskrit. O beloved inhabitants, if
you are to benefit the country through education, use Sanskrit as a
support to begin composing books, with one person helping another to spread the language of the country."[35] This of course as-
sumed that the reading public consisted mostly of men who resem-

bled the author: upper caste and Sanskrit-educated. Borrowing from Sanskrit was natural, "just as we would borrow or buy a plough if there was none in our home, just as we transplant trees and flowers from where they grow abundantly to our homes to create our own flower gardens, just as we bring water from the river to fill up our ponds."[36] This strong emphasis on the natural and inevitable character of linguistic borrowing was meant to reassure defenders of Asomiya who feared that its local roots might be compromised by Sanskrit forms.

These pronounced metaphors of place and home reveal how for local élites the evocation of homeland became increasingly important. This fervent advocacy of the Asomiya language was being articulated while new migrants were bringing their own languages and customs into Assam. Against a backdrop of migration and demographic change, the author framed his didactic message in strongly affectionate, almost intimate terms. He depicted his mission as a quest for a community of friends, united in a common love of mother-tongue and homeland: "In the country where we are born or where we live, and whose speech we cannot forget from the day of our birth until death, that language is what is called mother tongue."[37] Assam's inhabitants had an inalienable bond with their mother-tongue. When friends made common cause over "adoration" of learning, language, and land, they could achieve the all-important goal of progress. Yet although the author made repeated references to this community of friends, the community's boundaries remained undefined. The possibility that migrants to Assam might adopt the language and join this community on equal terms was still open.

Publicists like the author of these letters confronted the difficult issue of how to convince readers that an affiliation to mother-tongue was to be privileged over any other linguistic expertise. This was not yet something that most Assamese élites were willing to accept. In the *Orunodoi* epistles the author mounted a dual appeal to his countrymen on the grounds of utility and sentiment. He held it "advisable to consider which language can be easily learnt in a short time. Our countrymen need to first learn Asomiya, and when they know it beautifully, *then* they can think of learning other languages."[38] His clinching argument was borrowed from the rival's camp. Bengalis, he argued, made it a point to study different languages, and that was how they managed to render their language beautiful.[39]

The people of Assam needed to emulate the Bengali and the English peoples, since both had made great progress in modernizing themselves and their mother-tongues. "That very English language which is now at the head of all other languages, and possesses all manner of books which advance knowledge was formerly unloved; but now, in the eyes of the people of its country, it has become a prominent language."[40] While this dismal past of English might encourage a colonized people, the author did not evade the tricky issue of English and the vernaculars: "Just as many people in our country adore the Bengali language, similarly many Bengalis used to adore the English language, but now that their language has been improved they have been won over by it."[41] While the Bengali and English languages might be emulated, it was imperative to seize a separate space for Asomiya within its homeland. The author praised English as an example for Indian vernaculars to follow, albeit with a frisson of nervousness about its seductive danger. However, "adoration of mother-tongue" might avoid this danger. Love for mother-tongue would bring forth adornment for a language and a civilized status for its people. In a situation where artifice inexorably operated to modernize these vernaculars, it was essential to portray the process as natural. Therefore publicists often made explicit connections between language and the organic bonds of home, friendship, and patriotism.

The author of the *Orunodoi* epistles was at the vanguard of a new intelligentsia. The number of Assamese students in colleges in Bengal remained limited, but increasingly the gentry aspired to higher education for their sons. Their ultimate objective was the safe sinecure of a government appointment. However much it was desired, this world of *chakri*, the monotony of clerical drudgery, still required elevation to some higher purpose.[42] In this context publicists proclaimed the existence of an immutable self for the Asomiya language and its speakers, premised upon its dual status as mother-tongue and literary medium. From the 1870s Calcutta's Assamese sojourners established their own print enterprises. Despite slender material resources, they published magazines and wrote poetry, essays, and novels. In this manner they linked the progress of language, literature, and homeland. Through the literary public sphere they portrayed linguistic belonging as the mainspring of identity for individuals and community.

In 1885 the periodical *Assam Bandhu* appeared from Calcutta. Its editor and publisher, Gunabhiram Barua, belonged to the third generation of the Dhekial Phukan family. Almost thirty years after Anandaram articulated his vision of the Asomiya language's future, his cousin Gunabhiram helped realize its promise. Gunabhiram's editorials offered what was by now a familiar idiom of friendship and common purpose. Periodicals like his became the principal vehicle of literary expression and public debate all over British India. They chronicled literary and political activities as well as changes in taste and fashion.[43] This new public culture of Asomiya, despite handicaps of inadequate finances and technology, spread rapidly among "rural landholders, schoolmasters, and the clerical classes."[44] By now, for Gunabhiram and succeeding generations the Asomiya print vernacular was almost the only acceptable vehicle for literary expression.

While rejecting Bengali linguistic hegemony, these early generations of Assamese publicists maintained close personal connections with Bengali society. They credited Bengali culture with having facilitated their encounter with modernity even though they envied the greater sophistication and professional reach of the Bengali middle classes. Many of them married Bengali women and adopted Bengali social mores.[45] The best-known examples are the litterateurs Lakshminath Bezbarua and Bolinarayan Bora. Both worked and dwelt outside Assam (one as a timber merchant, the other as a civil engineer) and led private lives almost entirely within Bengali genteel circles. They wrote letters to family and friends which chronicled their most intimate thoughts in the Bengali language. Yet each defined his public persona exclusively as that of an Assamese intellectual and patriot. Both wrote on literary and political matters in the Asomiya language and established periodicals in that language. They remained wary of a public slippage into their domestic Bengali self. For instance, Lakshminath vehemently denied a rumour that he had become a *ghar jamai* (a scornful term for a son-in-law who lived at his wife's natal home). He narrated in his autobiography how immediately after his wedding he had returned to live in the Assamese students' mess rather than at the opulent mansion of his Tagore in-laws.[46] In an ironic parallel to the Bengali public's obsession with the effeminacy that the British attributed to them, Assamese élites constantly needed reassurance that they and their mother-tongue would avoid Bengali emasculation. Adoration of the Asomiya language would strengthen not only the homeland but also her sons.

An admiring emulation of Calcutta's progress was sometimes overwhelmed by darker feelings of victimization and sectarian competitiveness. By the early twentieth century anxieties over Bengali cultural and political dominance became stronger. Cultural resentments were exacerbated by the sectarian politics of aspiring communities within Assam's shifting political boundaries. For the majority of Assam's intelligentsia, student existence in Calcutta was succeeded by a return to Assam and service employment by the state, or by a plantation. The annexation of Bengal's Sylhet district to the Brahmaputra valley in 1874 impelled a large number of its Bengali-speaking educated youths to compete for clerical employment in a newly created Assam province. Educated men in the Brahmaputra valley now found themselves competing with rivals from Sylhet as well as from Bengal proper. Bengali educational and numerical superiority was resented as an undue advantage. Of the 938 students who matriculated from Calcutta University in 1872, only 4 graduated from schools in Brahmaputra valley. As late as 1898 the number was only 32. In 1888–1900 only 29 Brahmaputra valley residents obtained B.A. degrees, compared to 68 from Sylhet. A publicist observed that "in the British epoch, everything is a matter of reading and writing. Those who are in official posts, or impart education, they are the leaders of society, and so Bengalis became here."[47]

Against the background of this newly fierce competitiveness, the language encounters of the early colonial period were now reframed as a conspiracy by migrant Bengali amlahs (clerks) to eradicate the Asomiya language. In this narrative the British rulers of Assam were portrayed as blameless except insofar as they were misled by cunning Bengali subordinates who sought the death of the Asomiya language. Assamese publicists first articulated this conspiracy theory at public meetings during the 1890s. Their theory reached a wider audience in 1907, when Hemchandra Goswami and Padmanath Gohain Barua outlined it in their *Note on Assamese Language and Literature*. This amlah conspiracy theory became well grounded in local scholarly lore and nationalist rhetoric over the twentieth century.[48] Its longevity is apparent from its reappearance at crucial moments in postcolonial language politics of the region, for instance during Assam's language riots in the 1960s and 1970s.[49]

Standardizing Language, Creating Dialects

Missionary support proved central to the campaign for official recognition of the Asomiya language. But once the colonial state acknowledged Asomiya's claims to its patronage, a new generation of publicists challenged certain aspects of the Baptist language program. This caused them to clash with Nidhi Levi Farwell, the first local Christian convert. Nidhi was an orphan from a lower-caste background and the most energetic of the Assamese Christians who worked for the *Orunodoi*. Aside from his work at the press, he published pieces in almost every issue.[50] Nidhi's writings were as far removed in style as he was, socially speaking, from Assamese élites. He relied on a distinctive colloquial register which approximated as far as possible to the spoken vernacular. This style provoked strong attacks from Assamese élites who wished to emphasize Asomiya's Sanskrit roots. As these élites developed a modern literary style that refined Asomiya's syntax and orthography into a highly Sanskritized register, they fulminated at the tendency of the *Orunodoi* to promote spoken usage as the literary standard.[51]

The leading proponent of this linguistic challenge was Hemchandra Barua, the author of the anti-opium play *Kaniyar Kirtan*, who subsequently gained renown as a lexicographer. Well known as an iconoclast who attacked all forms of established religion, he was highly critical of Nidhi and the Baptists for what he saw as their deliberate watering-down of the Asomiya language. He was particularly opposed to Miles Bronson's dictionary, which employed a colloquial vocabulary. Since there was as yet no other published dictionary of the Asomiya language, Bronson's work was widely in use.[52] Its orthography, the author claimed, better corresponded with the actual pronunciation of the people than any other system.[53] But members of the Assamese intelligentsia were more interested in literary standardization than popular usage. They were deeply unhappy with the dictionary's simple syntax and orthography. Faced with immense local pressure, the missionaries capitulated. In its final years the *Orunodoi* adopted the newly Sanskritized orthography and syntax that local élites favoured. Nidhi Levi Farwell was deeply unhappy at this capitulation, but it was inevitable. The publishing monopoly of the missionary press no longer existed. If the *Orunodoi* was to retain credibility among its public, it had to conform to Asomiya's new norms. As part of this capitulation, in 1892 the mission published Hemchandra's new grammar textbook, explicitly modeled on Sanskrit grammar rules. In it, Hemchandra set down rules for spelling and syntax which might supersede older missionary usage.[54] He cautioned that the Rev. Bronson's "orthography is wholly incorrect and in respect of meanings too it is not what it should have been. Assamese learners are in no way benefited by it, nor will they be."[55] Colloquial usage might in fact aid critics who dismissed Asomiya as a rustic form of Bengali.

Hemchandra Barua also began to prepare a massive replacement for Bronson's dictionary, the *Hem Kosha*, modeled upon Webster's dictionary. But publication was delayed for lack of funds until ten years after its completion, in 1900, with support from some officials.[56] By then the *Orunodoi* had ceased publication. The new Baptist priority was to prepare educational and religious works for a fast-growing Christian flock in the Naga and Garo Hills. The mission relinquished the field of Asomiya literary activity to the plains intelligentsia.

From the 1870s, after the colonial state adopted Asomiya as its official vernacular, officials such as George Grierson, Edward Gait, and P. R. T. Gurdon became active in its modernization and refinement.[57] The linguist Grierson helped resurrect Anandaram Dhekial Phukan's ideas about the historical roots of the Asomiya language for an all-India audience.[58] In 1873 official support enabled Gunabhiram Barua to publish a new edition of his cousin Anandaram's primer. Thirty years after its writing it found commercial success as a school textbook.[59] The newly established Linguistic Survey of India, under Grierson's leadership, institutionalized colonial efforts to study and classify vernacular languages. In addition to the "Indo-European" vernaculars where written traditions had long existed, the survey examined unwritten idioms and dialects. Impressed by the region's multitude of languages, Grierson's report awarded Assam a prominent place among those "parts of India which seem to have had each a special Tower of Babel of its own."[60] The report further declared the Asomiya language preeminent within the region. It followed the direction set by the census report of 1881, which made an important distinction between Assam's caste and tribal populations on the basis of the caste population's Indo-Aryan mother-tongue. "The languages of the non-Aryan tribes do not seem to have contributed to the vocabulary of Assamese (which, like Bengali, rests in the main upon a foundation of Sanskrit) in any greater degree than Welsh has contributed to our modern English."[61]

Armed with this imprimatur for their mother-tongue, the members of Assam's intelligentsia sought to create a suitably modern infrastructure to advance it. On the one hand this involved the zealous production of printed books to support Asomiya's stature as a modern vernacular. On the other, the promoters of Asomiya wished to convince the region's entire population that the language needed their strongest public allegiance. This was no easy task in a region where so many other idioms existed. These included local forms of Asomiya such as Lower Assam's Kamrupi, the mother-tongues of tribal groups such as Kachari, and the myriad dialects and languages in use among migrants. Increasingly publicists emphasized a hierarchy of status between Asomiya and other local idioms. They depicted *bhasa* (language) as inseparable from *sahitya* (literature). Their argument strengthened Asomiya's claim to being the region's only true language, since most other local idioms were either unwritten or lacked a literary tradition. Periodicals such as the *Jonaki* carried at least one essay in every issue which elaborated grammatical rules and literary history.

Between 1923 and 1929 Hemchandra Goswami published a multivolume anthology of Asomiya literature, *Asomiya Sahityar Chaneki*. This work compiled selections from over the centuries to demonstrate the language's lengthy historical and literary pedigree. By doing so it sought to establish a standard literary canon for the Asomiya language. This anthology's publication costs were met through the munificent donation of Rs 10,000 from Bholanath Barua (1850–1923). Bholanath was a successful Assamese businessman with a timber empire spanning Assam, Bengal, and Orissa who became well-known for his educational philanthropy. Other contemporaries of Hemchandra — the noted Bengali literary scholar Suniti Kumar Chatterji, and his Assamese PhD student Banikanta Kakati — also published monographs which highlighted historical and philological research into the languages of eastern India.[62] After 1937 Calcutta University's introduction of vernacular languages as examination subjects expanded the audience for these academic works.

For today's readers Hemchandra Goswami's attempt at a "history of literature" appears curiously indiscriminate. He included Puranic legends, aphorisms, medicinal treatises, poetry, drama, and modern school textbooks. He separated them only into chronological periods. In the absence of generic boundaries, the parameter of selection was set by the bounds of the "Asomiya" language itself. By dint of this logic, Haliram Dhekial Phukan was not included as an author, despite his being the first Assamese to be widely published. But Hemchandra Goswami's strict linguistic standard was difficult to impose on the distant past. Therefore the selection of medieval devotional literature was characterized by a much more heterogeneous linguistic idiom than the modern examples. Other votaries of Asomiya noted this point. For instance, an anonymous compiler of Vaishnavite hymns expressed his puzzlement at what he regarded as the saint Sankardeb's indiscriminate use of words from "Assami, Kamrupi, Bangali, Hindustani, Brajbuli, Musalmani, Oriya etc."[63] Clearly an abyss was opening between a vernacular culture of the past, one adept at switching mood, vocabulary, and register to suit different purposes, and a burgeoning modern desire for language standardization.

As innovators and upholders of Asomiya literary standards, prominent publicists acted as patrons for aspiring authors. People on the social margins often displayed tremendous uncertainty about their command over the newly standardized vernacular. Maulvi Muhammad Shah Haji, who wrote an Asomiya work called the *Lukir Buranji*, is a case in point.[64] A Muslim mauzadar, he published this work in 1922, a short history of his locality of Luki. Its preface contained a statement of approval from two well-known litterateurs, Hemchandra Goswami and Sarbeswar Sarma. The condescending nature of these upper-caste publicists' endorsement is evident from their praise of "the standard of the language" used by "this member of the Musalman community."[65] It is noteworthy that the author was so lacking in linguistic confidence that he felt impelled to use their statement. It is even more striking when juxtaposed against the confident attitude of a caste Hindu figure from a comparable class background, the dramatist and philologist Hemchandra Barua, who declared, "Asomiya is my mother tongue and I have paid particular attention to it for upwards of eighteen years past and have also written and published four or five books in the language, one of which is a grammar of the same. I possess a tolerably fair knowledge of Sanskrit which is admittedly the parent of Asomiya."[66] *Sadhana*, the periodical published by the Asomiya Musalman Yuva Sanmilan (Assamese Muslim Youth Association), repeatedly exhorted Muslims to improve their command of Asomiya.[67] The association was evidently concerned that its members' linguistic expertise did not measure up to the standards set by their caste Hindu peers. The hegemony acquired by the equation between mother-tongue and official language ensured that the higher echelons of Assamese caste Hindu society easily extended their linguistic and educational dominance. They often stigmatized other social groups as speakers of vulgar, incorrect dialects. Peasants and women became key subjects for these publicists' efforts to improve discourse. The expanded linguistic dominance of Asomiya and its upper-caste speakers was even more obvious when juxtaposed against the many tribal and hill inhabitants of Assam whose mother-tongues boasted no Sanskritic lineage or written pedigree.

Finding Aryan Ancestors

Colonial Assam's discussions of language frequently overlapped with, and influenced ideas about, race, history, and social identity. Over the Victorian age studies of race diverged from linguistics and approached ethnology even as notions of progressive evolution emerged within a general theory of human "racial types." European science applied notions of evolutionary racial hierarchies and historic race conquests to South Asia. The belief that civilization was the unique achievement of ethnologically "advanced" races came to coexist with the search for the pure, refined languages which were the hallmark of these races. Assam's élites were morbidly conscious of their inclusion among the "barbarous hordes" who inhabited British India's frontiers. They used Aryanist arguments to contest this ascription. From the late nineteenth century Aryanism conflated the race rhetoric of the western ethnographer with the Sanskrit criteria of "Arya" respectability, offering caste Hindus a "civilized" lineage. The historians Joan Leopold, Thomas Trautmann, and Tony Ballantyne have variously mapped the tremendous reach of this imagery.[68] Assam's élites were all the more attracted to Aryanist imagery because it allowed them to connect their homeland to a broader Indic world. Aryanism offered a way for Assamese Hindus to grasp a place in Indic sacral space.

Gunabhiram Barua had a multifaceted career as a government functionary, social reformer, and literary entrepreneur. In 1875 he published a chronicle of Assam, *Assam Buranji*. His work's title proclaimed its position within a long-standing buranji genre, in the manner of Haliram Dhekial Phukan's text of 1829. But it also hid substantial discontinuities. First, the readership of buranjis had undergone substantial change. Gunabhiram wrote his work in the newly standardized Asomiya vernacular. He addressed a new print public for this language. Government patronage of Asomiya permitted his book's use as a history textbook for high schools. While the title suggested Gunabhiram's desire to work within the familiar buranji genre, the narrative employed the new Aryanist idiom then coming into favour all through the British Empire.[69] Gunabhiram explicitly connected Assam's origins with Aryan migration: "Some people say that as this land is bounded by hills it is called a-sama [uneven]. The area between the Himalayas and Vindhyas is Aryavarta. That is the adi [original] place of the Aryans in Bharatavarsha. That place was even. So when they came here, they called it A-sam."[70] This connection marked a radical departure from Haliram, who had linked the etymology of the name Assam to Ahom rule. Now Gunabhiram's narrative placed Assam's past as an Aryan frontier at centrestage. He sought to structure past migrations into Assam along racial and linguistic lines: "The first are the Arya [Aryan], the people who migrated from Aryavarta, whose languages are based upon Sanskrit. Among them are groups such as the Brahmins, Kalitas, and Keot, whose language is Asomiya, derived from Sanskrit. The second category is the on-Arya [non-Aryans], those who are not descended from the Arya, have lived in this land from the remote past, and have languages that are independent."[71] The binary pair of Arya and on-Arya was not new. It was one of several discursive classifications which had long constituted the Sanskrit cultural order. British Orientalists reworked this classification to unite the indigenous category "Arya" with the race scientists' category of "Aryan." William Jones's discovery of the Indo-European language family already revealed kinship between Sanskrit, Asomiya, Bengali, Greek, Latin, and other languages. Among Assam's locals only Assamese caste Hindus could claim descent from past Arya/Aryans.[72] Therefore the family romance with Indic language-cousins allowed Gunabhiram to distinguish caste Hindus from other locals such as Kacharis and Nagas.

Local knowledge already classified the latter groups as Assam's *par-batiya jatis* (hill people). Race science further categorized hill people as non-Aryans. Both local élites and colonial officials now began to describe hill groups as Dravidian and Mongoloid races. As such they were distinct from Aryan-descended caste Hindus.

Previously, in 1829 Haliram's *Assam Buranji* had described the pre-colonial Ahom rulers as the "descendants of the god Indra who defeated many hill groups to rule over Assam."[73] The defeated groups were the "Mikir, Kachari, Garo, Lalung and Miri who lived along the outskirts of the plains. Some worship spirits according to their past customs while others worship Hindu gods."[74] In this manner Haliram had structured his account through the relationship of the land to its people through these constituent groups. Even while according a subordinate position to the hill groups, Haliram depicted their identities as relatively easy to change. Haliram acknowledged that the princely Ahoms initially lived in "similar manner to hill groups."[75] Hill group status was largely contingent upon temporal and spatial moorings. His understanding was a relatively nuanced one that contrasted with the "savagery" later projected by colonial knowledge onto the subcontinent's "tribes." By the 1870s the influence of race science theories had made parbatiya jati, in Gunabhiram's rendering, almost indistinguishable from the colonial category of tribe. Tribes became an antediluvian, unchanging stratum of Indian society. Still, his analysis did not entirely deny the possibility of change for non-Aryans. Linguistically adept non-Aryans might venture upward and transform their status by acquiring the Asomiya language.[76] This notion of language as modifying social identity permitted this analysis of Assamese society to retain a degree of permeability.

A more exclusionary depiction of Assamese as Aryans appeared in Sonaram Choudhury's essay "Assamot Aryar Bosoti" (Assam as the Home of Aryans), published in the *Jonaki* in 1889. This essay offers yet another glimpse of the tortuous, often self-contradictory form taken by juxtapositions of colonial philology, race theory, and Indic desires. Sonaram argued that Assam's inhabitants were direct descendants of an ancient Aryan race. He reinforced his use of "Aryan" with reference to the "Turanian" race which older ethnographers such as Brian Hodgson had described. Sonaram began his analysis with what he called the "common knowledge" that the ancient Aryans initially dwelt in Central Asia. When barbaric Turanian neigh-bours constantly harassed them, the Aryans migrated to Afghani-stan's hills.[77] Since British ethnographers classified Assam's tea la-bourers as Turanians, this racially demarcated past might evoked a wealth of associations for readers.[78] Sonaram described the three occupational groups that made up this Central Asian population — hunters, pastoralists, and agriculturists. While the first two were brave and hardy, the third was ready to undertake any kind of toil. The hunters were fond of meat and alcohol, in contrast to the agri-culturists who only consumed them in moderation.[79] Readers could easily identify a reflection of the dichotomies of caste and tribe played out at that very moment, where alcohol use, for instance, was associated with lower-caste and tribal groups.

At this point the narrative sharply departed from standard Aryan-ist lore, as Sonaram, attempting to prove that Assam was the final destination of the Aryan race, introduced an inventive if fantastic instance of the etymologies that often accompanied quasi-scientific linguistic analysis: "According to the rules of grammar, the Sanskrit 's' is replaced by 'h' in primeval languages. It can be inferred that this was none other than the 's' pronounced as h in the Asomiya language of today. Thus, the Sanskrit 'Asur' is none other than the word 'Ahur.' "[80] In a mind-boggling leap of logic, Sonaram used the sim-ilarity between Asura and Ahura to deduce that Ahura Mazda was the head of the gods (the Asuras) of the agriculturists. Before Aryans separated into distinct groups on the basis of divergent living habits, "Asura" signified "divine being." As the cultural habits of Aryan groups began to differ, so did gods, and nomenclatures. This was a crucial step in Sonaram's argument. It allowed him to establish a direct equation between a "primeval" Aryan language, Sanskrit, and modern Asomiya. A bold stroke was to use the Asomiya pronuncia-tion of "s" as "h" (a feature which distinguished it from Bengali and other Indic vernaculars) to posit its status as the authentic Aryan tongue. This attention to phonetics removed the discussion from the realm of literary achievement, where Asomiya could not yet shine, to that of its demotic essence.

After he traced Asomiya as Aryan, Sonaram proceeded to identify Asomiya as Hindu: "One group among the agriculturists had al-ready, before the war, moved to that territory [of Bharatvarsha]. Since 's' was pronounced as 'h' in their language, as in modern Asomiya, they were known as Hindus. Later, when the hunters moved in, they too adopted that name."[81] The chief point of this analysis was that the Assamese, among all the Indic people, had the closest ties to the Aryan race. The key evidence was the linguistic genealogy. Sonaram asserted that the Asomiya language was older than even the Sanskrit. A lengthy account of Aryan migration into Assam provided the setting for this audacious assertion. He began with the apparent derivation of the term "Hindu" from a primeval tongue, a direct ancestor of Asomiya: "The fact that Hindu is derived from Sindhu is widely known. What is not a matter of common knowledge is that which follows, that Asomiya is a very ancient language as this term comes from it. It is only recently that Asomiya has sunk into the mists of obscure darkness."[82] In this manner Sonaram posited an imaginative leap into an antediluvian past.

This somewhat arid philological discussion was enlivened by the gendered and sexualized rhetoric which Sonaram employed in his closing paragraphs. Most publicists adopted a gendered anthropomorphism which simultaneously domesticated and venerated language through the trope of the "mother." In contrast, Sonaram represented language as a chaste and gentle maiden. He conveyed a strong suggestion of sexual violation when he alluded to the external foes that threatened the tender body of the young maiden, the Asomiya language.[83] Through his ascription of feminine grace to the Asomiya language, he signaled to his audience the danger of sullied female purity. Sonaram's essay on Assam as the cradle of the Aryan race culminated, therefore, in a call to arms for male readers to protect the feminized virtues of their language and homeland. This call would find resonance in the increased connections that Assamese publicists began to make between community status, historical achievements, and Hinduized female virtues.

Asomiya and Its "Others"

By the last decades of the nineteenth century a new official thrust toward "pacification" of the Assam hills shifted further eastward the political boundaries of the northeastern frontier of British India. The colonial state introduced an increased degree of administrative control into the Naga and Lushai Hills districts. On the ethnographic front, scholars such as Herbert Risley discarded Brian Hodgson's contention that language was the chief marker of race. Risley's new generation of ethnographer-officials viewed anthropometry and physical measurements as the most scientific method for race study. However, well into the twentieth century district officials who administered the Assam hills continued to emphasize language as a prime identification for race. They emphasized that there existed "no less than eighteen distinct languages within our border besides the multitude spoken by the wild tribes beyond the frontier."[84]

In 1908 Assam's chief commissioner, Charles Lyell, declared, "Without an understanding of the language of a tribe, there can be no adequate investigation of its institutions; the speech is the expression of the mind of the people who speak it, the measure of their culture and outlook upon the world."[85] He underlined for his charges the importance of studying language, race, and ethnicities: "It is, moreover, in Assam, with its vast diversity of ethnic stocks, the only safe index to the affinities of a tribe with its neighbours, and in the almost complete absence of historic record or remembered tradition, to the migrations which have brought the various units to their present sites."[86]

Colonial and official opinion did not constitute a rigid monolithic body. There were tremendous shifts in understandings of indigenous society across time, and also across space. Certainly many officials on this frontier held idiosyncratic views which ran counter to their colleagues elsewhere in British India. The colonial state supported the study of local languages and their speakers, in the belief that these would be invaluable in administering the region's remote hill terrain. In 1881 the governor of Assam, Sir Charles Elliott, called for compiling grammars, vocabularies, and phrasebooks of languages of the leading tribes, as well as records of customs and institutions. These texts, structured with copious appendices, sketches and photographs, vocabularies, and folktales, buttressed official claims of comprehensive knowledge of their subjects.[87] Through these materials colonial ethnography sought to trace the local histories of groups that it categorized within the Dravidian and Mongoloid races.

From the later nineteenth century British administrators welcomed missions as intermediaries to conduct "indirect rule" in the Assam hills, since their revenues barely recouped bare administrative costs. The state would oversee basic law and order, but the missions would undertake responsibilities such as providing education and healthcare. Their reward was unrestricted access to "souls" for conversion. The Welsh Methodist mission was based in the Khasi Hills, while the American Baptist Mission worked in the Garo, Naga, and Mizo Hills. For the inhabitants of these hills the shift to literacy was mediated by these missions and their message of Christian improvement.[88] The Inner Line regulations which governed Assam's hill tracts ensured that British officials and their attendant missionary groups were virtually the only non-locals permitted into these areas. As a result, the Christian missions enjoyed a near-monopoly as purveyors of religious, educational, and modern health services to the hills.

Over this period the American Baptists gradually discontinued their activities in the Asomiya language aimed at the higher classes of plains society. In the Brahmaputra valley, where the mission pioneered a vernacular print culture, it had developed against an existing infrastructure of a literate gentry and a written tradition. Despite decades of work, converts from the Assamese gentry and peasantry were few. The Baptists had more success among coolie migrants, but planters often blocked missionary activities aimed at their workers. As a result, the mission saw much more potential in the preliterate population of the hills. The "general information" agenda of the Asomiya-language periodical *Orunodoi* was no longer important. From the 1870s the Baptists replaced it with the creation of scriptural and pedagogical texts in newly enscripted tribal languages. They followed the example of the Welsh Methodists, who had already devised a Romanized script and standardized print form for the Khasi language. In the 1890s the Methodist and Baptist missionaries decided that the Roman script was best to transcribe different hill languages, so that future hill Christian congregations "could touch hands over the hills."[89] In Shillong a growing Khasi Christian middle class played an active role in commercial, educational, print journalism, political, and religious networks. Education and Christianity spread slowly but surely among the Garo, Mizo, and Naga groups, which encountered missionary modernity at a later date than the Khasi.

From the late nineteenth century onward the balance of power in the region's language politics shifted toward the standard Asomiya language, which now enjoyed state patronage. Increasingly there emerged a dissonance between the dynamic, multilingual character of Assam's population and the monolingual aspirations of its dominant caste Hindu intelligentsia. In 1917 the Asomiya literary public acquired an institutional base in the Brahmaputra valley with the foundation of the Asom Sahitya Sabha (Assam Literary Association).[90] The organization's main objective was the promotion of the Asomiya language and its culture. It regarded the region's other languages as far inferior. Its first president, Padmanath Gohain Barua, declared in his keynote address, "For the nation that does not possess a literature, its language is nothing but a dialect, only one rung higher than the cries of birds and animals."[91] Publicists like Gohain Barua adopted a strategy of linguistic aggression even though the region became increasingly multiethnic. They refused to accept the legitimacy of other languages and stigmatized them as unlettered dialects. In 1920 another president, Hemchandra Goswami, was even more explicit in his disdain for migrant groups whose mother tongues lacked a literature: "A literature-less nation becomes unable to keep itself alive as soon as it comes into the vicinity of another nation. We do not have to go far to find an example of this—those thousands of tea garden coolies who come into our country year after year."[92] The Sabha conducted "missionary work" in the Goalpara and Naga Hills districts, where it taught standard Asomiya to coolie and hill groups, but its activists adopted a condescending attitude toward these students. Asomiya enthusiasts belittled the recent emergence of a Khasi literary public in Shillong and envisaged its forcible takeover by their own language. This sort of exclusive cultural nationalism was easily constructed upon a foundation of colonial assumptions about "order, hierarchy, and evolutionary distance" as suitable principles for language policy.[93] Ironically, the influence and reach of the Asomiya language increasingly derived from the ability of its print publications to help constitute not just the dominant caste Hindu public but also the Kaivarta, Ahom, Bodo Kachari, and other newly emergent ones. However, residual uncertainty vis-à-vis other Indic vernaculars meant that publicists sought to ensure Asomiya's dominance by displacing "uncivilized" status onto tribal, non-Aryan languages.

Regional debates over language reveal the way in which colonial modernity depended not simply on the formation of print publics, but also on the shifting of the burden of primitiveness onto non-élites. The fraught relationship of the Assamese gentry with different languages and their speakers' claims upon the state shows how local and regional élites carved out a place for themselves within different nodes of colonial modernity. Language continued to be a flashpoint in political and cultural life. In 1945, the Assam Provincial Committee of the Indian National Congress declared, in its election manifesto, "Unless the province of Assam is organized on the basis of Asomiya language and Assamese culture, the survival of the Assamese nationality and culture will become impossible."[94] This declaration alarmed non-Asomiya speaking groups. In later decades, its attempted enforcement provoked much opposition and ultimately, the division of Assam into different political units.

After India's Independence, the state machinery was harnessed to further Asomiya's public dominance, particularly in the sphere of education. Subordinate groups such as tea labourers, East Bengali peasants, and Nepali graziers had little choice but to send their children to Asomiya-medium government schools. However, middle-class groups increasingly opted for more expensive private schools which taught the English, Hindi, or Bengali languages. During the 1960s, the state government's ill-judged attempts to make Asomiya the sole official language for educational and administrative purposes backfired spectacularly. There was upheaval in the Bengali-speaking districts and in the hill tracts which used English for official purposes. The tribal populations of the hill districts seceded to establish the new political units that currently form the states of Meghalaya and Nagaland. The Asomiya language remained confined to the Brahmaputra valley, where increasingly, its public dominance was challenged by locals who switched their public allegiance to other vernaculars. In the manner of upper classes elsewhere in South Asia, Assam's élites, whether Asomiya, Bengali, or Hindi-speaking, resorted to English for schooling and public use, but skirmished over the prestige attached to official languages. Continuing contradictions vis-à-vis multilingual and multiethnic populations and official policies keep language policy as a thorny and emotive issue in South Asia.

7. Contesting Publics
Raced Communities and Gendered History

In 1853 Maniram Barbhandar Barua, former courtier and tea entrepreneur, had written a lengthy memorandum for Justice Mills's report on the East India Company's governance of Assam. In his analysis of social conditions Maniram grouped Assam's population into various jatis: "Brahmun, Khetree, Boisto and Kyusts, Bor Koleeta, Soroo ditto, Keot, Koch, Koomar Koleeta, Mattee ditto, Hindoo Chooteea, Ahom, Boorook, Kacharee, Moran, Chandal, Toorook, Gooreea, Dom, Haree, Moreea."[1] In pre-modern South Asia the term "jati" designated a group of people who possessed relatively fluid, overlapping attributes of ritual, occupational, and spatial belonging. To Maniram and his peers, jati signified a broader, more porous entity than the English terms caste, tribe, race, and religion, one whose meanings might encompass them all.

Even when it appeared, Maniram's list was outmoded. Contemporary British observers viewed it as a strange mélange of otherwise distinct categories of castes, tribes, and religious communities. Administrators now took jati to mean caste or tribe even as they attempted to order British India's people into neat categories of tribes and castes. Scholar-officials such as George Campbell, William Hunter, Herbert Risley, and Edward Gait viewed the subcontinent as a composite social landscape defined by race. Those of "superior Aryan blood" constituted a hierarchical, Brahminically defined caste society ethnologically discrete from aborigines, wild tribes, and those of "mixed race" birth.[2] Hindus and Muslims too were distinct. Colonial modernity deemed unacceptable Maniram's classification, which placed the Brahmin caste alongside the Kachari tribe and the Goriya Muslim community, because of the divergent racialized origins of the two groups that ethnography claimed to have discovered.

Colonialism's absorption of jati into the modernizing framework of racialized categories was facilitated by the use of administrative tools to count and classify its subjects. The census was an important one. In 1866 the Indian government directed officials to compile comprehensive lists of races and classes.[3] These lists were later published in the census volumes. The theorist Sudipta Kaviraj argues that compilation and public dissemination of the lists hastened a definitive transition from "fuzzy" to "enumerated" boundaries of belonging.[4] As officials annexed jati into ethnographic categories of caste and tribe, they ensured that this indigenous category of social classification was redefined as a racial category. Victorian scientific thought reworked notions of indigenous alterity into unchanging race essences. Ethnographers viewed social classifications in terms of biological descent. They reworked Maniram's chaotic jatis into a neat framework of *varna* (fourfold caste order).[5] For example, the ethnographer Herbert Risley viewed caste and tribe as ethnologically defined relationships. Castes were really races. Distinctions between high and low castes and between castes and tribes signified superior and inferior racial endowment. Like geological deposits, humans were deposited in stratified layers. Recent strata were superior. Risley declared, "The lowest castes preserve the most primitive usages just as the oldest geological formations contain the simplest forms of organic life."[6]

By the late nineteenth century many high-caste élites welcomed these racialized arguments, which they felt affirmed their superior status. Several lower-caste intellectuals also adopted a racialized definition of caste, but these subaltern groups sought to use this logic for their own purposes. For instance, during the 1870s the Marathi publicist Jotiba Phule declared that the *bahujan samaj* (members of the lower castes) were the subcontinent's original inhabitants and its only authentic race, in contrast to later, high-caste interlopers who tricked the lower castes into *ghulamgiri* (slavery).[7] There were many such complex interactions between western-inspired race theories and South Asian intellectual and cultural movements.[8] Rather than a unilateral process of colonial fabrication, local groups actively acted to reinterpret jati as a race-based category.

Over the same period a new generation of Assamese publicists participated in multiple arenas of culture and politics, both within and without the region. Pre-modern conceptions of jati seemed even more obsolete as the local élites who succeeded Maniram's generation adopted broad caste or race categories which might bring them wider relevance. For example, the local caste of "Koleeta" (Kalita) sought a high-caste Hindu status that might be recognized throughout the subcontinent. Among "Kacharees" (Kacharis) the ethnographer's notion of an ancient Bodo race gained popularity. The universal category of "Musalman" replaced the older Assamese terms "Toorook" (Turk) and "Gooreea" (Goriya), which had denoted local Muslim groups.

By the early twentieth century the term jati acquired another, important new meaning. More and more often, jati appeared as a synonym for nation. Categories such as race, caste, and tribe acquired complex, protean meanings through this new signification of jati. In its broadest reading, Assamese jati denoted regional belonging. Simultaneously, the term might denote other identities, whether of caste, tribe, or religion. Through their common use of the term jati, Assamese, Bengali, and Marathi regional identities, as well as Hindu and Muslim religious ones, could all enter into the broad, overarching category of Indian. Yet at the same time as local jatis acquired broader affiliations with local, regional, and national networks, interested groups sought to tighten their boundaries. Some high-caste publicists projected a purified Assamese social identity, which placed monolingual Asomiya-speaking élite Hindus at the apex of the Assamese nation. Lower-caste and tribal publicists resented and actively contested these claims.

This final chapter examines how the appearance of new public arenas after the First World War challenged the dominance of upper-caste male intellectuals in the realms of cultural politics and social action. The wider reach of educational institutions, burgeoning print media, and greater possibilities for economic mobility and political representation brought lower-caste and tribal groups, and a few educated women, into the public domain. A critical mass of literati from previously marginalized groups demanded political rights based on re/formed jati affiliations. Diverse groups of lower-caste and tribal publicists reacted in different ways to a dominant-caste Hindu narrative of racial preeminence and superior entitlement to nationhood.

The colonial state was an important interlocutor through its selection of certain groups for political support and its recognition and rejection of others. Within the uneven and contradictory intersection of power structures, different publics jostled for visibility and state patronage. There were not only important internal hierarchies of class, gender, and status within each of these groups but also changing alliances across various axes. However, it is important for us to keep in mind that many autonomous attempts at assertion remain virtually obscured, with their historical traces scanty or altogether absent. For instance, until late in the twentieth century migrant groups of coolies, peasants, and graziers were less visible in these public areas. Thus far these groups were limited by difficult material circumstances which provided them little access to education and print culture. While publicists articulated divergent, competing accounts of the past and future, a common tendency was to valorize a heroic, gendered history for the region, whether through literature, scholarship, public assemblies, or film. As Assam and India moved toward independence from colonial rule, overlapping and diverging voices dominated the public sphere, seeking a new type of civic visibility and enunciating multiple versions of the visions of progress for women, men, communities, and nations.

"Kachari" Aspirations, "Bodo" Progress

Twentieth-century Bodo Kachari publicists contributed an important new voice to Assam's public sphere. Until the late nineteenth century few Kacharis had the wherewithal to obtain a high school or college education. Colonial officials and local élites alike described them as primitive aboriginals. In the 1840s the scholar-official Brian Hodgson conferred upon Assam's "oldest and most numerous non-Aryan races . . . the generic name of Bodo, being the title given to themselves by the most numerous branch."[9] His description of Bodos as a migratory non-Aryan people had lasting influence. In Hodgson's opinion a prehistoric Bodo race migrated from China into Assam. At a later date it disintegrated into groups of Kachari, Lalung, Rabha, Mech, and Garo tribals.[10] He applied Bodo as a common label for previously distinct Kachari groups living in Assam and North Bengal. While Hodgson classified Bodos within an ancient Turanian race, later ethnographers claimed them as part of a Mongoloid race.[11]

Based on his observations of local Bodo groups, Hodgson judged theirs a tribal society of perfect social equality. Unlike hierarchy-ridden caste society, Bodo Kacharis had "neither servants nor slaves, nor aliens of any kind."[12] This depiction of timeless aboriginal equality remained in force for many years. But in 1906 the British administrator and historian Edward Gait published an authoritative account of the medieval Kachari kings who ruled Lower Assam.[13] This history contradicted Hodgson's premise that Bodos had always been a non-hierarchical tribal society of primitive agriculturists. Another official, B. C. Allen, devised a historical theory of conquest and defeat to resolve this contradiction. Allen theorized that the Kachari kingdom was crushed by Shan newcomers from Burma. Under the name of Ahom, the Shan allied with "Aryan migrants from North India."[14] They reduced a previously complex Bodo Kachari society to "unthinking helot condition."[15] As a result "the ordinary Kachari of Kamrup is an illiterate villager quite innocent of history, has never heard of the Kachari Raj, and as a source of information of anything prior to the present day is completely useless."[16] Conquest, impoverishment, and racial amnesia worsted the once mighty Bodos.

Such colonial speculations about this group of people were often underpinned by utilitarian motives. Alone among Assam's inhabitants, nineteenth-century observers viewed Kacharis as ideal labouring subjects. Hodgson acclaimed their "high character as skilful, laborious cultivators and peaceable, respectable subjects."[17] The Assamese official Gunabhiram Barua described them as a hardy non-Aryan people who took advantage of new waged opportunities under colonial rule.[18] Tea work was one of the new employment avenues that attracted Kacharis. Yet their planter employers soon came to dislike the very propensity for equality that Hodgson had admired. Kachari resistance to plantation discipline gradually earned them the reputation of unruliness. By the late nineteenth century only Assamese planters employed Kachari workers in significant numbers; European planters preferred to import Dhangar coolies. Many Kacharis resorted to other waged openings such as construction or army and police recruitment. Educated young men gravitated toward school teaching and petty trade.[19]

As Kachari involvement in the British tea industry receded, the tone of colonial observations also changed. Instead of discussing Kacharis solely in terms of suitability for manual work, many observers focused on their ethnic and religious traits. This was the period when the British began to visualize themselves as protectors of primitive groups from Aryan and Hindu assault. They recorded the religious changes that affected Kachari and other tribal groups and brought them within the orbit of caste society. The census of 1872 observed, "Wherever they are not protected by mountains or by jungles, the non-Aryan residents invariably have yielded, and are yielding, to the overpowering fascination of the Hindu religion and of that higher civilization to which it is the key."[20] The early-twentieth-century Assam gazetteers compiled by B. C. Allen described how "Lower Assam Kacharis, when they are converted to Hinduism, are generally incorporated into the ranks of the Koch caste. In Sibsagar, most of them have foresworn pigs, fowls and liquor and live much as do the other humble Hindu castes."[21] Quite in Hodgson's fashion, the S.P.G. missionary Sidney Endle, who wrote about the Kacharis at the end of the nineteenth century, praised them as diligent aboriginals. But he was less interested in their economic redemption than in the spiritual. Endle's main objective was the Christian conversion of his Kachari flock.

Colonial officialdom viewed Kachari involvement with Assamese Vaishnavism and other Hinduizing sects as standard examples of the long-standing Brahminical practice of absorbing socially peripheral groups. Christianity, on the other hand, they viewed as providing a rescue from savagery and from being "overpowered" by Hinduism and caste tyranny. This top-down analysis missed the new feature distinguishing these movements for social and religious change — that educated young Kacharis were setting the agenda. This new generation was dynamic and eclectic in its adoption of novel identities and practices, whether from western race science or from the Hindu and Christian religious repertoires. Through new religious and social initiatives, modern Kachari reformers sought to reject caste hierarchies, reinterpret Vedantic thought, and devise new theories of Bodo race destiny.

By the early twentieth century a small Kachari public emerged from among petty traders, schoolteachers, and small-time contractors. Its participants sought out alternatives to the limited mobility offered by established Hinduism. Some, educated in mission schools, were attracted to Christianity. Others preferred a new, exclusive Hindu sect called "Brahma." The founder of this movement was Kalicharan (1860–1938), a Kachari trader based in Goalpara. A Bengali mendicant, Sibnarayan Paramhansa, inspired him to venerate Brahma, the Supreme Soul. Kalicharan summoned comrades to join him in a new, monotheistic faith whose members adopted a new surname, Brahma, in place of their older, demeaning tribal names.[22] Simultaneously they claimed a new Bodo identity.

The Brahma movement spread rapidly. By 1921 the census reported that many Kacharis had abandoned tribal names and were describing themselves as Bara [sic] by caste and language, and Brahma by religion.[23] These reforming Bodos rejected ritual and caste hierarchies. Brahmin priests had enjoyed a monopoly on the performance of religious ceremonies. They often refused to officiate for lower castes and tribals. On behalf of Bodos, Kalicharan challenged these inequities. In 1908 he took a momentous step when he acted as an officiating priest. A follower exulted at this: "No Brahmanical superiority is recognized. The Boros who adopted the new form of religion began to call themselves as Brahmas styling their religion as Brahma religion. They recite Gayatries, perform Homa sacrifice, and worship God through the sun."[24] Previously these Hindu rituals were reserved for higher castes. The Brahma movement challenged exclusivity. Kalicharan found the available models of Assamese religion to be unsatisfactory. In their place he sought to forge independent links to reformed Hindu churches beyond the region. His followers saw theirs as a new and higher form of Vedic religion which served the interests of educated Kacharis.[25]

The census report of 1921 gave wide publicity to this new generation of Kacharis, which included the Bodo politician Rupnath Brahma.[26] In a note for the census report Rupnath claimed that Kacharis always formed a separate society which "never allowed their tribal peculiarities to be merged into the Hindu society."[27] Previously, educated Kacharis like Rupnath possessed few options for social mobility other than absorption into the Hindu lower castes. The Brahma religion offered him and his peers a new opportunity to assert a respectable and autonomous Bodo identity. No longer subordinated to caste society, these modernizing Bodos sought to restore what they saw as lost racial glory. As they pledged to reform less advanced brethren, educated Bodos sought to reclaim a past when their ancestors were "the most influential people in the whole of the Brahmaputra valley."[28]

From 1919 Bodo publicists organized numerous conclaves and associations to forward their improving agenda. These included the Bodo Chatra Sanmilan (Bodo Students Association), Kachari Chatra Sanmilan (Kachari Students Association), and Bodo Maha Sanmilan (Greater Bodo Association).[29] The fifth annual session of the Bodo Students Association, held at Simbargaon in 1923, was attended by over eight hundred people. It called for village schools for boys and girls, a special educational fund for the poor, and reduced wedding expenses. Association members were urged to abjure pork, alcohol, and the practice of animal sacrifice to the gods. Bodo women were exhorted to follow the examples of legendary females such as the virtuous wife Sita of the *Ramayana* epic in their lives and conduct.[30] The association also resolved to establish a school and a cooperative society to promote spinning and weaving. It called for circulating Asomiya newspapers in Bodo villages to advance literacy and knowledge of current events.[31] The Bodo associations often sought patronage from established Assamese figures who showed sympathy to the Bodo cause. For example, the tea planter Bisturam Barua received the title of "Kachari Raja" for his financial support of the community's events.[32] Occasionally a liberal-minded religious head such as Pitambar Deb Goswami, the Gosain of the Goramur satra, was invited.[33] The presence of these public figures gave Bodo events prominence in the region's media.[34] Guests praised educated Bodos for their desire to ameliorate the lot of the backward segments of their community.

It is not easy to reconstruct the thoughts and actions of this nascent Bodo public, since constituents had limited access to social capital and print media.[35] Ideas and structures were constantly in flux as they flowed through multiple organizations and meetings. Fragmentary traces of Bodo publicists' ideas appear in the rare pamphlets that have survived in archives. These reveal the divergent approaches to social progress that were on offer. A parallel can be drawn with early-twentieth-century Bengal. The historians Sumit Sarkar and P. K. Datta describe a flood of printed pamphlet literature written by lower-caste and Muslim literati from obscure villages. These were cheap, flimsy pamphlets and booklets, imbued with an improvement ethic of education and social reform.[36] In early-twentieth-century

Assam too, despite its smaller concentration of print and literacy, a didactic pamphlet culture emerged whose participants included lower-caste, tribal, and Muslim males, and even a few women.[37]

Among the Bodo contributions to this genre a good example is the tract *Kacharir Katha* (The Story of the Kacharis; 1927) by the schoolteacher Jadunath Khakhlari, whose approach to social regeneration differed from the views of the Brahma sect. This pamphlet was a published version of the powerful address that Jadunath had delivered at the annual meeting of the Kachari Jatiyo Sanmilan (Kachari Community Association).[38] Jadunath accepted the notion of a greater Bodo race which would unite different groups. Yet in contrast to Kalicharan and his followers, he wished to retain the name Kachari. He criticized the term Bodo as a neologism which denied the Kachari historical legacy: "If we ourselves see the name Kachari as shameful so will other groups."[39] In this manner Jadunath sought to reclaim past Kachari contributions to Assamese culture and literature. He reminded his readers that "the Kachari language [was the one] from whose roots sprang the present Asomiya language, whose king was the first patron of the religion and its books."[40] Jadunath voiced the views of those Bodos who felt that they might lose their claim to the rich heritage of Assam's medieval Kachari and Koch kingdoms. In the vacuum created by the absence of an acknowledged history of state formation, colonial observers and Assamese élites had wrongly dismissed Bodo Kacharis as a primitive people. For example, colonial officials photographed Bodos as the Brahmaputra valley example of a primitive tribe.[41] Modernizing Bodos felt that they had to distinguish themselves from "savage" tribal neighbours such as Nagas even while resisting caste domination.

By the 1940s Bodos had adopted a variety of political and cultural strategies to achieve their objectives of social and political progress. Some sought to join a new political grouping that unified Assam's different "plains tribes" into one party. The basis for this was their common identity as "Mongolia people," that is, people of "Mongoloid" racial heritage who had lived in Assam far longer than the descendants of Aryans.[42] Other Bodos sought connections with national figures such as M.C. Rajah, who represented the political leadership of all-India "Depressed Class" organizations. Educated Bodos in the twentieth century employed a host of these local and national strategies even as they sought to create an autonomous cultural and political identity.[43] Yet the continued economic and educational weakness of the community, accentuated by rural dependence on remote, marginal tracts of land, made this project a peculiarly fragile one. It remained peculiarly prone to internal cleavages and fissiparous tendencies.[44]

"Dom," "Nadiyal," "Kaibarta": Journeys toward Caste

In British India a host of low-status groups seized new political and economic opportunities for economic and social mobility.[45] In the manner of Kacharis, these groups often renamed themselves. The census of 1901 interpreted the act of renaming as a "refusal of those at the bottom of the social scale to acquiesce in the humble positions assigned to them."[46] For Assam's Dom fisher caste, previously at the lowest end of the ritual hierarchy, this refusal took the form of claims to Aryanist belonging through the new names of Nadiyal and Kaibarta. In colonial Assam the upper echelons of Dom society succeeded for the most part in acquiring new, respectable caste identities within the larger Hindu fold, helped by commercial prosperity and Vaishnavite affiliations.

In his account of Assam published in 1829, the chronicler Haliram Dhekial Phukan acknowledged "the admirable qualities of Doms, despite their low ritual status."[47] Already Doms were prospering and sought the new name of Nadiyal.[48] The district official Captain Butler noted that even impecunious boatmen preferred the less opprobrious name of Nadiyal (watermen) to that of Dom, which carried associations of social degradation.[49] For the community as a whole, attempts at social mobility were linked to prosperity within a rapidly changing political economy. Most inhabitants of Assam caught fish for their consumption, but only Doms sold fish commercially. Higher castes considered this trade socially low.[50] The growing commercialization of the fish trade created considerable wealth. Many well-to-do Doms adopted surnames from other castes. But they needed official ratification for wider acceptance as a "clean" caste. The census listing of castes and tribes seemed the best instrument to advance their claims.

For Dom élites the acquisition of Nadiyal status would only be a first step. Assam already possessed an agriculturist caste of Kaibartas.

Prosperous Dom/Nadiyals aspired to join Kaibarta ranks while wishing to retain their profitable occupation of trade in fish. The acquisition of Kaibarta caste status, they felt, would allow them to claim an Aryan lineage. By the early twentieth century newly vocal Dom/Nadiyal publicists organized into associations such as the All Assam Kaibarta Sanmilan (Association) to lobby for state support. They sent numerous petitions to remind the chief commissioner that "during [the] Abor and Manipur expeditions, hundreds of boatmen performed one of the most arduous work[s] that was ever done by any civil community."[51] In return they asked him to recognize their new name of Kaibarta. They claimed that this renaming had acquired urgency because of the social changes tied to the tea economy. Coolie newcomers included members of Bengal's untouchable Dom caste, which did not exist in Assam. As a result, Assam's respectable and affluent Doms risked being confused with that "degraded and dirty Bengali coolie, the remover of filth and dead bodies."[52] Since the colonial state had introduced these coolies, it should take responsibility for the confusion.

The fisher people's growing prosperity made it easier for them to achieve their goals. Until 1901 census officials refused to reclassify Doms as either Nadiyas or Kaibartas. But the state was eventually forced to acknowledge the economic influence of fish traders. In the Lakhimpur district annual auctions of fishing rights fetched almost Rs 30,000 in revenues from Dom/Nadiyal traders.[53] Fish sellers conducted a lucrative trade with markets near plantations.[54] Each decennial volume of the census contained evidence of a new concession bestowed upon this increasingly important community by the colonial state. In 1911 officials recognized Doms by the name of Nadiyal.[55] In 1921 Nadiyals were upgraded to Kaibartas.[56] Ironically, even this promotion did not satisfy all members. An élite section began to lobby for a separate name, Mahishya Vaisya. This new title might allow them to build political connections with Bengal's powerful caste of the same name which had successfully made the transition from Kaibarta to Mahisya.[57] In the wake of the Government of India Act of 1919, which expanded political representation, Kaibarta hopes for advancement in this regard rested on strategic alliances with other marginal groups. In 1930 the increased social and economic power of the Kaibarta leadership enabled the establishment of the newspaper *Tinidiniya Asomiya* as a voice for their community and other socially subordinated groups.[58] These Kaibarta publicists, in the manner of their Bodo counterparts, sought to forge links with leaders of all-India "Depressed Classes" to press the state for increased representation.[59]

On the social front Kaibartas sought support for their improvement agenda from high-caste élites, even while publicly affirming a commitment to Vaishnavite religion and ritual norms. A vocal champion was Pitambar Deb Goswami, the Gosain of the Goramur satra, whose Gandhian ideology inspired him to support lower-caste reform movements.[60] His liberal views were in sharp contrast to those of other Gosains who still discriminated against the fisher community as a *heen* (degraded) caste which should be denied entry to places of worship.[61]

As part of their desire for upward social mobility, male Kaibarta publicists evinced a new hostility to women's labour and public activity. Previously, Dom women were noted for their active participation in numerous remunerative tasks. Fisher women collected whelk shells to make a lime condiment, which was commonly eaten with betel nut and pan.[62] These women sold fish, lime, and other goods at local markets. Observers described the Assam countryside as populated by these women, transplanting rice or fishing.[63] But Kaibarta publicists began to claim that women who worked outside the household in this manner stigmatized the entire caste and even the Assamese nation.[64] They believed that women should abjure such lowly commercial activities and asked Kaibarta men to prevent the women of their households even from visiting markets.[65]

In newly fledged public arenas there is often a tendency to portray women's work as marginal to the reproduction of the household economy. In a structured setting where cultural or ideological contest negotiation takes place among various publics, gendered opposition between the categories of "public woman" and "virtue" becomes an essential ingredient for social validation.[66] Over these years of social and political flux many Assamese publicists, as well as Kaibarta activists, advocated the withdrawal of female labour from the public domain as essential for respectability.[67] Efforts to restrict working-class women's waged activity and economic independence acquired additional meaning in the Assam setting, in which female coolies were stigmatized as sexually promiscuous women. A popular folksong of the Bihu harvest festival scornfully told of tea garden *sahibs* (white men) and their *mems* (mistresses) among the coolie workers.[68]

Kaibarta publicists viewed the woman fish trader who was exposed to the public gaze as the biggest threat to the community's respectability. Strictures against women's waged work became a recurrent theme in their writings. At the same time they created a prescriptive example of female virtue for Kaibarta women. They acquired this example from the annals of Vaishnavite devotionalism, from which they disseminated the tale of a virtuous fisherman's wife, Radhika, whose virtue was put to the test by the saint Sankardeb.[69] The humble Radhika triumphantly passed the test, which high-caste women failed. The saint bestowed on her the honorific title of Santi or Sati (chaste wife). From the 1920s an annual public festivity, the Radhika Santi Utsav, commemorated this heroic yet conformist ancestor.[70] In 1931 the All Assam Kaibarta Mahila Sanmilan (Women's Association) organized a public meeting to mark the occasion. A Kaibarta woman schoolteacher, Labanya Prabha Das, presided there.[71] Her example showed that it was becoming acceptable for respectable Assamese women to work outside the home, but only within a narrow range of new middle-class vocations.

Restoring "Ahom": A Place for Tribe and Race in History

From the early twentieth century a rapid and belatedly intense surge of activity transformed late colonial Assam's public arenas. Efforts proliferated to stratify, consolidate, and challenge ritual boundaries. Numerous lower-caste and tribal groups used the colonial apparatus of print, enumeration, and representation to accumulate political and cultural capital. This process was particularly complex for Ahom publicists as they dealt with the complex ramifications of caste and tribe, history, and national belonging.

With Ahoms, British administrators steered an uneasy course. They found it difficult to comprehend Ahom social ranking in precolonial Assam, since their practices and ritual stature differed from those of Kshatriya ruling groups elsewhere in South Asia. The historian Yasmin Saikia describes Ahom élites as a relatively open status group encompassing a diverse set of local peoples who participated in a warrior ruling ethos.[72] Rather than an inherited bodily identity, Ahom was a prestigious rank achieved by those in royal favour. This high social and economic status existed alongside a relatively low ritual rank. Stymied by this dissonance, early colonial observers preferred to portray Ahoms as an alien race of invaders rather than a local status group.[73]

The British takeover traumatized the Ahom warrior élite. The East India Company's officials reported the failure of British efforts to employ Ahom aristocrats, since they lacked any usable skills.[74] This did not mean that the Ahom upper classes lost everything. Most retained some land. Where they lagged significantly, in the manner of North Indian Muslim aristocrats, was in acquiring new educational and job opportunities. The educationalist, politician, and author Padmanath Gohain Barua (1871–1946) formed a rare exception. He was the best-known Ahom representative among the first generation of Assamese publicists. His unique position allowed him to take a pivotal part in linguistic and cultural politics and the creation of a modern Ahom political movement.[75] Padmanath was the son of a mauzadar who supplemented his landed income with elephant trapping.[76] From a comfortable rural home and small-town high school, Padmanath proceeded to a college education in urban Bengal. In Calcutta he became dedicated to the cause of Asomiya language and literature. Heated discussions about his mother-tongue's backwardness inspired him to write its first novel, *Lahori*.[77] At this time Padmanath's energies were focused on Mother Assam. He was a founding member of the ABUSS, which from 1872 aimed to bring about a renaissance of language, literature, and society. A British official commended Padmanath as "a rising young man [who] writes in pure Assamese and does not over-Sanskritise or introduce Bengali words unnecessarily. [He is a] real friend to his countrymen and their language."[78]

After his return to Assam, Padmanath remained active in the campaign to regenerate the Asomiya language. At the same time he discovered a new mission: to promote race recovery and progress for his own Ahom community. He united this specifically Ahom agenda with his long-standing activism on behalf of the Asomiya language. His return as an adult to Sibsagar, the former Ahom capital, had a profound impact. He relished the atmosphere of Ahom royal glory associated with the town's historic buildings.[79] As he commenced a career as a schoolteacher, he became increasingly obsessed with the objective of *jatiyo unnati* (national progress). Padmanath defined his quest as a twofold mission. He sought to reinvigorate both an Ahom *gyati* (kin group) and a larger Assamese jati. Doing so involved a crucial semantic disjuncture. In his writings Padmanath reserved the term gyati, and its intimate, familial resonances, for his Ahom kith and kin. He used the term jati to denote Assamese — a fictive community of friends, sympathizers, and fellow patriots.[80] For the rest of his political career Padmanath remained active in both the Ahom and Assamese causes.

Through the 1890s Padmanath travelled on elephant to remote parts of Upper Assam in his quest to regenerate his Ahom kin. In 1893 he organized the first public session of his new organization, the Ahom Sabha, at Sibsagar. Subsequently he established its branches all over Upper Assam. The Ahom Sabha's first activity was an anti-opium crusade. Padmanath adopted a modernizing platform that challenged the established values of Ahom notables for whom opium was indispensable for socialization and daily life. This anti-opium campaign gave him a prominent place among Assamese reformers eager to improve those whom they saw as their indolent and intemperate countrymen. Padmanath joined a new political body, the Assam Association, founded by distinguished Assamese and Bengali residents of the province such as Manik Chandra Barua, Prasanna Chandra Ghosh, Mathuramohan Barua, and Radhanath Changkakati. He attended its first annual convention, held at Dibrugarh in 1905. In 1911 he became the president of the association. Given the general unhappiness with the partition of 1905, which annexed Assam to Eastern Bengal, the Assam Association had consciously sought a commonality of interests between Assamese, Bengalis, Hindus, and Muslims. To this end its proceedings were conducted in the English language. But under Padmanath's presidency, the Asomiya language became the official vernacular. This shift signaled that its political agenda had begun to exclude non-Asomiya speakers. In 1917 Padmanath was elected the first president of the Asom Sahitya Sabha (Assam Literary Association). This prestigious post cemented his stature as a champion of Asomiya.

Padmanath continued to be active in Ahom culture and politics. In 1910 the Ahom Sabha was renamed the Ahom Association even as its agenda became overtly political and exclusionist. The shift from

Sabha to association was a significant one. Under Padmanath's leadership the new association aimed to establish Ahoms as a separate political force in Assam's political landscape. As with other local groups, claims to historical achievement easily developed into demands for current political representation. In 1912 Assam regained its status as a chief commissioner's province after revocation of the partition of 1905. The Government of India Act of 1909 had created a Legislative Council for Assam, but this was constituted only in 1913. The Government of India Act of 1919 raised the strength of the council to fifty-three members, of whom forty-one were to be elected and the remaining twelve nominated by the government. The constitution of the council provided an opportunity for sectional groups such as Ahoms to lobby for political representation.

On 21 February 1928 the Ahom Association issued a call for special seats and a separate electorate for Ahoms. It justified this demand on account of "their brilliant past and present backwardness."[81] Similarly, during 1928–29 several other lower-caste and tribal publicists advanced claims for separate electoral enumeration before the Simon Commission.[82] Impressed by the Ahom community's historical claims, the commission granted it a nominated seat in the council. In contrast, Bodo and Kaibarta petitions were turned down. Subsequently the government nominated Padmanath Gohain Barua as the first Ahom member of the Assam Legislative Council.

Padmanath's autobiography includes a mannered, retrospective description of this political victory that is silent on the differences and contestations within the Ahom community. There existed strong counter-movements to his Ahom Sabha. One opposing faction asserted that Ahoms belonged to the prestigious Kshatriya warrior caste. Like Kaibartas, these Ahoms sought state patronage for their claims to higher ritual status within Hindu society. To this end they established a Kshatriya Association. From 1902 the chief commissioner received numerous petitions from this association demanding that the state should recognize Ahoms as Kshatriyas,[83] but the administrators of the census of 1911 rejected this claim. Disappointed, the petition's organizers blamed their failure upon a prejudiced Brahmin lobby that sought to reduce Ahoms to a lowly position vis-à-vis other high-caste groups. They cited recent, widely publicized Brahminical attacks on Ahoms, including one by the orthodox Brahmin Tirthanath Goswami, whose book *Ripunjay Smriti* described Ahoms as *Antaryja* (outcastes) and prescribed penances for Hindus who associated with them.[84] A noted Bengali Brahmin scholar at Cotton College, Padmanath Vidyavinod, also provoked outrage when he described Ahom students as *Mlechhas* (outcaste non-Aryans) unworthy of Sanskrit learning.[85] There were strong protests when a circular of the Education Department classified Ahoms as a "Depressed Class."[86] Most Ahom élites were sensitive about their relative loss of position in the colonial era. Even for those who did not wish for Kshatriya status, the lowly attributions denied a glorious past and slandered their present standing.

In response to attacks from orthodox Brahmins, some leaders of the Ahom Association changed direction, calling for members to abjure Hinduism altogether and return to ancestral Bailung worship. Whether they did so or not, certainly after the 1920s Ahoms articulated fewer claims to high-caste status. Instead many publicists pressed the government to class Ahoms as a "racial minority" for electoral purposes. Others demanded political recognition of Ahoms as a distinct religious community. Yet another group, supported by yet another new political body, the Ahom Conference, enunciated a clear notion of racial separation from Hindu society. This group called for broad-based unity among "Mongoloid" communities such as Bodos, Deoris, Mishings, and Ahoms. Even as these Ahoms sought a common political front with other local groups, they claimed a leading role as the "foremost tribal race of Assam."[87] In January 1935 the Ahom Conference publicly urged noncooperation with Brahmin priests and the "social amalgamation of Ahoms, Kacharis, Deoris, and other Mongolian people."[88] This campaign resulted in the creation of a new organization, the Tribal League, which sought to maximize tribal political influence by exploiting the differences between the two leading political parties in the province, the Muslim League and the Congress.

During the 1940s, as Indian independence seemed imminent, several Ahom leaders renewed attempts for an electoral alliance of race-based "Mongolia groups" to increase political leverage after the British departure. An important initiative was taken in March 1945, when a convention of Assam tribes met at Shillong. Since this convention had representatives from Bodos, Ahoms, Chutias, Khasis, Manipuris, and Nagas, it plausibly claimed to represent most of the hill and plains tribes of the northeast frontier. This meeting on a common platform was indeed momentous, given the political, social, and linguistic divisions among its constituent groups. The convention pointedly excluded caste groups on grounds of their Aryan identity.[89] Its resolutions demanded a halt to nontribal immigration into tribal lands, a measure directed against time-expired coolies and East Bengali peasant settlers. Most controversially, the convention declared that Assam had never been a part of India, since its original tribes and races were ethnically and culturally different from the rest of the subcontinent. Therefore it opposed inclusion into any proposed partitioned nation. Neither Pakistan nor Hindustan was acceptable. In their place it demanded a separate "Free State."[90]

In 1945 the Assam government, in its report to Delhi superiors (which eventually rested in the files of the Department of External Affairs), was unperturbed by this demand. It declared the convention a mere symptom of the desire among tribes for some form of cohesion, a mere symbolic protest against the perceived domination of mainstream Hindu and Muslim communities. This was an oversimplification. Certainly in the first few years after Indian independence most Ahoms continued to live peaceably alongside other communities, as did most other Assamese. Bodos seemed preoccupied with internal linguistic and religious divisions. The only open defiance came from the inhabitants of the Naga Hills who were unhappy with forcible inclusion in India. Their small numbers and remote location made the Naga plight of little import to the Indian government, even when they resorted to violence. However, as events in subsequent decades showed, Assam's alternate publics were rapidly expanding their reach and their demands. Brahmaputra valley élites and the all-India political leadership misunderstood both the determination of tribal groups to resist the Assamese élite's hegemony and the determination in the adjacent Naga Hills for separation from an Indian nation-state. Eventually mainstream India's lack of respect for groups still perceived to be on the margins of Indic culture, continued underdevelopment of the region, and the seeming governmental indifference to local aspirations caused unrest and bloodshed in Assam and its adjoining territories of India's Northeast, which continue to the present day.

Heroic History and the Gendered Nation

By the early twentieth century other modes of nation making were also at work, not least in the sphere of cultural representations and historical mythologizing. For instance, in 1928 the Simon Commission, in its deliberations into the future of Indian constitutional reform, received a strongly worded letter of protest from Assam. A young lawyer expressed indignation that an exhibition at the Calcutta Museum classified Ahoms as an uncivilized hill tribe.[91] This affront to Ahom history seemed to represent an insult to the entire Assamese nation. Indic affiliation was at risk if Assam's pre-colonial rulers were compared to "savages such as the naked Nagas."[92] Since the late nineteenth century Assamese publicists had asserted the Brahmaputra valley's distinctiveness from its hill neighbours, the peoples seemingly without history. As Ahoms debated their relationship with Hindu society, local intellectuals wove incidents from the Ahom past into a heroic Assam history. This history coexisted alongside, albeit with considerable potential for tension, the grand narrative of Indo-Aryan belonging claimed by many Assamese.

The most prolific voice among the intellectuals was Assam's first professional historian, Surya Kumar Bhuyan (1894–1964). Bhuyan was loud in his assertions that the buranjis, Ahom-era chronicles, were the greatest asset possessed by modern Assam. He explicitly connected historical scholarship and nationalist pride. Bhuyan remarked, "Give me the buranjis of Assam and I will say what the people of Assam are. The buranjis are our strengthening tie to bind us with the past, maintain the solidarity of the Assamese people, and protect us from any threatened erosion of our nationalism."[93] Bhuyan began his career as a professor of English literature at Guwahati's Cotton College. He later earned a doctorate in history from the University of London and had a distinguished public career in Assam.[94] As someone who wrote copiously in both the English and Asomiya languages, Bhuyan was the most prominent figure among a host of history-minded publicists. In 1912 the growing interest in old inscriptions and manuscripts led to the foundation of the Kamrup Anushilan Samiti (Kamrup Research Society), at Guwahati. The society began as a private body, inspired by the Borendra Anusandhan Samiti in neighbouring North Bengal (Koch Behar), but soon acquired state patronage. From 1925 the Asom Sahitya Sabha's annual meetings included a special buranji session on historical writings. Bhuyan brought wide publicity to these past-minded endeavours when he forged links with eminent scholars in Bengal, Maharashtra, and Gujarat. He sought their advice and approbation for Assam's rich historical materials.[95]

By the 1920s the study of Assamese history had acquired considerable academic and institutional trappings. But the history's distinctiveness from myth and fiction remained blurred. Sudipta Kaviraj observes that colonial intellectuals wrote an enormous amount of history. Much of it was respectable in modern academic terms, but much of it was fictional. Often the authors viewed both types of writing as integral to the building of a comprehensive historical narrative.[96] Bhuyan's oeuvre displays this eclecticism in abundance. His works included numerous scholarly printings of old chronicles and well-regarded tomes on political history. Examples included his compilation of two old chronicles, *Assamor Padya Buranji* (Assam's Verse Histories), and his work based on his doctoral thesis, *Anglo-Assamese Relations*. A prolific writer, Bhuyan simultaneously produced various other works on the past, written in a faux-historical, semifictional vein.[97] The distinction between these works and his scholarly productions was left unclear. Readers had to plough through a work before they could know whether it was fictional or factual. For example, the verse ballad *Jaymati Upakhyan* (The Narrative of Jaymati) depicted the trials undergone by a seventeenth-century Ahom princess named Jaymati. In language and style it resembled historical chronicles. Nowhere was there any acknowledgement that this was a work of fiction by a modern author. Bhuyan's biography of a legendary Ahom warrior, *Lachit Barphukan and His Times*, was another work replete with long passages of fictionalized dialogue. While Kaviraj calls writings such as these fictionalized or imaginary history, the historian Kumkum Chatterjee's characterization of them as popular and romantic histories seems more apposite. As she shows, they combined and commingled fragments of historical "fact" with stories and accounts of cultural value and antiquity to better inspire and rejuvenate readers.[98]

A number of other Assamese publicists made similar creative excursions into the terrain of history. Their writings ranged from short, informative essays that became a staple of the vernacular periodical to historical novels and plays in the manner of Sir Walter Scott. In the field of historical prose Assam's best-known figure was Rajani Kanta Bordoloi (1867–1940). His works ranged from a tribal romance, *Miri Jiyari* (Daughter of the Miri Tribe), published in 1895, to a series of historical novels set against the Burmese invasion. He also wrote numerous ethnographic essays about tribal life and customs. Writers like Bordoloi and Bhuyan saw history's didactic agenda as equally well served by fiction and fact.

In these works publicists stated their desire to redress the scarcity of vernacular materials on history. As they employed a new, expanded meaning for the term jati, these writers claimed to speak for more than their actual readership. Throughout the subcontinent the reading public was small, and skewed toward urban male élites. Publicists tended to conflate this readership with the entirety of the new jati. In this manner participants in the vernacular print milieu imagined a fresh collective self, the nation, as they sought to construct its history. The historian Riho Isaka shows how there was a conscious and continuous move to describe history in a specific form and to spread this history among a wide range of the population.[99] Again, Kaviraj notes the ambiguity of the term jati as an index of the historical difficulty of discourse. Authors stretched the meaning of jati in unaccustomed directions as they attempted to shape its meaning away from caste and community, and toward that of nationality and nation.[100]

By the early twentieth century publicists began to transmute ingredients of an Ahom dynastic past into an Assamese allegory of sacrifice and redemption. Their most popular theme was the story of Jaymati, an Ahom princess who fell victim to her husband's enemies. This incident occurred in the seventeenth century, at a time when powerful ministers made and unmade puppet Ahom kings. The unscrupulous Lora Raja (boy king) and his minister viewed the prince Gadapani as a formidable rival. They conspired to arrest him, but his wife Jaymati had already persuaded him to flee to the Naga Hills. The king's men seized and tortured her. Jaymati's husband returned in Naga disguise and asked her to surrender him. She refused and sent him away. Soon after, the king's men tortured and killed Jaymati. Gadapani eventually defeated his rivals and founded a mighty dynasty. His virtuous wife Jaymati's sacrifice was not in vain.

After its first print appearance in 1899, the story of Jaymati was retold numerous times.[101] Its best-known literary versions were the plays by Padmanath Gohain Barua (1900) and Lakshminath Bezbarua (1915). There were also various retellings in the Bengali and Sanskrit languages.[102] The story reached a pinnacle of fame when it was filmed in 1935 by Jyotiprasad Agarwala (1903–51), a well-known tea planter and cultural entrepreneur. Assamese publicists emphasized the importance of Jaymati as a local icon. Her heroic narrative seemed to offer an authentic history of the Assamese nation. Through the decades of nationalist upheaval, Jaymati retained pride of place for the Assamese public. A variety of public commemorations kept her story in the public eye. The virtues that she embodied — female heroism, self-sacrifice, and conjugal virtue at a time of political danger — took centre stage in representations of Assam's past and present. One school primer declared, "Inspired by the example of Sati Jaymati are the daughters and mothers of our land."[103]

The mythology of origin that these publicists constructed for the Jaymati tale offers a telling example of the blurred line in national hagiographies between history, myth, and fiction. The story's modern retellers asserted that Ahom historical chronicles had preserved the legend of this exemplar of Assamese wifely virtue. In reality, extant chronicles did not even mention Jaymati. Two old manuscripts cited her, but only as a nameless "Prince Gadapani's woman."[104] Among Assamese publicists there was a telling silence about the sources of the Jaymati story. Those were the ballads and folklore transmitted orally by Upper Assam's women. Male literary figures such as Padmanath Gohian Barua subsequently appropriated and modified these oral folk materials. Their printed narratives elaborated a simple folktale into vivid descriptions of Jaymati's conversations with her husband, the palace conspirators, the fugitive's Naga Hills sojourn, and the tortures that the faithful wife suffered. The popular basis of these authors' inspiration went unacknowledged, as did the fictional nature of their literary embellishments to the tale. Through the publicists' claim that the buranji chronicles were their real source, this mythic history obtained an impeccable genealogy. The prestigious male authors claimed historical veracity for their literary productions while concealing their appropriation of a female-centred popular tradition.

Throughout colonial India gender played an important role in constituting nationalist and modernizing identities. Confronted with images of the "manly Englishman" and the "effeminate Native," the colonial intelligentsia tended to react in two ways.[105] Often they identified positively with the British diagnosis of the Indian condition and its advocacy of social reform for Indian redemption. At the same time, the intelligentsia felt constrained to prove Indian humanitarian instincts in the eyes of doubters. The feminist scholar Susie Tharu suggests that as a response to the British emphasis on native oppression of women, local publicists often privileged the image of a woman who voluntarily chose the path of suffering and death to save her people.[106] In this manner Asomiya narratives depicted Jaymati's spiritual strength overcoming her enemy's might. Her sacrifice allowed her consort to carve out a glorious Ahom destiny for Assam. Through suffering and self-sacrifice, the female hero made a moral point more powerful than any conventional tale of male military valour.

Simultaneously, another, more conservative rendition of the Jaymati tale began to appear. This was a representation of Jaymati as a sati (a virtuous and religious Hindu wife). An orthodox Brahmin publicist, Kumudeswar Barthakur, first bestowed the title of sati upon Jaymati in his brief tract *Jaymati Kahini* (1918).[107] The mythological Sati represented the embodiment of Hindu female chastity, the pure symbol of a life of self-abnegation, and devotion to husband and dharma. This Hinduized attribution shifted the Jaymati story closer to Indic values at the same time as it retained its local roots. The use of this sati framework allowed the Jaymati theme and its author admittance into a pan-Indian Hindu universe.

The term sati must be located within the larger historical context of its use in the Asomiya language. Although colonial Assam never experienced sati burnings of widows, its upper castes began to emulate their Bengali peers in gendered values. Female chastity and virtue became the normative standard by which a caste community could heighten its ritual status. Previously practices such as women's working in agriculture and petty trade, or the free interaction of the sexes during the Bihu harvest festivities, were widespread. Twentieth-century Assamese publicists sought to reform these aspects of local life, which they criticized as suitable only for people of low social standing. Against these practices they juxtaposed new middle-class ideals of conjugal compatibility and female formal education. These ideals, when translated into modern life, might train the nation's women to better perform the roles of wife and mother for its men. The image of a local sati asserted Assamese suitability for the elevated destiny of the new Indian woman.[108]

Occasionally authors displayed some discomfort at the inconsistencies in their claims. Kumudeswar Barthakur acknowledged that readers might be surprised at his reverence for "a non-Hindu woman who is ritually impure."[109] He sought to preempt such criticism when he asserted that although Jaymati was not a Hindu, she exemplified "all the virtues of Hindu goddesses such as Sita."[110] The title sati became Jaymati's because of her virtues, despite her Ahom husband's famed (non-Hindu) ability to eat an entire calf in one sitting. This Brahmin narrator impressively placed his Assamese sati within an Indo-Aryan pantheon of female virtue which included Sita, Draupadi, and Savitri.[111]

Kumudeswar Barthakur's avowed objective was to spread "knowledge about Jaymati among the ignorant sections such as women and rural folk, who were uninformed of her name and virtues."[112] This was an ironic claim. Male publicists had borrowed from women's folk ballads without any acknowledgement. Now they transmitted their literary borrowings, suitably embellished, to a new female audience. The Ahom princess Jaymati was reshaped into the image of a Hindu sati and assimilated into an Indo-Aryan model of chastity and virtue. From the 1920s a hagiography of ideal womanhood (which started with Sita and ended with Jaymati) entered girls' schoolbooks. Often Indic and Assamese heroes were joined by Queen Victoria, the British Empire's approved model of female domestic virtues.[113] Jaymati also inspired local imitations. For example, Kaibarta publicists in their quest for respectability "excavated" another sati from their own caste history, Santi Radhika. Another local group, the Chutias, found a virtuous princess, Sati Sadhani, for themselves. Assamese Muslims celebrated their own icon, Sati Rahima.[114]

It is important to note that the Jaymati theme, despite all its constraints, did provide opportunities for many women to participate in the public domain.[115] The gendered and classed limitations of the public sphere make it doubly essential to remember that its members seldom had any alternative but to form their identities within available discourses or, with difficulty, against them. The feminist theorist Michelle Rosaldo observes that often in societies where domestic and public spheres are firmly differentiated, women may win power and value only when they stress their differences from men. When they accept and elaborate upon the symbols and expectations associated with their cultural definition, they create the possibility of either goading men into compliance or managing to establish a society unto themselves.[116]

As Assamese women sought admission into the public sphere, Jaymati was their calling card. From the 1920s the Jaymati theme became the main topic for writings by a newly literate generation of élite women. An annual commemorative fete, Jaymati Utsav, was the occasion which inspired many of their works. This fete was first organized at Sibsagar in 1913. It commemorated Jaymati's martyrdom and aimed to inspire her "daughters" to achieve similar feats. The nationalist paper *Asomiya*, run by the Agarwala business clan, described these annual celebrations at great length. It carried appeals for women's participation, speeches, editorials, and letters. By the 1920s virtually the entire Brahmaputra valley celebrated the Jaymati Utsav. The Assamese community that resided in Calcutta also did so.[117] For the first time public deliberations were conducted by Assam's women. Male publicists continued to undertake a leading role either as speakers or as organizers. Prominent reformist men often introduced celebrations of the Utsav into their localities. Many female participants were their sisters, daughters, and wives. For example, the first-ever celebration of the Jaymati Utsav was organized by Tara Prasad Chaliha, a planter returned from England, with his mother, Nikunjalata, and his wife, Kamalaloya. From their Sibsagar home the two women edited a woman's magazine, *Ghar Jeuti*, which published many essays and poems on Jaymati.

A close study of these Jaymati texts reveals the gendered hierarchies which permeated the Assamese public sphere. Male publicists employed diverse genres, plays, epic verse, lengthy essays, and even a film script to flesh out the prescriptive discourse around Jaymati. Their essays, plays, and verse narratives received wide readership when they were published in Asomiya periodicals and newspapers. Oral readings from the plays and poems were the high points of the Jaymati Utsav celebrations. Ironically, in many of the plays about Jaymati the playwright assigned very little dialogue to the title character: while male characters expressed authorial opinions on weighty political concerns, the main female character stayed silent and suffering.[118]

Several essays and poems by women on this Jaymati theme have survived. During the 1920s and 1930s Assam's first women's magazine, the *Ghar Jeuti*, ran an annual writing competition for women. Unsurprisingly, the assigned theme was Jaymati. Many of the extant writings by women on Jaymati were written for this competition.[119] All these entries were written very simply. Unlike the writings of their male counterparts, Sati Jaymati's virtues and tribulations appeared as a didactic statement of fact with few narrative embellishments. These pieces bear marked similarity to other types of prescriptive literature written by the first generation of educated women in South Asia. The historian Tanika Sarkar notes that the weight of this literature lay in the dullness of constant repetition, not in literary flourishes.[120] Given the fairly limited facilities for female education, even élite Assamese women received little formal schooling. Likely these were their first ventures of paper to pen. The expectations of social conformity made it necessary to emphasize a commitment to conventional values. An essay on this heroic theme was an act of filial piety that simultaneously sought to appropriate a historical tale of bravery and sacrifice for the present. The Jaymati story was an ideal vehicle for modernizing young women who needed to display virtue as well as talent.

Despite nationalist obsession with the "woman's question," the predominantly masculine world of political discourse provided few formal roles for women in Assam, as on the all-India front. Yet the Gandhian call to action tugged large numbers of women out of their homes to join the noncooperation campaigns. In Sibsagar the Chaliha women organized a range of Gandhian initiatives. They opened a weaving centre and trained village women in handicrafts, as did two schoolteachers in Dibrugarh, Hemaprabha Das and Rajabala Das.[121] British observers disapprovingly noted that many Congress leaders encouraged women to take a prominent part in antigovernment demonstrations. Assam's women formed political associations, attended, sang at, and spoke at political meetings, and volunteered for picketing and boycotts.[122] At Sibsagar they opened the celebration of Jaymati Utsav in 1934 with "O Mor Apunar Des" (O My Beloved Homeland), the patriotic song composed by Lakshminath Bezbarua.[123] Still, the Gandhian vocabulary of politics largely limited women to domestic and nurturing concerns. Female participation in the political public often remained conditional and restricted, even while the Mahila Samitis (Women's Associations) in Assam acquired a strength of mobilization which they retain to the present day.

The complex imprint of this gendered Gandhian ideology is discernible in the making of the first Assamese film, *Jaymati Kunwari*, in 1935. Its auteur was Jyotiprasad Agarwala, a descendant of the Assamese Marwari business family founded by the Kaya trader Navrangram Agarwala in the 1820s. Jyotiprasad was steeped in the modernist imaginings of a new public sphere and alive to the possibilities of cultural entrepreneurship and nationalist self-fashioning.[124] In the manner of many cultural figures during the 1930s, Jyotiprasad was fascinated by socialism, especially the notion of social change through cultural activism. In later years he presided over the Assam branch of the Communist-associated Indian People's Theatre Association (IPTA). But he was also a staunch believer in Gandhi's *satyagraha*: the achievement of truth through passive resistance. Jyotiprasad was enthralled by the possibilities of film as a didactic and realistic medium for political education. In the 1930s he journeyed to the famous Universum Film AG (UFA) studios in Germany. There he encountered the cinema realism theories of the Russian thinker Lev Kuleshov, who had influenced filmmakers such as Sergei Eisenstein.[125] On Jyotiprasad's return to Assam, Lakshminath Bezbarua's play about Jaymati provided the basis for a screenplay.[126] For Jyotiprasad, Jaymati represented the perfect *satyagrahi* (truth seeker). Through her image he felt that he might represent both the glory of Assamese culture and the political ideals of Gandhi.[127]

Jyotiprasad's quest for authenticity was expressed through his determination to acquire an actor with the right lineage and virtue for his film's female lead.[128] This was no easy task, as no woman had ever appeared on an Assamese stage or screen. In Calcutta theatres most female actors were former prostitutes. Only a few years previously the pioneering Bombay filmmaker Dadasaheb Phalke had failed to find a suitable woman to play female film roles. Even prostitutes refused to act in his film, and he was forced to cast a young male actor in a female role. This strategy was unthinkable for Jyotiprasad. From his family's plantation he scoured the countryside. His choice fell on Aideo Sandikai, a fourteen-year-old Ahom girl. Astonishingly, he received permission for her to act from her aristocratic family, since she would depict an illustrious Ahom character. The female foil for Jaymati came not from history but from the playwright and screenwriter Lakshminath Bezbarua's pen. This was the fictional figure of the "noble savage" Dalimi, a Naga girl who sheltered Jaymati's fugitive husband and fell in love with him. Casting Dalimi seemed much simpler, since any attractive young girl would suffice. Unlike the all-important Jaymati, there was no necessity to cast an authentic Naga girl in this role.[129] Primitivity, it would appear, could be enacted, as Ahom regality could not.

Fittingly, this first Assamese film was shot on sets constructed against the verdant green landscape of an Agarwala tea garden. Plantation workers constructed the wooden sets which represented

Ahom royal buildings. One of the film's best-known sequences showed a nubile Dalimi dancing against a lush forest background while clad in a scanty tribal costume. Her dance and attire provided a sharp contrast to the sober visage of Jaymati, who was shown at worship, shrouded from head to foot. The film provided the civilized trappings of an Assamese Hindu past, juxtaposed against its necessary Other, the child of nature from the Naga hills. The figure of the virtuous Jaymati powerfully united the twin strands of Ahom heroism and Asomiya devotionalism as imagined by two generations of local publicists. Ironically, the absence of modern infrastructure in Assam left little option but for the film's première to be held at a cinema theatre in distant Calcutta. A combination of infrastructural and technical obstacles meant that few people in Assam ever managed to see the film. Only its melodious, patriotic songs reached far and wide, thanks to the ubiquitous reach of the new All India Radio. Despite its historical importance, both *Jaymati* and its talented auteur remained largely unknown to scholars and film lovers outside Assam. Yet the film retained its hold over the Assamese public imagination as a landmark of national commemoration and cultural assertion.[130] So did its maker, as a symbol of Assam's multiethnic cultural mosaic.

Public invocations of Jaymati continued to prove useful in defusing potentially subversive actions, as Assam's educated women pioneers sought to make the best of the limited opportunities on offer. The life and career of Chandraprabha Saikiani (1901–72), a lower-caste schoolteacher, nationalist agitator, women's activist, and single mother, reveals how her public veneration of Jaymati as an iconoclast served to legitimize her unconventional actions and lifestyle.[131] For instance, at a session of the Asom Sahitya Sabha in 1925, Chandraprabha insisted on sitting alongside male delegates in full public view, holding her young son on her lap, in defiance of the norm for women to sit in a curtained space.[132] Rajabala Das, one of a handful of university-educated women and the founding principal of the Guwahati Girls' College from 1939 to 1965, powerfully urged that Jaymati's example should inspire women to come out of their homes and seek empowerment through higher education and careers.[133] Jaymati as a cultural artifact provides a telling glimpse into the complex, tension-ridden discourses of inclusion and exclusion that attended the contested histories and national imaginings of Assam and India.

A fragile political and cultural unity did emerge in modern Assam. Even as twentieth-century Assam's public arenas were characterized by a paradoxical combination of segmentation, convergence, dissonance, contestation, and conflict, progress remained a mantra for all. However, the seeds of future, often violent contestations, whether among its constituent groups or directed outwards, were already present. By the last years of the twentieth century, these contestations often threatened to tear apart the nation's fabric. Common aspirations for progress were overtaken by nativist anxieties as well as the very real inequities of society, economy, and polity in Assam, and India.

Conclusion

Tea Narratives: Global, National, and Local

IN 2010, ALMOST TWO HUNDRED years after the establishment of the imperial tea garden, Assam's local tea plant and its indigenous tribal people again made newspaper headlines. Since 2006 a Canadian nonprofit organization had successfully sold organic tea, grown by Upper Assam's Singpho tribals, as an international fair-trade commodity.[1] One promising niche market for this Singpho tea was in North America, where there was a growing demand for alternative and "green" products. Another market was Thailand, which had ecological and past cultural bonds with Assam that had been sundered by Indian state policies dictating that the only legal travel connection between the Mekong and the Brahmaputra should be through distant Delhi. In a post-imperial setting the hierarchical, exploitative tie between the City of London and Assam seemed replaced by kinder, more equitable, more multilateral ones born of the twenty-first century's alternative eco-visions. Indigenous tribal groups, long written out of the garden project, appeared set to recover and disseminate some of their lost heritage, where artisanal tea-making skills might be repackaged for a new global commitment to sustainable living. This initiative marketed a positive face for globalization.

But fair-trade tea is a metaphorical single leaf in a plantation of bushes. The grand vision of fair trade sometimes obscures the ongoing reality of life in the postcolonial commodity garden. The negative impact of globalization remains starkly evident in the condition of the millions of people who still make up the plantation workforce and produce the bulk of Assam's tea. Encouraging as such new prospects might be for small-scale producers, they offer little scope to a proletariat deprived of land and capital, the descendants of colonialism's coolies. Frustrated with the inability of electoral politics and stagnant commodity markets to change their condition, the younger generation among the tea labour population recently began to unleash violent intimidation against plantation functionaries. Their tactics emulate the violent activities of other insurgent groups which have given contemporary Assam a reputation as one of the most strife-torn regions of South Asia.

Over the colonial period tea gardens became synonymous with verdant expanses and feudal lifestyles for "white sahibs." Assam's plantations produced more than a quarter of the world's tea. Until Indian independence, planters, with help from compliant British officials, resisted all pressures toward unionization. Left-oriented trade unions had already established a strong presence among railway and oil industry workers in Assam, but their attempts to penetrate tea plantations floundered. When decolonization loomed, the industry entered into an agreement which gave India's ruling-party-to-be, the Congress, through its trade union wing the Indian National Trade Union Congress (INTUC), a monopoly over organizing tea labour. This served to block rival Communist-affiliated unions such as the All India Trade Union Congress. After independence Congress unionists organized tea workers into the Assam Chah Mazdoor Sangh (ACMS), affiliated with the INTUC. Initially a large part of the ACMS leadership consisted of caste Hindu middle-class men from outside the labour communities, but over time an "insider" union élite developed. Despite the enactment of reformist legislation such as the Plantation Labour Act of 1951, neither trade unions nor governments provided long-term systemic change. After more than half a century of Indian independence, labour legislation provided access to subsistence level wages and worker benefits. Vertical mobility, though, remained mostly unobtainable. The older, pejorative identity of coolie was officially cast aside, but the newly adopted names "Tea Tribes" and "Adibasis" (original dwellers) could not conceal workers' continued existence as an economically disadvantaged and racially stigmatized people.

Independence had little impact on management lifestyles until the tea industry was forcibly nationalized in the 1970s. In ensuing decades, after more than a century of assured profits, the Assam tea industry no longer enjoyed its former confidence and prosperity. From the 1990s changing fashions in consumption and increased competition from new producers such as Kenya eroded India's share of the global tea market. Accustomed to paying dividends rather than investing capital, many tea firms abandoned older plantations along with their labourers, who usually lacked the skills and resources to find other employment. Other firms passed falling world commodity prices onto workers in the form of reduced bonuses and overtime pay. A vicious cycle of labour unrest, lockouts, and industry closures emerged.

Contests in the Garden, Claims for Post-nations

This book studies the Assam imagined by imperial science and commerce as a tea-growing Edenic garden, needing only the emancipatory force of European plantation enterprise to improve and thrive. Colonialism depicted Assam's people as placid, enervated, and indolent, the local version of its ever-present foe, the lazy native. As elsewhere in the British Empire, it found an alternative: coolie labourers whom state regulation and planter coercion induced to move, and toil. Tea labourers, the largest single group of newcomers, were impelled by adverse economic conditions to embrace a proletarian labouring existence. An indentured existence in the Assam garden racialized previously diverse groups into the status of "aboriginal coolies." Despite the subsequent easing of indenture bonds, their subaltern status kept the majority of coolies close to the plantations. As time-expired labourers they were localized as Asomiya-speaking baganiya people, their permanent home this destination whence an imperial commodity regime had brought them. In contrast to the coolie experience, Marwari traders (who originated from Rajputana), Nepali graziers (from the Himalayan borderlands of Nepal and India), and "Mymensinghia" cultivators (from East Bengal) exercised a greater variety of choices, both in the circumstances of their moves and in diverse lived experiences. They moved into Assam at different times and under differing circumstances. Their identities and ties were reformulated in the context of migration, the colonial economy, and the changing social milieu within and without Assam.

Each of these groups had a distinct and important niche in the making of modern Assam and India, and their debates over improvement and progress.

Although colonialism deemed Assam's locals to be lazy, their cooperation in the colonial enterprise was necessary to a limited degree. Indeed, the complicated course of colonial modernity enabled, for a while, local and colonial élite visions of progress to match. Race science theories, ethnographic wisdom, and Indo-Aryanist genealogies greatly influenced these visions. But as colonial structures of rule became unacceptable to the bulk of the region's inhabitants, local groups reached for alternative futures even while clinging to an ordered vision of a garden and a new nation. In the aftermath of empire, this vision too experienced violent challenges.

Ironically, the image of the tea garden as a symbol of Assam's natural endowment and potential for progress retains much of its force. Nothing reveals this more than the actions and rhetoric of the United Liberation Front of Assam (ULFA), which aims to establish a sovereign Assam through armed struggle. One of ULFA's main targets for extortion and violence remains the tea industry. ULFA has lambasted plantation managers for ostentatious lifestyles and highlighted the lack of progress for locals and workers. ULFA ties this critique to its larger grievance that the Indian state has exploited Assam and maintained it as a backward region despite its rich natural resources, notably tea, timber, and oil. This grievance, shared by many of Assam's inhabitants, initially earned ULFA a fair degree of public support. But its attacks on tea industry and government functionaries have not translated into sympathy for the plantation's historically displaced workers. Sadly yet unsurprisingly, most local groups at the forefront of identity-based political action remain profoundly sectarian in their actions. They display shocking callousness toward labouring migrants, both the descendants of coolies and recent entrants from other regions (such as the state of Bihar, or neighbouring Bangladesh), even as they portray political separatism as the sole route to economic and cultural independence.

While keeping in mind Frederick Cooper's warning of the pitfalls of "leapfrogging history," we might locate the antecedents of this nativism in Assam's long and complex journey into modern nationhood.[2] As India confronted independence and partition in 1947, the British province of Assam had one part of its territory enter East

Pakistan (later Bangladesh), while the remainder was incorporated into the Indian Union as the new state of Assam. Quite apart from its human costs, this partition brought about a severe long-term economic disruption. It cut off Assam from its natural markets and ports in East Bengal. Assam was linked to the rest of India only by a narrow strip of territory derisively called the "chicken neck." Transport and communication became immensely difficult and expensive. In Assam many local groups developed antagonistic relationships with a distant, unresponsive central government at New Delhi, and with an ineffectual state government largely dominated by an Asomiya Hindu élite. Local resentments at exclusion from decision making and developmental infrastructure were exacerbated by internal rivalries over the few available opportunities for advancement.

After 1947 Assam consisted of a predominantly Asomiya-speaking Brahmaputra valley, a Bengali-speaking Surma valley, and smaller hill districts dominated by indigenous tribal communities. Further political changes followed over the next half-century. Clashes over language policy, political representation, and slow economic growth brought about a decisive parting of the ways between the hill districts and the plains. By the 1960s the hill districts sought autonomy as distinct states and union territories of India's Northeast — located within the Indian Union, but external to Assam.[3] Subsequently other non-caste, tribal groups which had opted to stay within Assam expressed dissatisfaction and demanded similar political and cultural autonomy. In particular, many Bodo publicists reversed their earlier adoption of the Asomiya language and a Hinduized Brahma identity. They violently demanded a Bodo homeland. Some militant Bodo organizations carried out bloody campaigns of ethnic cleansing directed especially at the descendants of coolie labourers whom they deemed non-indigenous intruders. The transition of neighbouring East Pakistan into nationhood as Bangladesh in 1971 caused additional crises. In response to population movements across the porous Indo-Bangladesh border, politics in India's Northeast became dominated by a rhetoric of indigenous citizenship rights, with a marked animus against "outsiders."

From one perspective the cultural nationalisms of late-nineteenth-century and early-twentieth-century South Asia had gradually accommodated themselves, however uneasily, to the logic of the post-1947 nation-state. In Assam, for instance, almost all streams of political opinion in the 1940s (the notable exception was the Naga) accepted their position within a forthcoming Indian Union. Initially local nationalisms accommodated themselves fairly well to pan-Indian nationalism. The linguistic reorganization of states and frequent changes in nomenclature and boundaries can be interpreted as integral to the lengthy and painful course of the pan-Indian project. But once the nation-state was established, centralized governing structures responded hesitantly and unsuccessfully to local aspirations for improvement and progress. The Indian state was slow to redress economic, social, and cultural injustice and failed to institute a truly representative system of regionally equitable governance. Recent turbulent histories suggest that sixty-odd years of independence directly produced the different forms of extra-parliamentary dissonance which characterize today's political landscape.

Across the Indian Union many states found themselves in acrimonious relationships with the central government. This tension was particularly strong for the northeastern states, given their distance from New Delhi, both geographic and metaphoric. Even as the popularity of pan-Indian cultural forms such as Bombay cinema penetrated deep into the region, Indian governance became associated with systemic exploitation by a complex of bureaucracy, contractors, and the military, usurpation of local resources, racist stereotyping of locals, and a near total absence of infrastructural development. ULFA in particular found considerable support in the Brahmaputra valley because of widespread public anger at the blatant indifference of government functionaries to citizens' basic entitlements and their aspirations for progress. For many members of the Assamese middle classes, control of the Assam garden seemed to have moved almost seamlessly from a white Planter Raj to its brown counterparts from mainland India. In many cases the same managing agency houses still operated: only their managerial personnel had changed.

From the 1980s various regional groups in India openly and persistently challenged the vision of a grand nation-state narrative. Unfortunately New Delhi's stock response to these challenges involved heavy-handed military repression and encouragement of collaborationist lobbies. The clumsy tactics strained democratic institutions and further encouraged local identity politics based on nativist and protectionist sentiments. Many insurgent groups began to exhibit a violently exclusionist character by attacking migrant and labouring groups as exploitative outsiders.

Modern identities, like earlier varieties, exhibit many ambiguities.

The major difference is that modern identities emerge within a comprehensive intellectual framework which sharpens ambiguities and thereby becomes more difficult to accommodate. In this process the stakes of political conflict become much higher. Ironically, identity movements contesting existing inequities tend to declare dominance over other groups within the spatial boundaries of their new nation. In many parts of South Asia the ideological and political practices initiated by local intelligentsias and the colonial state laid the basis for an influential and exclusionist model of nationalism, which in turn caused equally chauvinistic forms of postcolonial nationality assertion. This was only part of a much larger crisis involving the local, the national, and the global. By the late twentieth century the vast majority of South Asia's dissenting groups articulated a deeply felt opposition to state policies for which existing structures of electoral politics did not provide a sufficient platform. Nonetheless, the violent and segregationist contours frequently taken by these movements demonstrate the nation-state's failure to sustain citizens' plural identities and multiple desires for self-respect and improvement.

In Assam an even broader set of processes exacerbates this troubled modernity. The largely suspicious relations between India, Pakistan, Nepal, and (from 1971) Bangladesh, and unsettled conditions in Burma, further aggravate the economic and political wounds that national boundary making created for this region. The workings of the globalized marketplace ensure that an extractive economy based on tea, timber, and oil continues in not very different form from its colonial antecedents. In the perception of Assam's insurgents, the imperial garden lives on. To them only the colour of its oppressors has changed. Both Assam and India remain incomplete and open to challenge. However, by a supreme irony, the ideology of the nation-state holds such a grip on human imaginations that groups contesting the logic of the Indian nation-state in turn seek their own new nation-states.

It is simplistic and inaccurate to characterize these combative movements as eruptions of primordial ethnic strife. They need to be understood as a modern phenomenon, a ground-level quest to "rescue history" (and possibly a future) from the grip of the nation.[4] But the language of these challenges does not necessarily include all the people for whom the movements claim to speak. Other critiques of the nation-state in its current form offer more innovative solutions.

For instance, a variety of citizens' groups advocate loosening India's rigid control over its frontier territories and opening economic and political linkages for these tracts to their neighbours on all sides, even while using such legislation as the recent Right to Information Act to promote better local governance and grassroots accountability. Again, on the larger international stage initiatives such as the Zomia network, which promote effective forms of cross-border association beyond the restrictions of national and area-study boundaries, have wide support from activists, academics, and local networks.[5] These initiatives hold promise for a less embattled and more inclusive future.

Tessa Morris-Suzuki argues that societies of the frontier are often ignored in the dominant histories being written, which tend to be about nation-states. The history of regions is for the most part relegated to obscure monographs of special-interest ethnography.[6] In like manner, on the world stage the forces of global economics and national politics often obscure the desires and longings of localities and the people who live there, who must wrestle with multiple identities, pasts, and presents. Perhaps this is where the historian can seek to intervene, to rescue the locality and region from the occlusion that they suffer by assimilation.

Notes

Introduction

1. B. Anderson, *Imagined Communities*, 121–22.
2. Ballantyne, *Orientalism and Race*, 1–17.
3. M. Goswami, *Producing India*, 9.
4. See Davis, *Late Victorian Holocausts*.
5. See Habermas, *The Structural Transformation of the Public Sphere*.
6. Eley, "Nations, Publics and Political Cultures"; Meehan, ed., *Feminists Read Habermas*.
7. Orsini, *The Hindi Public Sphere*, 3–16.
8. S. Joshi, *Fractured Modernity*, 1–31.
9. S. Sarkar, *Writing Social History*, 92.
10. See R. Guha, *A Rule of Property for Bengal*.
11. R. Guha, *Dominance without Hegemony*, 30–56.
12. Robb, *Liberalism, Modernity, and the Nation*, 133.
13. Arnold, "Agriculture and 'Improvement' in Early Colonial India."
14. See Drayton, *Nature's Government*.
15. See R. Das Gupta, *Labour and Working Class in Eastern India*; Behal and Mohapatra, "'Tea and Money versus Human Life'"; Samita Sen, "Questions of Consent."
16. Metcalf, *Ideologies of the Raj*, 28.
17. S. Sarkar, *Writing Social History*, 22.
18. M. Goswami, *Producing India*, 5.
19. Datta, *Carving Blocs*, 64–102.

Chapter 1. Nature's Jungle, Empire's Garden

1. Barpujari, ed., *The American Missionaries and North-East India*, 7.
2. Bray, *The Rice Economies*, i.
3. Eaton, *The Rise of Islam and the Bengal Frontier*, 3–21.

4. The classic translation of Mirza Nathan's writings is Bora, *Baharistan-i-Ghaybi.*

5. See Mackay, *In the Wake of Cook*; MacLeod, ed., *Nature and Empire*; Latour, *Science in Action.*

6. Schiebinger, *Plants and Empire*, 11.

7. Biswas, *The Original Correspondence of Sir Joseph Banks relating to the Foundation of the Royal Botanic Garden*, 185–236.

8. Drayton, *Nature's Government*, 121–24.

9. *British Parliamentary Papers*, vol. 39 (1839), paper 63: Wallich, "Observations on Cultivation of Tea Plant, for Commercial Purposes in the Mountainous Parts of Hindostan."

10. *British Parliamentary Papers*, vol. 39 (1839), paper 63: Walker, "Proposition to Cultivate Tea upon the Nepaul Hills, and Such Other Parts of the Territories of the East India Company as May Be Suitable to Its Growth."

11. Ibid.

12. *British Parliamentary Papers,* vol. 39 (1839), paper 63: Bentinck Memorandum, 24 January 1834.

13. Ibid., Tea Committee to Revenue Department, 15 March 1834.

14. Ibid., Tea Committee Report, 15 March 1834.

15. Robert Bruce, formerly a major in the Bengal Artillery Corps, traded in Assam from the 1820s. Charles Bruce, formerly a naval lieutenant, commanded a gunboat during the Anglo-Burmese War of 1825–26.

16. *British Parliamentary Papers,* vol. 39 (1839), paper 63: Charlton letter to Jenkins, 8 November 1834.

17. Ibid., Tea Committee Letter to Revenue Department, 24 December 1834.

18. Ibid., Griffith, "Report on the Tea Plant of Upper Assam," 20 June 1836.

19. "The Genuine Tea Plant in Upper Assam," *Times*, 10 January 1839.

20. Antrobus, *A History of the Assam Company*, 263–66.

21. Ibid., 35–40.

22. A. Guha, *Medieval and Early Colonial Assam*, 142–45.

23. Foreign Political Consultations and Proceedings 51, 7 May 1830, Scott letter to Swinton, chief secretary, Fort William, 17 April 1830, National Archives of India.

24. Ibid. 50, 10 June 1838, Scott letter to Swinton, 18 May 1831.

25. Ibid. 90, 11 February 1835, Jenkins letter to Swinton, 22 July 1833.

26. Philips, ed., *The Correspondence of Lord William Cavendish Bentinck*, vol. 1, xxx.

27. C. A. Bayly, *Imperial Meridian*, 155–60.

28. A. J. M. Mills, *Report on the Province of Assam*, 16.

29. *British Parliamentary Papers,* vol. 39 (1839), paper 63: Jenkins letter to Tea Committee, 6 January 1835.

30. Gardella, *Harvesting Mountains*, 10.

31. *Assam: Sketch of Its History, Soil, and Productions*, 24.

32. Warren, *Tea Tales of Assam*, 5.

33. *Assam Company Reports of the Local Board in Calcutta, 1840–42*, 8.

34. *British Parliamentary Papers*, vol. 39 (1839), paper 63: secretary's letter to Tea Committee, 4 April 1836.

35. Ibid., Tea Committee letter to secretary, 6 August 1836.

36. *Assam Company Reports of the Local Board in Calcutta*, 9.

37. Antrobus, *A History of the Assam Company*, 376–78.

38. *British Parliamentary Papers*, vol. 39 (1839), paper 63: Griffith, "Report on the Tea Plant of Upper Assam."

39. The Charter Act of 1833 permitted European land ownership in the East India Company's colonies. Specific Wasteland Rules were enacted for Assam in 1838 and revised in 1854 to attract more Europeans.

40. *Assam Company Reports of the Local Board in Calcutta*, 13.

41. *British Parliamentary Papers*, vol. 39 (1839), paper 63: Jenkins letter to Bentinck, 6 May 1838.

42. *Assam Company Reports of the Local Board in Calcutta*, 8.

43. Antrobus, *A History of the Assam Company*, 378–80.

44. Ibid.

45. Chang, "Chinese Coolie Trade in the Straits Settlements in [the] late Nineteenth Century," 4–7.

46. *Assam Company Reports of the Local Board in Calcutta*, appendix D.

47. Ibid.

48. Ibid., 7.

49. Ibid., appendix D.

50. Ibid.

51. Warren, *Tea Tales of Assam*, 8.

52. *Assam Company Reports of the Local Board in Calcutta*, appendix D.

53. Ibid., 12.

54. *British Parliamentary Papers*, vol. 39 (1839), paper 63: Wallich letter to Jenkins, 15 March 1836.

55. Foreign Political Consultations and Proceedings 96, 12 August 1843, letter from Beesa Gaum chief, National Archives of India.

56. *British Parliamentary Papers*, vol. 39 (1839), paper 63: Jenkins letter to Wallich, 5 May 1836.

57. S. K. Bhuyan, ed., *Assamar Padya Buranji*, part 1, by Dutiram Hazarika.

58. Macfarlane and Macfarlane, *Green Gold*, 8.

59. MacCosh, *Topography of Assam*, 33.

60. Drayton, *Nature's Government*, 80.

61. Philip, *Civilising Natures*, 48.

62. Barpujari, ed., *The American Missionaries and North-East India*, 10.

63. Ibid., 7.

64. *Assam Company Report of Local Directors to Shareholders at a General Meeting*, li.

65. Ibid.

66. Nilkumud [Indibar] Barua, *Jivandarsha*, 32.

67. Antrobus, *A History of the Assam Company*, 343–44.

68. Benudhar Sarma, *Maniram Dewan*, 92–95.

69. A. J. M. Mills, *Report on the Province of Assam*, 516.

70. Among its promoters were Dwarkanath Tagore, Prasanna Kumar Tagore, Rustomjee Cowasjee, Motilal Seal, and Haji Ispahani. Motilal Seal and Prasanna Kumar Tagore served in 1839 and 1839–41 as directors.

71. Kling, *Partner in Empire*, 168–75.

72. Auckland Papers, Addl. MSS 37689–718, Oriental and India Office Collection, British Library, London.

73. See Bagchi, *Private Investment in India*, for a penetrating analysis.

74. Anjan Baruah, *Assamese Businessmen from Maniram Dewan to Robin Dutta*, 10.

75. Anandaram Dhekial Phukan, "Inglandor Biboron," *Orunodoi*, April 1847.

76. Gunabhiram Barua, *Assam Buranji*, 169.

77. A. J. M. Mills, *Report on the Province of Assam*, appendix J, "Observations on the Administration of the Province of Assam by Baboo Anundaram Dakeal Phukan."

Chapter 2. Borderlands, Rice Eaters, Tea Growers

1. Plowden, *The Indian Empire Census of 1881*, 30; and Beverley, *Report: Census of Bengal, 1872*, 80.

2. "Bongali," *Assam Bandhu*, 1885, 95.

3. Thapar, "The Image of the Barbarian in Early India," 417.

4. Eaton, *The Rise of Islam and the Bengal Frontier*, 77–78.

5. The medieval *Kalika Purana* text and various Asomiya folktales attribute the building of the Kamakhya shrine to the Asura (demon) king Naraka, who later met his death at Lord Krishna's hands. Naraka was said to have settled many Brahmins in Assam. Usha, daughter of another Asura king, Ban, eloped with Krishna's grandson, Aniruddha.

6. Lahiri, "Landholding and Peasantry in the Brahmaputra Valley," 158–68.

7. Amalendu Guha, "The Ahom Political System."

8. Chakrabarti, "Texts and Traditions."

9. See Thapar, *Clan, Caste, and Origin Myths in Early India*, and Kulke, *Kings and Cults*.

10. See Talish, extensively quoted in J. Sarkar, "Assam and the Ahoms in 1660 A.D."

11. S. K. Bhuyan, "New Light on Mogul India from Assamese Sources," 335.

12. "Agar Din Atiyar Din," *Assam Bandhu*, 1885, 11.

13. Talish, in J. Sarkar, "Assam and the Ahoms in 1660 A.D."

14. P. D. Goswami, *Folk Literature of Assam*, 66.

15. Neog, *Pabitra Asom*, 105.

16. Mohammad Mansoor Alam, "Azan Fakir."

17. See Malik, *Asomiya Jikir aru Jari*.

18. S. K. Bhuyan, ed., *Deodhai Asam Buranji*, 80.

19. Talish, in J. Sarkar, "Assam and the Ahoms in 1660 A.D."

20. Ibid.

21. Ibid.

22. S. K. Bhuyan, ed., *Deodhai Asam Buranji*, 110.

23. S. K. Bhuyan, *Anglo-Assamese Relations*, 10, 49.

24. Elliot and Dowson, eds., *History of India as Told by Its Own Historians*, vol. 2, 27 n. 311.

25. Pemberton, *Political Mission to Bhutan*, 77.

26. Talish, in J. Sarkar, "Assam and the Ahoms in 1660 A.D."

27. S. K. Bhuyan, *Anglo-Assamese Relations*, 64.

28. Buchanan Hamilton, *An Account of Assam*, 5.

29. Firminger, ed., *Rungpore District Records*, vol. 2, 57, William Dow to George Bogle, 17 March 1780.

30. Martin, *The History, Antiquities, Topography, and Statistics of Eastern India*, 660–61.

31. S. K. Bhuyan, *Anglo-Assamese Relations*, 96.

32. Minute by Cornwallis, 3 October, *Bengal Political Consultations*, 1792, 17, Oriental and India Office Collection, British Library, London.

33. Letter 95 from Wade, 16 November 1795, Fowke Papers, vol. 22, MSS Eur. C 767, "Consultations, 1792," 17, Oriental and India Office Collection, British Library, London.

34. Kaviraj, "The Imaginary Institution of India."

35. "Notes on the Northeast Frontier of Assam, 1881," *India's North-east Frontier in the Nineteenth Century*, ed. Elwin, 284.

36. "Report on Captain Dalton's Visit to Membu, 1855," *India's North-east Frontier in the Nineteenth Century*, ed. Elwin, 249.

37. P. D. Goswami, *Tribal Folk-Tales of Assam*, 183.

38. S. Guha, "Lower Strata, Older Races, and Aboriginal Peoples."

39. See Ballantyne, *Orientalism and Race*, for an excellent study of Aryanist ideas.

40. See *Journal of the Assam Research Society* (*Kamarupa Anusandhan Samiti*), issues from 1933 to 1949.

41. Prafulla Chandra Barua, ed., *Uttam Chandra Baruar Jivani*, 6.

42. Hazarika and Barua were Ahom titles denoting official rank. Today they are common surnames.

43. Interview with Prof. Nurul Islam, Guwahati.

44. Entries on Assamese Muslims in *Census* and *Gazetteer* volumes.

45. See Gait, *A History of Assam*.

46. See Golap Chandra Barua, *Ahom Buranji*.

47. See works by O'Connor and Morey.

48. Timberg, *The Marwaris*, 43.

49. Barpujari, *An Account of Assam and Her Administration*, appendix, "Report of Captain Welsh."

50. Butler, *Travels and Adventures in the Province of Assam*, 244, 258.

51. Amalendu Guha, *Medieval and Early Colonial Assam*, 141, 166.

52. Foreign Political Consultations and Proceedings 106–8, 6 June 1833, National Archives of India.

53. *Selections from the Records of the Government of Bengal*, "Evidence from District Collectors."

54. Ibid.

55. Butler, *A Sketch of Assam by an Officer*, 35.

56. A. J. M. Mills, *Report on the Province of Assam*, "Petition from Moneeram."

57. K. N. Chaudhuri, ed., *The Economic Development of India*, 250–51.

58. A. J. M. Mills, *Report on the Province of Assam*, "Memorandum from Captain Matthie."

59. Ibid., 21.

60. Home Public Proceedings 15–18, 10 September 1858, communication from Rev. Mr. Higgs, National Archives of India.

61. "General Intelligence," *Orunodoi*, January 1846.

62. Skaria, "Shades of Wildness."

63. Endle, *The Kacharis*. See the introduction by the administrator J. D. Anderson.

64. Ibid., 1.

65. Hodgson, "On the Origin, Location, Numbers, Creed, Customs, Character and Condition of the Kocch, Bodo, and Dhimal People."

66. Arnold, "Race, Place and Bodily Difference in Early Nineteenth Century India."

67. Hodgson, "A Brief Note on Indian Ethnology."

68. See Grierson, *Linguistic Survey of India*.

69. See Risley, *People of India*.

70. Kaye and Forbes Watson, eds., *The People of India*, vol. 1, 27.

71. *British Parliamentary Papers*, vol. 39 (1839), paper 63: Jenkins Letter to Wallich, 5 May 1836.

72. See P. D. Goswami, *Folk Literature of Assam* and *Tribal Folk-Tales of Assam*.

73. Jenkins, "Report on the Revenue Administration of the Province of Assam," Department of Historical and Antiquarian Studies, Guwahati.

74. Ibid.

75. Home Public Proceedings 15–18, 10 September 1858, National Archives of India.

76. Barker, *A Tea Planter's Life in Assam*, 126.

77. Foreign Political Consultations and Proceedings 106–8, 6 June 1833, National Archives of India.

78. Hunter, *A Statistical Account of Assam*, vol. 1, 36.

79. Letters issued to government, vol. 24, Hopkinson to governor general, no 80/20, November 1861, Assam State Archives, Dispur.

80. Endle, *The Kacharis*, 14.

81. Ibid.

82. *Times*, 25 December 1841, "Assam Tea."

83. Ibid.

84. Home Public Proceedings 88, 30 November 1861, Hopkinson to secretary to Bengal Government, National Archives of India.

85. *Report of the Commissioners on the Tea Cultivation of Assam, 1868*, "Evidence of Haxell, Seconie Estate." This act was repealed only in the 1920s, well after penal contracts were abolished in 1908–15.

86. In comparison with coffee, tea required nearly nine months of diligent attention and a more stable work force, as well as a larger investment for factory facilities. This accounted for the late-nineteenth-century shift from smaller enterprises to domination by a few managing agency houses.

87. See works by Behal, Carter, Kale, Mohapatra, and Tinker.

88. *British Parliamentary Papers*, 1837–38, 52, 180.

89. See Campbell, "The Ethnology of India."

90. Ibid.

91. "Coolie/kuli" also can mean "bitter labour." Personal communication, James Scott.

92. Campbell, "The Ethnology of India."

93. Burnell and Yule, *Hobson-Jobson*, 249–51.

94. *Assam Labour Enquiry Committee*, "Remarks by Rev. E. Wuesti, German Lutheran Mission, Govindpur, Ranchi District."

95. *Moral and Material Progress and Condition of India during 1871–2*, 104.

96. *Report: Census of Assam for 1881*, 47.

97. Figures compiled from *Annual Reports on Inland Emigration and Labour Emigration into Assam*, quoted in Bates, "Regional Dependence and Rural Development in Central India."

98. Ibid.

99. Fawcett, "Note on the Recent Immigration of Khonds and Other Central Indian Tribes into the Jungle Country of Assam," 40.

100. See works by Gillion, Meer, Carter, and Kale.

101. *Report of the Labour Enquiry Commission of Bengal*, 15.

102. See Mohapatra, "Coolies and Colliers."

103. Quoted in Cotton, *Indian and Home Memories*, 264.

104. See works by the tea industry functionaries Deas and Crole.

105. See *Report of the Commissioners on the Tea Cultivation of Assam, 1868*. Jan Breman shows how the Batak people on the Sumatran East Coast were co-opted into becoming coolie hunters for planters.

106. Planters' illegitimate children do not appear in written records, but they are the subjects of my next research project, on mixed-race Anglo-Indian children. Assamese folklore talks openly, and maliciously, of coolie women's liaisons with white men.

107. Ramsden, *Assam Planter*, 24.

108. Ibid.

109. *Report: Census of Assam for 1881*, 10.

110. Mohapatra, "Assam and the West Indies."

111. Sen, "Questions of Consent."

112. *Assam Labour Enquiry Committee*, "Evidence from Assam Garden Managers."

113. Behal and Mohapatra, "'Tea and Money versus Human Life.'"

114. *Report of the Royal Commission on Labour in India*, chapter 20, "Recruitment for Assam: Difficulty of Return."

115. Allen, ed., *Assam District Gazetteers, Sibsagar*, 2.

116. Cronon, *Nature's Metropolis*, 266–67.

117. *Selections from the Records of the Government of Bengal*, 33, 812.

118. Allen, ed., *Assam District Gazetteers, Sibsagar*, 274.

119. Behal and Mohapatra, "'Tea and Money versus Human Life.'"

Chapter 3. Migrants in the Garden

1. John Carnegie, undated letter, MSS Eur. D 682, Consultations, 1792, 17, Oriental and India Office Collection, British Library, London.

2. Ibid.

3. Allen, *Census of India, 1901*, vol. 4, *Assam*, parts 1–2, 33.

4. Fielder, "On the Rise, Progress, and Future Prospects of Tea Cultivation in British India."

5. *Administrative Report of Bengal for 1867–68*, 204.

6. Allen, *Census of India, 1901*, vol. 4, *Assam*, parts 1–2, 34.

7. Lees, *Memorandum Written after a Tour through the Tea Districts of Eastern Bengal in 1864–5*, 2.

8. "Guinea and Assam," *Times*, 22 August 1867.

9. *Report of the Commissioners on the Tea Cultivation of Assam, 1868*, 17.

10. Ibid.

11. Ibid.

12. Moulton, "Early Indian Nationalism."

13. Lees, *Memorandum Written after a Tour through Tea Districts of Eastern Bengal in 1864–5*, 62.

14. Ibid.

15. Crole, *A Textbook of Tea Planting and Manufacture*, 7–23.

16. Bamber, *An Account of the Cultivation and Manufacture of Tea in India from Personal Observation*, 45.

17. *Report of Royal Commission on Opium*, vol. 2, "Evidence, S. E. Peal, Sibsagar," 7 December 1893.

18. *Assam Administrative Reports*, 1884–85, 168.

19. Tea Districts Labour Association, *Handbook of Castes and Tribes Employed on Tea Estates*, appendix A.

20. Bamber, *An Account of the Cultivation and Manufacture of Tea in India from Personal Observation*, 45–46.

21. Lees, *Memorandum Written after a Tour through Tea Districts of Eastern Bengal in 1864–5*, 43.

22. *Assam Labour Enquiry Committee*, "C. L. Wilkin, Manager, Hautley Tea Estate, Sibsagar."

23. Report by Henry Cotton (1899), quoted in Amalendu Guha, *Planter Raj to Swaraj*, 46.

24. Fuller, *Some Personal Experiences*, 120.

25. IOL Records, Economic Department, L/E/7/1181/57 and L/E/7/1354/3296, 26 May 1921 to 1 December 1922, and 1921–29, Consultations, 1792, 17, Oriental and India Office Collection, British Library, London.

26. A. J. M. Mills, *Report on the Province of Assam*, 16–17.

27. A. Guha, "'A Big Push without a Take-off.'"

28. Antrobus, *A History of the Assam Company*, 96.

29. Lees, *Memorandum Written after a Tour through Tea Districts of Eastern Bengal in 1864–5*, 34.

30. Allen, *Census of India, 1901*, vol. 4, *Assam*, parts 1–2, 162–63.

31. Industries and Overseas Dept, L/E/7/1181, file I&O 57, 1921: confidential letter 5842-F, 19 July 1921, Government of Assam to Government of India, Consultations, 1792, 17, Oriental and India Office Collection, British Library, London.

32. R. Chatterjee, "Legislative Control of Labour Migration in Assam Plantations."

33. *Report of the Indian Statutory Commission, 1930*, Memorandum submitted by Government of Assam, vol. 14, 359.

34. *Assam Labour Report, 1928–9*, 20.

35. Crole, *A Textbook of Tea Planting and Manufacture*, 80.

36. Khadria, "Internal Trade and Market Network in the Brahmaputra Valley," 152–73.

37. *Report of Royal Commission on Opium*, vol. 2, "Evidence, S. E. Peal, Sibsagar," 7 December 1893.

38. Swanson, *In Villages and Tea Gardens*, 65.

39. Bhowmick, "Recruitment Policy of Tea Plantations"; Chattopadhyay, "Storm in Tea Gardens."

40. See Timberg's fine work *The Marwaris*.

41. Hardgrove, *Community and Public Culture*, 1.

42. Timberg, *The Marwaris*, 98.

43. Hardgrove, *Community and Public Culture*, Introduction.

44. Buchanan Hamilton Papers, Rongpur Records, 49–59, MSS Eur. K 156–75, Consultations, 1792, 17, Oriental and India Office Collection, British Library, London.

45. Timberg, *The Marwaris*, 65–66, 197–201.

46. "General Intelligence," *Orunodoi*, March 1854.

47. Allen, ed., *Assam District Gazetteers, Darrang*, 181.

48. A. J. M. Mills, *Report on the Province of Assam*, 29.

49. B. K. Barua [writing as Rasna Barua], *Seuji Pator Kahini*.

50. *Notes on Some Industries of Assam from 1884 to 1895*, 62.

51. *Assam Administrative Reports*, 1880–81, 15; 1881–82, 14.

52. J. Sarma, ed., *Benudhar Sarmar Rasanavali*, vol. 1, *Majiyarpora Mejoloi*, 23, 97.

53. "Guwahatir Biboron," *Orunodoi*, June 1853.

54. Allen, Gait, Allen, and Howard, *Provincial Gazetteer of Bengal and Assam*, 587.

55. *Report of Provincial Banking Enquiry Committee, 1929–30*, 5.

56. Agarwala, *Haribilas Agarwala Dangariyar Atmajiboni*, 4.

57. Allen, ed., *Assam District Gazetteers, Sibsagar*, 505.

58. R. Saikia, *Social and Economic History of Assam*, 94.

59. "Aamar Manuh," *Assam Bandhu*, 1885, 130.

60. Bezbarua, *Mor Jivan Sowaran*, 77.

61. See West Bengal State Archives, Calcutta, Report into the Condition of People in the Lower Provinces of Bengal, 1888, "Note H. Z. Darrah."

62. Hardiman, "In Praise of Marwaris."

63. *Bengalee*, 17 October 1896.

64. *Report of Indian Statutory Commission*, "Memorandum, Government of Assam," vol. 14, 30.

65. See discussion in Hardgrove, *Community and Public Culture*, Introduction.

66. Hutt, "Going to Mugulan."

67. http://www.army.mod.uk/brigade_of_gurkhas/history/index.htm.

68. Imdad Hussain, "Soldiers and Settlers, Recruitment of Gorkhas."

69. Godwin-Austen, Journal of a Tour in Assam, Digital Himalaya Project, University of Cambridge.

70. Imdad Hussain, "Soldiers and Settlers, Recruitment of Gorkhas."

71. A. J. O. Pollock, *Sport in British Burmah, Assam, and the Cassyah and Jyntiah Hills*, 40.

72. Ibid.

73. Foreign Secret Consultations and Proceedings, 15 October 1832, "Report by Jenkins and Pemberton," 114, National Archives of India.

74. Allen, ed., *Assam District Gazetteers, Darrang*, 131–32.

75. Hunter, *A Statistical Account of Assam*, vol. 1, 100.

76. Allen, *Census of India, 1901*, vol. 4, *Assam*, parts 1–2, 122.

77. Allen, ed., *Assam District Gazetteers, Darrang*, 79.

78. IOL Records, MSS/EMR, confidential letter 892, 7607/1930, Consultations, 1792, 17, Oriental and India Office Collection, British Library, London.

79. C. S. Mullen, *Civil Service Census of India, 1931*, vol. 3, *Assam* (Shillong: Government Press, 1932), appendix 4.

80. Hutton, Tour Diary, 15 June 1922.

81. J. P. Mills et al., Tour Diaries and Administrative Notes from the North Cachar Hills, Assam, 1928–1940, Unpublished Government Papers, 31 July 1928, Centre for South Asian Studies Library and Archives, Cambridge. Also, Digital Himalaya Project, University of Cambridge.

82. IOL Records, MSS/EMR, confidential letter 892, 7607/1930, Consultations, 1792, 17, Oriental and India Office Collection, British Library, London.

83. Onta, "The Politics of Bravery."

84. Home Police Proceedings, Dundas to Botham, 23 April 1921, National Archives of India.

85. Ibid.

86. IOL Records, MSS/EMR, confidential letter 892, 7607/1930, Consultations, 1792, 17, Oriental and India Office Collection, British Library, London.

87. Chalmers, "'We Nepalis.'"

88. Rose, "The Nepali Ethnic Community in the North-east of the Subcontinent."

89. Hutt mentions *Basai*, a Nepali novel about migration by the Assamese Nepali writer Lila Bahadur Kshetri, published from Kathmandu and going into nineteen editions from 1957 to 1989.

90. Prominent Nepali political figures in Assam included Chabilal and Hariprasad Upadhyay, Dalbir Singh Lohar, and Bir Bahadur Chetri as Gandhian activists, and Bhakta Bahadur Pradhan as a leader of the Digboi refinery strike of 1929.

91. Bhandari, *Freedom Movement and Role of Indian Nepalese*.

92. "Bongali," *Assam Bandhu*, 1885, 95.

93. See works by Padmanath Gohain Barua, Lakshminath Bezbarua, et al.

94. "Desiyo Parisad," *Assam Bandhu*, 1885, 16–22; "Asomiya aru Bidesi Saaj," *Assam Bandhu*, 1885, 282–88.

95. Allen, *Census of India, 1901*, vol. 4, *Assam*, parts 1–2, 11.

96. Dasgupta, "Denial and Resistance."

97. H. C. Bhattacharya, *Origin and Development of the Assamese Drama and the Stage*.

98. Prafulla Chandra Barua, ed., *Uttam Chandra Baruar Jivani*, 45.

99. Padmanath Gohain Barua, *Mor Sowarani*, 67.

100. M. Kar, *Muslims in Assam Politics*, 145.

101. Monirul Husain, "Muslims of the Indian State of Assam."

102. Ullah, "An Account of the Development of Persian in Assam."

103. Binod Sarma, "A Note on the Assamese Jikir and Its Philosophy."

104. Allen, ed., *Assam District Gazetteers, Darrang*, 100.

105. Shah, *Lukir Buranji*.

106. Doullah, *Immigration of East Bengal Farm Settlers*.

107. McSwiney, *Census of India, 1911*, vol. 3, *Assam*, part 1, *Report*, 28.

108. Allen, Gait, Allen, and Howard, *Provincial Gazetteer of Bengal and Assam*, 538.

109. Lloyd, *Census of India, 1921*, vol. 3, *Assam*, part 1, *Report*, 72.

110. Allen, Gait, Allen, and Howard, *Provincial Gazetteer of Bengal and Assam*, 60.

111. Monahan, *Report on Jute Cultivation*.

112. *Report of Line System Committee*, 7.

113. Monirul Husain, "Muslims of the Indian State of Assam."

114. Dev and Lahiri, "The Line System in Assam."

115. Pegu, "The Line System."

116. In 1937 an impasse between the Muslim League and the Congress on the issue of abolishing the Line System led the Line System Committee to examine the impact of confining immigrants to certain zones.

117. Amalendu Guha, "East Bengal Immigrants and Maulana Abdul Hamid Khan Bhasani in Assam Politics."

Chapter 4. Old Lords and "Improving" Regimes

1. Gunabhiram Barua, *Anandaram Dhekial Phukanar Jivan Charitra*, describes this important clan.

2. Home Miscellaneous Proceedings 662, 173–75, National Archives of India.

3. Ibid.

4. Bimalakanta Barua and M. Das, eds. and trans., *Weissalisa*, 8.

5. Wilson, *The History of British India from 1805 to 1835*, 111.

6. See Marshall, *Trade and Conquest*.

7. Harakanta Barua, *Sadar Aminor Atmajivani*, 1–20.

8. British Secret and Political Consultations, 65–66, 26 August 1825, Consultations, 1792, 17, Oriental and India Office Collection, British Library, London.

9. British Political Consultations 89, 30 May 1833, Consultations, 1792, 17, Oriental and India Office Collection, British Library, London.

10. *Report of Royal Commission on Opium*, vol. 2, "Evidence, J. J. S. Driberg, Excise Commissioner, Assam," 22, 27, and 29 December 1893.

11. A. J. M. Mills, *Report on the Province of Assam*, 8–10.

12. Prafulla Chandra Barua, ed., *Uttam Chandra Baruar Jivani*.

13. Harakanta Barua, *Sadar Aminor Atmajivani*, 73–75.

14. A. J. M. Mills, *Report on the Province of Assam*, appendix J, "Observations by Anandaram Dakeal Phookun."

15. *Reports on Native Papers (Bengal)*, 1883, *Sahachar* (Calcutta), 4 April.

16. Barpujari, *An Account of Assam and Her Administration*, 75–76.

17. Butler, *A Sketch of Assam by an Officer*, 47.

18. Wilson, *The History of British India from 1805 to 1835*, 112.

19. Beverley, *Report: Census of Bengal, 1872*, 45.

20. B. B. Misra, *The Unification and Division of India*, 224.

21. Ibid.

22. "Memorials from Assam Tea Planters," *Times*, 19 June 1867.

23. *Report: Census of Assam for 1881*, 23.

24. Amalendu Guha, *Planter Raj to Swaraj*, 28.

25. *Reports on Native Papers: Bengal Presidency*, 1877–78: *Bharat Sang-charak* (Calcutta), 22 January, and *Bharat Mihir* (Mymensingh), 20 June.

26. *Report: Census of Assam for 1881*, 24.

27. Ibid.

28. Court of Directors' Letter to Bengal, 10 March 1830, Consultations, 1792, 17, Oriental and India Office Collection, British Library, London.

29. *British Parliamentary Papers*, 1834, paper 238: "On Slavery in the East Indies."

30. Indrani Chatterjee, *Gender, Slavery and Law in Colonial India*, 202–13.

31. Amalendu Guha, *Medieval and Colonial Assam*, 56.

32. Foreign Political Consultations and Proceedings 106–8, June 1833, National Archives of India.

33. Board's Collection, F/4/1115/29887, Scott to chief secretary, Bengal, 4 March 1828, Consultations, 1792, 17, Oriental and India Office Collection, British Library, London.

34. *British Parliamentary Papers*, 1834, 238, appendix VI, 3, Report from law commissioners; appendix VI, 5, Scott to chief secretary, Bengal, 10 October 1830.

35. *British Parliamentary Papers*, 1841, appendix VI, 3, Captain Neufville's report, 26 July 1830.

36. Ibid.

37. Nirode K. Barooah, "David Scott and the Question of Slavery in Assam."

38. *Reports on Native Papers: Bengal Presidency*, 1873; *Assam Mihir* (Guwahati), 30 July.

39. Harakanta Barua, *Sadar Aminor Atmajivani*, 41.

40. A. J. M. Mills, *Report on the Province of Assam*, appendix K.B., "Petition from Moneeram."

41. Ibid.

42. C. A. Bayly, "The Second British Empire," 54.

43. Home Public Proceedings 182–83, March 1875, secretary to chief commissioner to secretary, National Archives of India.

44. Letters to government 664, November 1877, "Note on the State of Public Opinion," Assam State Archives, Dispur.

45. "Agor Din, Etiyar Din," *Assam Bandhu*, 1885, 4–6.

46. *Report on Native Papers (Bengal)*, 1873, *Assam Mihir* (Guwahati), 30 July.

47. Rajput, Maratha, and Nepali regimes in pre-modern South Asia provide similar cases.

48. Vaishnavism as a belief system denotes followers of Vishnu, known as Vaishnavites.

49. See S. N. Sarma, *Neo-Vaishnavite Movement and the Satra Institution of Assam*.

50. The Auniati satra was said to have been founded at the order of an Ahom king by a Brahmin.

51. Amalendu Guha, *Medieval and Colonial Assam*, 56.

52. S. N. Sarma lists 380 satras founded over the seventeenth and eighteenth centuries.

53. While King Rudra Singha accepted the Auniati Gosain as guru, his successors were initiated by the Parbatiya Gosains of Kamakhya, who traced their lineage to Nadia, indicating the growing influence of Bengal Sakta worship, its absorption of the local Kamakhya mother-goddess cult, and a vogue for celebrating the Durga Puja festival of Bengal. But the Auniati Gosain remained the most important "spiritual lord."

54. Amalendu Guha, "Moamoria Revolution," and Neog, *Socio-political Events in Assam leading to Militancy of Mayamariya Vaishnavas*, offer divergent views.

55. Fort William Revenue Proceedings, 27–28 July 1855, Consultations, 1792, 17, Oriental and India Office Collection, British Library, London.

56. Bengal Political Consultations, 13C, 12 March 1830; and Bengal Secret and Political Consultations, 3 and 5 March, 1830, Consultations, 1792, 17, Oriental and India Office Collection, British Library, London.

57. Fort William Revenue Proceedings, 27–28 July 1855, Consultations, 1792, 17, Oriental and India Office Collection, British Library, London.

58. Ibid.

59. Harakanta Barua, *Sadar Aminor Atmajivani*, 20.

60. A. J. M. Mills, *Report on the Province of Assam*, appendix H.

61. Robinson, *A Descriptive Account of Assam*, 285.

62. A. J. M. Mills, *Report on the Province of Assam*, "Captain John Butler's Evidence."

63. Miscellaneous Letters, Judicial, 25 February 1843, Captain Gordon to Captain Brodie, Sibsagar, Assam State Archives, Dispur.

64. Ibid.

65. Benudhar Sarma, *Maniram Dewan*, 68.

66. Hunter, *A Statistical Account of Assam*, vol. 1, 29.

67. A. J. M. Mills, *Report on the Province of Assam*, "Captain John Butler's Evidence."

68. Ramsden, *Assam Planter*, 76.

69. Barpujari, ed., *The American Missionaries and North-East India*, 4.

70. Ibid.

71. Ibid., 77.

72. Ibid., 135–41.

73. Ibid.

74. Ibid., 33–36.

75. Ibid., 158.

76. Ibid.

77. See S. Das, "Beadon, Sir Cecil."

78. S. K. Bhuyan, ed., *Harakanta Barua's Assam Buranji.*

79. Ibid.

80. White, *A Memoir of the Late David Scott*, 164.

81. Harakanta Barua, *Sadar Aminor Atmajivani*, 75.

82. Ibid.

83. Letters received by government of Assam 13, 1862, Assam State Archives, Dispur.

84. Ibid.

85. Ibid.

86. Cohn, "Representing Authority in Victorian India."

87. Home Public Proceedings 182–83, March 1875, "Observations on Memorial Presented by Inhabitants of Guwahati and Sibsagar to Viceroy," secretary to chief commissioner to secretary, National Archives of India.

88. "Illegal Opium Cultivation," *Orunodoi*, February 1867.

89. See *Orunodoi*, February, March, and April 1867; and letter 105, 19 April 1867, A. N. Phillips, assistant commissioner, Sibsagar, to commissioner, Assam, District Record Office, Jorhat.

90. Letters received by Government of Assam 105, 1867, Assam State Archives, Dispur.

91. "Annual Meeting of Assam Mission, 1850," *Baptist Missionary Magazine*, May 1852.

92. *Friend of India*, 4 August 1836.

93. Barpujari, ed., *The American Missionaries and North-East India*, 56.

94. The *Orunodoi* was published from the American Baptist Mission Press, Sibsagar, from 1846 regularly until the 1860s, and then intermittently until 1880. The British Library possesses rare copies of the later issues.

95. Shri Modram Sarma Bar Pujari, "What Are the Advantages for Assamese People in Reading the *Orunodoi*?," *Orunodoi*, October 1856.

96. Lees, *Memorandum Written after a Tour through Tea Districts of Bengal in 1864–5*, 10.

97. See O'Hanlon, *Caste, Conflict and Ideology*, 50–87, for a useful analysis of missionary periodicals.

98. Fox Young, *Resistant Hinduism*, 82.

99. "Report of the American Baptist Mission to Assam, 1845," *Baptist Missionary Magazine*, August 1846.

100. See Copley, *Religions in Conflict*, and Forrester, *Caste and Christianity*.

101. Barpujari, *The American Missionaries and North-East India*, 83.

102. In a sermon delivered by Miles Bronson in 1850, he cited mission's three biggest obstacles as "caste, a venerated priesthood and sacred shasters . . . The priests declare they are superior to the sacred book! Why? Ours is not written by man, ours is as old as the world." Bronson Papers, North-Eastern Hill University, Shillong.

103. "General Intelligence," *Orunodoi*, March 1867.

104. "Letter from Auniati Gosain," *Orunodoi*, April 1867.

105. Allen, Gait, Allen, and Howard, *Provincial Gazetteer of Bengal and Assam*, 584.

106. "Memorial on Reassessment of Assam Valley Districts," Revenue Agriculture Proceedings, 22–24 March 1894, National Archives of India.

107. The one exception was Pitambar Deb Goswami of the Goramur satra, who became a follower of Gandhi in the 1920s. The British then confiscated most of his satra's lands.

108. Jnanabhiram Barua, "Agor Din," *Abahon*, 1929, 30. (The author's father, Gunabhiram Barua, and uncle, Anandaram Dhekial Phukan, were prominent supporters of the *Orunodoi*.)

109. Comaroff, "Missionaries and Mechanical Clocks," 7.

110. Apart from periodicals there were a few textbooks, such as *Itihas Mala* (1876), from the Dharma Prakash press. The normal periodical print run was 400, and 100–500 for other books.

111. O'Hanlon, *Caste, Conflict, and Ideology*, 50–87.

112. Swanson, *In Villages and Tea Gardens*, 74.

113. R. D. Grant, "Report of the Committee on Missions in Assam," *Baptist Missionary Magazine*, May 1891.

114. Copley, *Religions in Conflict*, 11.

115. "Mission to the Assamese: Fifty-fourth Annual Report," *Baptist Missionary Magazine*, July 1868.

116. Swanson, *In Villages and Tea Gardens*, 54–58.

117. M. C. Mason, "The People of Assam," *Baptist Missionary Magazine*, September 1880.

118. Swanson, *In Villages and Tea Gardens*, 141–47.

Chapter 5. Bringing Progress, Restoring Culture

1. J. Goswami, ed., "Dangariya Dinanath Bezbaruar Sangsikpta Jivan Charit," *Bezbaruar Granthavali*, by Lakshminath Bezbarua, vol. 1.

2. Harakanta Barua, *Sadar Aminor Atmajivani*, 4.

3. Gunabhiram Barua, *Anandaram Dhekial Phukanar Jivan Charitra*, 25.

4. Padmanath Gohain Barua, *Mor Sowarani*, 1–19.

5. Early students included Colonel Zalnur Ali (father of the future president Fakhruddin Ali Ahmed); a doctor, Colonel Sibram Bora; and an engineer, Bolinarayan Bora.

6. *Assam Administrative Reports*, 1875–76, 28.

7. See ibid., 1884–86.

8. Ibid., 1875–76, 30.

9. N. Talukdar, ed., *Lambodar Bora Rasanavali*, preface.

10. *Assam Administrative Reports*, 1883–84, 180–86.

11. Ibid.

12. Ibid.

13. Ibid.

14. *General Reports on Public Instruction in Assam*, 1880, 10.

15. N. Talukdar, ed., *Lambodar Bora Rasanavali*, 20.

16. *Report of Royal Commission on Opium*, vol. 2, "Evidence, U.N. Barooah, 22 December, 1893."

17. Borra, *Bolinarayan Bora*, 10.

18. Gunabhiram Barua, *Anandaram Dhekial Phukanar Jivan Charitra*, 33.

19. P. Sinha, "Calcutta and the Currents of History."

20. Padmanath Gohain Barua, *Mor Sowarani*, 26–33.

21. Berwick, "Chatra Samaj."

22. Omeo Kumar Das, independent Assam's first education minister, bitterly recollected the caste segregation of Cotton College hostels in his autobiography, *Jibonsmriti*, 20.

23. Acharya, "Education in Old Calcutta."

24. Padmanath Gohain Barua, *Mor Sowarani*, 29–33.

25. McGuire, *The Making of a Colonial Mind*, 55.

26. Pal, *Memories of My Life and Times*, 157.

27. B. Anderson, *Imagined Communities*, 57.

28. Padmanath Gohain Barua, *Mor Sowarani*, 19–26.

29. Mohanty, *Oriya Nationalism*, 78.

30. Home Revenue Proceedings, 8–10 August 1861, commissioner to Bengal government, 14 May 1861, National Archives of India.

31. Ibid.

32. Butler, *Travels and Adventures in the Province of Assam*, 144.

33. J. Sarma, ed., *Benudhar Sarmar Rasanavali*, vol. 1, *Majiyarpora Mejoloi*, 25.

34. Foreign Political Proceedings 93, 15 April 1831, Lamb to Hutchinson, Medical Board, Dacca, 30 March 1831, National Archives of India.

35. A. J. M. Mills, *Report on the Province of Assam*, appendix K.B., "Petition from Moneeram."

36. Ibid.

37. Butler, *Travels and Adventures in the Province of Assam*, 144.

38. Note on Condition of the People of Assam, by deputy commissioner, Sibsagar, Assam Secretariat File 824 R, 1888, Assam State Archives, Dispur.

39. "General Intelligence," *Orunodoi*, January 1846.

40. "General Intelligence," *Orunodoi*, March 1867.

41. The first reformist work in the Asomiya language on widow remar-

riage was probably Gunabhiram Barua's *Ram Nabami Natak* (Play of Ram and Nabami) of 1857, written in the wake of Pandit Vidyasagar's Bengali tracts, which were published in 1855.

42. See J. Goswami, *Hemchandra Barua*.

43. See Hemchandra Barua, *Kaniyar Kirtan*.

44. J. B. Brown, "Politics of the Poppy."

45. *Report of Royal Commission on Opium*, vol. 2, "Evidence, Driberg," 22, 27, and 29 December 1893.

46. *Assam Administrative Reports*, 1880–81, 27.

47. Ibid.

48. J. B. Brown, "Politics of the Poppy."

49. *Report of Royal Commission on Opium*, vol. 2, "Evidence, Peal, Sibsagar," 7 December 1893.

50. Ibid., "Evidence, Driberg."

51. Ibid.

52. *Report of Royal Commission on Opium*, vol. 2, "Evidence, U.N. Barooah and Gunabhiram Barua," 22 December 1893.

53. Ibid.

54. Ibid.

55. *Report of Royal Commission on Opium*, vol. 2, "Evidence, Jagannath Borooah," 22 December 1893.

56. Ibid., "Evidence, Rahmat Ali," 29 December 1893.

57. Ibid., "Memorial of Jorhat Sarbajanik Sabha," appendix xxxvi.

58. Ibid., "Evidence, Jagannath Borooah," 22 December 1893.

59. *British Parliamentary Papers*, Sessional Papers of the House of Commons, 1895, xlii; *Report of Royal Commission on Opium*, 94. Also see Royal Commission on Opium, *Report and Minutes of Evidences*, 1892–93.

60. *General Report on Public Instruction in Assam*, 1876–77, 14.

61. Calcutta had many associations operating in the city's main vernacular, such as the Society for Improvement of Bengali Language and Literature (1874), the Hindu Literary Society (1875), and the Calcutta Literary Society (1876).

62. Advertisement for mail-order remedy to stop opium cravings, *Asomiya*, 9 July 1922.

63. A. K. Sharma, *The Quit India Movement in Assam*, 126.

64. *Asomiya*, 7 December 1924, 1 February 1925, 15 February 1925.

65. In Java opium smoking, polygamy, and betel chewing became marks of being old-fashioned. Chambers of commerce were active in anti-opium propaganda. See Rush, "Opium in Java."

66. Bezbarua, *Mor Jivan Sowaran*, 37–48.

67. J. Sarma, ed., *Benudhar Sarmar Rasanavali*, vol. 1, *Majiyarpora Mejoloi*, 10.

68. Lloyd, *Census of India, 1921*, vol. 3, *Assam*, part 1, *Report*, 167.

69. See *General Reports on Public Instruction in Assam*, 1876–79.

70. Bamber, *An Account of the Cultivation and Manufacture of Tea in India from Personal Observation*, 55–56.

71. Ibid.

72. Ibid.

73. Bolinarayan Bora, "Sah Bagisar Kuli," *Mau*, 1886.

74. Ballantyne, *Orientalism and Race*, 169–87.

75. "Agar Din Etiyar Din," *Assam Bandhu*, 1885, 4–6.

76. Ganguli, *Slavery in British Dominion*.

77. Bannerjee, "History of Brahmo Activities in Assam."

78. Vidyaratna's account was later published as *Udeshi Satya Srabar Assam Bhraman*.

79. Home, *Kuli-Kahini*.

80. *Native Newspaper Reports* (Bengal), 1870–1890s.

81. *Lakshminath Bezbarua*, "Kuli," *Mau*, 1886.

82. See Robb on expectations of progress created by the state vis-à-vis Indian élites in "The Colonial State and Constructions of Indian Identity."

83. Lees, *Memorandum Written after a Tour through the Tea Districts in 1864–5*, 34.

84. *Agriculture and Revenue Records*, letter 267, 15 December 1870, District Record Office, Jorhat.

85. J. Bhuyan, *Unnisso Satikar Asom-Sangbad*, 157 (quoting from the Nagaon property register, 1872–73).

86. *Assam Labour Enquiry Committee*, "Evidence, Danish Muhammad."

87. Allen, ed., *Assam District Gazetteers, Sibsagar*, appendix.

88. Dutta, *The Khongiya Baruahs of Thengal*, 27–28, 42–45.

89. No better instance obtains of the colonial nature of tea entrepreneurship than that Indian independence made little difference. Not until the Indian state nationalized the industry did the Khongiya Baruah firm break loose from this patron-client relationship.

90. *Asomiya*, 8 May, 1 June, 15 June, 13 July, and 20 July 1924. This paper was owned and operated by the Agarwala business clan, which also owned tea plantations. Typically such local planters were not part of the migrant labour import networks, controlled by the European-dominated Tea Planters Association.

91. Tea labour unions were permitted only after 1946, and that too on terms that excluded Communist unions in favour of reformist Congress unions.

92. Personal account, Tulsi Bordoloi; also see the *Asomiya*, 8 May 1924, for an article by Kanak Sarma, "Gandhi's Name on Coolie Lips." Attempts to organize tea workers are narrated in Krishnanath Sarma's *Diary* and the biographies of Sarbeswar Bordoloi and Robin Kalita.

93. Kushal Konwar (1905–42) became an Assamese household name as a nationalist martyr; a believer in Gandhian non-violence, he was hanged after arrest for a derailment in 1942.

94. Padmanath Gohain Barua, *Mor Sowarani*, 32–34.

95. Ibid.

96. See Orsini, *The Hindi Public Sphere*.

97. Hemchandra Goswami was the son of Dambarudhar Goswami of the Gauranga Satra, near Nagaon. Educated at Calcutta, he was a founder of ABUSS. After a career in administrative posts he retired as an extra assistant commissioner. He assisted E. A. Gait and P. R. T. Gurdon in their quest for old manuscripts.

98. See *Assam Administrative Reports*, 1883–89.

99. Gunabhiram Barua mentions the New Press at Calcutta, a family concern.

100. Books from these presses are classified as vernacular tracts in the British Library. Consultations, 1792, 17, Oriental and India Office Collection, British Library, London collection. A few later ones are to be found in Calcutta's National Library.

101. S. K. Bhuyan, *Studies in the History of Assam*, 21–22.

102. A relatively large number of such devotional texts are extant, compared to fewer examples of the "high culture" texts to which literary historians have paid most attention.

103. *Orunodoi*, July 1857.

104. See *Proverbs* by Gurdon and Majid; also P. C. Barua's and P. D. Goswami's collections.

105. J. Goswami, ed., "Khohota Dimarur Satradhikar" and "Nomal," *Bezbaruar Granthavali*, by Lakshminath Bezbarua, vol. 2.

106. McSwiney, *Census of India, 1911*, vol. 3, *Assam*, part 1, *Report*, 11.

107. *Native Newspaper Reports*, Bengal, 1889, *Assam Mihir* (Guwahati).

108. Bezbarua, *Mor Jivan Sowaran*, 10.

109. J. Goswami, ed., "Sankardeb" and "Sri Sankardeb and Sri Madhabdeb," *Bezbaruar Granthavali*, vol. 1; and "Nomal," *Bezbaruar Granthavali*, vol. 2, by Lakshminath Bezbarua.

110. J. Goswami, ed., "Asomiya Bhasa aru Sahitya," *Bezbaruar Granthavali*, by Lakshminath Bezbarua, vol. 2.

111. Ibid.

112. Ibid.

113. Ibid.

114. J. Goswami, ed., "Kripabor Baruar Kakotor Tupula," *Bezbaruar Granthavali*, by Lakshminath Bezbarua, vol. 2.

115. Accounts of celebrations came from virtually all Calcutta sojourners from Assam.

116. See Dutta Baruah, *Assam Buranji-Path*.

117. See Bezbarua, *History of Vaishnavism in India*.

118. Ibid.

Chapter 6. Language and Literature

1. Fabian, *Language and Colonial Power*, 2–8.

2. S. Pollock, "The Cosmopolitan Vernacular."

3. Ramaswamy, *Passions of the Tongue*, 7–8.

4. Alam, "The Pursuit of Persian."

5. Ullah, "An Account of the Development of Persian in Assam and Its Influence on the Assamese Language."

6. Jones, "The Third Anniversary Discourse Delivered 1786."

7. Washbrook, "Language, Culture and Society in India."

8. Ramaswamy, *Passions of the Tongue*, 254; and Metcalf, *Ideologies of the Raj*, 66–159.

9. Gunabhiram Barua, *Anandaram Dhekial Phukanar Jivan Charitra*, 13–15.

10. Foreign Political Proceedings 81, 19 March 1832, Swinton to Fort William, National Archives of India.

11. S. K. Chatterji, *The Origin and Development of the Bengali Language*, 89.

12. Foreign Secret Consultations 44–45, 17 August 1827, Scott to Fort William, National Archives of India.

13. Haliram Dhekial Phukan, *Assam Desher Itihas Orthat Assam Buranji*, preface.

14. Ibid.

15. These buranji manuscripts were acquired by the Assamese historian S. K. Bhuyan for publication by the new Department of Historical and Antiquarian Studies (DHAS) in the 1930s.

16. Haliram Dhekial Phukan, *Assam Desher Itihas Orthat Assam Buranji*, preface.

17. S. Pollock, "The Cosmopolitan Vernacular."

18. Dalmia, *The Nationalization of Hindu Traditions*, 218; also King, *One Language, Two Scripts*.

19. Robinson quoted in Barpujari, ed., *The American Missionaries and North-East India*, 131.

20. Ibid., 130–35.

21. N. Brown, *A Grammatical Notice of the Assamese Language*.

22. Barpujari, ed., *The American Missionaries and North-East India*, 128–29.

23. N. Brown, *A Grammatical Notice of the Assamese Language*.

24. Gunabhiram Barua, *Anandaram Dhekial Phukanar Jivan Charitra*, 25.

25. Ibid., 44.

26. The legal works by Anandaram Dhekial Phukan in the Bengali language are *Phukan Dewan Quaidabandi*, *Sadar Dewani Nishpatti*, and *Ain O Byabastha Sangraha*.

27. A. J. M. Mills, *Report on the Province of Assam*, appendix J, "Observations by Anundaram Dakeal Phukan."

28. Ibid.

29. Ibid.

30. Neog, ed., *A Few Remarks on the Assamese Language*.

31. Ibid.

32. Ibid.

33. "Letter from Calcutta," *Orunodoi*, May 1853; "Second Letter from Calcutta," *Orunodoi*, July 1853; "Learning Assamese: A Friendly Word," *Orunodoi*, August 1853; "Fourth Letter from Calcutta," *Orunodoi*, October 1853. In all likelihood the anonymous writer of these improving epistles was Gunabhiram Barua.

34. *Orunodoi*, May 1853.

35. Ibid.

36. Ibid.

37. Ibid.

38. "Learning Assamese: A Friendly Word," *Orunodoi*, August 1853.

39. Ibid.

40. Ibid.

41. Ibid.

42. See S. Sarkar, *Writing Social History*, 186–215, for a penetrating analysis of chakri's colonial meanings.

43. See Dalmia, *The Nationalization of Hindu Traditions*, and Orsini, *The Hindi Public Sphere*, for fine analyses of periodicals in the Hindi-writing regions.

44. *Report of Indian Statutory Commission*, 1928–89, vol. 14, "Memorandum, Government of Assam," 37.

45. Amalendu Guha, *Planter Raj to Swaraj*, appendix.

46. Bezbarua, *Mor Jivan Sowaran*, 68.

47. "Bongali," *Assam Bandhu*, 1885, 95.

48. For an Oriya version of this conspiracy theory see Fakirmohan Senapati's *My Times and I*, 138.

49. M. Kar, "Assam's Language Question in Retrospect."

50. Neog, ed., *A Few Remarks on the Assamese Language*.

51. Hemchandra Barua and Gurdon, eds., *Hem Kosha*, "Introductory Remarks by Hemchandra Barua."

52. Bronson, *A Dictionary in Assamese and English*.

53. Ibid.

54. Hemchandra Barua, *Parhasalia Abhidan*, preface.

55. Ibid.

56. Hemchandra Barua and Gurdon, eds., *Hem Kosha*.

57. Ibid. Also Gurdon and Majid, eds., *Assamese Proverbs*.

58. See "Assamese Literature: Communicated by G. Grierson."

59. The British Library has various editions: the third to the seventh

published by the Goalpara Hitsadhini Press, the second and the eighth from New Arya Press in Calcutta. The print runs were one thousand copies each year, except for two thousand in the second edition. Therefore nine thousand copies were printed from 1873 to 1880.

60. Grierson, *Linguistic Survey of India*, vol. 2, 21.

61. *Report: Census of Assam for 1881*, 115.

62. S. K. Chatterji, *The Origin and Development of the Bengali Language*, and Kakati, *Assamese*.

63. *Bargeet*, preface.

64. Shah, *Lukir Buranji*.

65. Ibid.

66. J. Goswami, *Hemchandra Barua*, 28–29.

67. *Sadhana*, 1922–26.

68. See Leopold, "The Aryan Theory of Race"; Trautmann, *Aryans and British India*; and Ballantyne, *Orientalism and Race*.

69. See Ballantyne, *Orientalism and Race*.

70. Gunabhiram Barua, *Assam Buranji*, 5–6.

71. Ibid., 11.

72. J. Shri, "Prasin Bharatot Aryasabhyata," *Jonaki*, 1891.

73. Haliram Dhekial Phukan, *Assam Desher Itihas Orthat Assam Buranji*, 87.

74. Ibid., 88.

75. Ibid., 87.

76. Gunabhiram Barua, *Assam Buranji*, 10.

77. Sonaram Choudhury, "Assamat Aryar Bosoti," *Jonaki*, 1889.

78. Alhough the *Jonaki* published this piece, some editorial unease was evident, expressing itself in a footnote acknowledging that the piece contradicted what most "prominent scholars" believed, and asking readers to send in any reactions to engage the author's arguments.

79. Sonaram Choudhury, "Assamat Aryar Bosoti," *Jonaki*, 1889.

80. Ibid.

81. Ibid.

82. Ibid.

83. Ibid.

84. Ibid.

85. Hodson, *The Meitheis*, introduction by Sir Charles Lyall.

86. Ibid.

87. See Lyall, *The Mikirs*; Hodson, *The Meitheis*; Playfair, *The Garos*; Endle, *The Kacharis*; Hutton, *The Angami Nagas*; and J. P. Mills, *The Ao Nagas*, published successively from 1908 to 1926.

88. Downs, *The Mighty Works of God*, 47.

89. *Assam Mission Third Triennial Conference Report*, 1893, 8.

90. The Asom Sahitya Sabha's annual conferences began on a modest scale in 1917 but evolved into a unique literary festival held at a different

location in Assam each year. Today annual meetings are attended by thousands of people, at which writers and intellectuals officiate as delegates. The state government funds these sessions.

91. A. Hazarika, ed., *Asom Sahitya Sabhar Bhasanavali*, 60.

92. Ibid., 82.

93. Fabian, *Language and Colonial Power*, 48.

94. Assam Pradesh Congress Committee, *Election Manifesto*, 1945.

Chapter 7. Contesting Publics

1. A. J. M. Mills, *A Report on the Province of Assam*, appendix K.B., "Petition Moneeram."

2. S. Bayly, "Caste and 'Race' in the Colonial Ethnography of India."

3. Campbell, "The Ethnology of India."

4. Kaviraj, "Imaginary History."

5. S. Bayly, "Caste and 'Race' in the Colonial Ethnography of India."

6. Ibid.

7. See Jotiba Phule, *Ghulamgiri* (Mumbai: Raghuvasi Prakasana, [1872] 1986).

8. See O'Hanlon, *Caste, Conflict and Ideology*; Bandyopadhyay, *Caste, Politics, and the Raj*; Dube, *Untouchable Pasts*; Juergensmeyer, *Religion as Social Vision*.

9. Hodgson, "On the Origin, Location, Numbers, Creed, Customs, Character and Condition of the Kocch, Bodo, and Dhimal People."

10. Ibid.

11. Campbell, "The Ethnology of India."

12. Hodgson, "On the Origin, Location, Numbers, Creed, Customs, Character and Condition of the Kocch, Bodo, and Dhimal People."

13. Gait, *A History of Assam*.

14. Allen, ed., *Assam District Gazetteers, Kamrup*, 78–79.

15. Ibid.

16. Ibid.

17. Hodgson, "On the Origin, Location, Numbers, Creed, Customs, Character and Condition of the Kocch, Bodo, and Dhimal People."

18. Gunabhiram Barua, *Assam Buranji*, 12.

19. Assam Secretariat file 824 R, 1888, "Note on Condition of People of Assam by Rai Gunabhiram Sarma Borua Bahadur," Assam State Archives, Dispur.

20. Beverley, *Report: Census of Bengal, 1872*, 130.

21. Allen, ed., *Assam District Gazetteers, Sibsagar*, 86.

22. D. Sarma, *Guru Kalicharan Brahma*.

23. Ibid.

24. Lloyd, *Census of India, 1921*, vol. 3, *Assam*, part 1, *Report*, "Note by Rupnath Brahma."

25. *Asomiya*, 6 January 1929, reported on a huge conclave at Bodo Kachari presided over by Kalicharan Brahma and attended by people from all over Lower and Upper Assam.

26. Rupnath Brahma had a successful career in Assamese politics. In 1938 he became the first tribal minister from the Brahmaputra valley when he joined the Congress government headed by Nabin Chandra Bordoloi in 1938–39. In the following year he joined the Muslim League government headed by Muhammad Saadullah.

27. Lloyd, *Census of India, 1921*, vol. 3, *Assam*, part 1, *Report*, "Note by Rupnath Brahma."

28. Ibid.

29. D. Sarma, *Guru Kalicharan Brahma*.

30. *Asomiya*, 2 December 1923.

31. Ibid., 18 December 1931.

32. Dutta, *The Khongiya Baruahs of Thengal*, 27–28, 42–45.

33. *Asomiya*, 10 July 1927: a report on the Bodo Sanmilan's local meeting at Jolah village (near Guwahati), attended by people from three nearby mauzas, with a Brahmin chairperson, Durgeswar Gosain.

34. The newspaper *Asomiya* in the 1920s often mentioned noteworthy guest speakers at Bodo meetings, such as Nilmani Dutta, Rajanikanta Bordoloi, and Benudhar Rajkhowa. Speeches were often published in the periodical *Abahon*.

35. Early Bodo periodicals such as the *Prabhati*, the *Prantabasi*, and the *Basumati* have not yet come to light. In their absence we depend on news reports reprinted elsewhere, as in the periodical *Abahon* and the newspaper *Asomiya*.

36. S. Sarkar, *Writing Social History*, 175, 258; also Datta, *Carving Blocs*, 64–102.

37. The National Library and British Library have collections of Asomiya pamphlets.

38. *Asomiya*, 3 April 1927.

39. Khakhlari, *Kacharir Katha*.

40. Ibid.

41. See Dalton, *Descriptive Ethnology of Bengal*; Kaye and Forbes Watson, eds., *The People of India*; and Endle, *The Kacharis*, for such visual representations of Kacharis.

42. *Forward*, 5 January 1935.

43. See http://www.geocities.com/ndfb2001/index.html for a representative history of the Bodo people as written by the separatist National Democratic Front of Bodoland.

44. By the 1970s radical Bodos rejected the Brahma model as too assimilative. Instead they favoured the revival of older cults. They rejected the Asomiya language but disagreed over use of the Nagri and Roman scripts to write Bodo. Today a violent political struggle against the Indian state has

been in force for almost twenty years. The professed aim is to achieve an autonomous Bodoland, but methods differ among groups. Often militant Bodo fighters have resorted to ethnic cleansing of non-Bodo labouring groups.

45. Such low-status groups included Shanars, Chamars, and Namasudras. See Kothari, *Caste in Indian Politics*; Bandyopadhyay, *Caste, Politics, and the Raj*; Juergensmeyer, *Religion as Social Vision*; etc.

46. Allen, *Census of India, 1901*, vol. 4, *Assam*, parts 1–2, 117.

47. Haliram Dhekial Phukan, *Assam Desher Itihas Orthat Assam Buranji*, 88.

48. For caste associations and caste politics see Kothari, ed., *Caste in Indian Politics*; Mukherjee, "The Social Role of a Caste Association"; Carroll, "Colonial Perceptions of Indian Society and the Emergence of Caste(s) Associations"; also Dirks, *Castes of Mind*.

49. Butler, *Travels and Adventures in the Province of Assam*, 224.

50. Allen, ed., *Assam District Gazetteers, Kamrup*, 172.

51. Assam Revenue Proceedings "B," June 1908, 370–76, "Memorial, Kaibarta Jatiya Hitkari Sabha," Assam State Archives, Dispur.

52. Beverley, *Report: Census of Bengal, 1872*, 201.

53. Allen, ed., *Assam District Gazetteers, Lakhimpur*, 210–1.

54. Allen, ed., *Assam District Gazetteers, Darrang*, 93.

55. McSwiney, *Census of India, 1911*, vol. 3, *Assam*, part 1, *Report*, 135.

56. Lloyd, *Census of India, 1921*, vol. 3, *Assam*, part 1, *Report*, 145.

57. Bengal Kaibartas were fishermen and agriculturists. Agriculturists broke away and claimed the more prestigious name of Mahisya after a major agitation.

58. The paper *Tinidiniya Asomiya* was run by the Kaibarta leaders Beliram Das and Jogesh Saikia.

59. The *Asomiya*, 30 September 1932, reported a meeting of Kaivarta youth at Uzanbazar (Guwahati), which hailed Gandhi as a champion of Depressed groups. They voted for communications to be established with leaders of all-India Depressed Classes such as B. R. Ambedkar, M. C. Rajah, and B. S. Moonje.

60. *Asomiya*, 14 August 1927.

61. The *Asomiya* reported on 26 June and 7 August 1927 that the year's Kaibarta Sanmilan had first met at the Kurubahi Satra in Majuli, but Kaibartas then protested at its Gosain's depiction of them as a heen (degraded) caste. The *Asomiya* also reported on 14 February 1929 and 3 December 1930 that Majuli's Auniati and Dihing Gosains still refused to allow Kaibartas to enter their naamghars (prayer houses).

62. Ibid.

63. "Note on Condition of People of Assam by Rai Gunabhiram Sarma Borua Bahadur," Assam Secretariat Files, 1888, Assam State Archives, Dispur.

64. *Asomiya*, 3 March 1929. However, there were a few dissenting Kaibarta voices against such restrictions on women. Mahendra Hazarika expressed the hope that the Assam Mahila Sanmilan (Women's Association) would join his protest, as reported on 13 April 1929. On 12 April 1931 the paper reported that according to the newly set up Kaibarta Mahila Sanmilan, women might sell fish if they had no other income.

65. Lloyd, *Census of India, 1921*, vol. 3, *Assam*, part 1, *Report*, 178.

66. Eley, "Nations, Publics and Political Cultures."

67. *Asomiya*, 26 January 1930. Resolutions about fish trade, women, and markets were taken at Kaibarta and Mahila Kaibarta Sabha meetings at Jorhat, presided over by the reformist Goramur Gosain, who championed lower castes.

68. P. D. Goswami, *Bihu Songs of Assam*, 117.

69. The first printed account of the virtuous fishwife Radhika's encounter with Sankardeb, at which she proved her unsullied chastity over Brahmin and Kalita women, was collected by the antiquarian U. C. Lekharu in 1911. His book is not extant, but P. D. Goswami cites it in his folklore collection of 1960. Another account was J. Saikia, *Sati Radhika*.

70. The newspaper *Asomiya* reported annually on the Santi Radhika Utsav celebrations. It also reported activities of associations such as the Kaibarta Sanmilan.

71. *Asomiya*, 1 October 1931.

72. Y. Saikia, *Fragmented Memories*.

73. Foreign Secret Consultations 27, 5 April 1825, Agent on Northeast Frontier to Fort William, National Archives of India.

74. A. J. M. Mills, *Report on the Province of Assam*, 637–43.

75. Padmanath Gohain Barua, *Mor Sowarani*. He first published these reminiscences serially in the periodical *Abahon* through the 1930s. They were later published in book form.

76. Ibid.

77. Ibid.

78. Padmanath Gohain Barua, *Assam Buranji*, preface to the 1907 edition by P. R. T. Gurdon.

79. Ibid., *Mor Sowarani*, 130.

80. Ibid.

81. "Memorandum by Government of Assam," *Report of Indian Statutory Commission*, vol. 14, 37.

82. These publicists representing different lower-caste and tribal groups included Sonadhar Das (Baniya), Rai Pyari Mohan Das (Mahisya), Nilakanta Hazarika (Kaibarta), Jogesh Chandra Nath (Jogi), Mahendra Lal Das (Lalung and Miri), Kalicharan Brahma (Bodo), and Jaduchandra Khakhlari (Kachari).

83. "Kaibarta Petition to Assam Chief Commissioner," Assam Secretariat Files, 29 November 1902, Assam State Archives, Dispur.

84. Tirthanath Goswami was an orthodox Gosain, with rigid views on caste and gender.

85. Various alumni recalled this incident, including Omeo Kumar Das in his autobiography, *Jibonsmriti*.

86. *Asomiya*, 4 April 1922.

87. *Forward*, 5 January 1935.

88. Ibid.

89. External Affairs Proceedings 1–4, file 228-CA (secret), 1945, National Archives of India.

90. Ibid.

91. "Memorandum by Government of Assam," *Indian Statutory Commission*, vol. 14, 56.

92. Ibid.

93. S. K. Bhuyan, "Sources of Assam History."

94. See A. Saikia, "History, Buranjis, and Nation," for an appraisal.

95. S. K. Bhuyan was active at the annual meetings of the Indian History Congress. He corresponded frequently with G. S. Sardesai, Jadunath Sarkar, and other noted scholars of the time. From 1928 to 1947 he was on the Indian Historical Records Commission.

96. Kaviraj, *The Unhappy Consciousness*, 227.

97. See S. K. Bhuyan, *Bibliography of the Works of Dr. S. K. Bhuyan*.

98. K. Chatterjee, *The Cultures of History in Early Modern India*, 256–57.

99. Isaka, "Gujarati Literati and Construction of a Regional Identity," 263.

100. Kaviraj, *The Unhappy Consciousness*, 74.

101. Ratneswar Mahanta, "Jaymati" (1899); Padmanath Gohain Baruah, *Jaymati Kunwari* (1900); Ramdas Goswami (pseud. for Ratneswar Mahanta), "Jaymati Kunwari and Langi Gadapani," *Jonaki* (1900); Lakshminath Bezbarua, *Jaymati Kunwari* (1915); S. K. Bhuyan, *Jaymati Upakhyan* (1920) and *Asom Jiyari* (1935); Kunjabala Devi and Mahadev Sarma, *Jaymati Kunwari* (1932); Lakhidhar Sarma "Sati Jaymati Kunwari," *Abahon* (1935). Variations were a Sanskrit verse work by Bhabadev Bhagabati, *Sati Jaymati* (1933), Ganesh Gogoi's dramatic trilogy *Jerengar Sati* (1937), and Nakul Chandra Bhuyan's *Gadapanir Sesh Sidhanta* (1923).

102. See Purkayastha, "Restructuring the Past in Early-Twentieth Century Assam."

103. Kunjabala Devi and Mahadev Sarma, *Jaymati Kunwari*.

104. Mentions of "Gada's woman" occur in the *Tungkhungia Buranji*, the *Assam Buranji* (Sukumar Mahanta), and Dutiram Hazarika's manuscript, all handwritten chronicles edited and published by S. K. Bhuyan from Guwahati in the 1930s.

105. See M. Sinha, *Colonial Masculinity*.

106. Tharu, "Tracing Savitri's Pedigree."

107. Kumudeswar Barthakur (1893–1966) was a student in Calcutta

when he wrote on Jaymati. Later in life he wrote about other female heroes such as Lakshmibai of Jhansi and Joan of Arc.

108. Other Asomiya works on the Sati ideal were Dugdhanath Khaund, *Sati Haran Natak* (undated); D. Kalita, *Satir Kahini* and *Satir Tej*; and P. Das, *Sati Pradhika* (1933).

109. Kumudeswar Barthakur, *Jaymati Kahini*.

110. Ibid.

111. Ibid.

112. Ibid.

113. Queen Victoria was a role model in D. Kalita, *Sati Kahini*, and Burman, *Nari-Ratna*.

114. The *Asomiya* reported on a Sati Rahima festival at North Lakhimpur in its issue of 4 December 1931.

115. The *Asomiya* carried reports of Jaymati Utsav and Bihu festivities at Calcutta.

116. One such play was Lakhidhar Sarma's "Sati Jaymati Kunwari," published in the *Abahon*, 1935.

117. Women authors in the *Ghar Jeuti* were Jagyadalata Duara, Shantiprabha Gohain Baruah, Punyaprabha Gohain Baruah, and Kamalaloya Kakoti. Hardly any other works are extant. Some Utsav speeches were reprinted in the *Asomiya* and *Abahon*.

118. T. Sarkar, *Words to Win*, 251.

119. A. K. Sharma, *The Quit India Movement in Assam*, 125–75.

120. *Assam Administrative Reports*, 1930, ii.

121. *Asomiya*, 21 April 1934. Lakshminath Bezbarua's song was later adopted as the Assamese national song, sung at public gatherings alongside the Indian anthem, Rabindranath Tagore's *Jana Gana Mana*.

122. In a region fissured by linguistic and ethnic differences, Jyotiprasad Agarwala, the Asomiya descendant of a Marwari trading migrant, is a cultural and national icon.

123. Mazid, "Joymoti."

124. Jyotiprasad's script was based upon Bezbarua's play *Jaymati Kunwari*. The film opened in Calcutta in 1935. Since Assam lacked screening facilities, the Agarwala family showed it on a mobile screen. Later they set up the first cinema hall at Tezpur.

125. Personal communication, Vivekanand Agarwala and Hridayanand Agarwala, Tezpur.

126. Ibid.

127. In my interview of one of the few survivors from the shoot, Jyotiprasad's younger brother, Vivekanand, he told me that for the role of the Naga damsel any sexy girl would have done, as opposed to the regal presence that the role of the Ahom princess Jaymati required, which only breeding and virtue could convey.

128. The only footage of the film *Jaymati* that I could watch was from the

few extant reels which Bhupen Hazarika incorporated into a documentary on the subject in 1976. Recently Altaf Mazid has made a digital version available. Public attention has shifted from the iconic female hero Jyotiprasad to the fate of the flesh-and-blood woman who portrayed her, Aideo Sandikoi, who lived out her life in a remote village, unable to marry after she publicly addressed her co-actor on screen as her dear husband.

129. Few women had previously published in the Asomiya language. Perhaps the earliest was Padmabati Devi Phukanani, the daughter of Anandaram Dhekial Phukan, who wrote a short novel and various essays. Another was Snehalata Bhattacharya, who wrote a free-form novel titled *Aamar Bihu* in 1922.

130. Rosaldo, "Woman, Culture, and Society: A Theoretical Overview," *Women, Culture and Society*, ed. Rosaldo and Lamphere, 17–42.

131. Chandraprabha Saikiani, "Jaymati Utsav," *Abahon*, 1927, 25.

132. P. Banerjee, "Assamese Women: Victims or Actors?," 119–32.

133. *Asomiya*, 23 December 1928, 12 April 1930. The college that Rajabala Das founded is now the Handique Girls' College at Guwahati.

Conclusion

1. "Singpho Organic Tea: A Hit in International Market," *Sentinel*, 22 October 2010.

2. Cooper, *Colonialism in Question*, 17.

3. Northeast India is usually taken to comprise the seven states of Arunachal Pradesh, Assam, Manipur, Meghalaya, Mizoram, Nagaland, and Tripura. Except for the first, all have had long-running insurgencies contesting the Indian nation-state and local governments.

4. See Duara, *Rescuing History from the Nation*.

5. For the concept of Zomia see Scott, *The Art of Not Being Governed*, and Van Schendel, "Geographies of Knowing, Geographies of Ignorance."

6. Morris-Suzuki, "The Frontiers of Japanese Identity."

Glossary

adibasi / adivasi   Lit. original dweller. Adopted by radicals among the tea labour community in Assam, in emulation of groups in today's Jharkhand and Chattisgarh regions, where their ancestors originated. Also known as Tea Tribes, after the official usage modelled on the 6th Schedule of the Indian Constitution. Sometimes the term baganiya (people of the bagan / garden) is also used.

ahu   Short-maturing rice, suitable for dry farming. Often cultivated with hoes.

amla   Agent or clerk.

anna   A monetary unit equal to one-sixteenth of a rupee.

arkatti   Village recruiter.

babu   Indians who had some connection with the British, through employment or the wearing of westernized attire. Used by the British as a term of ridicule.

bailung   Shaman or ritual specialist for the Ahom community.

bandi / beti   Male and female servile labour in the pre-colonial household economy.

Bangal   Until the mid-nineteenth century this referred to any foreigner, irrespective of ethnicity; later referred to an inhabitant of Bengal.

bari   Garden.

barkandazi   Military mercenary from eastern or northern India.

Barua   An Ahom official with jurisdiction over a department of state or a *khel* of people, with the prefix indicating his responsibility (e.g. Hathi Barua, the official in charge of the royal elephants). Later became a surname, often with prefix dropped.

bhaal manuh   Respectable (lit. good man).

bhakat   Monastic acolyte attached to the *satras (Vaishnavite monasteries)*.

bhakti   Devotion to God.

bhasa / bhasha   Language, usually the commonly spoken vernacular. With *matri* (mother) as prefix, a new usage signifying mother-tongue.

bidesi Stranger (from outside the *des*/homeland).

bigha One-third of an acre.

Brahmin Priestly and learned caste groups. Patronized by later Ahom kings.

brahmottar Revenue-free grants to Brahmins.

buranji Chronicle; also used to denote history, text or discipline.

carit-puthi Devotional hagiographies, usually produced in the satras.

chakri Clerical job, with connotations of drudgery.

chapori, char Riverine shoals and islands resulting from silt deposits.

chatra samaj Student community.

Daivagna Astrologer caste (also called Ganak) which leveraged Ahom courtly patronage to claim ritual rank after Brahmins. This claim to the second rank in Assam's caste hierarchy was contested by other upwardly mobile castes such as Kalitas during British colonial rule.

dangariya An Ahom noble; later extended to mean anyone of high status.

des/desh Homeland or country.

devottar Revenue-free grants to *devalayas* (temples and shrines).

dewan Land agent (e.g. Maniram Dewan).

dharma Moral or religious path.

dubhashi Lit. someone who had two languages or bhashas, used here to refer to those members of the service gentry who translated for the early British.

durbar A court or levee.

eri A local silk of rough, heavy texture, used as an outer garment in cold weather.

gaon Village.

gohain An Ahom aristocrat. Later becomes a surname.

Gosain Lit. god. Respectful title for the head of a temple or satra (monastery). Another such term was Mahanta. Both terms, Mahanta and Gosain (in its Anglicized form Goswami), came into use as surnames.

gyati Kin.

haat A weekly or biweekly market serving a village or group of villages.

jat Endogamous caste grouping, also used here to refer to a species.

jati Different uses in a context of community, from caste to ethnie to nation.

Jatiyo/jatiya Usually denotes national.

Kalita A peasant caste with high status; many subcastes and occupational groups are within its ranks. Its higher sections were members of the service gentry.

kaniya Opium eater, from *kani* (opium).

kaya Local term for a Marwari (Rajasthani) trader.

khiraj Full revenue-paying land.

Kunwari Could denote *Aideo* (princess), but usually an aristocratic Ahom woman.

la-khiraj   Land exempt from paying revenue.

maund   A variable unit of weight, usually 36 kilograms in Bengal.

mauza   Villages grouped into a unit for revenue purposes. Could cover anywhere from 8 to 200 square miles depending on the number of villages.

mauzadar   Revenue collector in charge of mauza commissions.

mel   An assembly of people gathered for a common purpose.

mess   Rooms rented by a group of students, with a common kitchen.

mohurir   Supervisors in government courts and offices, or tea plantations.

muga   A thick silk with a golden sheen. Unique to Assam.

Munsif   See *Sadar Amin*, below.

Na-Asomiya   Lit. New Assamese, descendants of Bengali Muslim migrants.

namoni   Lower (as in Lower Assam).

nisf-khiraj   Land paying revenue at half the usual rate.

paik   A peasant subject to annual service obligations for the Ahom state.

parbatiya   Pertaining to *parbat* (hill).

Phukan   Superintendent of a khel in the Ahom period, with a jurisdiction over up to six thousand people. Later used as a surname. Usually confined to Brahmins and Ahoms.

rai   Public, or the subjects of the raja.

rupit   Land suitable for growing transplanted (wet) rice.

ryot   Peasant (also *raiyat*).

sabha   Meeting or assembly.

sabhya   Civilized; *a/sabhya* is used as its antonym, and *sabhyata* as the noun form.

Sadar Amin   Civil court judges; with *Munsifs*, so-called native judges, had limited jurisdiction. In Assam they had fewer powers and emoluments than in Bengal, since a Munsif drawing Rs 80 pm could not try civil cases above Rs 100. A Sadar Amin tried cases above Rs 100 and received Rs 150 pm.

sahitya   Literature.

sali   Long-maturing "wet" rice needing transplantation, frequent weeding, and use of ploughs. Much more labour-intensive than ahu and other "dry" varieties of rice.

Sardar   Plantation field supervisor and labour overseer.

sati   Chaste and true woman, typically a fount of wifely virtues.

satra   A Vaishvavite monastery in Assam, typically with lands attached to it.

Satradhikar   Head of a satra, often known as Gosain; or Mahanta if a non-Brahmin.

seer   Unit of weight; in British India it was 2.05715 pounds or 0.9331 kilogram.

Seristadar   A registrar or record keeper, especially a head "native" officer of a court or collector's office in charge of public records and official documents.

shish   Lay disciple of Gosains or Satradhikars.

Swargadeo   Lord of heaven, a title used by the Ahom kings.

tehsildar   Revenue official at the tehsil level of local administration, below districts.

tithi   Commemorative anniversary.

ujani   Upper (as in Upper Assam).

unnati   Progress.

utsav   Festival.

Bibliography

Unpublished Sources

PRIVATE PAPERS

British Library, London
   Auckland Papers
   Joseph Banks Memorial on Tea
   Francis Buchanan Hamilton Papers
   Carnegie Papers
   Carter Collection
   Curzon Papers
   Fowke Papers
   Indian Tea Association Papers
   Francis Jenkins Papers
   Note on John Peter Wade

Centre for South Asian Studies Library and Archives, Cambridge
   Hutton Papers
   Mills Papers

Department of Historical and Antiquarian Studies, Guwahati
   "Buranji Vivekratna." Maniram Barbhandar Barua, 1838 (transcript of
      original MSS).
   Jenkins, Francis. "Journals of a Tour of Upper Assam," 1838.
   ——. "Report on the Revenue Administration of the Province of As-
      sam," 1849–50.

Guildhall Library and Archives, London
   Assam Company Papers

Nehru Memorial Museum and Library, New Delhi
   Jyotiprasad Agarwala Papers

North-Eastern Hill University, Shillong
  Miles Bronson Papers (microfilm)

Asiatic Society, Calcutta
  "Sahibor Gun Bornona" (anonymous nineteenth-century MSS)

MANUSCRIPT SOURCES

British Library
  Bengal Judicial Proceedings
  Bengal Revenue Proceedings
  Bengal Political Consultations
  Bengal Secret and Political Consultations
  Board's Collection
  Court of Directors' Letters to Bengal
  Economic Department
  Fort William Revenue Proceedings
  IOL Records

Digital Himalaya Project, University of Cambridge
  http://www.digitalhimalaya.com
  H. H. Godwin-Austen, Journal of a Tour in Assam
  J. H. Hutton Tour Diaries
  J. P. Mills Tour Diaries

National Archives of India
  Emigration Proceedings
  External Affairs Proceedings
  Foreign Political Consultations and Proceedings
  Foreign Secret Consultations and Proceedings
  Home Miscellaneous Proceedings
  Home Police Proceedings
  Home Public Proceedings
  Home Revenue Proceedings
  Revenue and Agriculture Proceedings

West Bengal State Archives, Calcutta
  Papers of the General Committee for Public Instruction in the Lower
    Provinces of the Bengal Presidency, 1835–68
  Report into the Condition of People in the Lower Provinces of Bengal,
    1888

Assam State Archives, Dispur
  Assam Secretariat Files
  Letters issued to government
  Letters received from government, Assam Secretariat Files

Letters received from government (Foreign Department), Assam Secretariat Files
Miscellaneous Letters, Judicial
Miscellaneous Newspaper Clippings, ca. 1920–45
Revenue Proceedings

District Record Office, Jorhat
Agriculture and Revenue Records and Letters, Assam
Tour Diaries of Deputy Commissioners, Assam

Published Sources

Abahon (periodical), ed. Dinanath Sarma. Guwahati, 1929–.

Acharya, Poromesh. "Education in Old Calcutta." *Calcutta: The Living City*, ed. Sukanta Chaudhuri, vol. 1, *The Past*, 85–94. Calcutta: Oxford University Press, 1990.

Adam, William. *Queries and Replies respecting the Present State of the Protestant Missions in Bengal*. Calcutta: Thacker, 1824.

Administrative Report of Bengal for 1867–68. Calcutta: Bengal Secretariat Press, 1868.

Agarwala, Tapan. *Haribilas Agarwala Dangariyar Atmajiboni*. Guwahati, n.d.

Ahmad, Mohammad P. al-. *Sindhu Vijaya*. Calcutta, 1928.

Ahmad, Nasir al din. *Gohar-i-Islam*. Jorhat, 1928.

Ahmed, Faiz al din. *Hazrat Mohammad*. Jorhat, 1929.

Ahmed, Fazal Ali. *Asomiya Jatiyo Sanghotit Ajan Fakir*. Guwahati, 2002.

Akhtar, S. M. *Emigrant Labour for Assam Tea Gardens*. Lahore, 1939.

Alam, Mohammad Mansoor. "Azan Fakir: His Contribution to Persian and Islamic Learning in Assam." *Indo-Iranica* 38 (1985), 39–44.

Alam, Muzaffar. "The Pursuit of Persian: Language in Mughal Politics." *Modern Asian Studies* 32, no. 2 (1998), 317–49.

Alatas, Syed Hussain. *The Myth of the Lazy Native: A Study of the Image of the Malays, Filipinos and Javanese from the 16th to the 20th Century and Its Function in the Ideology of Colonial Capitalism*. London: Cass, 1977.

Allen, B. C. *Census of India, 1901*, vol. 4, *Assam*, parts 1–2. Shillong: Government Press, 1902.

———, ed. *Assam District Gazetteers*. Calcutta: Baptist Mission Press, 1905–14.

Allen, B. C., E. A. Gait, C. G. H. Allen, and H. F. Howard. *Provincial Gazetteer of Bengal and Assam*. New Delhi: Mittal, 1911.

Anderson, Benedict. *Imagined Communities: Reflections on the Origin and Spread of Nationalism*. London: Verso, 1991.

Anderson, Michael. "India, 1858–1930: The Illusion of Free Labor." *Mas-*

ters, Servants, and Magistrates in Britain and the Empire, ed. Douglas Hay. Chapel Hill: University of North Carolina Press, 2004.

"Annual Meeting of Assam Mission, 1850." *Baptist Missionary Magazine*, May 1852.

"Annual Report, Assam, 1838." *Baptist Missionary Magazine*, December 1839.

Annual Reports on the Land Revenue Administration. Shillong: Government Press, 1874–1936.

Antrobus, H. A. *A History of the Assam Company, 1839–1953*. Edinburgh: T. and A. Constable, 1957.

Appadurai, Arjun. *Modernity at Large: Cultural Dimensions of Globalization*. Minneapolis: University of Minnesota Press, 1986.

———, ed. *The Social Life of Things: Commodities in Cultural Perspective*. Cambridge: Cambridge University Press, 1986.

Arnold, David. "Agriculture and 'Improvement' in Early Colonial India: A Pre-history of Development." *Journal of Agrarian Change* 5, no. 4 (2005), 505–25.

———. *A New Cambridge History of India*, part 3, vol. 5, *Science, Technology, and Medicine in Colonial India*. Cambridge: Cambridge University Press, 2000.

———. *The Problem of Nature. Environment, Culture, and European Expansion*. Oxford: Blackwell, 1996.

———. "Race, Place and Bodily Difference in Early Nineteenth Century India." *Historical Research* 77, no. 196 (2004), 254–73.

———. *The Tropics and the Traveling Gaze: India, Landscape, and Science, 1800–1856*. Seattle: University of Washington Press, 2006.

Asomiya (newspaper), ed., Omeo Kumar Das, proprietor C. K. Agarwala. Dibrugarh and Guwahati, 1918–47.

Assam: Sketch of Its History, Soil, and Productions, with the Discovery of the Tea-Plant, and of the Countries Adjoining Assam, with Maps. London: Smith, Elder, 1839.

Assam Administrative Reports, Annual Series. Shillong: Government Press, 1874–1936.

Assam Bandhu (periodical), ed. Gunabhiram Barua. Calcutta, 1885–86.

Assam Company Report of Local Directors to Shareholders at a General Meeting. Calcutta: Bishop's College Press / Smith, Elder, 1841.

Assam Company Reports of the Local Board in Calcutta. Calcutta, 1840–44.

Assam Congress Opium Enquiry Report. Jorhat, 1925.

"Assamese Literature: Communicated by G. Grierson." *Indian Antiquary*, March 1896.

Assam Labour Enquiry Committee: Proceedings and Report. Calcutta: Superintendent of Government Printing, 1906.

Assam Labour Report, 1928–9. Shillong: Government Press, 1930.

Assam Mission Third Triennial Conference Report. Nowgong: Assam Mission, 1893.

Assam Valley Re-assessment Report. Shillong: Government Press, 1893.

Baak, Paul Erik. *Plantations, Production and Political Power*. Delhi: Oxford University Press, 1997.

Bagchi, A. K. *Private Investment in India, 1900–39*. Cambridge: Cambridge University Press, 1974.

Bahi (periodical), ed. Lakshminath Bezbarua. Calcutta and Guwahati, 1909–40.

Ballantyne, Tony. *Orientalism and Race: Aryanism in the British Empire*. Houndmills, Basingstoke, Hampshire: Palgrave Macmillan, 2002.

Bamber, E. F. *An Account of the Cultivation and Manufacture of Tea in India from Personal Observation*. Calcutta: T. S. Smith, 1866.

Bandhopadhyay, Brojendranath, ed. *Sambadpatre Sekaler Kotha: 1830–40*. Calcutta: Bangiya Sahitya Parishad Mandir, 1949.

Bandyopadhyay, Sekhar. *Caste, Politics, and the Raj*. Calcutta: K. P. Bagchi, 1990.

Banerjee, A. C. "The New Regime: 1826–1931." *The Comprehensive History of Assam*, vol. 4, ed. H. K. Barpujari, 1–27. Guwahati: Publication Board, 1992.

Banerjee, Paula. "Assamese Women: Victims or Actors?" *The Guwahati Declaration and the Road to Peace in Assam*, ed. Imdad Hussain, 119–32. New Delhi: Akansha, 2005.

Bannerjee, Amal Sankar. "History of Brahmo Activities in Assam." *Quarterly Review of Historical Studies* 32, nos. 3–4 (1992–93), 36–51.

Bargeet. Jorhat: Dharma Prakash, 1887.

Barkakati, Annada Devi. *Biyanaam*. Jorhat: Dharma Prakash, n.d.

Barker, George. *A Tea Planter's Life in Assam*. Calcutta: Thacker, Spink, 1884.

Barooah, Nirode K. "David Scott and the Question of Slavery in Assam: A Case Study in British Paternalism." *Indian Economic and Social History Review* 6, no. 2 (1969), 179–96.

———. *David Scott in North-East India, 1802–31*. New Delhi: Munshilal Manoharlal, 1970.

Barpujari, H. K. *An Account of Assam and Her Administration*. Guwahati: Spectrum, 1988.

———. *Assam in the Days of the Company, 1826–58*. Shillong: United Publishers, 1963.

———. *A Comprehensive History of Assam*. Guwahati: Publication Board, 1990.

———. *Problem of the Hill Tribes: North-East Frontier*. Guwahati: Lawyer's Book Stall, 1977.

———, ed. *The American Missionaries and North-East India, 1836–1900*. Guwahati: Spectrum, 1986.

Barthakur, Kumudeswar. *Jaymati Kahini*. Calcutta, 1918.

———. *Jhansir Rani*. Tezpur: Asom Sahitya Mandir, 1960.

———. *Joan ob Arc*. Guwahati, n.d.

Barthakur, P. C. *Lora Puthi*. Calcutta, 1934.

Barthakur, Sheela, ed. *Lekhikar Jivoni*. Tezpur: Sadau Asom Lekhika Samaroh Samiti, 1990.

Barua, Anandachandra Barua. *Hafizar Sur*. N.p., n.d.

Barua, Bhimkanta, ed. *Sangrung Phukanar Buranji*. Dibrugarh: Dibrugarh University, 1992.

Barua, Bimalakanta, and Mahendra Das, eds. and trans. *Weissalisa*. Dibrugarh: Dibrugarh University, 1997.

Barua, Bipinchandra, ed. *Lorar Sankardeb*. Jorhat, 1932.

Barua, Birinchi Kumar. *A Cultural History of Assam*. Guwahati: Lawyer's Book Stall, 1951.

———. *History of Assamese Literature*. New Delhi: Sahitya Akademi, 1964.

———. *Modern Assamese Literature*. Guwahati: Lawyer's Book Stall, 1957.

———. [Rasna Barua, pseud.]. *Seuji Pator Kahini*. Shillong, 1959.

———, ed. *Orunodoir Dhalpat*. Jorhat: Asom Sahitya Sabha, 1965.

Barua, Golap Chandra. *Ahom Buranji*. Calcutta: Baptist Mission Press, 1930.

———. *Anglo-Assamese Wordbook*. Calcutta: Baptist Mission Press, 1906.

Barua, Gunabhiram. *Anandaram Dhekial Phukanar Jivan Charitra*. Calcutta, 1880.

———. *Assam Buranji*. Calcutta, 1875.

———. *Lora Puthi*. Calcutta, 1874.

———. *Ram Navami Natak*. Calcutta, 1861.

Barua, Harakanta. *Sadar Aminor Atmajivani*, ed. Kirtinath Bordoloi. Guwahati, 1930.

Barua, Hemchandra. *Asomiya Lorar Adipatha*. Calcutta, 1875–76.

———. *Kaniyar Kirtan*. Sibsagar: Baptist Press, 1861.

———. *Lakshminath Bezbarua*. New Delhi: Sahitya Akademi, 1967.

———. *Parhasalia Abhidan*. Guwahati, 1892.

Barua, Hemchandra, and P. R. T. Gurdon, eds. *Hem Kosha*. Guwahati, 1900.

Barua, Joykanta. *Chutia Buranji*. Guwahati, 1926.

Barua, Lalit Kumar. *Birinchi Kumar Barua*. New Delhi: Sahitya Akademi, 1999.

Barua, M. N., and M. L. Kathabarua. *Bharat Buranji*. Jorhat, 1938.

Barua, Nilkumud [Indibar]. *Jivandarsha*. Calcutta, 1891.

Barua, Prafulla Chandra. *Assamese Proverbs*. Guwahati: Lawyer's Book Stall, 1962.

———, ed. *Uttam Chandra Baruar Jivani*. Calcutta, 1962.

Barua, Sridhar Chandra. *Rituvihar*. Jorhat, 1881.

Baruah, Anjan. *Assamese Businessmen from Maniram Dewan to Robin Dutta*. Jorhat: Meenakshi Kashyap Baruah, 1992.

Baruah, Sanjib. "Clash of Resource Use Regimes in Colonial Assam: A

Nineteenth-Century Puzzle Revisited." *Journal of Peasant Studies* 28, no. 3 (2000), 109–24.

———. *Durable Disorder: Understanding the Politics of Northeast India*. Delhi: Oxford University Press, 2005.

———. *India against Itself: Assam and the Politics of Nationality*. Philadelphia: University of Pennsylvania Press, 1999.

Baruani, Bhuvanmohini. *Biyanaam*. Guwahati, 1913.

Basu, Swaraj. *Dynamics of a Caste Movement: The Rajbansis of North Bengal, 1910–47*. New Delhi: Manohar, 2003.

Bates, Crispin. "Race, Caste and Tribe in Central India: The Early Origins of Indian Anthropometry." *The Concept of Race in South Asia*, ed. Peter Robb, 219–59. Delhi: Oxford University Press, 1996.

———. "Regional Dependence and Rural Development in Central India: The Pivotal Role of Migrant Labour." *Modern Asian Studies* 19, no. 3 (1985), 573–92.

Bayly, C. A. *Empire and Information: Intelligence Gathering and Social Communication in India, 1780–1870*. Cambridge: Cambridge University Press, 1996.

———. *Imperial Meridian: The British Empire and the World, 1780–1830*. London: Longman, 1989.

———. *Origins of Nationality in South Asia*. Delhi: Oxford University Press, 1989.

———. "The Second British Empire." *Historiography: The Oxford History of the British Empire*, ed. Robin W. Winks, 54–72. Oxford: Oxford University Press, 1999.

Bayly, Susan. "Caste and 'Race' in the Colonial Ethnography of India." *The Concept of Race in India*, ed. Peter Robb, 165–218. Delhi: Oxford University Press, 1995.

Beadon, F., and F. Bryant. *A Note of Inspection on the Forests of Assam*. Calcutta: Superintendent of Government Printing, 1912.

Behal, R. P. "Forms of Labour Protest in the Assam Valley." *Kolkata Historical Journal* 9, no. 1 (1984), 30–78.

Behal, R. P., and P. Mohapatra. " 'Tea and Money versus Human Life': The Rise and Fall of the Indenture System in the Assam Tea Plantations: 1840–1908." *Plantations, Proletarians and Peasants in Colonial Asia*, ed. E. Valentine Daniel, Henry Bernstein, and Tom Brass, 142–72. London: Frank Cass, 1992.

Behal, R. P., and Marcel van der Linden. *Coolies, Capital, and Colonialism: Studies in Indian Labour History*. Cambridge: Cambridge University Press, 2006.

Berwick, John. "Chatra Samaj: The Significance of the Student Community in Bengal c. 1870–1922." *Mind, Body and Society: Life and Mentality in Colonial Bengal*, ed. Rajat Kanta Ray, 232–86. Delhi: Oxford University Press, 1995.

Betts, Ursula. *Naga Path*. London: John Murray, 1950.

Beverley, H. *Report: Census of Bengal, 1872*. Calcutta: Superintendent of Government Printing, 1873.

Bezbarua, Lakshminath. *Asomiya Bhasha aru Sahityar Buranji*. Calcutta, 1933.

——. *History of Vaishnavism in India and Rasalila of Shri Krishna: The Baroda Lectures*. Calcutta, 1934.

——. *Jaymati Kunwari*. Calcutta, 1915.

——. *Mor Jivan Sowaran*. Guwahati, 1944.

Bhagabati, Bhabadev. *Sati Jaymati*. Guwahati, 1933.

Bhagavat Purana. Guwahati, 1879.

Bhagavat Purana. Jorhat, 1871.

Bhagavatratna. Jorhat, 1874.

Bhandari, Purushottam. *Freedom Movement and Role of Indian Nepalese*. Jagiroad: Rama Bhandari, 1996.

Bharati, Srichandra. *Kumar Haran*. Nagaon, 1879.

Bhattacharya, Achintya. "The Plain Tribes Movement in Assam." *People's Democracy* 4, no. 25 (1968), 11.

Bhattacharya, Hari Chandra. *Origin and Development of the Assamese Drama and the Stage*. Guwahati: Barua Agency, 1964.

Bhattacharya, Krishnakanta. *Mohammad Garah*. Jorhat, 1919.

Bhattacharya, Snehalata. *Aamar Bihu*. Calcutta, 1922.

Bhowmick, Sharit. "Recruitment Policy of Tea Plantations." *North-east Quarterly* 1, no. 2 (1982), 5–28.

Bhuyan, Arun Chandra, ed. *Political History of Assam*. Guwahati: Government of Assam, 1980.

Bhuyan, Jogendranath. *Unnisso Satikar Asom-Sangbad*. Dibrugarh, 1998.

——, ed. *Anandaram Dhekial Phukanor Asomiya Lorar Mitra*. Guwahati: Publication Board, 1992 [1857].

——, ed. *Ratneswar Mahanta Rasanavali*. Guwahati: Publication Board, 1994.

Bhuyan, Kulanath. *Brajabali Abhidan*. Jorhat, 2000.

Bhuyan, Nakul Chandra. *Asamar Buranjir ek Edhya Bara*. Sibsagar, 1916.

——. *Bidrohi Moran*. Sibsagar, 1938.

——. *Chandrakanta Sinha*. Sibsagar, 1931.

——. *Gadapanir Sesh Sidhanta*. Sibsagar, 1923.

Bhuyan, Surya Kumar. *Anglo-Assamese Relations, 1771–1826*. Guwahati: Lawyer's Book Stall, 1949.

——. *Asom Jiyari*. Guwahati: Kamrup Mahila Samiti, 1935.

——. *Bibliography of the Works of Dr. S. K. Bhuyan*. Guwahati: Department of Historical and Antiquarian Studies, 1964.

——. *Early British Relations with Assam*. Shillong: Assam Secretariat Press, 1928.

——. *Jaymati Upakhyan*. Guwahati, 1920.

——. *Lachit Barphukan and His Times*. Guwahati: Department of Historical and Antiquarian Studies, 1947.

———. *London Memories*. Guwahati: Publication Board, 1979.

———. "New Light on Mogul India from Assamese Sources." *Islamic Culture*, April 1928, 324–63.

———. *Report on the Work of the Department of Historical and Antiquarian Studies*. Guwahati: Department of Historical and Antiquarian Studies, 1932.

———. "Sources of Assam History." *Bulletin II of D.H.A.S.*, 23 February 1924.

———. *Studies in the History of Assam*. Guwahati, 1965.

———, ed. *Assamar Padya Buranji* [Two chronicles by Dutiram Hazarika and Bisweswar Vaidyadhip]. Guwahati: Department of Historical and Antiquarian Studies, 1932.

———, ed. *Deodhai Asam Buranji*. Guwahati: Department of Historical and Antiquarian Studies, 1962.

———, ed. *Harakanta Barua's Assam Buranji; or, A History of Assam from the Commencement of Assam in 1826 AD, Being an Enlarged Version of the Chronicle of Kasinath Tamuli Phukan*. Guwahati: Department of Historical and Antiquarian Studies, 1930.

———, ed. *Kachari Buranji*. Guwahati: Department of Historical and Antiquarian Studies, 1936.

———, ed. *Kamrupar Buranji*. Guwahati: Department of Historical and Antiquarian Studies, 1930.

———, ed. *Lakshminath Bezbarua: Sahityarathi of Assam*. Guwahati: Lawyer's Book Stall, 1972.

———, ed. *Purani Assam Buranji*. Guwahati: Department of Historical and Antiquarian Studies, 1922.

Billig, Michael. *Banal Nationalism*. London: Sage, 1995.

Bishop, Sydney Olive. *Sketches in Assam*. Calcutta: T. S. Smith, 1885.

Biswas, Kalipada. *The Original Correspondence of Sir Joseph Banks relating to the Foundation of the Royal Botanic Gardens*. Calcutta: Government Press, 1950.

Biyanaam. Jorhat: Dharma Prakash, 1916.

Bora, Moidul Islam, trans. *Baharistan-i-Ghaybi: A History of the Mughal Wars in Assam, Cooch Behar, Bengal, Bihar and Orissa*. Guwahati: Department of Historical and Antiquarian Studies, 1936.

Bordoloi, Hemanta, Prasenjit Goswami, and Maniklal Mahanta, eds. *Shramikpran Sarbeswar Bordoloi* [Assam Chah Mazdoor Sangha]. Jorhat: Sahitya Akademi, 1991.

Bordoloi, Rajani Kanta. *Miri Jiyari*. Calcutta, 1895.

Borra, J. N. *Bolinarayan Bora: His Life, Work and Musings*. Calcutta, 1967.

Bose, Sanat Kumar. *Capital and Labour in the Indian Tea Industry*. Bombay: All India Trade Union Congress, 1954.

———. "Tea Garden Labour in Assam." *Studies in the History of Northeast India: Essays in Honour of H. K. Barpujari*, ed. J. B. Bhattacharjee, 175–86. Shillong: North-Eastern Hill University, 1986.

Bose, Sugata. *Agrarian Bengal*. Cambridge: Cambridge University Press, 1986.

Bourdillon, J. A. *Report: Census of Bengal, 1881*. Calcutta: Superintendent of Government Printing, 1882.

Brahma, Sitanath. *Kamala Kali*. Dhubri, 1925.

Brahmachari, Hariprasad. *Jati Unnati*. Calcutta, 1923.

Brahmasumatari, Mahendranarayan. *Bishada*. Basugaon, 1930.

Bray, Francesca. *The Rice Economies: Technology and Development in Asian Societies*. Oxford: Basil Blackwell, 1996.

Breman, Jan. *Taming the Coolie Beast*. Delhi: Oxford University Press, 1989.

Brennan, Lance, and Ralph Shlomowitz. "Mortality and Migrant Labour in Assam." *Indian Economic and Social History* 27, no. 1 (1980), 85–110.

Brewer, John. *The Sinews of Power: War, Money, and the British State, 1688–1783*. London: Unwin Hyman, 1989.

British Parliamentary Papers: Papers Relating to Measures for Introducing Cultivation of Tea Plant in British Possessions in India, vol. 39 (1839), paper 63.

Bronson, Miles. *A Dictionary in Assamese and English*. Sibsagar: Baptist Press, 1867.

Brown, J. B. "Politics of the Poppy: The Society for the Suppression of the Opium Trade, 1874–1916." *Journal of Contemporary History* 8, no. 3 (1873), 97–111.

Brown, Nathan. "Alphabets of the Tai Language." *Journal of the Asiatic Society of Bengal* 61 (1837), 17–21.

———. "Comparison of Indo-Chinese Languages." *Journal of the Asiatic Society of Bengal* 63 (1837), 1023–37.

———. *A Grammatical Notice of the Assamese Language*. Sibsagar: Baptist Press, 1846.

Buchanan Hamilton, Francis. *An Account of Assam*. Guwahati: Department of Historical and Antiquarian Studies, 1940 [1820].

Buckingham, James. *An Account of the Burman Empire, and of the Kingdom of Assam*. Calcutta, 1830.

Bur Bhandaree Barrooa, Muneeram. "On the Mezangurree Silk of Assam and Plants Whereof the Worm Feeds." *Transactions of the Agricultural and Horticultural Society of India*, 1840.

———. "Native Account of Washing for Gold in Assam (Communicated by Captain Jenkins to the Coal and Mineral Committee)." *Journal of the Asiatic Society of Bengal* 79 (1838), 621–25.

Burhagohain, Hem, ed. *Jaymati Kunwari*. Guwahati, 1988.

Burman, Kasinath. *Nari Ratna*. Calcutta, 1929.

Burnell, Arthur Coke, and Henry Yule. *Hobson-Jobson: A Glossary of Colloquial Anglo-Indian Words and Phrases*. London: Murray, 1883.

Butler, John. *A Sketch of Assam by an Officer in the Hon. East India Company's Bengal Native Infantry*. London: Smith, Elder, 1847.

———. *Travels and Adventures in the Province of Assam during a Residence of Fourteen Years*. London: Smith, Elder, 1855.

Campbell, George. "The Ethnology of India." *Journal of the Asiatic Society of Bengal* 30, no. 2 (1865) [suppl. no.].

Cantlie, Audrey. *The Assamese*. London: Curzon, 1984.

Carey, William. *A Garo Jungle Book*. Philadelphia: Judson, 1919.

Carroll, Lucy. "Colonial Perceptions of Indian Society and the Emergence of Caste(s) Associations." *Journal of Asian Studies* 37 (1978), no. 2, 233–50.

Carter, Marina. *Servants, Sirdars, and Settlers: Indians in Mauritius*. Delhi: Oxford University Press, 1995.

Chakrabarti, Kunal. "Texts and Traditions: The Making of the Bengal Puranas." *Tradition, Dissent and Ideology: Essays in Honour of Romila Thapar*, ed. R. Champakalakshmi and S. Gopal, 55–88. Delhi: Oxford University Press, 1996.

Chakravarti, Jayachandra. *Lora Patha*. Calcutta, 1887.

Chakravarti, Ramakant. *Vaishnavism in Bengal*. Calcutta: K. P. Bagchi, 1985.

Chakravarti, Uma. *Rewriting History*. New Delhi: Kali for Women, 1998.

Chakravarty, Dipesh. *Rethinking Working-Class History*. Princeton: Princeton University Press, 1989.

Chaliha, Nikunjalata. *Stutimala*. Guwahati: Lawyer's Book Stall, 1967.

Champakalakshmi, R., and S. Gopal, eds. *Tradition, Dissent and Ideology*. Delhi: Oxford University Press, 1996.

Chandavarkar, Rajnarayan. *Imperial Power and Popular Politics: Class, Resistance, and the State in India, 1850–1950*. Cambridge: Cambridge University Press, 1998.

———. *The Origins of Industrial Capitalism: Business Strategies and the Working Classes in Bombay, 1900–1940*. Cambridge: Cambridge University Press, 1994.

Chandra, Sudhir. *The Oppressive Present*. Delhi: Oxford University Press, 1992.

Chang, Chen-Tung. "Chinese Coolie Trade in the Straits Settlements in [the] late Nineteenth Century." *Bulletin of the Institute of Ethnology, Academia Sinica* 65 (1988), 1–29.

Chatterjee, Indrani. *Gender, Slavery and Law in Colonial India*. Delhi: Oxford University Press, 1999.

Chatterjee, Kumkum. *The Cultures of History in Early Modern India*. Delhi: Oxford University Press, 2009.

Chatterjee, Partha. *Nationalist Thought and the Colonial World*. London: Zed, 1986.

Chatterjee, Partha, and Gyanendra Pandey, eds. *The Nation and Its Fragments*. Delhi: Oxford University Press, 1994.

———, eds. *Subaltern Studies VII*. Delhi: Oxford University Press, 1992.

Chatterjee, Ramkrishna. "Land Grant as a Method of Labour Control in Assam Plantations in Colonial Times." *Proceedings: Indian History Congress*, 1988, 520–23.

———. "Legislative Control of Labour Migration in Colonial Assam Plantations." Unpublished paper, Fourth International Labour History Conference, NOIDA, India, 2004.

Chatterjee, Suhas. *Frontier Officers in Colonial Northeast India*. New Delhi: Akansha, 2009.

Chatterji, Piya. *A Time for Tea*. Durham: Duke University Press, 2001.

Chatterji, Suniti Kumar. *The Origin and Development of the Bengali Language*. London: Allen and Unwin, 1926.

Chattopadhyay, Suhrid Sankar. "Storm in Tea Gardens." *Frontline* 22, no. 16 (2005).

Chaturvedi, Vinayak, ed. *Mapping Subaltern Studies and the Postcolonial*. London: Verso, 2000.

Chaube, S. K. *Hill Politics in Northeast India*. Hyderabad: Orient Longman, 1999.

Chaudhuri, K.N., ed. *The Economic Development of India, 1814–1858*. Cambridge: Cambridge University Press, 1971.

Chetia, Dadhiram. *Gadadhar Singha*. Calcutta, 1925.

Chichele Plowden, W. *The Indian Empire Census of 1881: Statistics of Population*, vol. 2. Calcutta: Superintendent of Government Printing, 1883.

Choudhari, Bancharam. *Lora Patha*. Guwahati, 1872.

Choudhury, Iswar Prasad. *Jyotiprasad Agarwala*. New Delhi: Sahitya Akademi, 1986.

Choudhury, Prosenjit. *Socio-cultural Aspects of Assam in the Nineteenth Century*. New Delhi: Vikas, 1994.

Choudhury, R. D. *Catalogue of Inscriptions in Assam State Museum*. Guwahati: Assam State Museum, 1987.

Chowdhuri, Indira. *The Frail Hero and Virile History*. Delhi: Oxford University Press, 1999.

Cohn, Bernard S. *An Anthropologist among the Historians and Other Essays*. Delhi: Oxford University Press, 1985.

———. "Representing Authority in Victorian India." *The Invention of Tradition*, ed. Eric Hobsbawm and Terence Ranger, 165–210. Cambridge: Cambridge University Press, 1983.

Comaroff, Jean. "Missionaries and Mechanical Clocks: An Essay on Religion and History in South Africa." *Journal of Religion* 71, no. 1 (1991), 1–17.

Cooper, Frederick. *Colonialism in Question: Theory, Knowledge, History*. Berkeley: University of California Press, 2005.

Cooper, Frederick, and Ann Laura Stoler. *Tensions of Empire: Colonial Cultures in a Bourgeois World*. Berkeley: University of California Press, 1997.

Copley, Anthony. *Religions in Conflict: Ideology, Cultural Contact and Conversion in Late Colonial India*. Delhi: Oxford University Press, 1997.

Cotton, H. J. *Indian and Home Memories*. London: Unwin, 1911.

Coward, Rosalind. *Female Desire, Women's Sexuality Today*. London: Paladin, 1984.

Crole, David. *A Textbook of Tea Planting and Manufacture*. London: Crosby, Lockwood, 1897.

Cronon, William. *Nature's Metropolis: Chicago and the Great West*. New York: W. W. Norton, 1992.

Dalmia, Vasudha. *The Nationalization of Hindu Traditions*. Delhi: Oxford University Press, 1997.

Dalton, E. T. *Descriptive Ethnology of Bengal*. Calcutta: Asiatic Society, 1872.

Das, Beliram. *Namasudra Sampraday*. Calcutta, 1933.

Das, Omeo Kumar. *Jibonsmriti*. Guwahati: Lawyer's Book Stall, 1983.

Das, Purnalata. *Sati Pradhika*. Guwahati, 1933.

Das, Suranjan. "Beadon, Sir Cecil (1816–1880)." *Oxford Dictionary of National Biography*. Oxford: Oxford University Press, 2004.

Das, Yajnarain. *Dak Bhanita*. Calcutta, 1885.

Dasgupta, Anindita. "Denial and Resistance: Sylhetti Partition 'Refugees' in Assam." *Contemporary South Asia* 10, no. 3 (2001), 343–60.

Das Gupta, Ranajit. *Labour and Working Class in Eastern India*. Calcutta: K. P. Bagchi, 1994.

Datta, Birendranath, N. Sarma, and P. C. Das, eds. *A Handbook of Folklore Materials of North East India*. Guwahati: Folklore Research Institute, 1994.

Datta, P. K. *Carving Blocs: Communal Ideology in Early-Twentieth Century Bengal*. Delhi: Oxford University Press, 1999.

Davis, Mike. *Late Victorian Holocausts: El Niño Famines and the Making of the Third World*. New York: Verso, 2001.

De, Amalendu. "Labour Immigration into Assam: Its History and Progress during the Period 1873–1882." *Journal of the Asiatic Society of Bengal* 22, nos. 3–4 (1980), 57–81.

Deas, F. T. R. *The Young Tea-Planter's Companion: A Practical Treatise on the Management of a Tea-Garden in Assam*. London: Lowrey, Swan Sonnenschein, 1886.

Deb Goswami, Pitambar. *Satriya Utsabor Porisoi aru Tatporjyo*. Dibrugarh: Auniati Satra, 2002.

de Groot, Joanna. "'Sex' and 'Race': The Construction of Language and Empire in the Nineteenth Century." *Cultures of Empire*, ed. Catherine Hall, 37–60. Manchester: Manchester University Press, 2000.

De Haan, Arjun. "Migration in Eastern India." *Indian Economic and Social History Review* 32, no. 1 (1985), 51–93.

Deshpande, Prachi. *Creative Pasts: Historical Memory and Identity in Western India, 1700–1960*. New York: Columbia University Press, 2007.

Dev, Bimal and Dilip Lahiri. *Cosmogony of Caste and Social Mobility in Assam*. Delhi: Mittal, 1984.

———. "The Line System in Assam." *Journal of the Asiatic Society of Bangladesh* 23, no. 2 (1978), 65–98.

Devi, Kunjabala, and Mahadev Sarma. *Jaymati Kunwari*. Jorhat, 1932.

Devi, Pragyasundari. *Randha Vada*. Calcutta, 1929.

Dhekial Phukan, Anandaram. *Ain O Byabastha Sangraha*. Calcutta, 1855.

———. *Asomiya Lorar Mitra*. Calcutta, 1857.

———. *Phukan Dewan Quaidabandi*. Calcutta, 1849.

———. *Sadar Dewani Nishpatti*. Calcutta, 1850.

Dhekial Phukan, Haliram. *Assam Desher Itihas Orthat Assam Buranji*. Calcutta: Samachar Chandrika, 1829.

———. *Kamakhya-yatra-paddhati*. Calcutta: Samachar Chandrika, 1829.

Dirks, Nicholas. *Castes of Mind: Colonialism and Making of Modern India*. New Haven: Yale University Press, 2001.

Doullah, Sujaud M. *Immigration of East Bengal Farm Settlers and the Agricultural Development of the Assam Valley, 1901–47*. New Delhi: Institute of Objective Studies, 2003.

Downs, F. S. *The Mighty Works of God*. Guwahati: Christian Literature Centre, 1969.

———. "Missionaries and the Language Controversy in Assam." *Indian Church History Review* 13, no. 1 (1979), 29–69.

———. "New Perspectives on the Missionary Role in the Nineteenth Century Language Agitation in Assam." *Indian Church History Review* 20, no. 1 (1986), 13–28.

Drayton, Richard. *Nature's Government: Science, Imperial Britain and the "Improvement" of the World*. New Haven: Yale University Press, 2000.

Duara, Prasenjit. *Rescuing History from the Nation*. Chicago: University of Chicago Press, 1995.

Dube, Saurabh. *Untouchable Pasts*. Albany: State University of New York Press, 1998.

Dutt, K. N. *Landmarks of the Freedom Struggle in Assam*. Guwahati: Publication Board, 1958.

Dutt, Srikant. "Migration and Development: The Nepalese in North-east India." *Economic and Political Weekly* 16, no. 28 (1981), 1053–55.

Dutta, Arup Kumar. *The Khongiya Baruahs of Thengal*. Guwahati: Bhupen Hazarika, 1990.

Dutta Barua, Harinarayan. *Assam Buranji-Path*. Nalbari: Dutta Baruah, 1924.

———, ed. *The Assamese Bhagavata*. Nalbari: Dutta Baruah & Co., 1959.

———, ed. *Mahapurush Sri Sankardeb aru Sri Madhabdeb Caritra*. Nalbari: Dutta Baruah, 1957.

Eaton, Richard. *The Rise of Islam and the Bengal Frontier*. Berkeley: University of California Press, 1993.

Eley, Geoff. "Nations, Publics and Political Cultures: Placing Habermas in the Nineteenth Century." *Habermas and the Public Sphere*, ed. Craig Calhoun, 289–339. Cambridge: Harvard University Press, 1992.

Elliot, H. M., and J. Dowson, eds. *History of India as Told by Its Own Historians*. London: Oxford University Press, 1866–77.

Elwin, Verrier, ed. *India's North-east Frontier in the Nineteenth Century*. Bombay: Oxford University Press, 1959.

Embree, Ainslie T. "Frontiers into Boundaries: From the Traditional to the Modern State." *Realm and Region in Traditional India*, ed. Richard G. Fox, 255–80. New Delhi: Vikas, 1977.

Endle, Sidney. *The Kacharis*. London: Macmillan, 1911.

Fabian, Johannes. *Language and Colonial Power*. Cambridge: Cambridge University Press, 1986.

Faruqee, Ashrufa. "Conceiving the Coolie Woman." *South Asia Research* 16, no. 1 (1996), 61–76.

Farwell, Nidhi. *Pardathavidyar Sar*. Sibsagar: Baptist Press, 1874.

Fawcett, F. "Note on the Recent Immigration of Khonds and Other Central Indian Tribes into the Jungle Country of Assam." *Man* 2 (1940), 40.

Fielder, Charles Henry. "On the Rise, Progress, and Future Prospects of Tea Cultivation in British India." *Journal of the Statistical Society of London* 32, no. 1 (1869), 29–37.

Firminger, W. K., ed. *Rungpore District Records*. Calcutta: Bengal Record Room, 1914–28.

Forbes Watson, J. *The International Exhibition of 1862: A Classified and Descriptive Catalogue of the Indian Department*. London, 1863.

Forrester, Duncan B. *Caste and Christianity*. London: Oxford University Press, 1980.

Fortune, Robert. *A Journey to the Countries of China*. London, 1852.

Fox Young, Richard. *Resistant Hinduism*. Vienna: De Nobili Research Library, 1981.

Fraser, Nancy. "Rethinking the Public Sphere: A Contribution to the Critique of Actually Existing Democracy." *Habermas and the Public Sphere*, ed. Craig Calhoun, 109–42. Cambridge: Harvard University Press, 1992.

Freitag, Sandria B. *Collective Action and Community*. Berkeley: University of California Press, 1989.

Fuller, Bampfylde J. *Some Personal Experiences*. London: Murray, 1930.

Furnivall, J. S. *An Introduction to the Political Economy of Burma*. Rangoon: People's Literature, 1931.

Gait, E. A. *Census of India, 1891, Assam*, part 1, *Report*. Shillong: Government Press, 1892.

——. *A History of Assam*. Calcutta: Thacker, Spink, 1906.

——. *Report on the Progress of Historical Research in Assam*. Shillong: Government Press, 1897.

Gallagher, John, Gordon Johnson, and Anil Seal, eds. *Locality, Province and Nation: Essays on Indian Politics, 1870–1940*. Cambridge: Cambridge University Press, 1973.

Ganguli, Dwarkanath. *Slavery in British Dominion*. Calcutta, 1886–87.

Gardella, Robert. *Harvesting Mountains: Fujian and the China Tea Trade, 1757–1937*. Berkeley: University of California Press, 1994.

Gellner, Ernest. *Nations and Nationalism*. Oxford: Blackwell, 1983.

General Reports on Public Instruction in Assam. Shillong: Government Press, 1875–1936.

Ghar Jeuti (periodical), ed. N. Chaliha and others. Sibsagar, 1928–32.

Ghose, Benoy, ed. *Selections from English Periodicals of Nineteenth Century Bengal*. Calcutta: Papyrus, 1978.

Ghosh, Kaushik. "A Market for Aboriginality: Primitivism and Race Classification in the Indentured Labour Market of Colonial India." *Subaltern Studies*, vol. 10, ed. Gautam Bhadra, Gyan Prakash, and Susie Tharu, 8–48. Delhi: Oxford University Press, 1999.

Gillion, Kenneth L. *Fiji's Indian Migrants*. Melbourne: Oxford University Press, 1962.

Gogoi, Ganesh. *Jerengar Sati*. Jorhat, 1937.

Gogoi, Lila. *The Buranjis: Historical Literature of Assam*. New Delhi, 1986.

Gohain, Hiren. *Assam: A Burning Question*. Guwahati: Spectrum, 1985.

——. "Origins of the Assamese Middle Class." *Social Scientist* 2, no. 16 (1973), 11–26.

——. "North-east: Roots of Separatism." *Mainstream*, 9 January 1988, 8–10.

——. *Sahitya aru Chetana*. Guwahati: Gauhati Book Stall, 1976.

——. *Swadhinata, Ancalikata, aru Asomor bhawisyata*. Guwahati: Students' Emporium, 1995.

Gohain Barua, Padmanath. *Assam Buranji*. Tezpur, 1899.

——. *Jaymati Kunwari*. Calcutta, 1900.

——. *Jivani Sangrah*. Calcutta, n.d.

——. *Lachit Barphukan*. Calcutta, 1920.

——. *Mor Sowarani*. Guwahati, 1968.

Gordon, Stewart. *The Marathas, 1600–1818*. Cambridge: Cambridge University Press, 1993.

Gosain, Dakhinpat. *Bidhav Bivah Samalohsana*. Jorhat: Dharma Prakash, 1914.

——. *Jati Mala*. Jorhat: Dharma Prakash, n.d.

Goswami, Dharmeswar. *Lorabodh Vyakaran*. Calcutta, 1884.

Goswami, Hemchandra. *Asomiya Sahitya Chaneki*. Calcutta, 1923–29.

Goswami, Hemchandra, and Padmanath Gohain Barua. *Descriptive Catalogue of Assamese Manuscripts*. Calcutta, 1930.

——. *A Note on Assamese Language and Literature*. Calcutta, 1907.

Goswami, Jatindranath. *Hemchandra Barua*. New Delhi: Sahitya Akademi, 1987.

——. *Jaganath Baruar Jivani*. Jorhat: Asom Sahitya Sabha, 1975.

——, ed. *Bezbaruar Granthavali*. Jorhat: Asom Sahitya Sabha, 1988.

Goswami, Manu. *Producing India*. Chicago: University of Chicago Press, 2004.

Goswami, Prafulla Datta. *Ballads and Tales of Assam*. Guwahati: Gauhati University, 1960.

———. *Bihu Songs of Assam*. Guwahati: Publication Board, 1988.

———. *Folk Literature of Assam*. Guwahati: Department of Historical and Antiquarian Studies, 1954.

———. *Tribal Folk-Tales of Assam*. Guwahati: Publication Board, 1955.

———, ed. *Baro Mahor Tero Geet*. Guwahati: Publication Board, 1962.

———, ed. *Padmabati Debi Phukananir Rasanabali*. Guwahati: Publication Board, 1994.

Goswami, Prakash, and Satish Chandra Choudhury, eds. *Buranjir Prakriti aru Swarup*. Jorhat, 1991.

Goswami, Shrutidev. *Aspects of Revenue Administration in Assam, 1826–1874*. Delhi: Mittal, 1987.

Goswami, Trailokyanath. *Attetor Katha*. Guwahati, 1989.

Greenfeld, Liah. *Nationalism: Five Roads to Modernity*. Cambridge: Harvard University Press, 1992.

Grierson, George A. *Linguistic Survey of India*. Calcutta: Superintendent Government Printing, 1927.

Griffith, William. *Journal of Travels in Assam, Burma, Bootan, Afghanistan and the Neighbouring Countries, Arranged by John M'Clelland*. Calcutta, 1847.

———. *Report on the Tea Plant of Upper Assam*. Calcutta, 1840 [orig. pubd. in *British Parliamentary Papers*, 1839].

Griffiths, Percival. *The History of the Indian Tea Industry*. London: Weidenfeld and Nicholson, 1967.

Grove, Richard H. "Colonial Conservation, Ecological Hegemony and Popular Resistance: Towards a Global Synthesis." *Imperialism and the Natural World*, ed. John M. MacKenzie, 15–50. Manchester: Manchester University Press, 1990.

Grove, Richard H, Vinita Damodaran, and Satpal Sangwan, eds. *Nature and the Orient*. Delhi: Oxford University Press, 1998.

Gruning, J. F. *Recruitment of Labour for Tea Gardens in Assam*. Shillong, 1909.

Guha, Amalendu. "The Ahom Political System: An Enquiry into State Formation in Medieval Assam: 1228–1714." *Social Scientist*, December 1983, 3–34.

———. "'A Big Push without a Take-off: A Case-Study of Assam: 1871–1901': Reply to Comment." *Indian Economic and Social History Review* 4, no. 4 (1974), 474–79.

———. "East Bengal Immigrants and Maulana Abdul Hamid Khan Bhasani in Assam Politics, 1928–47." *Indian Economic and Social History Review* 13, no. 4 (1976), 419–53.

———. *Medieval and Early Colonial Assam*. Calcutta: K. P. Bagchi, 1985.

———. "Moamoria Revolution: Was It a Class War?" *Assam Tribune*, 18 October 1950.

———. *Planter Raj to Swaraj*. New Delhi: Indian Council of Historical Research, 1977.

———. "The Pre-Ahom Roots of Medieval Assam." *Social Scientist*, December 1984, 1–2.

Guha, Ranajit. *Dominance without Hegemony*. Cambridge: Harvard University Press, 1997.

———. *A Rule of Property for Bengal: An Essay on the Idea of Permanent Settlement*. Paris: Mouton, 1963.

Guha, Sumit. *Environment and Ethnicity in India: 1200–1991*. Cambridge: Cambridge University Press, 1999.

———. "Lower Strata, Older Races, and Aboriginal Peoples: Racial Anthropology and Mythical History Past and Present." *Journal of Asian Studies* 57, no. 2 (1998), 423–41.

Gunamala. Jorhat: Dharma Prakash, 1872.

Gupta, Charu. *Sexuality, Obscenity, and Community*. New Delhi: Permanent Black, 2002.

Gurdon, P. R. T., and Abdul Majid, eds. *Assamese Proverbs*. Shillong: Government Press, 1920.

Habermas, Jürgen. *The Structural Transformation of the Public Sphere*, trans. T. Burger. Cambridge: Harvard University Press, 1989.

Hagan, James, and Rob Castle. "Unfree Labour on Assamese Tea Gardens and in the Australian Cattle Industry, 1860–1930." Unpublished MS, n.d..

Hanley, Maurice P. *Tales and Songs from an Assam Tea Garden*. Calcutta: Thacker, Spink, 1928.

Hardgrove, Anne. *Community and Public Culture: Marwaris in Calcutta, 1897–1997*. New York: Columbia University Press, 2002.

Hardiman, David. "In Praise of Marwaris: Review of D. K. Taknet's Industrial Entrepreneurship of Shekhawati Marwaris." *Economic and Political Weekly*, 14 February 1987, 273.

Hazarika, Atulchandra, ed. *Asom Sahitya Sabhar Bhasanavali*. Jorhat: Asom Sahitya Sabha, 1955.

Hazarika, B. B. *Political Life in Assam during the 19th Century*. Delhi: Gian, 1987.

Hazarika, Ganeshchandra. *Bihu aru tar Prakritik Chitra*. Calcutta, 1918.

Hazarika, Sanjay. *Rites of Passage. Border Crossings, Imagined Homelands, India's East, and Bangladesh*. Delhi: Penguin, 2000.

Headrick, Daniel R. *The Tentacles of Progress; Technology Transfer in the Age of Imperialism, 1850–1940*. Oxford: Oxford University Press, 1988.

Hints for Europeans Engaged in Commerce and Industry on Their First Arrival in India, with Special Reference to Conditions in Bengal and Assam. London: Worrall and Robey, 1946.

Hobsbawm, Eric. *Nations and Nationalism since 1780*. Cambridge: Cambridge University Press, 1990.

Hodgson, Brian Houghton. "A Brief Note on Indian Ethnology." *Journal of the Asiatic Society of Bengal* 53 (1849), 238–46.

———. *Miscellaneous Essays Relating to Indian Subjects*. London: Trübner, 1880.

———. "On the Origin, Location, Numbers, Creed, Customs, Character and Condition of the Kocch, Bodo, and Dhimal People, with a General Description of the Climate They Dwell in." *Miscellaneous Essays Relating to Indian Subjects*, vol. 1, sec. 1 London, 1880 [1847], 1–160.

Hodson, T. H. *The Meitheis*. London: David Nutt, 1908.

Home, Gagan Chandra. *Kuli Kahini*. Calcutta, 1888.

Hunter, W. W. *Imperial Gazetteer of India*. Oxford: Oxford University Press, 1909.

———. *A Statistical Account of Assam*. London: Trübner, 1879.

Husain, Monirul. *The Assam Movement: Class, Movement, and Ideology*. Delhi: Manak, 1993.

———. "Muslims of the Indian State of Assam." *Journal of the Institute of Muslim Minority Affairs* 8, no. 2 (1987), 397–402.

Hussain, Imdad. *From Residency to the Raj Bhavan: A History of Shillong Government House*. Delhi: Regency, 2005.

———. "Soldiers and Settlers, Recruitment of Gorkhas." *The Nepalis in Northeast India*, ed. A. C. Sinha and T. B. Subba, 67–105. New Delhi: Indus, 2003.

———, ed. *The Guwahati Declaration and the Road to Peace in Assam*. New Delhi, 2005.

Hussain, Ismail. *Assamor Char-Chaporir Lok-Sahitya*. Guwahati, 2002.

———. *Assamor Jatiyo Jivan aru Abhibasi Asomiya Mussalman*. Guwahati, 1997.

———, ed. *Char-Chaporir Galpa*. Guwahati, 1998.

Hutt, Michael. "Going to Mugulan: Nepali Literary Representations of Migration to India and Bhutan." *South Asia Research* 18, no. 2 (1998), 195–214.

Hutton, J. H. *The Angami Nagas, with Notes on Neighbouring Tribes*. London: Macmillan, 1921.

"Institution of a Horticultural Society." *Kolkata Monthly Journal*, 24 June 1816.

Isaka, Riho. "Language and Dominance: The Debates over the Gujarati Language in the Late Nineteenth Century." *South Asia* 25 (2002), 1.

Itihas Mala. Jorhat: Dharma Prakash, 1876.

Jain, Shobhita. "Gender Relations and the Plantation System in Assam, India." *Women Plantation Workers. International Experiences*, ed. S. Jain and Rhoda Reddock. Oxford: Oxford University Press, 1998.

———. *Sexual Equality. Workers in an Asian Plantation System*. Delhi: Sterling, 1998.

Jonaki (periodical), ed. Asomiya Bhasa Unnati Sadhini Sabha (C. K. Agarwala, Satyanath Bora, Kanaklal Barua, et al.). Calcutta and Guwahati, 1889–ca. 1898, 1901–3.

Jones, William. "Eighth Discourse Delivered 1791." *Asiatick Researches* 3 (1807), 1–16.

———. "Sixth Discourse Delivered 1789." *Asiatick Researches* 2 (1807), 43–66.

———. "The Third Anniversary Discourse Delivered 1786: On the Hindus." *Asiatick Researches* 1 (1798), 415–31.

Joshi, Chitra. *Lost Worlds: Indian Labour and Its Forgotten Histories*. Delhi: Permanent Black, 2003.

Joshi, Sanjay. *Fractured Modernity: Making of a Middle Class in Colonial North India*. Delhi: Oxford University Press, 2001.

Juergensmeyer, Mark. *Religion as Social Vision: The Movement against Untouchability in Twentieth Century Punjab*. Berkeley: University of California Press, 1982.

Jyotish Chandra Dutta. *Lachit Barphukan*. Guwahati, 2001.

Kakati, Banikanta. *Assamese: Its Formation and Development*. Guwahati: Department of Historical and Antiquarian Studies, 1941.

Kale, Madhavi. *Fragments of Empire: Capital, Slavery, and Indian Indentured Labor Migration in the British Caribbean*. Philadelphia: University of Pennsylvania Press, 1995.

Kalita, Dandinath. *Asom Sandhya Buranji*. Tezpur, n.d.

———. *Satir Kahini*. Tezpur, 1920.

———. *Satir Tej*. Tezpur, 1930.

Kalita, Somen. *Hajo Anchalor Itihas*. Guwahati, 1988.

Kar, Bodhisattva. "The Assam Fever." *Wellcome History* 23 (June 2003).

———. "Energizing Tea, Enervating Opium: Culture of Commodities in Colonial Assam." *Space, Sexuality and Postcolonial Cultures*, ed. Manas Ray, CSSS ENRECA Papers Series. Calcutta, 2002.

———. "Incredible Stories in the Time of Credible Histories: Colonial Assam and Translations of Vernacular Geographies." *History in the Vernacular*, ed. Partha Chatterjee and Raza Aquil, 288–321. Delhi: Oxford University Press, 2008.

———. "What Is in a Name? Politics of Spatial Imagination in Colonial Assam." CENISEAS Papers, ed. Sanjib Baruah, vol. 5. Guwahati: Omeo Kumar Das Institute, 2002.

Kar, M. "Assam's Language Question in Retrospect." *Social Scientist* 4, no. 2 (1975), 21–35.

———. *Muslims in Assam Politics*. Delhi: Omsons, 1990.

Kaviraj, Sudipta. "Imaginary History: Narrativizing of the Nation in Bankim Chandra Chattopadhyay." *Self-Images, Identity and Nationality*, ed. P. C. Chatterjee. Shimla: Indian Institute of Advanced Study, 1989.

———. "The Imaginary Institution of India," *Subaltern Studies VII*, ed. Partha Chatterjee and Gyanendra Pandey, 1–39. Delhi: Oxford University Press, 1992.

——. *The Unhappy Consciousness: Bankim Chandra Chattopadhyay and the Formation of Nationalist Discourse in India*. Delhi: Oxford University Press, 1996.

Kaye, J. W., and J. Forbes Watson, eds. *The People of India*. London: India Museum, 1868.

Khadria, Nandita. "Internal Trade and Market Network in the Brahmaputra Valley, 1826–73." *Indian Historical Review* 17, nos. 1–2 (1990–91), 152–73.

Khakhlari, Jadunath. *Kacharir Kotha*. Jorhat, 1927.

Khaund, Dugdhanath. *Sati Haran Natak*. Jorhat, n.d.

King, Christopher R. *One Language, Two Scripts: The Hindi Movement in Nineteenth Century North India*. Delhi: Oxford University Press, 1994.

Kirtanghosha. Nagaon, 1880.

Kling, Blair B. *Partner in Empire: Dwarkanath Tagore and the Age of Enterprise in Eastern India*. Berkeley: University of California Press, 1976.

Kolff, Dirk H. A. *Naukar, Rajput and Sepoy: The Ethno-history of the Military Labour Market in Hindustan, 1450–1850*. Cambridge: Cambridge University Press, 1990.

Kooiman, Dick. *Conversion and Social Equality*. New Delhi: Manohar, 1989.

Kothari, Rajni, ed. *Caste in Indian Politics*. New Delhi: Orient Longman, 1970.

Kulke, Hermann. *Kings and Cults: State Formation and Legitimation in India and Southeast Asia*. New Delhi: Manohar, 1993.

Kumar, Deepak. "The Evolution of Colonial Science in India." *Imperialism and the Natural World*, ed. John M. MacKenzie, 51–66. Manchester, 1990.

Kurmi, Ganesh Chandra. *Sah Jan-Jatir Kimbadanti*. Jorhat: Asom Sahitya Sabha, 1997.

Kurmi, Sushil. *Sah Bagisar Asomiya Sampraday*. Jorhat: Asom Sahitya Sabha, 1983.

Lahiri, Naynjot. "Landholding and Peasantry in the Brahmaputra Valley, c. 5th–13th Centuries A.D." *Journal of the Social and Economic History of the Orient* 33, no. 2 (1990), 158–68.

Land Revenue Administration Report of Assam Valley Districts. Shillong: Government Press, 1885.

Latour, Bruno. *Science in Action: How to Follow Scientists and Engineers through Society*. Cambridge: Harvard University Press, 1987.

Leach, Edmund. *Political Systems of Highland Burma*. London: London School of Economics, 1954.

Lees, W. Nassau. *The Land and Labour of India: A Review*. London, 1867.

——. *Memorandum Written after a Tour through the Tea Districts of Eastern Bengal in 1864–5*. Calcutta, 1866.

———. *Tea Cultivation, Cotton, and Other Agricultural Experiments in India. A Review*. London: W. H. Allen, 1863.

Leopold, Joan. "The Aryan Theory of Race, 1870–1920: Nationalist and Internationalist Visions." *Indian Economic and Social History Review* 2, no. 1 (1970), 271–98.

Lévi-Strauss, Claude. *The Savage Mind*. London: Weidenfeld and Nicholson, 1972.

Lilamala. Jorhat: Dharma Prakash, 1871.

Lloyd, G. T. *Census of India, 1921*, vol. 3, *Assam*, part 1, *Report*. Shillong: Government Press, 1923.

Longley, P. H. *Tea Planter Sahib: The Life and Adventures of a Tea Planter in North East India*. Auckland: Tonson, 1969.

Ludden, David. "Maps in the Mind and the Mobility of Asia." *Journal of Asian Studies* 62, no. 4 (2001), 1057–78.

———. *Reading Subaltern Studies: Critical History, Contested Meaning, and the Globalization of South Asia*. London: Anthem, 2001.

———. "Where Is Assam? Using Geographical History to Locate Current Social Realities." CENISEAS Papers, ed. Sanjib Baruah, vol. 1. Guwahati: Omeo Kumar Das Institute, 2001.

Lyall, Charles. *The Mikirs*. London: D. Nutt, 1908.

Lynn, Martin. "British Policy, Trade and Informal Empire in the Mid-Nineteenth Century." *The Nineteenth Century: The Oxford History of the British Empire*, ed. Andrew Porter, 101–21. Oxford: Oxford University Press, 1999.

MacCosh, John. *Topography of Assam*. London, 1837.

Macdonald, Ellen E. "The Growth of Regional Consciousness in Maharashtra." *Indian Economic and Social History Review* 3, no. 2 (1968), 233–44.

Macfarlane, Alan, and Iris Macfarlane. *Green Gold: The Empire of Tea*. London: Ebury, 2003.

Mackay, David. *In the Wake of Cook: Exploration, Science, and Empire, 1780–1801*. London: Croom Helm, 1985.

Mackenzie, Alexander. *History of the Relations of the Government with the Hill Tribes of the Northeast Frontier of Bengal*. Calcutta: Government Press, 1884.

MacLeod, Roy, ed. *Nature and Empire. Science and the Colonial Enterprise. Osiris* 15 (2000) [special issue].

Mahanta, Ratneswar. "Jaymati." *Ratneswar Mahanta Rasanavali*, ed. Jogendranath Bhuyan. Guwahati: Publication Board, 1994.

Mahato, Pashupati Prasad. "World-view of the Jharkhand as Depicted in Songs of the Tea Garden Labourers of Assam." *Folklore* 26, no. 8 (1985), 141–51.

Majeed, Javed. 1995, "'The Jargon of Indostan': An Exploration of Jargon in Urdu and East Company English." *Languages and Jargons*, ed. Peter

Burke and Roy Porter, 182–205. Cambridge: Cambridge University Press, 1995.

Majumdar Barua, Durga Prasad. *Mohorir*. Calcutta, 1896.

Malhotra, Anshu. *Gender, Caste, and Religious Identities: Restructuring Class in Colonial Punjab*. Delhi: Oxford University Press, 2002.

Malik, Syed Abdul. *Asomiya Jikir aru Jari*. Jorhat: Asom Sahitya Sabha, 1958.

———. *Surya Mukheer Swapna*. Guwahati, 1990.

Markovits, Claude, Jacques Pouchepadass, and Sanjay Subrahmanyam. *Society and Circulation. Mobile People and Itinerant Cultures in South Asia*. Delhi: Oxford University Press, 2003.

Marshall, Peter. *Trade and Conquest: Studies on the Rise of British Dominance in India*. Aldershot: Variorum, 1993.

Martin, Montgomery. *The History, Antiquities, Topography, and Statistics of Eastern India*. London: W. H. Allen, 1838.

Mau, or the Bee (periodical), ed. Harinarayan Bora. Calcutta, 1886–87.

Mazid, Altaf. "Joymoti: The First Radical Film of India." *Himal*, 2006, http://www.himalmag.com/tbc.php?bid=26.

McGuire, John. *The Making of a Colonial Mind*. Canberra: Australia National University, 1983.

McSwiney, J. *Census of India, 1911*, vol. 3, *Assam*, part 1, *Report*. Shillong: Government Press, 1912.

Medhi, Kaliram. *Assamese Grammar and Origin of Assamese Language*. Guwahati: Publication Board, 1934.

Meehan, Johanna, ed. *Feminists Read Habermas: Gendering the Subject of Discourse*. New York: Routledge, 1995.

Meer, Y. S. *Documents of Indentured Labour: Natal, 1851–1917*. Durban: Institute of Black Research, 1980.

Metcalf, Thomas R. *Ideologies of the Raj*. Cambridge: Cambridge University Press, 1995.

Meyer, Eric. 1992, "'Enclave' Plantations, 'Hemmed-In' Villages and Dualistic Representations, Colonial Ceylon." *Plantations, Proletarians and Peasants in Colonial Asia*, ed. E. Valentine Daniel, Henry Bernstein, and Tom Brass, 199–228. London: Cass, 1992.

Mills, A. J. Moffat. *Report on the Province of Assam*. Calcutta: Superintendent of Government Printing, 1854.

Mills, J. P. *The Ao Nagas*. London: D. Nutt, 1926.

Milner, Anthony. *The Invention of Politics in Colonial Malaya*. Cambridge: Cambridge University Press, 1995.

Mintz, Sidney. *Sweetness and Power: Place of Sugar in Modern History*. New York: Viking, 1985.

Miri, Sonaram. *Miri Duyana*. Dibrugarh, 1915.

Mishra, Sanghamitra. "Changing Frontiers and Spaces: The Colonial State in Nineteenth-Century Goalpara." *Studies in History* 21, no. 2 (2005), 215–46.

———. "Redrawing Frontiers: Language, Resistance and the Imagining of a Goalparia People." *Indian Economic and Social History Review* 43, no. 2 (2006), 199–225.

Misra, B. B. *The Unification and Division of India*. Delhi: Oxford University Press, 1990.

Misra, Prafulla. "The Communist Party of India in Assam: A Brief History." *North-east Quarterly* 2, no. 1 (1984), 5–23.

Misra, Tilottama. *Literature and Society in Assam*. Guwahati: Omsons, 1987.

———, trans. *Gunabhiram Barua, Ramnabami-Natak: The Story of Ram and Nabami*. Delhi: Oxford University Press, 2007.

Misra, Udayon. *The Periphery Strikes Back: Challenges to the Nation-State in Assam and Nagaland*. Shimla: Institute of Advanced Studies, 2000.

Mohammad, Munshi Yar. *Lora Darsaka*. Goalpara: Hitsadhini, 1876.

Mohanty, Nivedita. *Oriya Nationalism*. New Delhi: Manohar, 1982.

Mohapatra, Prabhu. "Assam and the West Indies, 1860–1920: Immobilising Plantation Labour." *Masters, Servants, and Magistrates in Britain and the Empire, 1562–1955*, ed. Douglas Hay, 455–80. Chapel Hill: University of North Carolina Press, 2004.

———. "Coolies and Colliers: A Study of the Agrarian Context of Labour Migration from Chhotanagpur, 1880–1920." *Studies in History* 1–2 (1985), 247–303.

Monahan, F. J. *Report on Jute Cultivation*. Shillong: Government Press, 1898.

Money, Edward. *The Tea Controversy (A Momentous Indian Question): Indian vs. Chinese Teas*. London: W. B. Whittingham, 1884.

Moore, Mrs. P. H. *Twenty Years in Assam: Leaves from My Journal*. Calcutta, 1901.

Moral and Material Progress and Condition of India during 1871–2. London: HMSO, 1873.

Morey, S. D. "Tai Languages of Assam: A Progress Report: Does Anything Remain of the Tai Ahom Language?" *Language Maintenance for Endangered Languages: An Active Approach*, ed. David and Maya Bradley, 98–113. London: Routledge Curzon, 2002.

———. "Tonal Change in the Tai Languages of Northeast India." *Linguistics of the Tibeto-Burman Area* 28, no. 2 (2005), 139–202.

Morris-Suzuki, Tessa. "The Frontiers of Japanese Identity." *Asian Forms of the Nation*, ed. Stein Tonnesson and Hans Antlov, 41–66. Richmond: Curzon, 1996.

Morton, Rev. W. "Remarks on a Comparison of Indo-Chinese Languages." *Journal of the Asiatic Society of Bengal* 73, no. 1 (1838), 56–64.

Moulton, Edward. "Cotton, Sir Henry John Stedman (1845–1915)." *Oxford Dictionary of National Biography*. Oxford: Oxford University Press, 2004.

———. "Early Indian Nationalism: Henry Cotton and the British Positivist and Radical Connection." *Journal of Indian History* 60 (1982), 125–59.

Muirhead-Thomson, R. C. *Assam Valley: Beliefs and Customs of the Assamese Hindus*. London: Luzac, 1948.

Mukherjee, Sibsankar. "The Social Role of a Caste Association." *Indian Economic and Social History Review* 31, no. 1 (1994), 89–100.

Mullen, C. S. *Census of India, 1931*, vol. 3, *Assam*, part 1, *Report*. Shillong: Government Press, 1932.

Myint-U, Thant. *The Making of Modern Burma*. Cambridge: Cambridge University Press, 2001.

Naregal, Veena. "Language and Power in Pre-colonial Western India: Textual Hierarchies, Literate Audiences and Colonial Philology." *Indian Economic and Social History Review* 37, no. 3 (2000), 259–94.

Nath, Lopita. *The Nepalis in Assam: Ethnicity and Cross Border Movements in the North-east*. Calcutta: Minerva, 2003.

Neog, Maheswar. *Anandaram Dhekial Phukan*. New Delhi: Sahitya Akademi, 1980.

———. *Guru Charit Katha*. Guwahati: Gauhati University, 1999.

———. *Nidhi Levi Farwell*. New Delhi: Sahitya Akademi, 1985.

———. *Pabitra Asom*. Jorhat: Asom Sahitya Sabha, 1958.

———. *Socio-political Events in Assam Leading to Militancy of Mayamariya Vaishnavas*. Calcutta: CSSS, 1982.

———, ed. *A Few Remarks on the Assamese Language*, by Anandaram Dhekial Phukan. Jorhat: Asom Sahitya Sabha, 1959 [1855].

———, ed. *Lakshminath Bezbarua: Sahityarathi of Assam*. Guwahati: Gauhati University, 1972.

———, ed. *Orunodoi*. Guwahati: Publication Board, 1983 [1846–54].

———, ed. *Prachya Sasanavali: An Anthology of Royal Charters Inscribed on Stone, Copper etc of Kamarupa, Assam, Koch Behar etc., 1205–1847 A.D.* Guwahati: State Museum, 1974.

Neog, Maheswar, and H. K. Barpujari, eds. *S. K. Bhuyan Commemoration Volume*. Guwahati: Department of Historical and Antiquarian Studies, 1966.

Neogy, Ajit K. *Partitions of Bengal*. Calcutta: A. Mukherjee, 1987.

Notes on Some Industries of Assam from 1884 to 1895. Shillong: Assam Secretariat Printing, 1896.

O'Connor, Richard A. "Agricultural Change and Ethnic Succession in Southeast Asian States: A Case for Regional Anthropology." *Journal of Asian Studies* 54, no. 4 (1995), 968–96.

O'Hanlon, Rosalind. *Caste, Conflict, and Ideology*. Cambridge: Cambridge University Press, 1985.

Okihiro, Gary Y. *Pineapple Culture: A History of the Tropical and Temperate Zones*. Berkeley: University of California Press, 2009.

O'Malley, L. S. S. *Bengal District Gazetteers*. Calcutta: Bengal Secretariat Book Depot, 1910.

Ong, Walter. *Orality and Literacy*. London: Routledge, 1982.

Orsini, Francesca. *The Hindi Public Sphere, 1920–40*. Delhi: Oxford University Press, 2002.

Orunodoi (periodical), ed. American Baptist Foreign Mission. Sibsagar, 1846–80.

Pai, Anant, ed. *Lachit Barphukan (Amar Chitra Katha)*. Mumbai: India Book House, 1978.

Pal, Bipan Chandra. *Memories of My Life and Times*. Calcutta: Modern Book Agency, 1932.

Patgiri, Nabadipranjan, and Kanakchandra Deka, eds. *Gandhibadi Neta Robin Kalita*. Guwahati, 1996.

Pathak, Balaram Sarma, trans. *Yogavasistha*. Jorhat, 1872.

Pemberton, Robert Boileau. *Political Mission to Bhutan*. Calcutta: Bengal Secretariat Office, 1839.

———. *Report on the Eastern Frontier of British India*. Calcutta: Baptist Mission Press, 1835.

Philips, C. H., ed. *The Correspondence of Lord William Cavendish Bentinck, Governor-General of India, 1828–1835*. Oxford: Oxford University Press, 1977.

Phillip, Kavita. *Civilising Natures: Race, Resources, and Modernity in Colonial South India*. New Delhi: Orient Longman, 2003.

Phrases, Assamese and Dhekeri. Sibsagar: Baptist Press, 1849.

Phukan, Jotindranath. *Mahabir Lachit*. Jorhat, 1981.

Playfair, A. *The Garos*. London: D. Nutt, 1909.

Pollock, A. J. O. *Sport in British Burmah, Assam, and the Cassyah and Jyntiah Hills*. London: Chapman and Hall, 1879.

Pollock, Sheldon. "The Cosmopolitan Vernacular." *Journal of Asian Studies* 57, no. 1 (1988), 6–37.

Porter, Andrew, ed. *The Nineteenth Century: The Oxford History of the British Empire*. Oxford: Oxford University Press, 1999.

Prabhakara, M. S. "Identity and Grievances." *Frontline* 22, no. 16 (2005).

———. "Manufacturing Identities?" *Frontline* 22, no. 20 (2005).

———. "In the Name of Tribal Identities." *Frontline* 22, no. 24 (2005).

———. "Separatist Strains." *Frontline* 24, no. 10 (2007).

Prakash, Gyan. *Bonded Histories: Genealogies of Labour Servitude in Colonial India*. Cambridge: Cambridge University Press, 1990.

Proceedings of Assam Legislative Council. Shillong: Government Press, 1912–36.

Purkayastha, Sudeshna. "Restructuring the Past in Early-Twentieth Century Assam." *History in the Vernacular*, ed. Partha Chatterjee and Raza Aquil, 172–208. Delhi: Oxford University Press, 2008.

Rafael, Vicente L. *Contracting Colonialism: Translation and Christian Conversion in Tagalog Society under Early Spanish Rule*. Ithaca: Cornell University Press, 1988.

Rahman Barua, Abdur. *Islam*. North Lakhimpur, 1911.

Rai, Mridu. *Hindu Rulers, Muslim Subjects: Islam, Rights, and the History of Kashmir*. London: Hurst, 2004.

Rajkhowa, Benudhar. *Assamese Popular Superstitions and Assamese Demonology*. Guwahati: Gauhati University, 1920.

———. *Historical Sketches of Old Assam*. Dibrugarh: Dibrugarh University, 1917.

Ramananda. *Bhakti Ratna Sindhu*. Guwahati, 1875.

Ramaswamy, Sumathi. *Passions of the Tongue: Language Devotion in Tamil Nadu, 1891–1970*. Berkeley: University of California Press, 1997.

Ramsden, A. R. *Assam Planter: Tea Planting and Hunting in the Assam Jungle*. London: John Gifford, 1944.

Ray, Rajat Kanta, ed. *Mind, Body and Society: Life and Mentality in Colonial Bengal*. Delhi: Oxford University Press, 1995.

Ray Choudhuri, Subir, ed. *Early History and Growth of Calcutta*. Calcutta: Romesh Chandra Ghose, 1905.

Report: Census of Assam for 1881. Calcutta, 1883.

Report of Indian Franchise Committee. Calcutta: Bengal Secretariat Press, 1932.

Report of Indian Statutory Commission. London: HMSO, 1930.

Report of Line System Committee. Shillong: Government Press, 1938.

Report of Provincial Banking Enquiry Committee, 1929–30. Shillong: Government Press, 1931.

Report of the Royal Commission on Labour in India, 1929–30. London: HMSO, 1931.

Report of the Royal Commission on Opium. London: HMSO, 1894.

"Report of the American Baptist Mission to Assam, 1845." *Baptist Missionary Magazine*, August 1846.

Report of the Commissioners on the Tea Cultivation of Assam, 1868: Papers regarding the Tea Industry of Bengal. Calcutta: Bengal Secretariat Press, 1873.

Report of the Committee Appointed to Enquire into Certain Aspects of Opium and Ganja Consumption [Botham Committee]. Shillong: Government Press, 1913.

Report of the Committee Appointed to Enquire into Certain Aspects of Opium and Ganja Consumption [Nichols-Roy Committee]. Shillong: Government Press, 1933.

Report of the Labour Enquiry Commission of Bengal. Calcutta: Bengal Secretariat Press, 1896.

Reports on Native Papers, Bengal Presidency. Calcutta: Bengal Secretariat Press, 1868–1920.

Richards, John F., and James Hagan. "A Century of Rural Expansion in Assam, 1870–1970." *Itinerario*, 1987, 193–209.

Risley, Herbert. *People of India*. London: Thacker, 1908.

Robb, Peter. "The Colonial State and Constructions of Indian Identity: An Example on the Northeast Frontier in the 1880s." *Modern Asian Studies* 31, no. 2 (1997), 245–83.

——. *Liberalism, Modernity, and the Nation*. New Delhi: Sage, 1997.

——, ed. *Dalit Movements and Meaning of Labour in India*. Delhi: Oxford University Press, 1993.

Robinson, William. *A Descriptive Account of Assam*. Calcutta: Baptist Mission Press, 1841.

Rogers, John D. "Post-Orientalism and the Interpretation of Pre-modern and Modern Political Identities: The Case of Sri Lanka." *Journal of Asian Studies* 53, no. 1 (1994), 10–23.

Rosaldo, Michelle Z., and Louise Lamphere, eds. *Woman, Culture, and Society*. Berkeley: University of California Press, 1974.

Rose, Leo. "The Nepali Ethnic Community in the North-east of the Subcontinent." *Ethnic Studies Report*, 12 January 1994, 105–20.

Rukminiharan. Jorhat, 1873–79 (several editions).

Rukminiharan. Nagaon, 1882.

Rukminiharan Natak. Jorhat, 1886.

Rush, James R. "Opium in Java: A Sinister Friend." *Journal of Asian Studies* 54, no. 3 (1985), 549–61.

Sadhana (periodical), ed. All Assam Muslim Students Association. Guwahati, 1922–26.

Saikia, Arupjyoti. "Forest Land and Peasant Struggles in Assam, 2002–7." *Journal of Peasant Studies* 35, no. 1 (2008), 39–59.

——. "Gait's Way: Writing History in Early-Twentieth Century Assam." *History in the Vernacular*, ed. Partha Chatterjee and Raza Aquil, 142–71. Delhi: Oxford University Press, 2008.

——. "Gunabhiram Barua." *Gariyashi*, December 2009, 53–56.

——. "Haliram Dhekial Phukan." *Gariyashi*, November 2009, 89–94.

——. "History, Buranjis, and Nation: Suryya Kumar Bhuyan's Histories in Twentieth-Century Assam." *Indian Economic and Social History Review* 45, no. 4 (2008), 473–505.

——. *Jungles, Reserves, Wildlife: A History of Forests in Assam*. Guwahati: Wildlife Areas Development and Welfare Trust, 2005.

Saikia, J. *Sati Radhika*. Barpeta, 1957.

Saikia, Mohini Kumar. *Asomiya Sankritit Islamiyo Prabhav*. Jorhat, 1985.

Saikia, Nagen, ed. *Buranji Vivekratna by Maniram Dewan*. Dibrugarh: Dibrugarh University, 2002.

Saikia, Rajen. *Social and Economic History of Assam*. Delhi: Manohar, 2001.

Saikia, Yasmin. *Fragmented Memories: Struggling to Be Tai-Ahom in Assam*. Durham: Duke University Press, 2004.

——. *In the Meadows of Gold*. Guwahati: Spectrum, 1997.

Samaddar, Ranabir. *The Marginal Nation: Transborder Migration from Bangladesh to West Bengal*. New Delhi: Sage, 1999.

Sandikai, Radhakanta. *Mula Gabharu*. Jorhat: Asom Sahitya Sabha, 1924.

Sangari, Kumkum, and Sudesh Vaid, eds. *Recasting Women*. New Delhi: Kali for Women, 1989.

Sangwan, Satpal. "From Gentlemen Amateurs to Professionals: Reassessing the Natural Science Tradition in Colonial India, 1780–1840." *Nature and the Orient*, ed. Richard H. Grove, Vinita Damodaran, and Satpal Sangwan, 210–36. Delhi: Oxford University Press, 1998.

Sankardeb aru Madhabdebor Kirtan. Nagaon, 1880.

Sankardebor Kirtanmala. Calcutta, 1903.

Sankruti (periodical), ed. Assam Association. Calcutta, 2001–.

Sardesai, G. S. *The Main Currents of Maratha History*. Patna: Patna University, 1926.

Sarkar, Jadunath. "Assam and the Ahoms in 1660 A.D." *Journal of the Bihar Research Society* 1, no. 2 (1915), 179–95.

———. *Shivaji and His Times*. Calcutta: M. C. Sarkar and Sons, 1919.

Sarkar, Sumit. *Beyond Nationalist Frames: Relocating Postmodernism, Hindutva and History*. New Delhi: Permanent Black, 2004.

———. *Writing Social History*. Delhi: Oxford University Press, 1997.

Sarkar, Tanika. *Hindu Wife, Hindu Nation*. New Delhi: Permanent Black, 2001.

———. *Words to Win: Making of "Amar Jiban," a Modern Autobiography*. New Delhi: Kali for Women, 1999.

Sarma, Anjali. *Among the Luminaries in Assam: A Study of Assamese Biography*. New Delhi: Mittal, 1990.

Sarma, Benudhar. *Congressor Kasiyali Rodot*. Guwahati, 1959.

———. *Maniram Dewan*. Guwahati, 1950.

———, ed. *An Account of Assam by J. P. Wade*. North Lakhimpur, 1927.

Sarma, Binod. "A Note on the Assamese Jikir and Its Philosophy." *Folklore* 20, no. 12 (1979), 277–80.

Sarma, Debendranath. *Guru Kalicharan Brahma*. Jorhat, 1983.

Sarma, Jogeswar, ed. *Benudhar Sarmar Rasanavali*. Guwahati: Publication Board, 1985.

Sarma, Kantabhusan. *Sankardeb Jivan Charit*. Goalpara, 1877.

Sarma, Krishnanath. *Jatiya Siksa*. Jorhat, 1921.

———. *Krishna Sarmar Diary*. Guwahati: Publication Board, 1972.

Sarma, Mahadev. *Asomiya Lora Katha Ramayan*. Jorhat, 1929.

Sarma, Satyendra Nath. *Assamese Literature*. Wiesbaden: Harrassowitz, 1976.

———. *Neo-Vaishnavite Movement and the Satra Institution of Assam*. Guwahati: Gauhati University, 1966.

Sarma, Someswar. *Assam Companir Biboron*. Sibsagar, 1875.

Sarma, Someswar Dev. *Nityakritram*. Jorhat, 1926.

Sarma, Tirthanath. *Auniati Satrar Buranji*. Majuli: Auniati Satra, 1975.

Sarma, Umakanta. *Bharanda Pakhir Jak*. Guwahati: Lawyer's Book Stall, 1991.

———. *Ejak Manuh aru Ekhon Aranyo*. Pathsala: Bani Prakash, 1986.
Sarma Bezbarua, Tulsiram. *Hitopadesa*. Jorhat, 1884.
Sarma Bordoloi, Kirtinath. *Sandipika*. Jorhat, 1933.
Saunders, Kay, ed. *Indentured Labour in the British Empire, 1834–1920*. London: Croom Helm, 1984.
Schiebinger, Londa. *Plants and Empire: Colonial Bioprospecting in the Atlantic World*. Cambridge: Harvard University Press, 2004.
Scott, James C. *The Art of Not Being Governed: An Anarchist History of Uplands Southeast Asia*. New Haven: Yale University Press, 2009.
———. *Domination and the Arts of Resistance: Hidden Transcripts*. New Haven: Yale University Press, 1990.
———. *Weapons of the Weak: Everyday Forms of Peasant Resistance*. New Haven: Yale University Press, 1985.
Selections from the Records of the Government of Bengal, no. 37, *Papers Relating to Tea Cultivation in Assam*. Calcutta: Bengal Secretariat Press, 1859–61.
Sen, Samita. "Questions of Consent: Women's Recruitment for Assam Tea Gardens, 1859–1900." *Studies in History* 2 (2002), 231–60.
———. *Women and Labour in Late Colonial India: The Bengal Jute Industry*. Cambridge: Cambridge University Press, 1999.
Senapati, Fakirmohan. *My Times and I*, trans. John Boulton. Bhubaneswar, 1985 [1918].
Shah, Muhammad. *Lukir Buranji*. Calcutta, 1922.
Sharma, A. K. *The Quit India Movement in Assam*. New Delhi: Mittal, 2007.
Sharma, Jayeeta. "Assam's Lachit, India's Missile Man: History, Nation and Gender in India." *The Politics of Cultural Mobilization in India*, ed. Andrew Wyatt and John Zavos, 166–94. Delhi: Oxford University Press, 2004.
———. "British Science, Chinese Skill and Assam Tea: Making Empire's Garden." *Indian Economic and Social History Review* 43, no. 4 (2006), 429–55.
———. "'Lazy' Natives, Coolie Labour, and the Assam Tea Industry." *Modern Asian Studies* 43, no. 6 (2009), 1287–1324.
———. "Making Garden, Erasing Jungle: The Tea Enterprise in Colonial Assam." *The British Empire and the Natural World: Environmental Encounters in South Asia*, ed. Deepak Kumar, Vinita Damodaran, and Rohan D'Souza, 119–41. Delhi: Oxford University Press, 2010.
———. "Religion, Science and General Knowledge: The Orunodoi Periodical of the American Baptist Missionaries in Assam." *Christians and Missionaries in India*, ed. Robert Frykenberg, 256–73. London: Routledge Curzon, 2002.
Sharma, Manorama. *Social and Economic Change in Assam*. Delhi: Ajanta, 1990.
Sharma, Mukunda Madhab, ed. *Inscriptions of Ancient Assam*. Guwahati: Gauhati University, 1978.

Siddique, Muhammad Abu B. *Evolution of Land Grants and Labour Policy of Government: The Growth of the Tea Industry in Assam, 1834–1940.* New Delhi: South Asian Publishers, 1990.

Sinha, Mrinalini. *Colonial Masculinity: The "Manly Englishman" and the "Effeminate Bengali" in the Late Nineteenth Century.* Manchester: Manchester University Press, 1995.

Sinha, Pradip. "Calcutta and the Currents of History, 1690–1912." *Calcutta: The Living City,* vol. 1, *The Past,* ed. Sukanta Chaudhuri, 31–44. Calcutta: Oxford University Press, 1990.

Sircar, Kalyan K. "Coolie Exodus from Assam's Chargola Valley, 1921: An Analytical Study." *Economic and Political Weekly* 22, nos. 1–2 (1987), 184–93.

Sivaramakrishnan, K. "British Imperium and Forested Zones of Anomaly in Bengal." *Indian Economic and Social History Review* 33 (1996), 225–42.

Skaria, Ajay. "Shades of Wildness: Tribe, Caste and Gender in Western India." *Journal of Asian Studies* 56, no. 3 (1997), 726–45.

Smith, Anthony D. *Theories of Nationalism.* London: Duckworth, 1983.

Srinivas, M. N. *Cohesive Role of Sanskritisation and Other Essays.* Delhi: Oxford University Press, 1989.

Srivastava, B. K. "Trade Union and Politics: A Study of the Assam Chah Mazdoor Sangh." *Social Research* 6, no. 1 (1986), 10–14.

Stocking, George. *Victorian Anthropology.* New York: Free Press, 1987.

Stoler, Ann Laura. *Capitalism and Confrontation in Sumatra's Plantation Belt, 1870–1979.* New Haven: Yale University Press, 1985.

Swanson, O. L. *In Villages and Tea Gardens: Forty-three years of Missionary Work in Assam.* Chicago: Conference Press, 1944.

Talukdar, Bishnurav. *Asomiya Ramayan—Kishkandh Kand.* N.p., 1929.

Talukdar, Gaurikanta. *Jati Samasya.* Guwahati, 1929.

———. *Kalitar Vratyodharar Avasyakala.* Guwahati, 1929.

Talukdar, Nanda, ed. *Lambodar Bora Rasanavali.* Guwahati: Publication Board, 1983.

Tamuli, Babul. "Assam Sahitya Sabha." *Assam Tribune,* 9 February 2001.

Tamuli Phukan, Kasinath. *Assam Buranji-Sar.* Sibsagar: Baptist Press, 1844.

Talish, Shihabuddin. *Fathyah-i-Ibriyah,* in H. Blochmann, "Koch Bihar, Koch Hajo, and Assam in the 16th and 17th Centuries, According to the Akbarnamah, the Padshahnamah, and the Fathiyah-i-Ibriyah," *Journal of the Asiatic Society of Bengal* 41, no. 1 (1872), 49–101.

———. *Fathyah-i-Ibriyah,* in Jadunath Sarkar, "Assam and the Ahoms in 1660 A.D.," *Journal of the Bihar Research Society* 1, no. 2 (1915), 179–95.

Taylor's Maps of Tea Districts. Calcutta: Thacker, Spink, 1910.

Tea Districts Labour Association. *Handbook of Castes and Tribes Employed on Tea Estates in North-east India.* Calcutta: Catholic Orphan Press, 1924.

Terwiel, B. J. "Recreating the Past: Revivalism in Northeastern India." *Bijdragen tot de taal: Land en volkenkunde* 152, no. 2 (1996), 275–92.

Thakur, Usha. "Workers' Initiative on Sick Tea Plantations in Assam and Bengal." *South Asia* 19, no. 2 (1996), 35–58.

Thapar, Romila. *Clan, Caste, and Origin Myths in Early India*. Shimla: Institute of Advanced Study, 1992.

———. "The Image of the Barbarian in Early India." *Comparative Studies in Society and History* 13, no. 4 (1971), 408–36.

Tharu, Susie. "Tracing Savitri's Pedigree: Victorian Racism and the Image of Women in Indo-Anglian Literature." *Recasting Women*, ed. Kumkum Sangari and Sudesh Vaid, 254–68. Delhi: Kali for Women, 1989.

Thurnton, J. H. *Memories of Seven Campaigns*. Westminster: A. Constable, 1895.

Timberg, Thomas. *The Marwaris: From Traders to Industrialists*. New Delhi: Vikas, 1978.

Times (London), 1785–1985.

Tinker, Hugh. *A New System of Slavery: The Export of Indian Labour Overseas, 1830–1920*. London: Institute of Race Relations, 1974.

Trautmann, Thomas. *Aryans and British India*. Berkeley: University of California Press, 1997.

Ullah, Syed Hassan. "An Account of the Development of Persian in Assam and Its Influence on the Assamese Language." *Islamic Culture*, April 1985, 83–94.

Van Schendel, Willem. *The Bengal Borderland: Beyond State and Nation in South Asia*. London: Anthem, 2005.

———. "Geographies of Knowing, Geographies of Ignorance: Jumping Scale in Southeast Asia." *Locating Southeast Asia: Geographies of Knowledge and Politics of Space*, ed. Paul Kratoska, R. Raben, and H. Nordholt, 275–307. Singapore: Singapore University Press, 2005.

Van Schendel, Willem, and Md. Mahbubar Rahman. "'I Am Not a Refugee': Rethinking Partition Migration." *Modern Asian Studies* 37, no. 3 (2003), 551–84.

Vansina, Jan. *Oral Tradition as History*. London: James Currey, 1985.

Vicziany, Marika. "Imperialism, Botany, and Statistics in Early Nineteenth Century India: The Surveys of Francis Buchanan (1762–1829)." *Modern Asian Studies* 20, no. 4 (1986), 625–60.

Wagoner, Phillip B. "Pre-colonial Intellectuals and the Production of Colonial Knowledge." *Comparative Studies in Society and History* 45, no. 4 (2003), 783–814.

Warren, W. Kenneth. *Tea Tales of Assam*. Liss: W. K. Warren, 1975.

Washbrook, David. "Language, Culture and Society in India." *Language, History and Class*, ed. P. J. Corfield, 179–203. Oxford: Basil Blackwell, 1991.

Weatherstone, John. *The Pioneers, 1825–1900: The Early British Tea and Coffee Planters and Their Way of Life*. London: Quiller, 1986.

White, Adam, ed. *A Memoir of the Late D. Scott*. Calcutta, 1832.

Wilson, H. H. *Documents Relating to the Burmese War*. London: W. H. Allen, 1827.

———. *The History of British India from 1805 to 1835*. London: James Madden, 1858.

Wolf, Eric R. *Europe and the People without History*. Berkeley: University of California Press, 1982.

Yang, Anand. "Peasants on the Move: A Study of Internal Migration in India." *Journal of Interdisciplinary History* 10, no. 1 (1979), 37–58.

Zutshi, Chitralekha. *Languages of Belonging: Islam, Regional Identity, and the Making of Kashmir*. Delhi: Oxford University Press, 2004.

Unpublished Theses and Dissertations

Chalmers, Rhoderick. "'We Nepalis': Language, Literature and the Formation of a Nepali Public Sphere in India, 1914–1940." PhD diss., University of London, 2003.

Goswami, Mahesh. "Satra and Society." PhD diss., Dibrugarh University, 1999.

Isaka, Riho. "The Gujarati Literati and the Construction of a Regional Identity in the Late Nineteenth Century." PhD diss., University of Cambridge, 1999.

Mohapatra, Pragati. "The Making of a Cultural Identity: Language, Literature and Gender in Orissa in Late Nineteenth and Early Twentieth Centuries." PhD diss., University of London, 1997.

Onta, Pratyush Raj. "The Politics of Bravery: A History of Nepali Nationalism." PhD diss., University of Pennsylvania, 1996.

Orsini, Francesca. "The Hindi Public Sphere." PhD diss., University of London, 1996.

Pegu, Rinku. "The Line System: Boundaries, Identities, and the Shaping of a Public Sphere in Colonial Assam, 1873–1947." M. Phil. thesis, Jawaharlal Nehru University, 2005.

Saikia, Sayeeda Yasmin. "A Name without a People: Searching to Be Tai-Ahom in Modern India." PhD diss., University of Wisconsin, 1999.

Interviews

Agarwala, Hridayanand, Meena, Monisha (Behal), Vivekanand: Tezpur and Delhi, 2001.

Basu, Meenakshi (Debjani Chaliha): Calcutta, 2001.

Bordoloi, Tulsi: Jorhat, 2003.

Chaliha, Reena: Guwahati, 2001.

Islam, Nurul: Guwahati, 2003.

Index

Bureaucracy, 120, 121–24, 143, 163; education for, 189, 191; Gosains and, 138–41, 144, 171–72; language policies and, 179–85. *See also* Service gentry

Burma, 240; Ahom trade with, 55; Assam invasions by, 3, 27, 29, 32, 42, 119–20, 149–50; Bengal and, 120; Konbaung regime in, 27; language of, 134; missionaries in, 44, 134; rice cultivation in, 60; United Kingdom vs., 3, 27, 29, 32, 93, 119–20

Butler, John, 64, 122, 144, 214

Cachar district, xvi, 81, 84, 119, 123. *See also* Kachari people

Calcutta, 7–8; Agricultural and Horticultural Society of, 13; educational facilities of, 147–48, 152–55; Hindu School of, 1, 152, 185; publishing in, 169–71, 181; Royal Botanical Garden in, 27, 29

Calcutta New Press, 171

Calcutta University, 191, 194

Campbell, A. C., 157

Campbell, George, 72–73, 205

Canning, Lord, 137

Carey, William, 186

Caribbean colonies: manumission in, 124; tea workers from, 71, 73, 75

Carnegie, John, 79

Carr, Tagore and Co., 32, 47

Carter, George, 133

Cash, 33, 62–63, 74; communal lands and, 40; "native" workers and, 39–41; transition to, 121–22, 127

Caste system, 45, 49, 50; Ahoms in, 217–22; *babus* in, 163; effects of education on, 128, 153; *jati* and, 207; missionaries on, 145–46; race and, 59, 66, 164, 196–200, 205–8; status taboos and, 126; tribal groups and, 67; untouchables of, 74, 215; Vashnavite sects and, 129. *See also* Élites

Censorship, 165. *See also* Print culture

Census-taking, 49, 122–23, 172, 206

Chaitanya (saint), 172

Chakrabarti, Kunal, 52

Chaliha, Tara Prasad, 229

Changkakati, Radhanath, 219

Chantra samaj (student community), 153

Chargola walkout (1921), 84

Charlton, Andrew, 30

Charter Acts (1813, 1833), 28, 34, 37

Charua Muslims, 101–2

Chatterjee, Kumkum, 224

Chatterji, Suniti Kumar, 194

Chattopadhyay, Dakshinacharan, 165

Chevalier, Jean Baptiste, 56

Chidananda Press, 170

China, 158, 162, 208; Assam trade with, 55, 122; migrant workers from, 35–38, 70, 71; Opium Wars of, 64–65; rice cultivation in, 60; tea cultivation in, 28–32

Cholera, 79, 81, 100

Chotanagpur migrant workers, 72–75, 83–84

Choudhury, Sonaram, 198–200

Chronicles (*buranjis*), 137, 182–83, 186, 197, 223–24

Chutias, 221–22, 228

"Civilizing mission": of East India Company, 27, 165; language standardization and, 180; of missionaries, 136–37

Civil service, 120, 121–24, 143, 163; education for, 189, 191; Gosains and, 138–41, 144, 171–72; language policies and, 179–85. *See also* Service gentry

Clark, Edward, 145

Coal mining, 32, 75, 80–81

Cohn, Bernard, 139–40

Comaroff, Jean, 144

Communist Party, 84, 168; theatre group of, 231; unions affiliated with, 235

Coolies, 36, 71–80, 236–37; *babus*
vs., 163; cholera among, 79, 81; as
Doms, 215; etymology of, 73;
intoxicants used by, 155, 156, 158,
160, 164; living conditions of, 81–
82, 164–66, 168; missionaries of,
202; population of, 49, 83, 85–86;
prejudices against, 76, 164;
rebellions by, 70, 84; women, 216–
17. *See also* Slavery; Workers
Cooper, Frederick, 237
Copley, Antony, 142
Cornwallis, Lord, 57
Corvée, 33, 121, 125, 129. *See also*
Taxes
Cotton, Henry, 82, 84
Cotton College (Guwahati), 152,
153, 221, 223
Crawfurd, John, 65
Crole, David, 83
Crystal Palace, 32
Curzon, Lord, 101, 123

Dakhinpat satra, 129, 140–41, 144,
166
Dangariyas (great men), 42, 120,
130–31, 155
Darjeeling, xv, 19, 31, 96
Darrang district, xvi, 66, 90, 94,
100, 123
Das, Labanya Prabha, 217
Das, Rajabala, 232
Dasgupta, Anindita, 98
Datta, P. K., 15, 212
Davidson, Captain, 121
Davis, Mike, 6
Deb, Pitambar, 212, 216
Deb, Raja Radhakanta, 29
"Depressed Classes," 213, 216, 221
Devi, Pragyasundari, 152
Devotional texts, 156–57, 171–76,
181–82, 193, 195
Dharma Prakash Press, 145, 169–71
Dhekial Phukan, Anandaram, 1–3,
56, 122, 150; as advocate of
Asomiya, 183–87, 193; education
of, 152; writings of, 4, 14–15,
47–48, 185–87, 190

Dhekial Phukan, Haliram, 4, 119;
on Doms, 214; on education,
150; as interpreter, 181; writings
of, 181–83, 195, 197–98
Dhimal people, 67
Dhubri (Goalpara), 80
Dialects, 134–35, 154, 173, 183–87,
193–94, 203
Dibrugarh, xvii, 80, 88–89, 101,
219, 230
Dom people, 155, 214–17
Dramatic Performances Act (1876),
165
Drayton, Richard, 13, 28, 43
Driberg, J. J. S., 158, 159
Drug abuse. *See* Opium
Duariya Baruas (revenue farmers),
56
Dubhashis (interpreters), 181
Dundas, W. C. M., 95–96
Durga Puja festival, 96
Dutta Baruah, Harinarayan, 171,
175
Dutt, R. C., 152

East India Company, 25–31, 56–
57, 121–23, 218; Burmese vs., 3,
120; "civilizing mission" of, 27,
165; government takeover of,
137; during Great Rebellion of
1857, 132, 133; language and,
135, 179–80, 183–85; missionaries and, 43–45, 134; opium
trade of, 28, 64–65; Singpho vs.,
41–42; slavery and, 124–28
Eaton, Richard, 51
Edgar, John, 81–82
Education, 8–9, 97–98, 163; of
Assam élites, 147–54, 189; for
civil service jobs, 189, 191; colonial, 150, 152, 179–80; demographics of, 150–51; in English,
150, 177, 185, 189, 204; language
and, 183–86; missionary schools
for, 151, 153, 193, 202; modernization and, 147–48, 153–54,
188, 212–13; religious taboos
and, 152; student housing for,

Great Rebellion of 1857, 47, 93,
127, 132–33, 140
Grierson, George, 67, 193
Griffith, William, 30–31, 37
Guha, Amalendu, 51, 125
Guha, Ranajit, 12–13
Guha, Sumit, 59
Gupta, Ranajit Das, 14
Gurdon, P. R. T., 193
Gurkhas, 93, 95–96
Guwahati, 80, 98, 182; Beadon's
visit to, 138; Cotton College at,
152, 153, 221, 223; English
school of, 150, 185; Girls' Col-
lege of, 232; Indian National
Congress at, 168; map of, xvii;
markets of, 88–89; missionaries
in, 136, 146; publishing in, 170;
slavery in, 127; temple complex
at, 51–52; as trading center, 55

Haats (markets), 45, 86, 88–89
Habermas, Jürgen, 9–10
Haji, Maulvi Muhammad Shah,
100, 195
Hajo mosque, 54, 55, 100. *See also*
Muslims
Hamilton, Francis Buchanan, 56, 87
Hardiman, David, 91–92
Hastings, Warren, 57, 179–80
Hazarika, Ali, 60
Hazarika, Dutiram, 43
Health care: by missionaries, 202;
by native doctors, 147, 163;
opium use in, 155–56, 158–60
Hindavi, 178, 179, 199–200
Hindi language, 173, 184, 187, 200
Hinduism, 205–7, 210; Assamese,
148, 172–76, 196–200. *See also*
Caste system; Vaishnavism
Hindu School (Calcutta), 1, 152,
185
Hitasadhini Press, 170
Hitopadesa, 170
Hodgson, Brian, 66–67, 72, 198,
201, 208–9
Holroyd, Captain, 133
Home, Gagan Chandra, 165

Hunter, W. W., 94, 205
Hutton, J. H., 92, 95

Indentured workers, 74, 77, 81–86,
126; emancipation of, 128; slav-
ery and, 75–76, 140; women as,
125, 128. *See also* Coolies;
Workers
India General Steam Navigation
Co., 80
Indian Forest Act (1920), 94
Indian National Congress, 84, 168,
204, 230
Indian National Trade Union Con-
gress (INTUC), 235
Indian People's Theatre Association
(IPTA), 231
Indian Tea Association, 166
Indigo plantations, 33, 72, 165
Indo-Aryans, 217–23; languages of,
178, 180, 193–94; migrations of,
49–52; races of, 67; religion of,
52; rice cultivation by, 26. *See also*
Aryanism
Indo-European languages, 180,
193, 197–98. *See also* Languages
Inland Emigration Act (1893), 77
Inner Line Restrictions (1873), 61,
202
INTUC (Indian National Trade
Union Congress), 235
Isaka, Riho, 225

Jadugiri (black magic), 53. *See also*
Witchcraft
Jagat Seth bankers, 87
Jati, 50, 90, 100, 205–7, 219, 225.
See also Caste system
Jatiyo unnati (national progress),
219
Jaymati (Ahom princess), 224–27;
annual festival for, 228–29; film
about, 230–31
Jenkins, Francis, 33–34, 41, 65; on
decline of élites, 130–31; on
Kacharis, 68, 69
Jikir (Assamese Sufi songs), 54, 99
Jinnah, Muhammad Ali, 103
Jogini Tantra, 52

Paramhansa, Sibnarayan, 211
Parbatiya Gosains, 97, 130
Parvati (goddess), 181
Patronage, literary, 157, 168–71, 182–83, 194. *See also* Print culture
Peal, Samuel, 83, 158
Pegu, Rinku, 102–3
Persian empire, 137
Persian language, 53–54, 55, 177, 183; literary uses of, 180; Sanskrit and, 179–80
Phalke, Dadasaheb, 231
Pharmacy Act (1868), 158
Philip, Kavita, 43
Philology, 180, 186. *See also* Languages
Phukan, Majindar & Co., 168
Phule, Jotiba, 206
Physiocratic ideas, 12, 28
Pilgrimages, 50, 55, 97, 182; Muslim, 54, 100; "secular," 1, 6, 153–54
Pitt, William (the Younger), 27
Plantation Labour Act (1951), 235
Poddar, Ramdayal, 89
Presbyterian missionaries, 151
Presidency College (Calcutta), 153
"Primitivism," 31, 66–67, 72, 203–4, 231
Prinsep, William, 13, 32, 45, 47
Print culture, 10, 89, 184; Asomiya literature and, 91, 147–48, 154–57, 168–71, 185, 194; Bengali literature and, 181, 212–13; of Calcutta, 148; censorship and, 165; of devotional texts, 156–57, 171–76, 181–82, 193, 195; Doms and, 215–16; financing of, 157, 168–71, 185, 186, 194; of Gosains, 144–45; linguistic studies and, 180, 186; of missionaries, 47, 65, 120, 134–37, 141–42, 180, 202; periodicals and, 141–45, 165–66, 170, 175, 190, 229; scripts and, 150, 202
Punjab, 14, 143

Rabha people, 208
Race, 76, 205, 207–12, 214; "aboriginal," 151, 206, 235; anthropometry and, 201; climate and, 37, 63, 68; élite genealogies and, 50–51, 196–200; ethnic violence and, 20, 238–41; as explanation for slavery, 206; *jati* and, 207; language and, 9, 67, 178, 180, 196; "Mongoloid," 198, 201, 209, 213, 221; "primitivism" and, 31, 66–67, 72, 203–4, 231; tea planters and, 166–68; tribal peoples and, 67, 72–73, 197–98; workers and, 37, 66–71. *See also* Caste system
Radhika, Santi, 217, 228
Rahima, Sati, 228
Railways, 80–81, 101
Rajah, M. C., 213
Rajasthan, 87, 89, 92
Ramayana, 60, 212
Ramsden, A. R., 76
Rebellion of 1857, 47, 93, 127, 132–33, 140
Religious endowments, 125, 128
Rice, 52; communal land for, 40; irrigation technology for, 60; varieties of, 26, 62; workers' wages in, 162
Rice beer, 68, 155, 161
Ripon College (Calcutta), 153
Risley, Herbert, 67, 201, 205, 206
River Steam Navigation Co., 80
Robb, Peter, 12–13
Robinson, John, 56
Robinson, William, 135, 184
Rosaldo, Michelle, 228
Rowlatt, Captain ??, 64
Roy, Acharya Prafulla Chandra, 161
Royal Botanical Garden (Calcutta), 27, 29
Rupnath Brahma, 211

Sadhana (periodical), 170, 195–96
Sadhani, Sati, 228
Sadiya, 41–44, 134
Sadullah, Muhammad, 103
Saikia, Yasmin, 217–18
Saikiani, Chandraprabha, 161–62, 232

Vaishnavism (*continued*)
of, 148, 173–76; Sankardeb and, 128, 148, 157, 172–76; sects of, 129, 130; Sufis and, 99, 130; texts of, 171–75, 181; theater of, 156–57. *See also* Gosains; Monasteries
Vamsavali, 50–51, 59–61, 196–200, 206–8, 225
Varna. See Caste system
Varua, Bisturam, 212
Vedantism, 174, 210
Victoria (queen of England), 137, 140, 228
Vidyapati (poet), 173
Vidyaratna, Ramkumar, 165

Wade, J. P., 57
Wallich, Nathaniel, 29, 30, 41
Warren, James, 36
Wastelands Rules, 32
Weissalisa chronicles, 120
Wellesley, Lord, 28
Welsh, Captain, 57, 62
Welsh missionaries, 151, 202
White, Captain, 121
Whiting, Samuel, 136
Williamson and Magor Group, 47, 167
Wilson, H. H., 122
Witchcraft, 6, 50, 53, 141, 144
Women: associations for, 162, 230; Christian publications for, 136; in chronicles, 225–27; "feminine" virtues of, 200, 216–17, 226–28; as indentured workers, 125, 128; magazine for, 229; marriage customs and, 154, 157, 174, 212; opium use among, 155, 156, 159, 162; rights of, 230, 232–33; sati and, 217, 227–28; on tea plantations, 75–77, 83, 216–17
Workers, 61–62, 64–65; Chinese migrant, 35–38, 70, 71; indentured, 74–77, 81–86, 125–26, 128, 140; land leases to, 85–86; legal protections for, 81–82; "native," 39–41; racial ideas about, 37, 66–71, 206; regulation of, 74–77, 83–84; shortage of, 63, 126, 130; supervisors of, 45, 76, 82–83, 142, 163; wages for, 68, 70, 77, 83, 158, 162–63. *See also* Coolies; Migrant workers
Workers Breach of Contract Act (1859), 70

Yandaboo Treaty (1826), 121
Yuvaraj, Ghanakanta, 131, 137–38

Zamindars (landlords), 12, 150, 169
Zomia network, 241

Jayeeta Sharma is an assistant professor of history at the University of Toronto. She was born in Tezpur and educated at Guwahati, Delhi, and Cambridge. After a nomadic academic existence in India, the United Kingdom, the United States, and Canada, she calls Toronto home and savours its global confluence of cultures, people, ideas, and foods. She is working on her second book, on race, labour, and migrations from the Eastern Himalayas across the British Empire.

Library of Congress Cataloging-in-Publication Data
Sharma, Jayeeta.
Empire's garden : Assam and the making of india
/ Jayeeta Sharma.
p. cm. — (Radical perspectives)
ISBN 978-0-8223-5032-3 (cloth : alk. paper)
ISBN 978-0-8223-5049-1 (pbk. : alk. paper)
1. Assam (India) — History. 2. British — India — Assam —
History — 19th century. 3. Tea trade — India — Assam — History.
I. Title. II. Series: Radical perspectives.
DS485.A88S537   2011
954'.16203 — dc22
2011006517

Made in the USA
Middletown, DE
12 September 2017